One-Day Trips through
HISTORY

*More than 200 Museums, Battlefields, Plantations,
Colonial Churches, Monuments, Historic Homes,
Forts, and Parks within 150 Miles of the
Nation's Capital*

JANE OCKERSHAUSEN

EPM Publications
An imprint of HOWELL PRESS
Charlottesville, Virginia

Library of Congress Cataloging-in-Publication Data

Ockershausen, Jane.
    One-day trips through history : More than 200 museums,
    battlefields, plantations, colonial churches, monuments,
    historic homes, forts, and parks within 150 miles of the
    nation's capital / Jane Ockershausen.-- 2nd ed.
        p.   cm.
    Includes index.
    ISBN 1-57427-090-7
    1. Washington Region--Guidebooks. 2. Historic sites--
    Washington Region--Guidebooks. I. Title.

    F192.3.O26 2000
    917.9704'43--dc21   00-024544

EPM Publications is an imprint of Howell Press, Inc.,
1713-2D Allied Lane, Charlottesville, VA 22903
www.howellpress.com

Printed in the United States of America

Front cover: The Fife and Drum Corps, Colonial Williamsburg.
(Courtesy of Colonial Williamsburg Foundation, Williamsburg, Va.)

Back cover: The *Susan Constant* replica, Jamestown Settlement.
(Courtesy of Jamestown-Yorktown Foundation)

Cover and book design by Carolyn Weary Brandt
Page layout by Scott Edie, E Graphics

One-Day Trips through
HISTORY

For My Mother,
Jessie Bradley Ockershausen,

Whom I Miss Each and Every Day.

Contents

The Declaration of Independence 175

Revolutionary War Years 195

Recent History

Geographical Cross-Reference

Index

Introduction

This book offers the American history no school has time to teach—the story of the men and women who really made this country—the brave, funny, and very human account of their individual lives. This enduring saga fills all who become involved in it with enormous pride; they, too, are a part of this continuing story.

When history is studied, it is the facts that are learned, not the spirit. Here is the spirit, captured in the stories of the soldiers, politicians, farmers, tavern keepers, housewives, and educators who made history happen. To understand their pasts, it helps to walk in their footsteps: Visit the homes where they lived, the churches where they worshiped, the taverns where they relaxed, the stores where they shopped, and, all too often, the battlefields where they died.

One-Day Trips through History meets a genuine need because most history books that mention significant historic sites give no indication when, or even if, the public can explore a particular spot. And travel books rarely provide the historical background that leads to an appreciation of these sites.

Those of us who live in the Middle Atlantic region are particularly fortunate because we can literally relive the history of the United States from its earliest days. Names that are part of our American heritage—Jamestown, Valley Forge, Yorktown, Gettysburg, Appomattox—are here.

A family's experience can be as varied as "acting" on a jury in a treason trial at St. Mary's City; riding on the prototype of today's railroad, the Tom Thumb; practicing eighteenth-century domestic skills at the Colonial Pennsylvania Plantation; barging up the C&O Canal; or enjoying warm gingerbread made from Mary Washington's own recipe at Kenmore. The excursions are as colorful and varied as our historical past. These sites also have much to *teach* us.

Just how rewarding these trips will be depends to a large extent on an understanding of the significance of the particular site or event. It isn't enough simply to trudge along the Antietam battlefield trail or stand on the ramparts of Fort Monroe. You must view each trip as a time tunnel to the past. Knowing the historical background is the key.

Armies of the colonies and England marched across the Middle Atlantic area. Later, in the same region, brother fought brother in the Civil War. Here are the cities and roads they fortified and the rivers they crossed. Many of the book's excursions mark sites that played a strategic role in knitting a group of disparate colonies into a nation. Other historic sites sustained the people's spirits when the country was challenged from within. To travel from Morristown to Yorktown or from Bull Run to Appomattox establishes a kinship with those who were there before.

Many feel that the diminishing of our sense of history contributed to the spiritual crises of the 1970s. We benefit from the sense of historical continuity that this book provides. We need to feel related to those who forged our past and will create our future. We also need to look more closely at the historical buildings that serve as tangible reminders of earlier times.

All you need to know about how, when, and why any particular historic site should be explored is in these pages. The outstanding advantage of these excursions is that they can be made in a day, providing an inexpensive minivacation. Sites can be combined to provide a weekend family adventure. Many of these historic sites are under the jurisdiction of the federal or state government; so the only cost for a fun-filled, educational one-day outing is the gas required to get there.

There are four different ways to begin exploring these historical sites. The first and most organized approach is the chronological. Children can be given a thorough picture of our country's development by choosing one or more outing from each time period. A visit to the Pamunkey Indian Reservation, with its reproduced tribal village, will give a representative look at the native peoples that Europeans encountered when they reached the New World. But expanding this visit to include a stop at nearby Mattaponi Reservation, continuing to the Jamestown Settlement, and including Moyaone will broaden your perception of the diversity of these first Americans.

Second, you can resort to the random approach. Each selection in this book is written so that it can be used independently. A visit to Sherwood Forest, an exploration of Independence National Historical Park, a look at the old trains at Strasburg Rail Road, a trip to retrace events of the War of 1812, or a trip to listen to the walls talk at the Nelson House in Yorktown are historically diverse and exciting options for a day's trip.

The third method, a mixing of different periods because of their geographical proximity, will appeal to the practical, economy-minded traveler. In the area around Frederick, Maryland, for instance, you can span the years from the colonial Rose Hill Manor to the Revolutionary War's Fort Frederick. Moving ahead, the Barbara Fritchie House is of the Civil War period. Lastly, the Roaring Twenties is evoked at the Blue Blazes Whiskey Still in Catoctin Mountain Park. This one-day trip covers two hundred years of American history.

The fourth approach follows the calendar, exploring why we have our national holidays. Learning the meaning and background personalizes each celebration. Being at a historic site on the same date that history was made there will also heighten your appreciation of the event or person.

Beginning in January, Robert E. Lee, one of the most brilliant of America's military men, was born on January 19, 1807. Choose that day to visit his boyhood home in Alexandria, Virginia, or one of the Civil War battlefields so closely associated with General Lee. In February visit Arlington House, where Robert E. Lee married Mary Anna Randolph Custis, the only surviving child of George Washington's foster son, George Washington Parke Custis.

February is the perfect time to visit one or all of the six homes in the area associated with the Washington family. Or visit the sites associated with the many aspects of George Washington's life: his gristmill, the church where he worshiped, the headquarters and battlefields from which he planned and fought the American Revolution, and his beloved Mount Vernon, where he is buried.

Maryland Day celebrations in March commemorate the founding of the colony by the Calverts. March is also an excellent time to discover the many diverse attractions at Historic St. Mary's City.

On April 14, 1865, John Wilkes Booth assassinated Abraham Lincoln at Ford's Theatre. Retracing the dramatic events of that night and Booth's flight provides an excursion with all the suspense of an adventure serial.

During May there is the yearly re-enactment of the Battle of New Market and the solemn Memorial Day ceremony at the Tomb of the Unknown Soldier. Flag Day is in June, and the celebration at Fort McHenry can be combined with a visit to the Mary Pickersgill House, now called the Star-Spangled Banner Flag House, where the story of the flag that inspired our national anthem comes to life.

The yearly commemoration of the signing of the Declaration of Independence on July Fourth provides an added impetus to those considering a visit to any one of the nine homes of the signers.

August begins the harvest season, and agricultural sites such as the Accokeek Foundation National Colonial Farm and the Claude Moore Farm at Turkey Run are at their peak of production. Frontier crafts are celebrated at the Hager House.

September is believed to be the month when the new-fangled horseless engine, Tom Thumb, raced his four-footed competitor. This month is an ideal time to check out the B&O Railroad Museum or the Ellicott City B&O Railroad Station Museum.

They are really trying to get in touch with the past at the Ghost Walk, held each October in Point Lookout State Park, scene of a Civil War prison camp. Berkeley Plantation, one of the most distinguished houses of the colonial period, was the location of America's first Thanksgiving, and a big celebration is held there on the first Sunday in November. Holidays in history end with a grand finale as many historic homes from all eras re-create Christmas from years past.

These historic trips will renew and restore a person's pride in being an American!

Prehistory

The small man, standing barely five feet tall, faces the huge elephant-like mastodon. He is armed with only a stick, to which is attached a sharpened stone. He is an Ice Age man, and he lived more than eleven thousand years ago in America, right in this area.

Early people, called Paleo-Indians by archeologists, were hunters. They crossed a land bridge of fourteen hundred miles that connected Asia with North America. Their survival depended on bravely attacking great roaming herds of gigantic mammals, which they killed for food and clothing. The harsh and rigorous existence of these hunters required courageous strength to kill these massive creatures with skillfully made spears and stone tools and the determination to track the beasts on their prolonged migrations.

As the giant glaciers of the Ice Age melted over a period of hundreds of years, the hunters followed their food supply south, settling along the new waterways. The melting ice in the Susquehanna River overflowed its banks to form the Chesapeake Bay.

The weather continued to moderate. Large animals began moving northward again and eventually became extinct, thus ending what is known as the Paleo-Indian period.

Animals with which we are more familiar—such as deer, turkey, and rabbits—then moved into this region. The Archaic Indians hunted these smaller animals using gradually improved Clovis-point spears, which today verify the presence of hunters from the Paleo-Indian period. Unlike those first spears, which had only a few rough longitudinal flakes struck from each flat face, the Archaic Indians developed a spear called the "atlatl," which allowed for greater distance and more strength of thrust. Other tools helped to enrich the American Indians' food supply and to build their communities; fishing gear and axes were used for the first time.

Gathering also became a principal source of food and was the job of the women in the tribe. Even as they moved from one camp to another, the women would use their digging sticks to obtain food. There was, however, some danger involved in discovering which plants could be eaten. The women developed a carefully graduated testing system. One woman would put a small piece of the leaf, root, berry, flower, or pod in her mouth and hold it for a short time. If there were no uncomfortable symptoms, a small amount would be swallowed. If the woman still experienced no ill effects, a new source of food would be added to the diet of the group. Women also accompanied the men on their hunts so that they could butcher and preserve the meat.

When they began to plant their own food, the age which we call the Archaic period ended, and a new stage began. By this time—Early Woodland period—the basic problem of survival had been solved, giving men the chance to develop in other ways.

Several important social changes took place during the Early Woodland period. The family unit was enlarged to encompass the clan, and religious ceremonies assumed greater importance for the new group. Travel on the rivers brought one clan in contact with another, and objects were traded. Every event in the life of a clan member was circumscribed by the past. Consequently, the shamans, or priests, gained considerable power as the guardians of the old ways.

During the Middle Woodland period, there were two noteworthy accomplishments: the bow and arrow was introduced, and ceramic making became more sophisticated.

The Late Woodland period was the final stage of prehistoric man in this area. By this time individual clans had established their own protected villages. The plentiful supply of fish and game, augmented by the cultivation of additional crops, made travel away from the tribal region unnecessary. Territory began to be fiercely protected. Conflicts between tribes began to occur when hunting parties from one clan strayed into another clan's territory.

It was at this stage of development that the first Europeans arrived to settle the North American continent.

Meeting House Galleries

Learning about prehistoric man provides a strong sense of continuity with those who lived, and died, in this region long before we did.

Increased political sensitivity has led to the closing of many archeological sites where remains used to be exhibited in their original positions, or in situ. Now, artifacts and paintings from early grave sites are preserved in museum settings, as is the case with material from the Island Field Site, a Native American burial ground near Bowers Beach, Delaware.

The Island Field Site is a Middle Woodland burial site where, for many years, glass covered graves in which bodies rested in their original positions surrounded by the individual's personal belongings. Like the ancient Egyptians, these Middle Woodland people buried tools and trinkets along with their dead.

At **Meeting House Gallery**, you will see many artifacts from Island Field, including spears, fish hooks, pipes, cups, pendants, and knives. These items provide a gauge of tribal development and are on display in Dover's 1790 Presbyterian Church. Adjacent is Meeting House Gallery II, in the 1880 Sunday School building, with an exhibit on *Main Street Delaware*, where you'll gain an overview of the economics, history, and culture of Delaware communities during the early 1900s.

The Meeting House Galleries are open at no charge (although donations are gratefully accepted) Tuesday through Saturday from 10:00 A.M. to 3:30 P.M. They are closed on Sundays, Mondays, and state holidays. Call (302) 739-4266 for additional information.

Directions: From the Washington Beltway, I-495/95, take the John Hansen Highway Exit, Route 15, and proceed east over the Bay Bridge. When Route 301 splits from Route 50, take Route 301 north to Route 300. From Route 300, take a right onto Route 44, which will become Route 8 and take you into Dover. The Meeting House Galleries are located at 316 South Governor's Avenue, one block from the Green in the heart of Dover.

Piscataway Park

Some places are important not for what remains, but for what once existed. **Piscataway Park** has no prehistoric artifacts to beguile visitors, but the fact that five separate prehistoric groups once lived on this spot makes it significant.

Beginning as early as the Archaic Period, man camped here beside the Potomac River. The first group known to have stopped at this site were the Marcey Creek people. Next, between 100 B.C. and 300 A.D., the Pope's Creek people lived here. The different techniques used by the two groups in their pottery making tell archeologists that they were entirely different groups, not just a cultural evolution from one group to the next.

During the Middle Woodland period, two groups lived in the Piscataway area: the Accokeek group, which began simple farming, and, later, the Mockley people. The Potomac Creek people of the Algonquins were the last prehistoric men to reside here. As they evolved into the Piscataway tribe, they crossed the line into the historic period (see Moyaone selection).

Directions: From the Washington Beltway, take Exit 3 south on Indian Head Highway and go approximately ten miles. Then turn right on Bryan Point Road and follow it until it ends at Piscataway Park.

Native American Epoch

Throughout history, the Native American has been misnamed, mistreated, and misplaced. Columbus reached the New World and called the inhabitants *Los Indios*, believing he had landed on an island off Asia. Even if Columbus had realized the enormity of his conquest, he would have incorrectly identified the natives. They were different peoples who fought constantly to retain their tribal autonomy.

Though the indigenous tribes were of diverse cultures, they did share certain fundamental ideas that were radically opposed to European ideas. A major difference, which caused discord and eventually war, concerned the right of land ownership. For Native Americans, land and its produce, like air and water, were free for the use of the group. The idea of an individual owning land and forbidding others the use of that land or passage across it was foreign to tribal thinking.

The first North American tribal groups to come in contact with the European settlers were the Native Americans of Virginia and Maryland. The tribes of Virginia were loosely linked in the Powhatan Confederation and those in Maryland in the Piscataway Empire. All were of the Algonquin family. Their language is part of our daily life—Patuxent, Potomac, Portoback, Piscataway. But how much do we really know about the once powerful groups who lived in this area?

The first settlers were befriended by the Algonquins of the Atlantic Coast. The Native Americans taught them new methods of hunting, fishing, and farming and how to construct the smaller boats used on inland waterways. They also introduced new foods to the Europeans: corn, potatoes, tomatoes, beans, and squash.

But this harmony did not endure and conflict arose, primarily caused by the settlers' demands for land. The intrusion by the Europeans into tribal homelands exposed the newcomers to reprisals such as horse theft, torture, and even cannibalism and human sacrifice. Though these practices had long been a part of American Indian tribal warfare, they angered and repelled the Europeans.

Although it is certainly true that were it not for the intrusion of the Europeans into Native American territory the conflict would not have occurred, it is also true that many tribal leaders invited the newcomers to battle with them against neighboring tribes and thus to participate in the destruction of rival groups.

In 1587, an English colony was established by Sir Walter Raleigh on Roanoke Island in North Carolina. Ninety-one men, seventeen women, and nine children, including Virginia Dare, the first child born of English parents in America, were left in the New World to establish a settlement. But this colony was not fated to endure. When supply ships returned four years later with new settlers, they found no trace of what has since been called the "Lost Colony."

In 1607, the first permanent English settlement was established at Jamestown, Virginia. This area was under the control of Powhatan, a strong chief who headed a confederation of some two hundred villages. This network of thirty Algonquin-speaking tribes with roughly twelve thousand members extended across most of Tidewater Virginia.

The Jamestown colonists dealt with Powhatan as they would with a European prince. They negotiated treaties of alliance for trade and defense purposes and cemented relations through marriage. Pocahontas, Powhatan's daughter, was converted to the Christian faith and later married John Rolfe. Folklore often embellishes the story of Pocahontas's heroic rescue of Capt. John Smith with romantic implications, but at this time she was just a young girl of twelve while Smith was a fatherly figure of twenty-seven.

Powhatan recognized the advantage of trade with the English. He was in his sixties when the settlers arrived, and at his death in 1618, the harmony that had existed between the two groups ended. The friction caused by the colonists' desire to plant more land with highly profitable tobacco, thus reducing tribal hunting grounds, caused resentment. Also, the efforts begun in 1620 to Christianize the Native American children led to mistrust. These two factors prompted Opechancanough, Powhatan's brother, to lead a surprise attack on the English, which killed 350 colonists. Nine years of warfare followed this massacre.

Due to these wars, by 1669 the Native Americans in this area were reduced from approximately fifteen thousand to about thirty-five hundred, about a quarter of the population of 1607. These

Native Americans were dispersed among remnant tribal groups re-establishing themselves on the eastern shore of the Chesapeake Bay. A few small groups remained in Virginia. Their descendants, the Pamunkeys, Mattaponis, and Chickahominys, reside there today.

In 1608, Capt. John Smith left the Jamestown settlement in hopes of finding gold among the tribes in the north. On his journey up the Potomac River, he stopped at a Piscataway village on Accokeek Creek, which he named "Moyaone." It was one of the main towns of the Piscataway Empire, which covered the western part of Tidewater Maryland. It is believed that the Piscataways lived in the Maryland area from the fourteenth century A.D.

In 1622, Maryland settlers attempted to massacre the Piscataway tribe at Moyaone. Conditions between the American Indians and the whites continued to deteriorate, and in 1623 the village was burned. The Piscataways also were suffering from repeated raids by the Senecas from the north, and so they abandoned this location.

Another Piscataway site in Maryland that was deserted by the tribe in fear of Susquehannock raids was St. Mary's. In 1634, the first Maryland settlement was made by English colonists at St. Mary's.

Jamestown Settlement

Just outside the boundaries of Jamestown, The Original Site (Colonial National Historical Park, see selection), is **Jamestown Settlement.** This state-operated, living-history museum of seventeenth-century Virginia has re-creations that help young and old gain a deeper understanding of the past. It's one thing to read about a confined cabin, rustic fort, or spartan Native American village and quite another to climb aboard the *Susan Constant*, to hear the wind whistle through a wattle-and-daub house, or to step inside a Powhatan dwelling. Jamestown Settlement offers these options as well as the chance to explore extensive gallery exhibits.

Start your visit with *Jamestown: The Beginning*, a twenty-minute docudrama that describes the origins and early years of America's first permanent English colony. Three themed exhibit galleries featuring artifacts from the sixteenth and seventeenth centuries explore the circumstances that led to English colonization of the New World, the culture of Virginia's Powhatans, and the colony's development in the seventeenth century.

The first English settlers in the Jamestown area were sponsored by the Virginia Company of London. Men and company alike were

Full-scale replicas of the three ships—Susan Constant, Godspeed, and Discovery—that brought America's first permanent English colonists to Virginia in 1607 are moored at Jamestown Settlement. The largest, Susan Constant, can be boarded.

anxious to make fortunes by taking advantage of their foothold on the continent. Within two months of their arrival on May 14, 1607, they planted a few crops and built a rough stockade and crude huts. Capt. John Smith traded for food with the local tribes. Explorations led by Smith in the spring and summer of 1608 enabled him to map much of the surrounding area.

A fire in January 1608 burned the first fort. The harsh winter weather likely helped to convince the settlers that sturdy houses were essential. The second time they built, they were more careful in their construction of the fort, church, storehouse, and guardhouse. These and other buildings from the fort have been re-created at Jamestown Settlement. You'll also see replicas of the three ships that brought settlers to America. Interpreters dressed in period clothes are at the fort and dock to answer questions.

Perhaps the best known Native American to become involved with the Jamestown settlers was Pocahontas. The museum has a small permanent exhibit that features several portraits of Pocahontas, favored daughter of Powhatan, the leader of about thirty Algonquian-speaking tribes in coastal Virginia. A European engraving depicts the legendary December 1607 incident when twelve-year-old Pocahontas rescued Capt. John Smith from execution by her father. The only reference to this occurrence was in Smith's subsequent account of his experiences with the Native Americans, and many historians doubt the incident took place. Two items on display—a cameo brooch and small stoneware jug—were reputedly given to Pocahontas when she and her English husband John Rolfe visited London. A seventeenth- or eighteenth-century painting of Pocahontas shows her in English attire.

A vivid evocation of the Powhatans who inhabited Tidewater Virginia awaits you at the tribal village and its ceremonial dance circle. Youngsters are amazed to learn that Native Americans in the East did not live in tepees. The dwellings in the village are based on archeological findings and drawings made by an Englishman during an earlier attempt to colonize Virginia.

Authentically dressed interpreters explain how the Native Americans prepared their food and constructed their utensils and tools. The houses are furnished as they would have been in the early seventeenth century, with fur-covered ledges along the walls for sleeping, woven mats on the earth, and a central fire for warmth. Extended families shared the houses. The dance circle may have been used by the Powhatans to celebrate harvests, seasonal changes, and other significant events.

Jamestown Settlement is open daily 9:00 A.M. to 5:00 P.M. except Christmas and New Year's Day. Admission is charged. A combination ticket with the Yorktown Victory Center is available. For information, you can call (757) 253-4838 or toll-free (888) 593-4682. You also can log onto their Web site at www.historyisfun.org.

Directions: From I-95 in the Richmond area, take I-64 east to the Williamsburg area. Then take the Colonial Parkway nine miles to Jamestown Island. Turn right to reach Jamestown Settlement. An alternate route is to take I-64 to Exit 242A and turn onto Route 199 west. Drive five miles to the intersection with Route 31 and turn left. Jamestown Settlement and Jamestown, The Original Site (see selection) are four miles farther on the left.

Moyaone

Although nothing remains but the ghosts from the past, those tracing the path of the American Indians of Maryland should visit Piscataway Park, as it figured so prominently in the history of the Piscataway Empire.

When Capt. John Smith stopped at this Native American town in 1608—one of the principal towns of the Piscataway Empire—it was already more than three hundred years old. Smith, trying to map his route, called the town "**Moyaone**."

Archeological work has uncovered the burial sites of the early inhabitants of this town. In the 1970s, at the request of Chief Turkey Tayak, the surviving Piscataway leader, the burial sites were recovered. Chief Turkey Tayak is now buried here with his ancestors.

When the digging was begun at what was called the Accokeek Creek site, archeologists discovered that this town was the location of five early prehistoric groups. Unfortunately, the few artifacts that remained at this significant site were stolen, and now nothing of these early people remains except the land and the river. It is a sad reminder of just how fragile our historical links can be.

Directions: From the Washington Beltway, take Exit 3 south on Indian Head Highway and go approximately ten miles. Then turn right on Bryan Point Road and follow it until it ends at Piscataway Park.

Pamunkey and Mattaponi Indian Reservations

Reservations of the Pamunkey and Mattaponi, surviving tribes of the powerful Powhatan Confederation, are located side by side. Ten thousand years before the birth of Christ, the Pamunkey Indians were working the soil of an area that would eventually become the Commonwealth of Virginia. When many of their neighboring Powhatans fled, leaving their homeland to the English settlers, the Pamunkey stayed. They remain on their Virginia reservation to this day.

Residents of the reservation, which is near West Point, worked for years developing their interpretive museum. Displays trace the tribe's origins in prehistoric Paleo-Indian days. Specific examples of implements as they developed from archaic to modern forms illustrate the advances in both tools and agriculture during the Woodland period. You can see the gradual improvement of tools in seven separate areas: cutting, hammering, chopping, grinding, piercing, scraping, and tying.

The **Pamunkey Museum** also has an exhibit on changing styles of Native American pottery, from the primitive beauty of Woodland work to the designs of the 1990s. It is noteworthy that the 1940s and 1950s produced a garishly colored unauthentic-looking design, whereas the more recent pieces resemble very early works in form, clay, color, and texture. Some fine examples of recent work are on sale at the gift shop, where you will also find Native American jewelry and souvenirs designed to appeal to young visitors. Museum hours are 10:00 A.M. to 4:00 P.M. Monday through Saturday and 1:00 to 4:00 P.M. on Sunday.

The nearby **Mattaponi Museum** eschews the organized, educational approach. Here, the collection of an entire people is jumbled together in a one-room display. Stuffed birds and local wildlife overlap ceremonial drums. Fossils dating from archaic man rest beside modern newspaper clippings about political figures. The artifacts span the entire history of the Mattaponi and the Powhatan Confederation. A headdress reputedly worn by Powhatan, a necklace that once belonged to Pocahontas, and a tomahawk of Opechancanough, which reminds visitors of the more violent history between the Native Americans and the English settlers, are on display.

Opechancanough (pronounced Ope-can-canoe) is a tribal hero to the Mattaponi, who consider him a member of their tribe despite some historians' belief that he came from the West Indies. The Mattaponi revere him as one of the few Native Americans to perceive the eventual catastrophe of English domination. The museum includes several items that once belonged to Opechancanough.

One unusual item is a "mercy" tomahawk, used by the medicine men for those they could not heal. Several medicine bags, in which powerful amulets were carried, are on display. There is also a replica of the execution club, a snake-like club used for ritual killings. It was reputedly a club like this that Powhatan raised to kill Capt. John Smith before Pocahantas's timely intervention. The museum is open by appointment only; call (804) 769-2194. A nominal admission is charged.

Directions: From I-95 just north of Richmond take Route 360 north for approximately twenty miles to Route 30; then head south for seven miles to Route 633. Turn right on Route 633 and travel eight miles to the Pamunkey Indian Reservation. Signs will direct you to the museum. The Mattaponi Reservation is almost directly across Route 30 from the Pamunkey Reservation. From Route 30, turn right on Route 640 and go one mile. Then make a left on Route 625 and travel 1.3 miles to the reservation.

Colonial Period

First Settlements

Imagine what it must have been like for the first English settlers leaving their homes for the wilderness of the New World. It was Christmas 1606, an occasion for festive gatherings and the renewing of family bonds. These men, however, were severing all bonds, heading into an unknown future. Few would ever see England again.

What motivated them? Why did they risk so much? They were all men who hoped to better their lot, many of whom dreamed of finding gold and becoming rich. The London Company, which outfitted their three ships—the *Susan Constant, Godspeed,* and *Discovery*—also believed that gold was available in the New World and that exploration of the area might reveal a shorter route to the South Seas. The voyage itself was arduous and long and made under difficult and cramped conditions. Both the company and the adventurers must have been haunted by thoughts of an earlier group of Englishmen who had attempted a settlement at Roanoke Island and had vanished without a trace in 1587. The uncertainty of the voyage ended after four months, when the three ships entered the Chesapeake Bay on April 26, 1607.

The Englishmen explored the banks of the James River for eleven days before picking Jamestown as the site of their settlement. Although marshy, the location had excellent anchorage and could easily be protected.

Spurred by threats from the London Company to abandon them if they did not find riches, the original settlers of Jamestown did not spend any time preparing shelters or planting crops. All their efforts were directed toward finding gold.

By summer's end more than half the original group had died of dysentery or malaria. Discouraged, the settlers faced the cold winter housed only in tents and woefully short of food.

John Smith was responsible for the survival of the group. He supervised the building of crude log cabins, which were enclosed by a fence stockade—the first James Fort. He also traded with the local Powhatans for much needed food. As the Native Americans were reluctant to sacrifice food, which was essential for their own welfare, Smith had to expand his efforts and visit tribes on nearby waterways and upriver. His explorations provided information on the Native American population in the area and allowed him to estimate that within sixty miles of Jamestown, there were roughly five thousand tribal members.

The food John Smith obtained from the American Indians literally made the difference between life and death. By early spring of 1608, the brave band that had left England were gaunt scarecrows, but still alive. Despite these heroic efforts, Jamestown might well have been another "Lost Colony" had new supplies not arrived when they did.

The English supply ship also brought a hundred new settlers. Renewed efforts were undertaken to make Jamestown more habitable; crops were planted, and prospects improved. A summer fire that destroyed all their buildings was actually a benefit because it forced the settlers to erect more durable structures. Having shivered through one long winter, they recognized that a little extra effort would be worthwhile. In the fall of 1608, another English ship brought seventy additional settlers, including the colony's first two women. John Smith also was chosen that fall as council president, a position tantamount to being the colony's governor. This development seems rather ironic because Smith had been excessively quarrelsome on the voyage over, and was, in fact, kept in irons for much of the journey. He was sentenced to be executed in the West Indies, and the gallows were constructed before he was reprieved. The group would later be grateful for their charity toward Smith; he certainly proved his worth under difficult circumstances.

John Smith returned to England in 1609 after being badly burnt when a spark ignited his powder bag. Smith's absence was sorely noted. The winter of 1609–10 was called the "starving time," and Jamestown was decimated by this famine. The colonists were reduced to eating mice, snakes, dogs, cats, and horses—hides and all. Only sixty-five settlers were left when spring finally came. They were determined to return to England, and when Sir Thomas Gates arrived, they demanded that he immediately set sail for their return trip.

Jamestown was abandoned, and the colonists were sailing out of the James River when they sighted ships approaching. It was the new governor, Lord De La Warr, with 150 new settlers, food, and supplies. He had arrived just in time to save the colony. The sixty-five survivors reluctantly returned, and Jamestown was saved.

Twenty-seven years after the arrival of the Jamestown expedition, the *Ark* and the *Dove* sailed from England. Lord Baltimore had been granted land along the Chesapeake Bay above Virginia to establish the Maryland colony as a haven for persecuted Catholics.

The one hundred and forty settlers bound for Maryland spent four rough months crossing the Atlantic. Violent storms separated the two ships, and each feared the other lost. When they finally sighted each other, there was great rejoicing.

First landfall was St. Clement's Island on March 25, 1634.The English were met by five hundred armed bowmen from a local Piscataway tribe. Governor Leonard Calvert learned that these American Indians owed allegiance to the "Emperor of the Piscataways." He took the *Dove* down to Moyaone on Accokeek Creek to obtain the Indian leader's permission to settle. The "Tayac," or Indian ruler, did not encourage the English to settle in his domain, but neither did he forbid it.

Satisfied with his meeting with the Piscataway emperor, Calvert returned to St. Clement's. He negotiated the purchase of land that was to become St. Mary's City from the Yoacomico Indians, a tribe that was planning to relocate anyway because they feared Susquehannock raids.

The settlers were able to use Yoacomico Indian huts as temporary shelters until they could build more substantial homes. As they had arrived in March, they luckily were able to take advantage of the spring planting season. This, combined with the harvest from the abandoned Yoacomico fields and the substantial amount of supplies they had brought with them, prevented the cruel starvation that had caused the death of so many early Virginia settlers.

Somewhat later, Father White, spiritual leader of the Maryland colony, returned to Moyaone and converted the emperor to Christianity. He also baptized the emperor's only daughter, Kittamagund. She returned with Father White to St. Mary's. Kittamgund, now called Betty, was raised and educated by Margaret Brent, one of the first women's activists in America. Betty married Margaret Brent's brother, Capt. Giles Brent.

Their son, Giles Brent, Jr., inherited the land that George Washington was later to buy and call River Farm. In July 1675, Giles, Jr. was involved in the series of events that precipitated the last major

American Indian war on English settlements in this region. Giles, Jr. and his cronies, seeking to avenge the death of an Englishman named Henn, attacked the wrong tribe. The resultant Susquehannock war led directly to the colonial insurrection known as Bacon's Rebellion, which left Jamestown a burnt ruin.

Flowerdew Hundred Plantation

On the south bank of the James River is **Flowerdew Hundred**, one of the earliest of the "particular plantations" or "hundreds" established in the New World. Sir George Yeardley acquired the plantation in 1619 and named it in honor of his wife, Temperence Flowerdew.

In 1612, the first wind-powered gristmill in English North America was built. A commemorative eighteenth-century style windmill was built in 1978 on what is now called Windmill Point.

The point has been occupied continuously, despite a Native American massacre in 1622 that decimated the original colony. In 1804, John W. Wilcox married the orphan of the property's last owner. Wilcox purchased an additional fourteen-hundred-acre tract, which when added to his wife's inheritance encompassed the entire original thousand-acre land grant. The plantation remained in the Wilcox family until the mid-twentieth century.

From 1971 through 1995, extensive archaeological excavations were done at Flowerdew Hundred. Artifacts were found from the Paleo-Indian occupation, dating from 10000 B.C. through to the nineteenth century. Today, visitors can explore an archaeological/historical museum, see a replicated nineteenth-century kitchen on the site of the original kitchen and the commemorative windmill.

Flowerdew Hundred Plantation is open April through mid-December, Tuesday through Saturday from 10:00 A.M. to 4:00 P.M. On Sundays, it opens at 1:00 P.M. The last tour is always at 3:30 P.M. At other times it is open by appointment; call (804) 541-8897. Admission is charged. Picnic facilities are on the grounds.

Directions: From I-95 head south of Richmond to the Hopewell Exit, Route 10 east. Follow Route 10 through Hopewell and continue approximately twelve miles east; then turn left onto Flowerdew Hundred Road, Route 630. Flowerdew Hundred is located 3.5 miles off Route 10.

Henricus Historical Park

Born in 1595 (approximately), Pocahontas was the favorite daughter of Chief Powhatan, a significant distinction as it is reported that he fathered approximately one hundred children. When the English settlers arrived in Virginia, they encountered the Mattaponi tribe ruled by Powhatan as part of his confederation (see Mattaponi Indian Reservation and Jamestown Settlement).

The inquisitive Pocahontas (called by the English "Princess") was fascinated by the English, and she frequently visited their fort. Some historians believe that her 1607 "rescue" of Capt. John Smith, when she was twelve, was part of an adoption ritual intended to welcome a foreign captive into the tribe. Soon after, Pocahontas discovered what it was like to be a captive. In 1613, two years after Capt. John Smith returned to England, Pocahontas was kidnaped by Capt. Samuel Argall. After ransom negotiations between Argall and Chief Powhatan broke down, Pocahontas was taken to the new Citie (*sic*) of Henricus.

Henricus was the second permanent English settlement. Although John Smith claimed Jamestown was the "fittest place for an Earthly Paradise," its low-lying terrain proved to be too swampy. In 1611, on a bluff above the James River, Henricus was established by 350 settlers led by Sir Thomas Dale, a military officer and governor of the Virginia colony.

The threat of attack from Native Americans was constant, and it was, perhaps, in hopes of securing peace, that Argall took Pocahontas hostage. She was taught Christianity by Reverend Alexander Whitaker and at age eighteen or nineteen was baptized in Henricus's church, taking the name Rebecca. In 1614, Rebecca married John Rolfe, a young English planter, and had a son, whom they named Thomas. John Rolfe developed a sweeter tasting tobacco hybrid while living near Henricus. From 1616 to 1617, the Rolfes traveled to London, where Pocahontas charmed the English court and the English people. Pocahontas died in London in 1617 after a brief illness and is buried in Gravesend, England.

The peace achieved by Pocahontas's presence at the settlement broke down after Powhatan's death and a massacre in 1622 virtually destroyed Henricus. On Good Friday, May 22, 1622, Powhatan's warriors came to Henricus as they did other areas of the Virginia colony. All the colonists who remained alive were ordered to return to Jamestown for their safety.

This historic site was overlooked for centuries, but in 1985 the **Henricus Historical Park** opened (although it wasn't until 1995 that the access road to the park opened) and is still a work in progress.

The Henricus Foundation is in the process of re-creating the original four-acre village along with a re-creation of Mt. Malady, the first hospital in North America, as well as the home of the Reverend Alexander Whitaker and the church where Pocahontas was baptized.

Additional palisades, watchtowers, and other settlement buildings will be constructed. There is a visitor center with a museum store and education center. Already in place is partial fortification with a watchtower and a wattle-and-daub settler's home (intended for six men since women didn't arrive in the colony until 1608) and several small fence-enclosed gardens planted with corn, tobacco and other crops, herbs, and plants that were grown in 1611. Several walking paths also wind along the James River and through the marshlands. A free boat dock is available for those who travel to the park by water.

The reconstruction of the 1611 Citie of Henricus is open at no charge Tuesday through Sunday from 10:00 A.M. to 4:00 P.M. In the spring and summer months, the hours on the weekends are extended to 5:00 P.M. The park area is open March through October from 8:00 A.M. to 8:00 P.M. and until 6:00 P.M. the rest of the year.

A weekend-long event in late September is a lively celebration that includes historical re-enactors, seventeenth-century crafts, children's games, musket companies, a Native American exhibit, and period food, such as Indian corn soup, Brunswick stew, roasted turkey legs, gingerbread cookies, and sassafras tea. For information on this event and the Henricus Historical Park, you can call the Henricus Foundation office at (804) 796-2671 or the Henricus Historical Park and Dutch Gap Conservation Area Visitors Center at (804) 706-1340.

Directions: From I-95, just south of Richmond, take Exit 61A, and travel east on Route 10 for about one block to Old Stage Road. Take Old Stage Road north for two miles to Coxendale Road and make a right; continue on Coxendale for 0.5 mile to Henricus Park Road and turn right to enter the park.

Historic St. Mary's City

Historic St. Mary's City is a National Historic Landmark, a site of incredible archaeological and historical richness. While the area around the city faded into obscurity, the original seventeenth-century city was preserved by its remote location to be rediscovered by future generations. Other seventeenth-century settlements have been destroyed by the tides of time and development. Neglect has been kinder to St. Mary's City. Today you can explore Maryland's early history at a number of exhibits and archaeological sites. Most outdoor

21

exhibits are open daily from the Maryland Day celebration in late March through the last weekend in November. The visitor center, housed in twentieth-century barns, is open year-round.

The colonization of Maryland dates to November 22, 1633, when two ships, the *Ark* and the *Dove,* sailed from Cowes on the Isle of Wight. On board were Leonard and George Calvert, representing their brother, Cecilius Calvert, the second Lord Baltimore. Eighteen British gentlemen and about 140 indentured servants were also on the ships.

The forty-ton *Dove* was a pinnace owned in share by the Calverts and others and purchased for the Maryland expedition. The three-hundred-ton *Ark* was a sailing ship rented specifically for this voyage. The ships arrived in Port Comfort, Virginia on February 26, 1634. In early March, Leonard Calvert, governor of the new colony, sailed up the Potomac to Piscataway to meet with the Indian Tayac (emperor) Wannas. During his journey he met a fur trader named Capt. Henry Fleete (also spelled Fleet), who then served as Calvert's intermediary and interpreter. When Wannas perceived that the colonists were not a threat to his people, he allowed Calvert to make the decision about where to settle. After celebrating mass on March 25, 1634 (the date now celebrated as Maryland Day), Calvert, his men, and Fleete sailed down the Potomac to a site that Fleete recommended near the mouth of the river. There they found a Yoacomico settlement, which consisted of two hamlets on either side of the St. Mary's River (which Calvert originally named the St. George's River). Calvert negotiated for the site with the peaceful fanning and hunting tribe, giving them a supply of hatchets, hoes, and cloth. The bargain called for one hamlet to be turned over immediately and the remaining part of the land over the coming year. Calvert named the settlement Saint Maries.

Soon, the *Ark* sailed back to England. The *Dove* remained and was used for local trade, since its small size meant it could easily negotiate narrow inland rivers. In August 1635 the *Dove* was loaded with beaver pelts and timber and set sail for England. She never arrived. According to some accounts, she was "much worme eaten." She may have encountered a violent storm.

The **Dove** you'll see anchored at St. Mary's is not an exact reproduction of the original because no plans survived. It is, however, a reproduction of a typical 1634 pinnace like the vessel that brought the first settlers to Maryland.

The *Dove* had a crew of seven who lived in crowded quarters. They had to find sleeping space on spare sails or even atop coils of rope. If they were lucky, they had a hammock to rig from the beams.

The Ark and the Dove *left England for the Calvert property, in what would become Maryland, on November 22, 1633. The* Dove, *a forty-ton pinnace, has been reproduced and can be boarded at Historic St. Mary's City.* MARYLAND DEPARTMENT OF ECONOMIC AND COMMUNITY DEVELOPMENT

The master's "great cabin" wasn't all that great. He had a berth and a table that was used for the passengers' dining table as well as the navigation chart and general work area. It was spartan and a small craft on which to brave the Atlantic.

On the hilltop above the pier where the *Dove* is anchored is the **Reconstructed State House of 1676**. St. Mary's City was the capital of the Maryland colony for sixty years, but for the first forty-one years, the colonial legislative body met in taverns and private homes. By 1674 the need for permanent headquarters was apparent, and Maryland's first state house was finished in 1676. Eighteen years later the capital was moved to Annapolis, and the State House was converted to a parish church. It was torn down in 1829.

You can see a slide presentation and tour the orientation exhibit in the visitor center. That's also where you'll purchase your admission ticket, which gives you access to all the exhibits. Nearby, there is a **Woodlands Indian Hamlet** with long houses of the type constructed by the Native Americans along the Chesapeake Bay.

Archaeological exploration continues to help twentieth-century scholars and visitors understand seventeenth-century life. Excavations at the first capital have yielded millions of artifacts and amplified what is known from the historical record.

Work on the Chapel Field uncovered the remains of a wooden Catholic chapel, which constitutes the founding site of the American Catholic Church in the English colonies. Already discovered are the cross-shaped remains of the Great Brick Chapel of the 1660s. Reproduction of this chapel was done using old brickmaking methods.

Directions: From Baltimore take I-97 south to Route 3/301. Continue south of the intersection with Route 4 in Upper Marlboro. Go south on Route 4 at Solomons; cross the Governor Thomas Johnson Bridge over the Patuxent River into St. Mary's County. Turn left onto Route 235 south and continue until you see the sign for Historic St. Mary's City. Make a right onto Mattapany Road and follow the signs to the visitor center. From I-495/95, the Washington Beltway, take Exit 7, Route 5, south to St. Mary's City.

Jamestown, The Original Site (Colonial National Historical Park)

If you arrive at **Jamestown, The Original Site (Colonial National Historical Park)**, with a proficient seventeenth-century vocabulary, you'll be able to banter with your colonially attired interpreter on one of the frequent walking tours. Try dropping a "heaven forfend," "shodikans," or "fie on it" in your conversation. Substitute "nay" or "aye" for "no" or "yes." Use "a" in place of "to" as in "go a town." Or try "me" to replace "I" as in "me feels" and "me thinks." You'll have a wonderful time.

Visitors to this historic site are often greeted as if they have just stepped off a ship from England. Interpreters in the guise of settlers at James Cittie, as it was originally called, act enthusiastic about the opportunities for advancement in Virginia. They will tell you that the road to riches is tobacco, not gold as the first arrivals so mistakenly believed. Such first-person tours are given daily in the summer and on weekends in the spring and fall. Uniformed park rangers also conduct site tours on a regular basis, year round.

Although only foundations and a tower from the 1639 church remain from that early era, the visitor center helps your imagination rebuild and repopulate the once thriving town. A fifteen-minute film provides the background on those first intrepid adventurers who set sail from England at Christmas time in 1606 on the *Discovery, Susan Constant,* and *Godspeed.*

After a four-month Atlantic crossing made under difficult and cramped conditions (you can board a reconstruction of one of their ships at Jamestown Settlement adjacent to the national park), the settlers arrived at a land where they had to hunt, grow, and build everything necessary for their survival. The exact site of their James Fort has been pinpointed. Artifacts that have been recovered from the site are on display in the visitor center museum and at the archaeology lab nearby. A museum shop also offers some fine reproductions of the pottery and glassware once made at Jamestown.

The seven-mile loop drive gives a clear picture of the natural environment the first settlers tamed in order to establish their community. The marsh and woodland is little changed since the early 1600s.

Before leaving the park, be sure to stop at the **Glasshouse**, located just inside the entrance. Here, in an open-sided timber and thatch shelter, craftsmen reproduce the first "factory-made" exports of the colonies. The green-colored glass, its tint due to the iron oxide in the sand, was sent back to England. You can watch craftsmen deftly blow down a long tube to form a jug or pitcher. A second glassmaker quickly adds a molten piece to form a graceful handle. The glass is at a temperature of between two thousand and three thousand degrees when first removed from the dome-shaped furnace. Soon after shaping, it's returned to another eight-hundred-degree oven for slow cooling, which prevents cracking.

Jamestown, The Original Site (Colonial National Historical Park), is open daily, except Christmas, from 9:00 A.M. to 4:30 P.M. An admission is charged.

Directions: From I-95 in the Richmond area, take I-64 east to the Williamsburg area. Then take the Colonial Parkway nine miles to Jamestown Island. An alternative route is to take I-64 to Exit 242A and turn onto Route 199 west. Drive five miles to the intersection with Route 31 and turn left. Follow Route 31 four miles to Route 359; then follow Route 359 approximately 0.25 mile and turn right onto the Colonial Parkway.

Virginia's Explore Park

Virginia's Explore Park aptly quotes T.S. Eliot: "We shall not cease from exploration and the end of all our exploring will be to arrive where we started and know the place for the first time." This is indeed what happens when you visit this eleven-hundred-acre, frontier, living-history museum and wilderness park. Many current area residents' great-great-grandparents started in Blue Ridge mountain cabins like those you will see at this historic park. Settlers turned the Native American's "Warriors Path" into a wagon road.

The park's nineteenth-century interpretive area includes the Hofauger Farm complex of home, barn, shop, garden, and orchard. Samuel Hofauger was of German descent, although his wife, Elizabeth Hays, was English. This farm, where they raised four children, was near Cave Spring in Roanoke County. Old-fashioned breeds of farm animals, such as Dominique chickens, geese, Ossabow hogs, and Hog Island sheep, fill the pens, graze in the fields, and roam the yard. Not far from the farm are the circa 1860 one-room Kemp's Ford Schoolhouse, early nineteenth- century German-style bank barn, and a country blacksmith shop.

In the eighteenth-century interpretative area are the long hunter camp and the settler's cabin. At the long hunter camp visitors can study the daily lives of colonial woodsmen. In the settler's cabin a variety of pioneers' daily tasks are performed including gardening, tool making, cooking, and cabin repairs.

At the Native American area, costumed interpreters replicate eastern woodland culture and lifestyles within an authentically reconstructed village atmosphere. You will learn how Native Americans fashioned tools and clothing from western Virginia's natural resources. The skills demonstrated here are typical of those used by the Monacan/Tupelo people hundreds of years before the arrival of the first Europeans in North America.

Two other public buildings were almost always found in early settlements: They are represented by the 1880 Mountain Union Church, which served as a meeting house for Presbyterians and Lutherans, and the 1790s' Brugh Tavern. This German inn, offering Parkway travelers lodging, food, and drink, was once situated on the Great Wagon Road just north of what is now the city of Roanoke.

Explore Park has horse-drawn wagons that carry visitors around the park. If you take a wagon ride, you will get a real feeling for why the first shops established on the frontier were blacksmiths and wheelwrights. The rutted, steep, rocky, muddy roads made travel hazardous. Wagons frequently lost or damaged their wheels, necessitating repairs. The expression "I'll be there with bells on" is derived from the custom of wagons with lost or damaged wheels giving their bells to any wagon that stopped and helped them back on the road. Thus, if you arrived with bells on your wagon, that usually meant you arrived without misadventure.

Natural history is also part of the story at Explore Park. Six miles of hiking trails provide the opportunity of exploring the dense hardwood forest with its abundant wildflowers and wildlife. Hiking and mountain bike trails wind through scenic Roanoke River Gorge with its striking shale cliffs. There is also fishing in the Roanoke River.

Virginia's Explore Park is open in April on Friday and Saturday from 10:00 A.M. to 6:00 P.M. It opens at noon on Sunday. From the end of April through October, the park is open Monday through Sunday at the hours listed above. Admission is charged. Before heading out into this woodsy setting, an application of insect repellant is a wise precaution. The welcome center and Brugh Tavern are open year round, but the mountain biking and hiking are subject to weather conditions. For additional information call (800) 842-9163 or log onto the Web site at www.explorepark.com.

Directions: Take I-81 to Roanoke, Exit 143, and go twelve miles on I-581/US Route 220 to the Blue Ridge Parkway. Take the parkway north for seven miles. Virginia's Explore Park is at Milepost 115 between Route 220 and Route 24.

Colonial Agriculture

Communism in America's first settlement at Jamestown? Libelous? What else do you call it when the proceeds of each individual's labor are put in a common pot to repay the collective debt to the London Company? Well, it also could be called a failure. The communal system was totally unsatisfactory, and in 1611 each settler was given three acres for his own use and profit.

Agriculture was the basis of the colonial economy; tobacco was actually the "coin of the realm." A horse cost roughly five hundred pounds of tobacco, while a slave cost five thousand pounds. A fair-sized house also could be built for that. The farm house where Washington was born cost his father five thousand pounds of tobacco. A man could even use tobacco notes to gamble, but he was risking the rewards of back-breaking labor.

Roughly 113 ten-hour days of hard work were required to produce a tobacco crop. A hard working planter would grow about fifteen hundred to two thousand pounds of tobacco a year on three or four cultivated acres, which works out to five thousand plants an acre yielding about five hundred pounds of tobacco per acre. The average size of a farm was one hundred and fifty to two hundred acres, but one man with his family's help could only cultivate four acres successfully.

The middle class planters were the largest group in the colonies. These planters were able to produce enough food on their farms to feed their families plus grow enough tobacco to acquire essential manufactured goods. It was a constant struggle, however, to prevent a downward spiral into debt, which would reduce their status to that of tenant farmer.

Everybody in the family worked except the very young—those under seven were exempt from field work. Frequent childbearing was one of the few ways for a family to obtain additional workers. This rough life, combined with yearly pregnancies, meant that few women lived through middle age. Serial monogamy was the rule, and it was not uncommon for a man to marry three times, thus siring three families.

Subsistence crops were an important element for all middle class planters. Corn was a major food crop, averaging about fifteen or twenty bushels for each acre planted. Planters tried to grow at least fifteen bushels of corn for each member of the family, which meant cultivating one acre per person.

Corn was a good crop to grow because not only did it provide food, but the leaves, husks, and stalks also could be fed to the livestock or even stuffed in a mattress for more comfortable sleeping. Wheat, which provided flour for bread, was another important crop. Farmers took their wheat to a mill, paying part of their crop for the convenience of having it ground.

Also important to the livelihood of the family was the kitchen garden, which was the women's responsibility. A wide variety of leafy green vegetables, root crops, and an assortment of peas, beans, and melons were grown. Herbs were another significant part of the kitchen garden. Herbs served three purposes: as a spice to add variety to diet, as medicinal aids, and as cosmetics.

Leisure time was nonexistent on the farms. Although work in the fields was curtailed in the winter, buildings and fences needed repair. Wood had to be cut to heat the house. New fields needed clearing, and farm implements had to be repaired. The livestock also needed tending.

For the women there was never a respite. Most colonial farm women bore at least ten children, with about half dying in infancy. The continuing job of food preservation and preparation was awesome. The meals were simple but still the result of long labor. A typical dinner would be meat, cornbread, and a vegetable. Women generally tended the kitchen garden with their children's help. Being well versed in the uses of different herbs, they doctored the family as best they could with homemade remedies.

Life on these small farms was hard. Many historians feel that families were not overly affectionate because the mortality rate was so high that life was a tenuous thing. The church usually provided the only respite from this grinding and unending fight to survive.

The Accokeek Foundation National Colonial Farm and Ecosystem Farm

Visitors to the **National Colonial Farm**, created by the Accokeek Foundation within the forty-seven-hundred-acre **Piscataway Park**, get a strong sense of being part of America's evolving history. The National Colonial Farm is growing more than crops; the site itself is growing, adding farm buildings, including a reconstructed farmhouse, circa 1775. The Accokeek Foundation also stewards additional gardens, walking trails, a native tree arboretum, fishing pond and pier, and the **Ecosystem Farm.**

Imagine standing along the farm's Potomac River bank in March 1634, watching the first Maryland settlers sail past on the *Dove*. Governor Leonard Calvert was on his way to meet the "Emperor of the Piscataway" to obtain his "permission" to settle in Maryland. This exchange marked the beginning of European settlement and the beginning of the end for the Piscataway tribe.

Move the clock forward to March 1799, the last year of George Washington's life. If you were standing on this farm looking through powerful field glasses, you might spot George relaxing on the porch of Mount Vernon. What is amazing is that the farm Washington would have seen across the river from his home has remained unchanged through all the subsequent years! What he saw then and what you see today is a late-eighteenth-century, middle-class tobacco farm. The colonial farm site includes a circa 1780 farm dwelling, an eighteenth-century tobacco barn, smokehouse, necessary, and out-kitchen. Workers in eighteenth-century attire till the fields and prepare food in the rustic out kitchen using handmade tools and implements. Many of the kitchen tools are carved from gourds that, like the ingredients for the meals, are grown at the farm. A few steps away from the kitchen is the Museum Herb Garden, featuring hundreds of varieties of vegetables, herbs, and even wild plants. All of these crops have a long history in Maryland. There are four sections to the garden: Crops of the Americas, Crops Brought from Europe, Crops of Africa, and Gathered Plants. Corn and squash were cultivated by the Piscataway Indians, while cabbage and carrots were brought from Europe's cooler areas. Okra and watermelon originated in Africa. The garden is a living reminder of how these crops relate to both the environment and the people from many cultures who have shaped Maryland.

The fields at this farm are planted, tended, and harvested as they would have been during colonial days. One departure from bygone days is that some animals, once allowed to roam, are now penned. Tobacco was the cash crop, but corn and wheat were, and are, also planted. An orchard, like the one here, provided fruit for wine and cider (the colonists did not drink the water).

If time permits, take one of the park's five nature trails that lead through the woods and along the Potomac shore. From the farm's riverbank, you can see Mount Vernon across the river. Walking these trails is indeed like walking back into history. Archeologists have found reminders of five prehistoric groups who crisscrossed this land. The Piscataway Indians settled here in a town Capt. John Smith called Moyoane (see selection).

The Persimmon Trail takes you to the wildfowl pond, where, if you're lucky, you might spot a bald eagle. An island in the pond is a nesting place for geese, ducks, and in the spring a variety of nesting birds. The Ken Otis Bluebird Trail, with more than fifty bluebird houses, borders the Native Tree Arboretum, with 128 species of trees and shrubs native to Southern Maryland. The Pawpaw Trail begins at the arboretum. Narrow and somewhat primitive, it proves rewarding in April and May when the columbines and Jack-in-the pulpit bloom. The Pumpkin Ash Trail is named for the northernmost stand of these trees in the country. A boardwalk along this trail takes you over a freshwater tidal swamp to the Ecosystem Farm, which also can be accessed from the Blackberry Trail (often very wet and demanding of old shoes or hiking boots).

The Ecosystem Farm is a certified organic demonstration farm that provides a practical demonstration to visitors of what it really means to practice land stewardship along with sustainable agricultural practices. The farm follows the principles of SHARE—sustainable harvest, adaptive research, and education. The surrounding community can purchase shares of the harvest before planting, and the harvest is distributed each week during the growing season. The farm has ongoing research projects, such as a solar-powered irrigation system that moves water from the Potomac River to the fields, innovative tillage practices that improve soil structure, modification of insect habitats to promote beneficial insect populations, and methods of controlling insects and diseases by growing resistant varieties and carefully using biological insecticides.

You can explore the National Colonial Farm Tuesday through Sunday from 10:00 A.M. to 5:00 P.M. A nominal admission fee is charged. The farm offers daily tours; call (301) 283-2113 for specific times and information on their weekend craft and cooking demonstrations. Boaters on the Potomac River may dock at the farm pier while they visit. Those with fishing licenses may try their luck from the pier.

Directions: From the Washington Beltway, I-95/495, take Exit 2A or 3A onto Indian Head Highway, Route 210 south. Take Route 210 for 9.2 miles. After you pass Farmington Road, take the next right onto the Bryan Point access road; look for the National Colonial Farm sign. Go left at the first stop sign and right at the second stop sign onto Bryan Point Road. Follow Bryan Point Road about 3.5 miles to the end.

Claude Moore Colonial Farm at Turkey Run

Most agricultural re-creations portray the plantations of the prosperous. A few represent the freeholders' farms. But far too few show us the common tenant farmer's homestead, which gives twentieth-century visitors a distorted view of life in colonial times—we don't see how the majority of people actually lived. This oversight is corrected at the **Claude Moore Colonial Farm at Turkey Run**, a privately operated national park, which provides a glimpse of just such a low-income tenant farm of the eighteenth century.

The farm is run as it would have been more than two centuries ago in the 1770s. It is easy to believe that you have stepped back in time when the "farm family" greets you. Dressed in period clothing, the "farm wife" tends the kitchen garden, supervises her children, and cares for the cows and chickens while the "farmer" hoes, plants, and harvests the field crops. Talk with the family, and you will learn about their many chores. You can even pick up a reproduction nineteenth-century tool and join in the work!

The one-room cabin is surrounded by an apple orchard, kitchen garden, and fields of tobacco, wheat, and corn. The farmer grows tobacco to pay the rent and for items of necessity he cannot produce himself. Subsistence crops like beans, pumpkins, squash, corn, and melons feed the family. Various foods are dried, smoked, or salted to make the lean wintertime a little easier. The farm raises livestock appropriate to the period: chickens, hogs, cattle, turkeys, and a horse.

You can watch the never-ending tasks that made up life on a colonial farm. Soap is made from lye and tallow and linen thread from flax. Milk from the cow is made into cheese and the cream churned into butter. Water is fetched from a nearby stream. Gourds are hollowed out for serving bowls and utensils. Although the farm family only comes in by the day, they present a masterful illusion that they actually live here and that you have stepped into a time machine, which has transported you back to colonial Virginia.

Bring a picnic; several tables near the parking lot provide a shady place to eat your lunch. The farm is open April through mid-December, Wednesday through Sunday from 10:00 A.M. to 4:30 P.M. A small admission is charged and should be placed in the collection tube along the path into the farm. During the farm season, the family presents nine interpretive programs focusing on such topics as: salting fish, making cheese and butter, herbal remedies, pickling produce, drying vegetables, and smoking meat. Three eighteenth-century market fairs also are hosted, on the third full weekends of May, July, and October. Several other special farm events focus on the agricultural cycles and harvesting. For a schedule please call (703) 442-7557.

Directions: From I-495/95, the Washington Beltway, take Exit 13, Route 193, Georgetown Pike east toward Langley for approximately 2.3 miles. Turn left onto Colonial Farm Road at the sign for the Claude Moore Colonial Farm.

The Colonial Pennsylvania Plantation

Did you know that houses could be dissected? Through painstaking architectural research at **The Colonial Pennsylvania Plantation**, it was possible to trace about 90% of the changes to this old farmhouse and uncover its past: when it was first constructed, how the original design was altered, and when different rooms were added.

Though the farm was started between 1705 and 1724, the 1760s through 1790s are re-created here. Drop-in visitors occasionally lend a hand with the farm chores—cutting the curd for cheese, carding wool, or dipping candles. The staff practices old-fashioned cooking over the fireplace as well as spinning and weaving.

Like the Peter Wentz Farmstead (see selection), this plantation appears as it would have looked during the eras that are re-created. The furnishings and equipment are not preserved in a hands-off museum format, but rather are there to be used. In many cases the furniture, utensils, and tools are made right at the farm, using old methods. And the colors of the paint and fabric are bright and unfaded; there is no mellowing with age.

It is interesting to note that although a farm family at that time would have been sufficiently well-off to set aside a room for formal entertaining, the furniture was still sturdy and practical rather than comfortable. It wasn't until the Victorian period that seats were upholstered and provided the comfort of springs.

Although the area around the Colonial Pennsylvania Plantation was primarily Quaker and many of the farmers did not leave to fight in the Revolutionary War, the farms were nevertheless affected by the fighting. A local farmer, Benjamin Hawley, made these entries in his diary

28 August 1777	"Clear morn, then some Clouds, Draw'd in all the hay."
11 September	"Very hot; finished harrowing the rye; the English Engaged the Americans; the latter defeated with much loss."
12 September	"Cloudy; putting up fences that the American Soldiers (broke) in their retreat."
13 September	"Some Clouds; Some of ye English Soldiers had Sundries to ye value of 8 shillings and did not pay."

The Colonial Pennsylvania Plantation re-creates farm life in surprising detail: fields, orchard, kitchen garden, still room, root cellar, spring house, and barns. As early as the colonial period, Pennsylvania farmers practiced crop rotation. A field of clover or grass is likely to be interspersed with the major crops of wheat, potatoes, rye, and oats. The plantation has instituted a breeding program to develop animals that more closely resemble those of two hundred years ago. On a farm this size, records indicate that a family would likely have kept two or three horses, three or four cows, five or six sheep, a sow and boar, plus an assortment of fowl. By visiting at least once during the spring, . summer, and fall, you'll get a picture not only of the daily chores but also of the larger seasonal activities such as planting, shearing, and harvesting. The plantation is open on weekends from 10:00 A.M. to 4:00 P.M., April through November. There is an admission fee. The Colonial Pennsylvania Plantation is located within the Ridley Creek State Park. Picnic facilities are available in the park.

Directions: Take I-95 from the Philadelphia area to Route 476 west; then exit at the Lima-Springfield exit at Route 1. Take Route 1 south to Route 252; exit right toward Newtown Square; continue through the first traffic light, pass Rose Tree Park, and make a left onto Providence Road. Stay on Providence Road to second four-way stop and make a left on Cradyville Road into Ridley Creek State Park. At first stop sign turn right and follow the park road to the Colonial Pennsylvania Plantation.

Historic St. Mary's Governor's Field

Historic St. Mary's Governor's Field is the seventeenth-century name for the area that included the Town Center of the old capital. Here you will find a large number of exhibits and archeological sites with a wide range of time periods. Along this promontory overlooking the St. Mary's River, archaeologists have found evidence of over ten thousand years of Native American settlement. In the seventeenth century the Governor's Field was the colony's center of social, political, and economic life.

As the capital of a growing colony, St. Mary's became a village of taverns and lawyers' offices after 1670. **Farthing's Ordinary** represents an inn of the period, whose customers came to the capital from near and far to attend court and Assembly sessions and to conduct business. In places like Farthing's, gossip and news were dispensed along with food, drink, and lodging. Today, visitors can purchase carryout meals. **The Brome-Howard Inn,** which was moved to the historic town lands, offers dining and lodging. This nineteenth-century plantation house with its outbuildings formerly stood on the site of the seventeenth-century capital's Town Center.

On the town lands is the site of Van Sweringen's Council Chamber Inn, a real colonial victualing and lodging house of the 1680s, which has been partially reconstructed. You can view portions of the seventeenth-century brick floor in the kitchen, where members of the Governor's Council and other visitors enjoyed some of the best cider in the colony.

At the Town Center archaeologists have uncovered and identified the remains of the home of Governor Leonard Calvert (The Country's House ca. 1635), Smith's Ordinary, and Cordelia's Hope. Pope's Fort dates to 1645 and Maryland's "times of troubles," when the colony was almost lost to a hostile and Protestant Virginia. The discovery of these sites and associated fence lines and roadbeds has helped provide the missing map to "St. Maries." In addition, excavations in the Town Center have uncovered evidence of thousands of years of Indian occupation. The reconstruction of some of the important buildings, connecting roadways, fences, and historic gardens has re-created this important seventeenth-century "city."

St. Mary's City takes its name from the Virgin Mary, while the colony is named after Queen Henrietta Maria. The history of this settlement is known because of several authentic colonials who lived in this area between 1650 and 1660. One settler, Robert Cole, unknowingly made an enormous contribution to the unfolding of St. Mary's story. Cole had a plantation twenty miles from St. Mary's between 1650 and 1662, and his ten-year account book was recovered. It provided invaluable assistance to the St. Mary's living-history project.

Cole's detailed day-to-day record showed that although tobacco was a cash crop, a limited amount of corn was also grown. Corn was primarily used on the plantation, but some farmers did sell their excess. The yearly production of tobacco per man was three or four hogsheads (large barrels) or thirteen hundred to fifteen hundred pounds. To compute the value of this yield, it helps to know that you could purchase a horse for roughly five hundred pounds of tobacco, whereas a slave cost five thousand pounds. The farmhouse where George Washington was born cost his father five thousand pounds of tobacco.

The Cole records were used to make St. Mary's City's **Godiah Spray Tobacco Plantation** typical of plantations of the period. A kitchen garden is close to the house. A picket fence encloses the vegetables and herbs to protect them from foraging livestock. According to Cole's records, his farm had thirty-three cows, twenty-nine hogs, several horses, and dunghill fowl, the old name for chickens.

The daily labor on a colonial farm was backbreaking. Hoeing roughly cleared forestland was a grueling chore, as you will see when you visit. If the men had to endure hours in the hot sun, the women had to endure equally long hours at the fireplace—baking, boiling, roasting, and frying meals.

This plantation house is far removed from such gracious eighteenth-century plantations as Sotterley and Montpelier (see selections). This is the house of a "prosperous" Chesapeake planter, meaning that he worked hard enough and lived long enough to be able to afford a few civilizing touches for his home. The house is of English design and has wood floors instead of dirt, windows with glass and lead panes, and plastered walls. An old barn, also of English construction, is heavily framed and elaborately jointed. A second barn and a tenant's house reveal architectural innovations from the Old World to the New.

Directions: From Baltimore take I-97 south to Route 3/301. Continue south to the intersection with Route 4 in Upper Marlboro. Go south on Route 4; at Solomons, cross the Governor Thomas Johnson Bridge over the Patuxent River into St. Mary's County. Turn left onto Route 235 south and continue until you see the sign for Historic St. Mary's City; make a right onto Mattapany Road and follow the signs to the visitor center. From I-495/95, the Washington Beltway, take Exit 7, Route 5 south to St. Mary's City.

Museum of American Frontier Culture

Visitors would have a better idea of the breadth and scope of this fascinating seventy-eight-acre living-history park if it was called "Roots" of America's Frontier Culture. Farmsteads have been rebuilt here in the heart of the Shenandoah Valley with buildings transported from settlers' homelands in Germany, Northern Ireland, and England. A fourth farmstead illustrates how these cultures met and merged by the nineteenth century.

These are not reconstructions or re-creations, but actual farms with their original clusters of houses and farm buildings and, to the extent possible, appropriate elements of the landscape. Living history brings to life the culture and lifestyle settlers brought to America when they immigrated in the eighteenth century. Authentically clad interpreters go about their farm work as they would have done in the old country.

After an informative fifteen-minute video explaining the background of the **Museum of American Frontier Culture**, you'll follow a sandy country lane to the 1688 half-timbered German farmhouse transported from Hordt in the Rhineland-Palatinate. In addition to the main house, a barn with a wagon-shed addition and a tobacco barn sit on the homestead. The house and barn are both built in the fachwerk style, a timber frame filled in with wattle-and-daub panels. These panels are formed by weaving strips of wood, then covering the strips with a mix of clay, sand, lime, and straw. An element of the German barn that was incorporated into the design of frontier farms was the central-entry double door to a threshing bay flanked by animal pens (often filled with pigs). Germans introduced pork and smoked meats to the frontier diet as well as sauerkraut. Furnishings in the front parlor, small bed chamber, kitchen, and hall reflect the 1750s; the first half of the eighteenth century was the time of the heaviest German immigration to this part of Virginia. Influences from other countries that made their way to western Germany can be seen, like the curtains of Egyptian cotton and the Roman hearth. Garden plots beside the buildings are enclosed by the traditional wattle and wooden picket fences.

The path to the past next leads visitors to the Scotch-Irish (Ulster) farm, which was originally built in the early nineteenth century near the village of Drumquin. The house and outbuildings were presented by the Ulster-American Folk Park, whose director, Eric Montgomery, was one of the visionaries who help found this living-history museum. Specialists from Northern Ireland assisted in the reconstruction, and two Irish thatchers completed the roof using a pattern common in County Tyrone. The farm has three buildings: the two-room house with a barn addition, a small outbuilding in front of the house, and a long four-room outbuilding at the end of the house. All have white-washed sandstone walls. Floors are made of blue clay and flagstone. One part of the longer outbuilding was used as a turf shed to store the peat used in Ireland for fuel. In the kitchen, which also served as the main living area, the parents' bed was located in the "outshot" near the fireplace. Notice the "creepy stools," so called because they were set low to avoid the peat smoke. Those sitting on these low stools would gradually move them closer and closer to the warm stove. The second room was used for spinning, weaving, churning, and other household chores as well as providing additional sleeping quarters. Visitors learn that colcannon is virtually the national dish in Northern Ireland—it's mashed potatoes, scallions, milk, butter, and kale. Hedgerows and stone walls enclose this farmstead.

Split-rail fences line the footpath that crosses a spring-fed creek, delivering visitors to yet another farm, which reveals our English heritage. Here you'll find outbuildings from a West Sussex farm once situated on the outskirts of Petworth as well as a farmhouse from Worcestershire near the village of Hartlebury in the West Midlands. The lifestyle of the seventeenth-century yeoman farmer is captured at the English farmstead. Two seventeenth-century barns, a mid-seventeenth-century house, and a late-eighteenth-century cattle shed were built using the English timber-frame construction. All were moved from the Garlands' Sussex farm; but the main house was protected by English preservation laws and was not allowed to be moved out of England. In its place is the Worcesterhire House, circa 1630, which was dissembled before the new preservation law became operational and so is likely to be the last historic dwelling that will be permitted to leave England. The position of the Petworth farmhouse is marked by a stone foundation and partial framework. The Worcestershire house is located in a separate area on the English exhibit site. Furnishings in the house are accurate reproductions based on original seventeenth-century probate inventories from this house and neighboring yeoman-class houses. As part of the museum's food ways program, authentic English dishes are prepared in the kitchen using brass cookware. There is a wooden trestle table, where a great deal of the food preparation was done. The family ate their meals at the carved wooden table in the hall. Notice the pond near the wagon shed, which was a typical design so that the wagons could be driven into the water to keep the wheels swollen and tight. The design of the English cattle shed and, later, the American smokehouse used a wooden frame construction with a hip roof.

The Appalachian farm from Botetourt County, which is southwest of Staunton, reveals the synthesis of these Europeans traditions. John Barger settled in Virginia in 1832 and built his farmhouse soon after. He eventually built two barns and enlarged his house—all of these as well as additional outbuildings are part of the American farm. The oldest buildings use the European-style log construction. Later additions are more varied, like the stone masonry of the spring house and the wood framing for the square-framed smokehouse. A variety of fencing also is seen on this farm: board fencing, picket fencing, and split-rail fences. Meal preparation, field work, and household chores all remind visitors of a vanished era.

The Museum of American Frontier Culture is open daily 9:00 A.M. to 5:00 P.M. Hours from December through mid-March are 10:00 A.M. to 4:00 P.M. It is closed on Thanksgiving, Christmas, and New Year's Day. Be sure to wear walking shoes, and remember that you will be outside a good portion of the time, so dress appropriately.

Many special programs conducted by museum staff are held in the Octagonal Barn Activities Center. This 1915 barn is one of only two octagonal barns in the state. Before leaving be sure to stop at the museum store, where they have a wide selection of handcrafted items. For a schedule of special events call (540) 332-7850. The highly popular Holiday Lantern Tours in December require advance reservations.

Directions: From I-81 take Exit 222, Route 250 west. Just off the interstate you will see the entrance to the Museum of American Frontier Culture on your left. If you come in on I-64, head north on I-81 for one exit.

Peter Wentz Farmstead

Did you ever stop to think that when you visit most historic sites you see the past through the patina of time? The quilt colors are faded, the upholstery frayed, the rugs well-trod, and the furniture chipped and worn. This is not the case at the **Peter Wentz Farmstead;** the exception demonstrates how much of the original we do lose over the years. Nothing has aged or dimmed at this colonial farm. Its motto is "As It Was."

A slide presentation at the reception center will take you back to the year 1777, thus establishing the correct mood for your tour. The ambience is enhanced by the period dress worn by the guides. You'll quickly discern the difference this approach makes. The main house has shutters so sparkling they appear to be newly painted. Far from having mellowed with age, everything has a crisp brightness. The colors used here are not the subtle Williamsburg shades so popular in our modern colonial style homes. In fact, the colors and manner of painting on the walls at this farmstead astound visitors. Knowing that visitors wonder whether the bright stripes, spots, diagonals, and squiggles are original, the restorers carefully left a small portion untouched as proof that what you see is "As It Was."

What exactly will you see? In the parlor, downstairs hall, and upstairs bedroom the walls below the chair rail are painted bright red with a white dots. In the upstairs bedroom this design is further embellished by the addition of white diamond stripes with commas in the center of each diamond. The wall below the chair rail in the master bedroom is white with black dots, a design also found on an entire wall in the winter kitchen.

It was decided to restore the farmstead to the way it was in 1777

The Peter Wentz Farmstead looks as it did in 1777, when George Washington stayed there on two occasions during his Revolutionary War struggles. The rooms he used have remained structurally intact; one is furnished to suggest his office, the other his bedroom.
WILLIAM LANDIS

because that was the year the Peter Wentz house had its brush with history. On two occasions, George Washington, who made it a practice whenever possible to avail himself of the hospitality of the grandest home in the area, stayed at this farm. This distinction was fully appreciated, and the rooms used by the general have remained structurally intact through the years. One of the rooms has been furnished as **Washington's office;** one of the upstairs chambers served as his bedroom.

Another room at the farm, the winter kitchen, is also closely associated with Washington's visits. The story is told that Washington's fellow officers so feared for their leader's life that his cook was seldom permitted to leave the kitchen. To prevent poisoning, the cook protected the food supplies served to the general both day and night. The food preparation areas reflect Peter Wentz's German heritage. The dining room has a traditional five-plate heating stove. The tile roof on the beehive bake oven was also a reminder of his native land. The farmstead has a **German kitchen garden,** laid out with a crossed path that forms four raised beds. More than a hundred different seasonal herbs, vegetables, and flowers serve a variety of purposes: culinary, medicinal, olfactory, and aesthetic. Demonstration crops in the fields and an orchard complete the picture of a prosperous eighteenth-century farm.

An active crafts program on Saturday afternoons supports the farmstead's goal of keeping the past alive. Costumed volunteers using authentic tools and old-time techniques demonstrate a wide variety of colonial crafts. On a given weekend you'll see such unusual crafts as scherenschnitte (scissor cutting), theorem painting, broom making, or fraktur painting. More common crafts include spinning, quilting, weaving, candle making, basketry, carving, block painting, and cooking demonstrations using the hearth and beehive oven. For information on craft programs call (215) 584-5104.

The farmstead, considered by the Pennsylvania Travel Industry Advisory Council to be one of the top ten tourist attractions in the state, is open year-round. Hours are Tuesday through Saturday from 10:00 A.M. to 4:00 P.M. On Sunday it opens at 1:00 P.M. The farm is closed Mondays, Thanksgiving, and Christmas. In December there are candlelight tours of the house. There is no admission charged, but donations are encouraged with the proceeds going to the furnishing fund.

Just a few blocks from the Wentz Farmstead is an even older homestead. The **Morgan Log House,** dating back to 1695, was built by Welsh Quaker Edward Morgan, the only surviving son of Sir James Morgan, fourth and last Baronet of Llantarnum Abbey in Wales.

This splendid example of early architecture is over 90% intact. The exterior dressed horizontal logs are chinked with stones laid in a diagonal pattern. All of the paneling and five of the eight interior doors are original. The house is now restored and furnished with period pieces from the Philadelphia Museum of Art and the Deitrich Brothers Collection in addition to its own collection.

While touring the log house, imagine the Morgans living here with their ten children. Three of the boys inherited two hundred acres of the property prior to their marriages. Subsequently, two of the sons left the homestead and moved to Winchester, Virginia. It was in Virginia that Joseph and Elizabeth Lloyd Morgan raised their family.

Their son Daniel became a brigadier general in the Revolutionary Army. Their youngest daughter, Sarah Morgan, married Squire Boone. They were the parents of Daniel Boone. Other notable Americans are descended from the Morgan family. The Morgan Log House is open April through November on weekends from noon to 5:00 P.M. It opens year-round by appointment; call (215) 368-2480.

Directions: Take I-76, the Pennsylvania Turnpike NE Extension, to the Lansdale exit. Travel east on Sumneytown Pike to Route 363, Valley Forge Road, and make a left. From Valley Forge Road turn left on Route 73 east to the entrance for the Peter Wentz Farmstead. For the Morgan Log House, from Valley Forge Road turn left at the sign for the historic property at Snyder Road. Continue several blocks and turn right on Weikel Road. The Morgan Log House is two blocks down on your left.

Colonial Plantations

Plantations all had to have names for accurate record keeping, but what a variety of names there were. Some simply reflected the owner's name or family home back in England; others were more imaginative and gave some indication of the struggle necessary to obtain the land—for example, I Looked Many Places None I Liked Plantation; I Have Been A Great While At Plantation; Aha, the Cow Pasture Plantation; Penny Come Quick Plantation; or Long Looked For, Come At Last Plantation.

But whether the name was elaborate or simple, the physical layouts were similar. Each plantation had a main house. In Virginia builders often copied the English Georgian style or the Palladian style, as at Thomas Jefferson's Monticello. Maryland houses also followed the Georgian five-part plan. That is, they had a central section with narrow side passages called hyphens. Smaller buildings were attached on each side; usually the kitchen, with house servant rooms above, was on one side and the chapel, with a schoolroom above, was on the other. The main house would have a large central hall with two entryways; one the approach, or carriage, entrance and the other overlooking the river and garden area. There would be a library, study, withdrawing room, ladies' parlor, and dining room. The bedrooms were upstairs.

Plantations were designed to be self-sufficient. Food was grown on the grounds, and most of the clothes and other necessities were provided by skilled workers. Two rows of dependencies, which were used as workrooms, were located down from the main house.

The shoemaker, cooper, carpenter, and tanner each had his own building. There would also have been a saw pit, stable, and barn area. The noisier and smellier occupations were farther from the house.

Women's work buildings included the spring house, weaving and spinning house, laundry, storehouse, soap making house, dovecote, and chicken run. Women also were in charge of the herb and kitchen gardens.

Even on the large plantations, the owner personally supervised his estate, though there was an overseer as well. The planter's wife personally ran the household. Unlike their European counterparts, plantation owners were compelled to exhibit resourcefulness. To hold and improve their position, they had to direct their agricultural empire tirelessly, which prevented them from leading the leisurely life of the English aristocracy.

The large estates were located on the water to permit the shipping of the cash crop tobacco directly to England. One of the high spots of plantation life was the arrival at the wharf of a ship to pick up the year's tobacco harvest. This ship would bring news from London as well as from those plantations it had already visited. A representative of a London merchant, known as a "factor," would take orders for the goods required from London. Planters ordered furniture, farm implements, horses and guns; their ladies, after being apprised of the latest fashions, ordered clothes. No money changed hands; the tobacco sent on board by the planter paid for the order. If the tobacco did not cover the order, the merchant gave credit. Many planters went deeply into debt to support an increasingly lavish eighteenth-century lifestyle. It is thought that by the time of the Revolution, colonial Virginians were two million British pounds sterling in debt. Some families stayed in debt for as much as 150 years.

An expensive part of this lavish lifestyle was the fabled plantation hospitality. The isolation of many of these estates encouraged long visits by relatives, friends, and often by travelers who had acquaintances in common with the planter. After 1751 when the ballroom was added to the Governor's Palace in Williamsburg, many of the plantations also added ballrooms. Large balls in the spring became a colonial custom to break the monotony of winter's enforced isolation.

By 1785 when Virginia abolished the English rule of primogeniture, the exclusive right of the elder son to inherit the entire estate, the dissolution of the plantations had already begun. Wartime losses during the Revolution, soil exhaustion, and the indebted state of many planters also contributed to the end of the plantation era.

Virginia

Abram's Delight

In 1682, Valentine Hollingsworth traveled to the New World with William Penn. His family continued to seek new frontiers, sometimes with tragic results. His son Thomas was killed by a wounded buffalo while exploring the wilderness. But the third generation established a homestead that is still associated with the Hollingsworths.

When Abram Hollingsworth came upon the Shawnee camp beside a natural spring, he declared the site "a delight to behold." He purchased 582 acres from the Native Americans for a cow, a calf, and a piece of red cloth. Abram built a log cabin beside the spring and, later, the area's first gristmill. The family prospered and added a flour mill and then a flax seed-oil mill.

In 1754, Abram's son Isaac built a two-story limestone house, which is the oldest house now in Winchester, having survived in part because of its two-and-a-half-foot-thick walls. A wing was added in 1800 by Jonah Hollingsworth, who needed extra room for his fifteen children. The house was "modernized" in 1830 in the Federal style. By 1943, when **Abram's Delight** was purchased by the city, it was in ruins. Restoration was undertaken by the Winchester-Frederick County Historical Society and upon completion, it was furnished and opened as a house museum.

David Hollingsworth's daughter Annie was the last Hollingsworth to live in the house. It seemed to be filled with more than memories for her. She spoke of hearing people singing and playing the piano in her empty home. Some of the family pieces that augment the eighteenth-century furnishings are an oil painting done by Mary and several Quaker quilts.

An herb garden and a formal boxwood garden are outside the house. You'll also see a log cabin on the grounds of the same type Abram first built. You can visit Abram's Delight Monday through Saturday 10:00 A.M. to 4:00 P.M. and on Sunday from noon to 4:00 P.M. from April through October and by appointment off-season. Admission is charged.

Directions: From I-95 at Fredericksburg take Route 17 west to Marshall and pick up I-66 west to I-81. Proceed north on I-81 to the Winchester exit at Millwood Avenue. Head into Winchester on Millwood Avenue and turn right on Pleasant Valley Road for Abram's Delight, which will be on your right.

Carter's Grove and Wolstenholme Towne

Your journey to **Carter's Grove** will take you from the bustling town of Williamsburg to the splendid country estate of Carter Burwell. A return trip to Williamsburg along a one-lane country road through quiet woods and across wooden bridges will offer an opportunity to reflect on the well-dressed burgesses who passed the same scenery on their way to an evening's entertainment at Carter's Grove.

Current visitors to Carter's Grove stop at a reception center where exhibits trace four centuries of history on this remarkable land. In the 1970s, when archaeologists were digging for the plantation outbuildings, they uncovered a historical bonanza: the remains of **Wolstenholme Towne**, the seventeenth-century Martin's Hundred settlement that all but disappeared after an Indian uprising in 1622.

A group of British adventurers settled at Martin's Hundred and obtained a patent for 21,500 acres from the Virginia Company. Then, in 1618, the company sent 220 settlers to Virginia who established a palisaded fort, which they named in honor of Sir John Wolstenholme.

The remains of the fort have been uncovered as well as the remains of farmsteads, storehouses, dwellings, and graves of settlers, some of whom were buried in haste after the Native American attack of March 22, 1622. The attack cost fifty-eight settlers their lives; twenty more were captured, and the homes and fields of almost all were destroyed. That was the end of Wolstenholme Towne.

The short two-year life of the town plus its abrupt end makes this an archaeological time capsule. Many of the uncovered artifacts, some from sites that survived the massacre, have been of inestimable value. Two closed helmets are unique discoveries; no others have been recovered in North America. The helmets have details not found on those exhibited in England. A dish made in 1631 is the oldest dated example of British colonial pottery-making. Artifacts are exhibited in the **Winthrop Rockefeller Archaeology Museum**.

After viewing the fourteen-minute orientation film, *A Thing Called Time*, at the visitor center, you will follow a path to the overlook pavilion, where you will hear the site archaeologist, Ivor Noel Hume, narrate a recorded drama about one settlement. Recorded messages are delivered at nine locations along the walk. A detailed painting also will help you to imagine what the town looked like more than three and a half centuries ago. Because insufficient data did not permit a complete reconstruction, only the outlines and partial building facades of the 1620 site have been reconstructed.

In total, six sites dating from 1619 to 1645 have been explored. Others are still awaiting excavation, including small farmsteads that survived the massacre and date from the period 1650 to 1750, the year when Carter Burwell began building his plantation house.

Burwell inherited the land from his mother, Elizabeth, the daughter of Robert "King" Carter, whose vast estate encompassed three hundred thousand acres. In his will King Carter stipulated that this portion of his land must always bear the name Carter's Grove.

Over a million bricks were used to build Carter Burwell's imposing Georgian mansion. Great care was expended on the carved interior woodwork. Burwell brought English carpenter Richard Baylis and his family to Virginia so that he could devote all his energies and skills to creating the elaborate designs you can see today. It took five hundred days just to complete the hallway design. Carter Burwell did not have much time to enjoy his completed home. He died six months after it was finished, but it was held by the Burwell family until 1838.

Carter's Grove is furnished with period pieces collected by Mr. and Mrs. Archibald McCrea, who purchased the plantation in 1928 and restored it to its colonial elegance. No description of this historic estate is complete without the two legends told and retold about events that are reputed to have occurred here before and during the American Revolution. According to one story, George Washington and Thomas Jefferson had their marriage proposals rejected while courting at Carter's Grove. The Refusal Room is where Washington is supposed to have asked Mary Cary, a Carter cousin, to marry him and where Jefferson is said to have proposed to Rebecca Burwell, his "fair Belinda."

The second legend dates from 1781, just before the Battle of Yorktown, when British colonel Banastre Tarleton was headquartered at Carter's Grove. Tarleton, believing that the Virginians were looting his supplies, wanted to rouse his sleeping men, so he rode his horse up the grand staircase slashing the stair rails with his saber. Though the story may be fictitious, the scars on the stair rails are real.

Carter's Grove is open daily from 9:00 A.M. to 4:00 P.M. During the summer months it stays open until 5:00 P.M. It can be toured independently for a fee; but the tour cost is also included as part of the Williamsburg Patriot's Pass. Tickets are available at the Colonial Williamsburg Visitor Center or the Carter's Grove Reception Center.

Directions: From I-95 in the Richmond area, take I-64 east, Exit 238, to Colonial Williamsburg. Follow the Carter's Grove signs to Route 60. You will return to Williamsburg by the Country Road.

Gunston Hall Plantation

George Mason built for the future: Both his words and his house endure. Mason built a framework of freedom with his words in the 1776 Virginia Declaration of Rights, stating: "That all men are by nature equally free and independent and have certain inherent rights... namely, the enjoyment of life and liberty, with the means of acquiring and possessing property, and pursuing and obtaining happiness and safety." His immortal document served as the inspiration for the US Declaration of Independence, Federal Bill of Rights, and the French Declaration of Rights of Man as well as many other emerging democracies. It also served as a model for the United Nations' Declaration of Human Rights.

Mason's concern for detail, so evident in the careful choice of words in his documents, reveals itself again and again in his plantation home, **Gunston Hall**, in northern Virginia. His keen powers of concentration, you'll learn, sometimes caused him to lose track of some very important details, however, such as the whereabouts of his nine children. His son John said, "I have frequently known his mind, tho' always kind and affectionate to his children, so diverted from the objects around him that he would not for days together miss one of the family who may have been absent, and would sometimes at table enquire for one of my sisters who had perhaps been gone a week on a visit to some friend, of which he had known but forgotten."

George Mason suffered from gout and therefore served the cause of the Revolution primarily with his pen from the confines of his study at Gunston Hall. He did, in spite of his handicap, attend every session of the Constitutional Convention in Philadelphia during the long hot summer of 1787. He made dozens of speeches and helped draft the Constitution. But when he lost the battle to include a bill of rights and a ban on the slave trade, he refused to sign the finished document.

For the most part, he did not travel great distances, content to travel instead in his mind. John Mason recalled, "The small dining room was devoted to (my Father's) service when he used to write, and he absented himself as it were from his family sometimes for weeks together, and often until very late at night during the Revolutionary War... " Mason's walnut writing table was salvaged from a fire in July 1880 and has been returned to the study at Gunston Hall.

It is the interior woodwork that places Gunston Hall among the most attractive of Virginia's colonial plantations. The house, unassuming from the outside, is unrivaled in its exquisitely carved interior woodwork, which was designed by William Buckland, a twenty-one-year-old indentured carpenter whom George Mason's brother engaged in England. He chose well, for Buckland went on to achieve distinction in the roughly five buildings he designed before his early death. He was one of the first to use chinoiserie in America. He used the new style in the dining room at Gunston Hall, designing scalloped frames over the windows and doors, each with intricate fretwork, or designs. Gunston Hall's dining room is the only room with a chinoiserie woodwork scheme to survive from the colonial era.

Buckland's delightfully designed drawing room combines the strong classicism typical of mid-century English design, reflecting the influence of Andrea Palladio, with rococo elements, which were a popular part of the "modern" or French-influenced style that was fashionable in Mason's day. On the wall is a portrait of Ann Eilbeck Mason, of whom her devoted husband, George, said, "She never met me without a smile."

If you think you've seen a representative sampling of Virginia colonial houses, you haven't until you see Gunston Hall, which is not only beautifully built and decorated but also features a picturesque Colonial Revival garden. From the main house you can gaze down a 230-foot boxwood allée, planted by George Mason. The allée extends to the Potomac River overlook and is the only truly original feature of the garden. Flanking the garden on raised knolls are twin gazebos. The garden design was based on the remembrances of John Mason combined with current understanding of colonial garden design. Ongoing archeological digging is helping Gunston Hall portray the garden as George Mason would have known it.

The gazebos offer a view of the house, garden, river, and Deer Park, which was once stocked with white-tailed deer. You can take the two-mile Barn Wharf Nature Trail, which begins at the front of the house. The trail offers the chance to enjoy spring wildflowers and nesting bluebirds. Hours at Gunston Hall are 9:30 A.M. to 5:00 P.M. daily except Thanksgiving, Christmas, and New Year's Day. Admission is charged. An orientation film about George Mason is shown at the visitor center. For more information you can call (703) 550-9220 or visit their Web site at GunstonHall.org.

Directions: From I-95 northbound in the direction of Washington, take Exit 161 onto Route 1 north. Turn right at the light onto Gunston Road, Route 242. The Gunston Hall entrance drive is about 3.5 miles on the left. From I-95 southbound in the direction of Richmond, take Exit 163. Turn left onto Lorton Road and then turn right onto Armistead Road. At the light turn left onto Route 1 south. At the third light turn left onto Gunston Road, Route 242. The Gunston Hall entrance is about 3.5 miles on the left.

Red Hill, The Patrick Henry National Memorial

No one visits **Red Hill** by accident; greater numbers should visit by design. Red Hill is the last home and burial place of Patrick Henry, the "Voice of the Revolution." Henry argued against the ratification of a United States constitution containing no bill of rights. Some attribute his lack of prominence to his Revolutionary role of speaker, not writer. He left few papers or letters behind. This neglect lends irony to his gravestone inscription, "His Fame His Best Epitaph," since Henry's fame has diminished. Although school children recognize his famous quote "Give me liberty, or give me death," they know nothing about the man.

His diminished fame is quite an eclipse for a man once heralded as the "first national hero," the "idol of the country," and "the noble patriot." A visit to Patrick Henry's last home, Red Hill, near Brookneal, will introduce you to this fascinating Founding Father. Patrick Henry was the first elected governor of Virginia, which declared independence from England on June 29, 1776. He served five one-year terms in all and was so popular among Virginians that he could have served more. In 1794, the fifty-seven-year-old lawyer retired from from his lucrative practice and moved to Red Hill, which was his favorite of the four Virginia plantations he owned at the time of his death. He called it "one of the garden spots of Virginia," no doubt because of its sweeping view of the Staunton River Valley, which remains little changed today.

Today's visitor is greeted at the visitor center, where a fifteen-minute video on Patrick Henry and Red Hill is shown. The center's museum room houses the largest existing collection of Henry artifacts and memorabilia. Perhaps the most famous of these is Peter Rothermel's painting *Patrick Henry before the Virginia House of Burgesses*. This impressive canvas, measuring eight feet by seven feet, depicts Henry's Stamp Act speech, during which he defied fellow members of the colonial legislature who criticized his opposition to taxation without representation by declaring, "If this be treason make the most of it."

You'll explore the Red Hill buildings and grounds with the help of a self-guided walking tour brochure. The house, a reconstruction of the original, which burned in 1919, has three downstairs rooms—the master bedroom, children's bedroom, and family room. The last two of the Henry's seventeen children were born in the master bedroom. Several pieces of furniture are Henry originals.

The Henry family relaxed and entertained in the parlor, where two of their daughters were married and where Patrick Henry died on June 6, 1799. A Chippendale corner chair is identical to the one he was resting in when he died.

Leaving the house, the visitor can explore its dependencies, which include a kitchen, privy, smokehouse, servants' quarters, carriage house, and stables. Although Henry had finished riding the circuit of county courthouses by the time he retired to Red Hill, he did continue to practice law in the office building you'll see on the estate. Henry also taught law here to several of his sons and grandsons.

In the Henry house's front yard stands the national champion Osage orange tree, certified as such by the National Forestry Association. This multitrunked giant with its gnarled roots and striated bark rises to a height of sixty feet and has a crown spread of eighty-five feet. It is an impressive sight.

You can take the garden walk to the family graveyard, which contains the graves of Patrick Henry, his wife Dorothea, and several members of his family, including his youngest son, John, in whose family Red Hill remained until it was purchased by the Patrick Henry Memorial Foundation in 1944. In 1986 it became a national memorial, although it is still operated and maintained by the foundation.

Red Hill is open daily 9:00 A.M. to 5:00 P.M. except from November through February when it closes at 4:00 P.M. It is closed on Thanksgiving, Christmas, and New Year's Day. Admission is charged.

Directions: From I-95 in the Richmond area, pick-up Route 360 southwest to Keysville. Then take Route 15 until it intersects with Route 40. Take Route 40 to within two miles of Brookneal and follow the well-marked signs to Red Hill.

Scotchtown

As Robert Burns once said, "The best laid schemes of mice and men often go astray." This certainly was the case with the scheme of Charles Chiswell, who wanted to establish a Scottish town in Virginia with himself as laird. It was a grandiose dream that inspired Charles Chiswell in 1717 to obtain a land grant from the King of England of 9,976 acres in New Kent County, now Hanover, Virginia. He hired Scottish architects and laborers to build his transplanted Scottish community.

The main house (Chiswell named **Scotchtown**), mill, and a small group of outbuildings were all that were finished when disease decimated the workers and the project was abandoned. A disillusioned Chiswell lived in the main house until his death in 1737.

Scotchtown's next owner, Charles's son John Chiswell, also had his dreams shattered—his by a too hastily delivered sword thrust. Chiswell's intemperate remarks in a tavern in Cumberland County provoked Robert Routledge into throwing his drink into Chiswell's face. Without thinking Chiswell unsheathed his sword and killed Routledge on the spot. He was immediately arrested and, again acting hastily, committed suicide rather than face certain conviction. Perhaps he was correct in assuming the trial would go against him. Feelings were strong because of Chiswell's unprovoked attack on Routledge, and the young man's family was suspicious that Chiswell's death may have been faked. To make sure that it was Chiswell in the coffin, the Routledges demanded it be opened before burial to prove he had indeed perished by his own hand.

Things did not run smoothly for Patrick Henry's family either after they acquired Scotchtown in 1771. Sarah Shelton Henry was left at this rural Virginia home with six children and thirty slaves while Patrick Henry fulfilled his many political commitments. In the seven years the Henry family lived at Scotchtown, he served in the House of Burgesses in Williamsburg, the First and Second Continental Congresses in Philadelphia, and the Second Virginia Convention at St. John's Church in Richmond (see selection).

Some historians have conjectured that, when he delivered his famous "Liberty or Death" speech at St. John's Church, his thoughts may have included, in addition to the plight of the American colonists under British tyranny, the unfortunate curtailment of his own wife's liberty. Due to her deteriorating mental condition, she was kept locked in one of the cellar rooms at Scotchtown until her death in 1775 at the age of thirty-six. She was cared for there by Dr. Thomas Hinde and a nurse, as well as by Patrick Henry's mother and sister.

Patrick Henry's second wife, Dorothea Dandridge, whom he married in 1777 while living in the Palace at Williamsburg, did not want to live at Scotchtown, and the plantation was advertised for sale in the *Virginia Gazette* in 1778. The years of Patrick Henry's residency are recaptured in this restored plantation house.

The personality of Patrick Henry is imprinted on the house. Henry enjoyed holding dances in the Great Hall and playing a spinet similar to the one exhibited in the Ladies' Parlor. An enthusiastic, versatile musician, he taught himself to play the flute while recovering from a broken collarbone. One of the most evocative family pieces is the writing desk in his bedroom, which is believed to have been made by his father.

It was said you could always tell when Henry was approaching the main thrust of his political speeches by his habit of raising his glasses to the top of his head, allowing his eyes to pierce his audience. That well-known pose is captured on canvas in a portrait of Henry hanging at Scotchtown.

Portraits of the Sheltons, his first wife's family, hang throughout the house. Many are primitive paintings, so called because the body was painted before the subject sat for the portrait. There are two portraits of Dolley Payne Madison, wife of President James Madison, who lived at Scotchtown from the age of eleven months until the age of three while her father rented the property. Some historians believe he was the overseer of the plantation.

Eighteenth-century furnishings reveal a great deal about life in colonial America. The rocker in the children's bedroom has two distinct sections on the back enabling either young or older ladies to use it for drying their hair. They would drape their hair through one of the two openings so it would not get the back of their garments wet. It was the custom of the day to take baths only seasonally. Patrick Henry was frequently accused of being untidy; Thomas Jefferson particularly chafed at his countrified ways.

Wandering around the grounds looking at Patrick Henry's old law office and the other outbuildings, it is not hard to imagine the great man himself strolling beneath the trees. Scotchtown is open April through October on Monday through Saturday from 10:00 A.M. to 4:30 P.M. and on Sunday from 1:30 to 4:30 P.M. Admission is charged. There are picnic tables in a tree-shaded grove.

Directions: From the Washington Beltway, take Exit 4 (I-95 south). While still north of Richmond, take Route 54 to Ashland. Go through Ashland for 8.5 miles to Route 671 and turn right. Make another right on Route 685 for Scotchtown. Parking is available on the grounds.

Shirley Plantation

It did not take many years for the English who settled at Jamestown in 1607 to discover that one path to the wealth they craved was tobacco. To that end they began spreading out, establishing plantations to grow the golden weed. One of the earliest of these plantations was **Shirley**, whose name first appeared on records in 1611, although it would be two more years before the estate was inhabited.

For three centuries and eleven generations Shirley has been held by the Hill-Carter family. Though the intricate family tree dates back to 1660, the house was not built until 1723, when Edward Hill III began constructing it for his daughter Elizabeth and her husband, John Carter, son of Robert "King" Carter. Shirley Plantation is designed in the Queen Anne style with a basement and three stories. The brick house is built in the Flemish bond pattern, as are its numerous dependencies. On the roof is a carved pineapple, symbol of hospitality.

Shirley is noted for its hospitality—to horses as well as presidents. The family silver has been used to serve George Washington, Thomas Jefferson, John Tyler, and Theodore Roosevelt. Not one of the presidents, however, had his own silver cup like Nestor, the family's champion racehorse. After a victorious race, Nestor was offered wine from his cup, reversing the practice of offering the loving cup to the owner.

Family lore abounds at Shirley. One story that is told and retold concerns the frieze over the fireplace in the parlor. In fact, it may have been told one too many times. One of the current younger generations at Shirley, after hearing repeatedly about an earlier Carter youngster who whittled all but four acorns out of the carved frieze, decided to make his own mark and eliminated all but one acorn before his mother stopped him in mid-crime.

Fortunately, the frieze is not the carved work for which Shirley is noted. That honor belongs to the hanging staircase. This square, not curved, staircase rises three stories without visible means of support, and each tread is gracefully scrolled. It is the only one of its kind in North America.

The parlor at Shirley is historically, rather than architecturally, significant. It was here that Ann Hill Carter married Governor Henry "Lighthorse Harry" Lee. Their son Robert would spend several boyhood years at Shirley. History also marked this plantation during America's early struggles. Like so many of the James River plantations, Shirley had troops on her soil during both the Revolutionary War and the War between the States.

Shirley is still a working plantation, producing corn, cotton, wheat, and soy beans. The grounds have a full complement of dependencies—a pair of two-story buildings housing the kitchen and laundry, smokehouse, dovecote, stable, and a pair of L-shaped barns. You can visit Shirley daily except Christmas Day from 9:00 A.M. to 5:00 P.M. Admission is charged, and the last tickets for the day are sold at 4:30 P.M. If you want to visit in January and February, call (800) 232-1613 to check on the hours the plantation is open.

Directions: From I-295, traveling either north or south to the Richmond area, take Route 5 east for 10 miles to Route 608, Shirley Plantation Road, on the right.

Smith's Fort Plantation and Bacon's Castle

Originally part of the Jamestown colony, the land across the James River was included in Surry County when it was established in 1652. The name provided a link with Surrey, England, which most settlers would never see again. Today **Smith's Fort Plantation** offers a chance to see where Virginia's leading crop was developed.

Capt. John Smith built a fort in 1609 on the banks of Gray's Creek across from Jamestown. Five years after Smith's fort was built, John Rolfe, who settled in Virginia in 1610 and lost his wife shortly after arriving, remarried. In 1614, he wed Pocahontas, daughter of the Powhatan chief (see Henricus Historical Park selection).The Powhatan Indian chief gave the couple tribal land that the English settlers had already commandeered. Rolfe used the land for experimenting with tobacco strains. Among the varieties he planted was the West Indian blend that became Virginia's number one cash crop.

The house you can see today at Smith's Fort Plantation was not built until the eighteenth century. It is noted for its fine woodwork and period furniture. Considerable information is known about Jacob and Ann Foulcon and their five children, who inhabited the house during the eighteenth century. There is a small English garden, and a trail leads to the ruins of the old fort. Smith's Fort Plantation is open for tours Tuesday through Saturday 10:00 A.M. to 4:00 P.M. and Sundays, noon to 4:00 P.M. from April through October and weekends only in March and November. Admission is charged.

Just as John Smith never lived at Smith's Fort Plantation, Nathaniel Bacon never lived at **Bacon's Castle**. This stately Jacobean house, once known as "Allen's Brick House," was built in 1665 by Arthur Allen, Speaker of the House of Burgesses and a good friend of Royal Governor Berkeley. Visiting Bacon's Castle will give you an opportunity to see where rebels ruled a century before the Revolution, where farm land has been tilled since 1619, and where evidence of what may be the oldest formal garden in the United States exists.

The house is one of if not the oldest brick house in English North America. Although not the fortress its name suggests, it looks formidable with its Flemish gables and their matched triple chimney stacks. The house has been extensively renovated both inside and out.

The house became a pivotal stronghold during the full-scale rebellion against Royal Governor William Berkeley a century before the American Revolution. The rebels, led by Nathaniel Bacon, burned Jamestown to the ground in September 1676. Bacon then retreated to Gloucester and sent one of his lieutenants, William Rookings, to establish a base of operations in Surry County. On September 18, Rookings and his band of seventy men seized Arthur Allen's house. From there they ruled the county for the next three months until the rebellion was crushed.

Extensive archeological work has been done on the grounds of Bacon's Castle. Archaeologists uncovered evidence of a seventy-two-thousand-square-foot garden that may date from 1680, possibly the oldest formal garden ever found in the United States. Although arranged in six sections with bisecting and surrounding paths, this was not an ornamental garden with mazes and decorative beds, it was a vegetable and herb garden (some of which flowered). Bacon's Castle is open concurrently with Smith's Fort Plantation from April through October, 10:00 A.M. to 4:00 P.M., Tuesday through Saturday. Sunday hours are noon to 4:00 P.M.

Another nearby plantation, in **Chippokes Plantation State Park** (named for a Native American chief, Choupoke, friendly to the early settlers), has a model farm that demonstrates agricultural methods and crops from the seventeenth to the twentieth century.

Chippokes has historical and horticultural significance. This land has been in continuous use for more than three hundred years, since it was first patented by Capt. William Powell in 1619. Powell's heirs sold the land to Sir William Berkeley, the Royal Governor.

The antebellum plantation house, the **Jones-Steward Mansion**, was built in 1854. The mansion and out-kitchen can be toured, providing a look at life on a rural plantation in the days immediately preceding the Civil War. Behind the house is a six-acre garden, in bloom from spring through fall, with the peak season being late summer when the abundant crape myrtle blossom. There are eighteenth- and nineteenth-century buildings on the grounds. The Jones-Steward Mansion is open for tours Memorial Day through October, Wednesday through Sunday from 1:00 to 5:00 P.M. Admission is charged. Chippokes may be visited daily from sunrise to sunset.The visitor center is open only from Memorial Day weekend to Labor Day weekend.

Directions: Take I-95 south of Richmond to the Route 10 Exit. Take Route 10 past Hopewell. All three attractions are just a short distance off Route 10. For Smith's Fort Plantation turn left on Route 31. For Chippokes turn left on Route 634 and for Bacon's Castle turn left on Route 617.

Weston Manor

Christian Eppes Gilliam, whose mother was descended from Pocahontas and whose cousin was married to Thomas Jefferson's daughter, was delighted with her wedding present. Who wouldn't be happy with a vast plantation overlooking the Appomattox River? By 1789 Christian and her husband William had completed **Weston Manor**, an elegant, formal thirteen-room dwelling—the very essence of the Tidewater plantation house.

The house was rich in architectural details, and the land rich in history. In 1607, around the time Jamestown was settled, Capt. Christopher Newport led an exploratory party thirty miles up the James River. They were entertained on the banks of the Appomattox River by Queen Opusoquoinuske and a group of Appomattox Indians. Later in 1635, the land on which they met was included in the seventeen hundred acres granted to Capt. Francis Eppes by crown patent.

Weston Manor, the three-story colonial frame farmhouse that you can see today, is a classic example of Virginia Georgian architecture. The manor's distinctive moldings, wainscoting, and chair rails are 85% original. The central arch, accented with a paneled keystone in the twenty-eight-foot entrance hall, is particularly attractive. The spiral stairway features concave paneling, a walnut handrail, and hand-carved supports. The old, heart-of-pine floor still shines despite its long and hard use. If you look closely you will see some of the original wooden floor pegs.

Although now beautifully restored and furnished with antiques and carefully selected period reproductions, the house did suffer damage during the War between the States. The house was shelled by a Northern gunboat. In fact, a cannonball was fired through the dining room window into the ceiling, which may well have served as a reminder of the hazards of war to the officers under General Grant's command, who were billeted at Weston Manor during the siege of Petersburg. Gen. Philip Sheridan was one of the officers quartered here. A windowpane scratched with his authenticated signature is displayed in the parlor.

Before its occupation by Union troops, Weston was the temporary residence of twelve-year-old Emma Wood, who wrote her memoirs for her children and grandchildren. Visitors hear about little Emma's wartime adventures and of post-war ghosts that "ran rampant" in the manor.

Today this stately manor house serenely overlooks the Appomattox River. A community outdoor stage has been built on the riverbank. Afternoon concerts are given during the summer months. Weston Manor is open for tours Monday through Saturday from 10:00 A.M. to 4:30 P.M. April through October. The tour lasts one hour and a nominal admission is charged.

Directions: From I-95 head south of Richmond to the Hopewell Exit, Route 10, East. Follow Route 10 and immediately after crossing the Charles Hardaway Marks Bridge into Hopewell, take a right on Riverside Loop Road. Turn left on Riverside Avenue at the Hopewell Yacht Club and follow historic marker signs, which will direct you to Weston Lane.

Wilton and Tuckahoe

Wilton, a Georgian-style, brick plantation house, was built for William Randolph III between 1747 and 1753. William, like others in his family, served in the Virginia militia (as a colonel) and was a delegate to the House of Burgesses. William married Ann Carter Harrison of Berkeley (see selection) in 1743 and reared eight children at Wilton. Many noted historical figures enjoyed the hospitality of his two-thousand-acre plantation.

An entry in George Washington's diary reads, "March 25, 1775. Returned to the Convention in Richmond. Dined at Galt's and went to Mrs. Randolph's of Wilton. 26 Stayed at Wilton all day." One of the bedrooms is decorated to look as it did during Washington's visit. Thomas Jefferson frequently visited his cousins at Wilton. His mother was a Randolph from nearby Tuckahoe.

At the end of the American Revolution, from May 15 to 20, 1781, General Lafayette made Wilton his headquarters. He moved on to Richmond when Cornwallis crossed the James River and headed in Wilton's direction.

Today you can enjoy the hospitality of Wilton, thanks to the efforts of The National Society of the Colonial Dames of America in the Commonwealth of Virginia. In 1933, Wilton faced demolition, and a museum was negotiating for the parlor paneling. The Colonial Dames, under the direction of Mrs. Granville Gray Valentine, saved the house. Although Wilton stood empty for years, it has now been beautifully restored and furnished with eighteenth- and nineteenth-century period pieces.

Your tour will begin in the central hallway. The so-called back door was the main, or river, entrance when the James was the main highway between plantations. One of the finest antiques at Wilton is the mahogany tall case clock in the hallway, made in 1795 by Simon Willard. Before you leave the hall, be sure to take a close look at the stair railing crafted from a single piece of walnut.

The parlor is included in Helen Comstock's book, *100 Most Beautiful Rooms in America* (now out of print). The twelve carved pillars are among the most attractive features of the room. The alcoves that flank the marble fireplace add to the parlor's symmetry. The earliest record of furnishings is an 1815 family inventory, the basis for the current furnishing and interpretation of the period rooms.

In all, you'll see copies of ten family portraits painted to hang at Wilton around 1755. The originals are owned by the Virginia Historical Society. The Garden Club of Virginia also has made a contribution by landscaping the grounds. Be sure to stroll around the grounds after your tour.

Wilton is open Tuesday through Saturday from 10:00 A.M. to 4:30 P.M. and Sunday 1:30 to 4:30 P.M. The last tour begins at 3:45 P.M. It is closed on Monday (except by advance appointment), national holidays, and during the month of February. Admission is charged.

After touring Wilton, why not head just a little farther out of town to **Tuckahoe Plantation**. You will need to call (804) 784-5736 or 784-3493 for an appointment. If you feel you recognize the house on your first visit, it is probably because you remember the country scenes filmed here for Williamsburg's orientation film, *The Story of a Patriot*.

Thomas Jefferson lived at Tuckahoe, his mother's home, between the ages of two and nine. The schoolhouse where Jefferson began his studies is matched on the other side of the main house by the plantation office. The rare outbuildings and H-shaped house are, according to the late architectural historian Frederick Nichols, "the most complete plantation layout in North America dating from the early eighteenth century."

Tuckahoe's interior features some of the most important architectural ideas of the early Georgian period. The house is still a home, and the family who live at Tuckahoe often conduct the guided tours. They have a wealth of old stories to share with visitors.

Directions: From Richmond center take Main Street to Cary Street, Route 147 west. At the 6900 block of Cary Street, turn south on Wilton Road. Follow Wilton Road to the James River. Ample parking is available on the grounds. To reach Tuckahoe from Wilton turn left on Cary Street and continue to River Road. Bear right on River Road. When you pass Parham Road South, Tuckahoe's entrance is 4.6 miles farther down River Road, on the left. The entrance road is flanked by white pillars, and there is a historical marker.

Maryland

Hager House

Jonathan Hager, a twenty-two-year-old German, emigrated to America on the *Harle,* a Dutch ship that arrived in Philadelphia on September 1, 1736. For the next three years, he explored the wildernesses of Virginia, Maryland, and Pennsylvania. On June 5, 1739, he purchased two hundred acres he called Hager's Fancy. The land he bought already had "3 acres of corn field fenced in and two sorry [poorly built] houses."

Hager built a two-and-a-half-story stone house on part of the foundation of one of the earlier dwellings. His stone house rested over two springs, giving him a protected water supply in the event of Indian attack. Its twenty-two-inch walls could serve as a frontier fort if necessary. (You'll notice the windows on the lower floor are wider on the inside than on the outside, making it easier to defend the house.)

Hager met Elizabeth Kershner, who was a neighbor on this western Maryland frontier. They were married a year after he settled in present day Hagerstown. When Hager formed the town in 1762, he named it Elizabeth Town, but everyone else called it Hager's Town.

Because Hager House was a frontier home, it is quite different from the coastal colonial plantations. You can still see the mud and straw insulation. The house is original, but the furnishings are not; they do, however, represent life on the frontier in the eighteenth century. You'll notice Hager's front room also served as a trading post. A variety of hides on the table indicate what kind of game was found in the region in the 1740s: rabbit, deer, beaver, bear, and even buffalo.

From the front room you'll move to the kitchen, the center of family life. It has far more dishes and utensils than typically would have been found in a frontier home, but they represent the simple pottery and pewter you would have seen at the time. Pewter dishes contained lead, which was responsible for some of the ill health and early deaths of this period. The old brick fireplace is surrounded by cooking pots and dried herbs.

At **Hager House** you can explore both upstairs and downstairs.

In the master bedroom there is a four-poster canopy bed. It was customary during the eighteenth century to use the bedroom, even if it was upstairs, as a social center, so you'll also see table and chairs as well as a 1735 clavichord. Next you'll see the basement, where the two springs still flow. The large fireplace was used for cooking during the summer and by Hager for minor forging jobs.

In six years his family had outgrown their place and he sold it at four times its initial per-acre cost to Jacob Rohrer, in whose family the property remained until the twentieth century. Hager purchased a 1,780-tract two miles away. He called his second home Hager's Delight, but nothing remains of this house. He later built a stone townhouse that fronted on City Square. On November 6, 1775, Hager was accidentally killed when a log hit him in the chest while he was supervising the building of the German Reformed Church on land he had donated to the town. Hager has been called the Father of Washington County. The Hager House is open Tuesday through Saturday 10: 00 A.M. to 4:00 P.M. and Sunday 2:00 to 5:00 P.M. It is closed Mondays and from January through March. Admission is charged.

Directions: From Baltimore take I-70 west to Exit 32 (Route 40) into Hagerstown. Route 40 becomes Franklin Street. Turn left at Prospect Street for City Park, where you will find both the Hager House and the Washington County Museum of Fine Arts.

Montpelier Mansion

Is it possible to be too wealthy? When Thomas and Ann Snowden married in 1774, their combined wealth was so great that they were forbidden to attend Quaker services until they divested themselves of a portion of their bounty. They sold a hundred slaves to satisfy the Quaker requirements.

At Montpelier, the eighteenth-century mansion built by the Snowdens around 1783, you will see indications of the Snowden wealth in the gracious and lavish Georgian architecture and indications of their religious commitment in the interior and exterior design. The door design suggests a wooden cross, with the bottom panels representing Bible pages.

The religious motif is continued in the garden, where the boxwoods are planted in the shape of a cross. The boxwood allée, or path, leads to the oldest surviving eighteenth-century belvedere, or summer house, in the United States. It is one of the few to survive from this early period in America and contributes to the historic ambiance of the gardens.

Montpelier was on the main road connecting the northern and southern colonies. The Snowdens kept open house for a steady stream of distinguished travelers. George Washington often stopped here as he went back and forth to Philadelphia. Martha Washington stayed here before heading to New York to see her husband inaugurated as first president. Another First Lady, Abigail Adams, enjoyed the Snowden hospitality before joining John Adams in the White House.

Montpelier Mansion is open on Sunday, noon to 3:15 P.M. and at other times by appointment; call (301) 953-1376. The Montpelier Cultural Arts Center, located adjacent to the mansion, contains galleries where artists and craftsmen display their work (much of it created in the studios that the center rents to artists). It is open daily, except holidays, from 10:00 A.M. to 5:00 P.M. Classes, workshops, and performances are regularly scheduled at the center; call (301) 953-1993 for a schedule.

Directions: From the Washington Beltway take Exit 22, the Baltimore-Washington Parkway, to the Laurel exit, Route 197. Proceed west toward Laurel for a short distance to the Muirkirk Road. At the traffic light turn left onto Muirkirk Road; almost immediately, turn right into the Montpelier grounds.

Rose Hill Manor and Schifferstadt Architectural Museum

Rose Hill Manor is a historical house museum planned with children in mind. The downstairs rooms contain hands-on exhibits that give youngsters a chance to be actively involved in the eighteenth century.

This rural Georgian manor house was built in the early 1790s by John Grahame and his wife, Anne Johnson Grahame. The house was built on land given to the couple by the bride's father, Thomas Johnson, the first elected governor of Maryland. One of the most significant contributions of Thomas Johnson's long and distinguished political career was his nomination of George Washington as commander-in-chief of the Continental Army. After Governor Johnson retired, he spent the last years of his life living at Rose Hill with his daughter and son-in-law.

Rose Hill Manor guides recall the days when Governor Johnson lived with the Grahames. The costumed interpreters invite visitors into the touch-and-see parlor, allowing time for younger guests to enjoy the eighteenth-century toys and dress-up clothes. The textile room gives visitors a chance to try their hand at quilt making or at carding wool to prepare it for spinning. A sizeable number of the three hundred items included in the Rose Hill children's museum are found in the kitchen, where youngsters can churn imaginary butter, turn the hand of a vegetable chopper, or roll dough for beaten biscuits. The hands-on approach is not followed in the upstairs rooms. The bedrooms and governor's study are furnished with valuable period pieces.

The manor house is but one part of this forty-three-acre park. There are five additional areas to explore. On weekends when Rose Hill hosts special events, a blacksmith demonstrates old world skills in the fully stocked work area. Speaking of Old World, a log cabin has been moved onto the park grounds. The rustic home, furnished with handmade furniture and utensils, takes you back to the days of the settlers who made Frederick County their home in the early eighteenth century.

As you make your way from one area of the park to the next, take time to smell the flowers. The eighteenth-century garden is filled with such aromatic herbs as mint, lavender, oregano, and basil. A vegetable patch, like the one that once served the manor's needs, is in full growth by mid-summer. Flowers were grown to grace the table. Sour cherry, apple, pear, and plum trees fill the orchard beyond the gardens.

Two museums, the Farm Museum and the Carriage Museum, provide exhibits of the nitty-gritty tools of trade for farming and the conveyances of an earlier era. Hundreds of farm implements are in the bank barn and dairy barn. Exhibits depict the evolution from wooden plows to steam tractors. The Carriage Museum has more than twenty restored vehicles, ranging from the buggy with the fringe on top to a Russian sleigh.

Walk-in tours of Rose Hill Manor are available Monday through Saturday from 10:00 A.M. to 4:00 P.M. and Sunday 1:00 to 4:00 P.M. April through October, and weekends in November and December. The house is closed January and February. Throughout the year colonial craft demonstrations are scheduled, highlighting such nineteenth-century skills as soapmaking, candle dipping, quilting, carpentry, broom making, spinning, and weaving. Check the calendar of events for specific happenings.

Just a mile from Rose Hill along Carroll Creek is **Schifferstadt Architectural Museum,** another eighteenth-century house, but one that is far more modest. Schifferstadt, a stone manor house, was completed in 1756, making it the oldest house still standing in Frederick. It provides a window into life in the 1750s as well as early German-American construction techniques. A historically accurate eighteenth-century German garden completes the story of everyday farm life at the site.

The house was built by Joseph Brunner and his son Elias. They named it after their family's birthplace near Mannheim, Germany. The Brunner family name is first mentioned in the Frederick area rent rolls in 1744, two years before Joseph Brunner purchased the land on which Schifferstadt was built. The 303 acres cost ten English pounds, or about half of a year's salary at that time.

The walls of locally quarried sandstone measure over two and a half feet thick. The stones, though uniformly laid at the front, are haphazard on the back and sides. The native oak beams are all hand-hewn. You can still see the wooden pegs that pin the braces together. The house tour gives you a chance to see the underside of the wooden roof beams in the attic, where you'll also get an unusual perspective of the huge vaulted "wishbone" chimney. This architectural tour covers the cellar as well as the attic. The cellar, also vaulted, extends beneath the northern half of the house, which was the original portion. The wing was added during the 1820s. Though the house is not furnished, you will see the original five-plate jamb stove dated 1756, which was cast in Mannheim, Germany, and bears a German inscription, "Where your treasure is, there is your heart." The brick wing has a seven-foot, squirrel-tail, brick bake oven.

The wing also houses the museum shop, with an eclectic mix of gifts, many handmade, as well as books, items of local interest, and specialty foods. Schifferstadt is open Tuesday through Saturday 10:00 A.M. to 4:00 P.M. and Sunday noon to 4:00 P.M. from April to December.

Directions: From Baltimore take I-70 west to US 15 north in Frederick. For Rose Hill take Motter Avenue Exit off US 15. For Schifferstadt take Rosemont Avenue Exit; the museum is at the intersection of the exit ramp.

Sotterley Plantation

A five-hundred-year-old rivalry and a reckless roll of dice are both part of the story behind **Sotterley,** an eighteenth-century working plantation in Hollywood, Maryland.

The families Plater and Satterlee were English political rivals in 1471, when King Edward IV confiscated the original Sotterley Hall estate from the Satterlees and gave it to the Platers. In 1717, when later Platers established this American colonial plantation, they named it for the home their ancestors had been given. Alas, in 1822 George Plater V gambled the whole property away in a dice game. The Satterlees gained some measure of revenge for the king's theft when a descendant, Herbert Satterlee, purchased the plantation in

The history of Sotterley, an eighteenth-century working plantation in Hollywood, Maryland, is rich with rivalry, gambling, and marauding pirates. Hidden stairways and secret compartments can be discovered right along with elegant architectural touches. D. MILLER

1910. Herbert Satterlee was the son-in-law of J.P. Morgan.

The brilliant red parlor where the notorious dice game occurred offers visitors still more drama. A narrow, hidden staircase leads from the parlor to an upstairs bedroom, otherwise accessible only by the bedroom next to it. It is easy to weave that staircase into a romantic scenario. The parlor also contains a secret compartment that was used to hide messages carried by a network of Confederate sympathizers. Although Maryland was a Union state, many southern Marylanders supported the South. During the Civil War the Briscoe family lived at Sotterley, and three of their sons served in the Confederate army.

The secret staircase may not have served romance. During the

Plater residency, when plantations along the water were frequent victims of marauding pirates, the staircase may have been used for hiding. A story is told about one time when pirates did stop. The pirates chose to stop early in the morning, thinking the men would be at work in the fields. Unluckily for them, a hunt breakfast was in progress, and the gentlemen riders routed the pirates, leaving two attackers fatally wounded. It is said that the slain pirates were buried in the field at Sotterley between the house and the river.

The large drawing room has the elegance we expect from the best of the southern plantations. Indeed, it is included in Helen Comstock's *100 Most Beautiful Rooms in America*. The Great Hall, as it is called, was exquisitely carved by Richard Boulton, an indentured carpenter. Architectural experts consider the shell alcoves he carved on each side of the ornate fireplace to be some of the finest work ever done for an eighteenth-century house.

Boulton also carved the delicate tracery of the mahogany Chinese Chippendale staircase. It is said that his indenture expired when he had only a small bit of molding on the stairs left to be carved. To this day it is still not finished.

In the library you'll see a rare jail Agra rug. Queen Victoria ordered Muslim prisoners—jailed because they wouldn't handle cartridges they believed to be greased with pig fat—to weave these rugs. The rugs are highly prized for their singular origin and limited number. Another rare find is the painting of George Washington floating on a cloud. His head is encircled with a halo, and the angels that surround him all bear Washington's visage.

The dining room, copied from Brighton pavilion, enchants visitors; antique buffs especially rhapsodize over the partners' desk. Those who enjoy an actual taste of the past may want to purchase a smoked ham from Sotterley's smokehouse. Garden fanciers should stroll through the restored eighteenth-century garden; it is particularly attractive in the spring when the lilacs bloom.

Sotterley still has a number of dependencies, including a gate house now furnished to represent an old-fashioned schoolhouse and one remaining cabin from a row of slave cabins along the rolling road leading to Sotterley's dock. This plantation was a port of entry into the colony, and tobacco from Sotterley and nearby plantations was loaded at the wharf.

Sotterley's grounds and walking trail are open November through April on Tuesday through Sunday from 10:00 A.M. to 4:00 P.M. From May through October visitors can take guided tours of Sotterley. For additional information you can call (301) 373-2280 or (800) 681-0850. Another option is to access their Web site at http://www.eaglenet.com/sotterly.

Directions: From Baltimore take I-695 to Route 97 south exit. Take Route 97 to Route 3/301. Continue south to Route 4. Follow Route 4 south toward Solomons and proceed over Patuxent River Bridge into St. Mary's County. At intersection of Route 4 and Route 235 make a right turn onto Route 235 north. Follow Route 235 to Hollywood and at the intersection of Route 235 and Route 245 make a right turn onto Route 245. Take Route 245 approximately three miles to Sotterley. From Washington take Route 95/495 to Branch Avenue, Route 5 south exit. Follow Route 5 south to Waldorf. In Waldorf at the intersection of Route 5 and Route 301, make a left turn and follow Route 5 south to Hollywood (after approximately twenty miles Route 5 will turn into Route 235). At the intersection of Route 235 and Route 245 make a left turn onto Route 245 and follow the signs to Sotterley.

Pennsylvania

Conrad Weiser Homestead

When Conrad Weiser was a young boy, his family emigrated from Germany to New York. Growing up in the New York colony, the youngster became fascinated with the Iroquois, who also considered this area their home. His interest and friendship with the Native Americans deepened when he spent the winter of 1712–13 as the adopted son of the Iroquois Chief Quahant in the Schoharie Valley. This experience proved invaluable to him as Pennsylvania's "ambassador" to the Iroquois nation.

In 1729, Conrad Weiser, his wife, and his children moved south, joining a group of Germans from the Schoharie, who settled at the foot of Eagle Peak in the Tulpehocken Valley of Pennsylvania. He built a one-room cabin for his family with an upstairs sleeping attic. In 1751, he added a second room to accommodate his family (of the fourteen children he fathered, seven survived). This rustic homestead is now a museum filled with period pieces reflecting the simple life on the frontier during America's earliest years, 1750–1800.

With the help of his large family, Weiser operated a farm, which eventually included more than eight hundred acres and a tannery. He also served as the colony's liaison with the indigenous tribal groups. Weiser was highly regarded for his skills in communicating with the

Native Americans and his grasp of tribal affairs. Working with James Logan, the Pennsylvania provincial secretary, he helped formulate and carry out a policy that maintained peace with the Iroquois.

Today, on twenty-six acres of this once-extensive holding, you can visit the graves of Weiser, his wife, and several of their children. Legend adds that Native Americans also are buried here, reflecting the harmony of Weiser's long years of peaceful coexistence. Near Conrad Weiser's grave, you'll see a statue of his Iroquois friend, Shikellamy, who was responsible for overseeing the Lenapes in the Susquehanna River Valley.

A visitor center provides background information on the contributions of Conrad Weiser to early American history. You can visit Wednesday through Saturday from 9:00 A.M. to 5:00 P.M. On Sunday the homestead opens at noon. Although the house is closed on Monday and Tuesday, the grounds are open daily from 9:00 A.M. to dusk for picnicking and recreation. Admission is charged. For guided tours administered by the Pennsylvania Historical & Museum Commission, you can call (610) 589-2934.

Directions: From I-76, the Pennsylvania Turnpike, take Exit 20, Lebanon/Lancaster. Take Route 72 north to Route 419. Proceed north on Route 419 to Womelsdorf, then make a right on High Street to West Park entrance. From I-78, head south on Route 419 to Route 422, then take Route 422 east for one mile to the Conrad Weiser Homestead at Womelsdorf.

Daniel Boone Homestead

The **Daniel Boone Homestead** was built in the untamed part of Pennsylvania that is now the Hopewell area. Daniel Boone was born and lived here until he was sixteen. In the woods around his home, he learned to hunt and trap. Only the foundations remain of the log cabin that was Daniel Boone's birthplace. A two-story stone house built by the Boones and fully completed in the late eighteenth century has been furnished to re-create rural life in this part of Pennsylvania. It is interesting to compare this independent rural life with that of the iron workers at nearby Hopewell Furnace (see selection).

The Boone house is now furnished to tell the story of the three families who lived on this site in the eighteenth century: the Boone, Maugridge, and DeTurk families. These families represent English and Germanic rural traditions, and their stories provide details about early settlers in this part of the state.

The homestead has a working blacksmith's shop. Daniel Boone's father practiced this trade, and as a young boy Daniel learned how to fix his own rifle and musket. Additional outbuildings include the smokehouse, barn, Bertolet log house, bake oven, and sawmill. The visitor center provides orientation and an extensive collection of publications on sale related to Boone and Pennsylvania colonial history. Tours and historical programs are presented year-round.

There are trails extending through part of the homestead's 579 acres of rolling countryside. The area around the farm is a game sanctuary, where deer, raccoon, rabbits, pheasants, and quail can occasionally be spotted, just as it was when young Daniel learned to hunt.

The grounds also boast a picnic area, lake, and overnight camping facilities, both indoor and outdoor, for organized youth groups. Admission is charged to the historic area. For additional information call (215) 582-4900.

Directions: From I-76, the Pennsylvania Turnpike, take Exit 22 at Morgantown and pick up Route 10; then bear left at the McDonalds. Proceed to the intersection and make a right; then very shortly, bear right again on Route 176, north. Follow Route 176 until you see a sign for Pottstown. This will take you to Route 422 east. Continue for approximately four miles to the highway division. Stay in the left lane and proceed through a traffic light at Route 82. Take the first left turn onto Daniel Boone Road. Proceed a half mile to the homestead.

Graeme Park

Were they to make a movie of Elizabeth Graeme's life, it would be a two-handkerchief film, for hers was a tragic tale. She was the youngest child of Dr. Thomas Graeme, who traveled to the New World in May 1717 as the personal physician of Sir William Keith, deputy-governor of Penn's colony.

Graeme, a single twenty-nine-year-old, lived in Keith's Philadelphia home, where he met and married the governor's stepdaughter Ann Diggs. Graeme's career progressed. He became physician of the port of Philadelphia and a judge of the Supreme Court. Meanwhile, Keith's career floundered. After a dispute with the Penn family, Keith was removed from office. He returned to England to raise funds to obtain passage for his family to return to England or to secure a new appointment in the New World. Keith died before realizing either goal.

While in Pennsylvania in 1722, Keith had commissioned a country mansion. He called his estate **Fountain Low** because of the natural springs running through the seventeen hundred acres. Graeme purchased the estate in 1739, remodeling the interior to reflect current English style and taste. He added elaborate paneling, fine marble, and imported ceramic delft tiles around the fireplaces.

At Graeme's death in 1772, the estate was inherited by his sole surviving child, Elizabeth. Unlike most women in the colonial era, she was well educated with an interest in literary pursuits and a talent for poetry. She hosted some of the country's first literary gatherings and was the only woman to be an informal associate of the Swains of the Schuylkill, a group of budding intellectuals who staged what member Benjamin Rush called "attic evenings."

Although of a romantic nature, her own affairs of the heart were tragically unfulfilled. At seventeen she fell in love with William Franklin, the illegitimate son of Benjamin Franklin. Both fathers opposed the match and broke up the relationship. In late 1771, six years after the death of her mother, while acting as her father's hostess, Elizabeth met Henry Hugh Ferguson, a poor Scottish immigrant ten years her junior. In little over four months, she married him, despite her father's disapproval and without his knowledge. The very day she had determined to tell him of her marriage, her father died. Henry then moved into **Graeme Park** with Elizabeth. They spent only two and a half years together. In 1775 Ferguson traveled to Great Britain. He returned to Philadelphia two years later but remained in the city, working for the British as commissary of prisoners. As a Loyalist, Ferguson was opposed to the American cause. He fled the country after the war, and he and Elizabeth never reunited.

Elizabeth's position during the Revolution was pitiable. Now in her forties, she remained alone at Graeme Park, cut off from family and friends. It is thought she favored the America cause; she contributed food and clothing to the army when it was camped at Whitemarsh. Mad Anthony Wayne's troops camped on the grounds of Graeme Park before the Battle of Germantown. Only the intervention of family friends prevented her home from being sold as a spoil of war because of her husband's Tory connections. Most of the contents were sold at public auction. She kept furniture for three rooms and eventually bought back some of the forfeited pieces. In 1791, Elizabeth sold Graeme Park to her niece Anna Young's husband. She had been living on less than two hundred dollars a year. The money she received for the house supported her until her death in 1801.

Through all the subsequent owners, the original stone exterior built for Keith survived, as did the exquisite details added by Thomas Graeme. The house is an architectural treasure and is presented with only a few pieces of period furniture in order to focus attention on the details of design and ornamentation. Paint pigments enabled restorers to return the rooms to the colors enjoyed during the years the Graeme family entertained at their country estate. The parlor retains the original eighteenth-century paint. The Georgian-style parlor is the most elaborate room. Portraits of members of the Graeme family adorn the walls.

The summer kitchen behind the mansion was reconstructed and a physic garden planted with medicinal and culinary herbs that would have been grown in the eighteenth century. The visitor center is in the nineteenth-century bank barn, added by the Penrose family, Quakers who farmed the land in the early 1800s. There are exhibits and a video introduction to Graeme Park. The house is open Wednesday through Saturday 10:00 A.M. to 4:00 P.M.; on Sunday it opens at noon. The last tour begins at 3:00 P.M. Admission is charged. Throughout the year, special events including the Scottish Heritage Festival and living-history programs are scheduled at Graeme Park; call (215) 343-0965 for details.

Directions: From I-76 take the Willow Grove Interchange and head north on Route 611. At the intersection with County Line Road, bear left; Graeme Park is at 859 County Line Road.

The Grange

During the **Grange's** three-hundred-year history, it has had at least ten owners, three names, and numerous architectural revisions. This layering effect makes the Grange historically, architecturally, and horticulturally interesting.

The present estate is just a small part of the five hundred acres claimed in 1682 by Henry Lewis, a Welsh Quaker, who was one of the first three European settlers in the area. He named his new home Maen Coch, which means Redstone, after his homeland in Wales. It is not his house that endures, but a later one built by his son Henry Lewis, Jr., circa 1700. The son's house forms the drawing room of The Grange and the rooms directly above. The part that is now the library and stair hall were added around 1730.

In 1750, the house acquired a new owner, a new name, and a new look. Capt. John Wilcox named it Clifton Hall and added a large room for formal entertaining. After only eleven years, he sold the property to Charles Cruikshank, a Scot. Cruikshank did not support the American Revolution and left the country when the colonists won the war, selling the estate in 1782 to his daughter's husband, John Ross. Ross helped finance the patriot's cause, an activity that certainly upset his father-in-law. Ross procured clothes, arms, and gunpowder for the Continental Army. Like so many who supported the cause of independence, he often paid out of his own pocket. Ross renamed his new home the Grange, after Lafayette's French estate.

Lafayette, Washington, and many members of the first cabinet enjoyed the hospitality of John Ross. Entries in Washington's diary refer to visits, such as the one on June 17, 1787: "Went to church. After wch rid 8 miles into the country and dined with Mr. Ross in Chester County. Retd. to town about dusk."

Today, you will see the house and dependencies so essential to an eighteenth- and nineteenth-century gentleman's country home. The estate grounds include ten acres of woodland with a number of record size specimens. One of the last owners of the Grange, Benjamin R. Hoffman of Philadelphia, greatly enhanced the gardens. Blooming from early spring to late fall, boxwood-enclosed terraced beds offer nearly continuous color through the seasons. Close to the house is a rose garden, an herbal bed with more than fifty different herbs, and an old-fashioned knot garden. In the spring daffodils, narcissus, and native wildflowers brighten the woodland trails.

The English Gothic appearance of the house is the result of alterations made from 1850 to 1863. This period is reflected in the interior furnishings as well. The property is now owned by the Township of Haverford, and operational activities are coordinated by the Friends of the Grange, Inc.

Guided tours of the mansion, gardens, outbuildings, and woodlands are held from April through October on weekends from 1:00 to 4:00 P.M. Admission is charged. To arrange a tour at other times or to obtain a schedule of special summer and December evening tours, call (610) 446-4958.

Directions: From I-76, take the Schuylkill Expressway from Philadelphia north to US 1. Take US 1 south about four miles to Earlington Road and turn right. Following Grange signs from Earlington, turn right on Bennington Road, then left on Myrtle Avenue. Make a right into the Grange entrance at Warwick Road next to St. James Church, which was once the Grange's dairy barn.

Historic Rock Ford Plantation

Historic Rock Ford Plantation in Lancaster is a quiet eighteenth-century oasis virtually unchanged from the time Gen. Edward Hand— physician, Revolutionary War hero, and close friend of George Washington—lived there over two hundred years ago.

The Hand family lived in the gracious 1794 Georgian-style brick mansion in the latter years of the new republic. The house still has

90% of the original floors, woodwork, window glass, and beautiful built-in cupboards. Costumed guides point out a window pane in the dining room on which two of the Hand children, John and Sarah, scratched their names. The estate inventory taken immediately following the general's death in 1802 was used to accurately furnish the house with appropriate period antiques.

Edward Hand rose to the rank of adjutant general during the American Revolution. In the grand hallway you will see the general's field desk, complete with three secret compartments. His personal chair, thought to have been constructed in Ireland to accommodate his six-foot, four-inch frame, can be seen in the study. A dinner invitation from President Washington is on display in the elegant blue parlor. Also seen in this formal room are a silver cream pitcher and sugar tongs that are believed to be the gifts President Washington sent to Mrs. Hand as a thank you for serving him tea when he visited Lancaster on July 4, 1791.

The kitchen fireplace is used periodically to demonstrate eighteenth-century cooking practices. During the spring and summer, the plantation's foursquare, raised bed in the kitchen/herb garden can be seen after you leave the mansion house.

On the site of the original barn is an eighteenth-century stone barn housing the **Kauffman Collection of Pennsylvania Folk Arts and Crafts**, which features more than four hundred examples of fraktur, pewter, copper, tin, glassware, firearms, and furniture typical of southeastern Pennsylvania artisans and craftsmen from 1750 to 1850. It is open by appointment only; call (717) 392-7223.

Historic Rock Ford is open April through October on Tuesday through Saturday from 10:00 A.M. to 4:00 P.M.; on Sundays it opens at noon. Special candlelight tours are offered in December.

Directions: From I-76, the Pennsylvania Turnpike, take Exit 21, Route 222 to Lancaster. Rock Ford Plantation is located in Lancaster County Central Park, just off Route 222 on Rock Ford Road.

Pennsbury Manor

Somehow when you read the history books you get the idea that William Penn, proprietor of the Pennsylvania colony, seeking to oversee his great social experiment personally, settled permanently in his domain in the New World. This is far from accurate, although it may have been close to Penn's original intentions.

Instead, Penn returned to England after only two years in his colony, intending to return promptly and bring his family with him. He went back in response to a threat to his land claims, which were based on a charter he received from King Charles II in 1681. From England, William Penn sent regular letters detailing his instructions for his house, gardens, and grounds to James Harrison, his steward.

Penn's estate was twenty-six miles north of Philadelphia on eighty-four hundred acres of land. Although he held title to the land through his land grant from the British king, Penn also acknowledged the rights of the indigenous population. He purchased his land from the native Lenapes, paying them 350 fathoms (a fathom equals six feet) of white wampum, a score (a set of twenty) each of blankets, guns, coats, shirts, and stockings, 40 axes, 40 pairs of scissors, 200 knives, and a handful of fishhooks.

William Penn returned to Pennsylvania in 1699 and in the following spring moved with his second wife to his completed country estate, **Pennsbury Manor**. Their son, John, had just been born in Philadelphia. Their stay was to be brief; after only two years, financial problems forced them back to England—this time for good. By the end of his life, Penn was in debtor's prison. He considered selling Pennsylvania back to the crown, but his wife wouldn't let him; she wanted it for her children.

Pennsbury Manor had fallen into disrepair and ruin by the time of the American Revolution. By the twentieth century no trace of Pennsbury survived above ground. In 1932, ten acres encompassing the ground on which the main house once stood were given to the state by the Charles Warner Company as a memorial to William Penn. A major restoration program restored the Manor House, plantation outbuildings, and the landscape to its appearance when William Penn was in residence.

You may notice that the furniture is not like that in the restored homes of Independence National Historical Park. Here the furniture is of an earlier era—the style of Charles II and William and Mary. Some of the pieces were made a hundred years before the American Revolution. Pennsbury Manor has the largest collection of seventeenth-century furnishings exhibited in the state. The collection reflects the breeding and wealth of the Penn family. Although he was a Quaker, Penn had a taste for gracious living. He never adopted the simple lifestyle typical of most members of his sect.

William Penn's letters to his steward also detailed his plans for the gardens. Skilled gardeners were sent to Pennsbury from England and Scotland. During his first visit to Pennsylvania, 1682 to 1684, Penn wrote to England requesting "a few fruit trees 9 of... Lord Sunderland's... rare collection." Tradition holds that when Penn returned, he brought with him eighteen rose plants from London. Penn also instructed his gardener to obtain native flowers. The kitchen garden grew large quantities of common vegetables plus specialty crops like artichokes, asparagus, and ten to twenty types of greens. A wide variety of herbs also were grown for culinary, medicinal, and cosmetic purposes. The garden also included apples, plums, pears, cherries, grapes, quince, apricots, and a wide variety of berries. The garden today is considerably smaller than it was in Penn's day, but it does reflect its style and substance and contains only historically authentic plants. The farm animals are also historically accurate.

Penn's concerns extended to the outbuildings, or dependencies. Today you will see twenty-one buildings, including the icehouse, stone stable, smokehouse, plantation office, wood house, and bake and brew house. Historically garbed guides conduct tours of the forty-three-acre historic site and explain the functions of the buildings. Don't miss the boathouse, which contains a replica of the barge Penn used for the five-hour trip back and forth to Philadelphia.

Pennsbury Manor is open Tuesday through Saturday from 9:00 A.M. to 5:00 P.M.; on Sundays it opens at noon. Tours take approximately one and a half hours. Admission is charged. An audiovisual program in the visitor center provides background on this historic property. From April through October on Sunday afternoons from 1:00 to 4:00 P.M., there are living-history programs for families. In the activity room visitors can try writing with a quill pen, carding wool, and playing a variety of seventeenth-century games like ball and cock and drop spindle.

Directions: From I-76, the Pennsylvania Turnpike, take Exit 29 to Route 13 north. Then make a right onto Green Lane at the first traffic light. When you reach a dead end, make a left onto Radcliffe Street and continue for 4.6 miles (the road changes names twice, becoming Main Street and then Bordentown Road). Make a right onto Pennsbury Memorial Road, which leads into the parking lot for Pennsbury Manor.

Wright's Ferry Mansion

Massachusetts had Abigail Adams, and Maryland had Margaret Brent, but Pennsylvania had its own inspirational woman, Susanna Wright. When she was twenty-nine years old, Susanna purchased a hundred acres of land along the Susquehanna River and became known as "the bluestocking of the Susquehanna."

One of her hopes in coming to this virtually uninhabited area was to be instrumental in Christianizing the Native Americans. She learned the Shawnah dialect in order to achieve her goal. She operated a ferry on the Susquehanna, and the settlement formerly called Shawnahtown became known as Wright's Ferry. Susanna served as the prothonotary, drawing up documents and writing letters for the other settlers in the area. She also practiced medicine; one of the upstairs rooms of the mansion contains drying herbs and plants she would have used. She wrote poetry and kept up a spirited correspondence with many of the country's leading thinkers. She was a particular favorite of Benjamin Franklin and they exchanged ideas and advice.

Wright's Ferry Mansion was built for Susanna Wright in 1738 and reflects her Quaker heritage as well as her links with England and Philadelphia. The house has been singled out as "the best effort to achieve an exact re-creation of eighteenth-century reality." It has one of the finest collections in the country of Pennsylvania furnishings and accessories made before 1750. The pieces have been chosen because of their historical significance and their architectural purity.

Susanna Wright's austerity can be seen in the curtainless windows and the bare scrubbed floors, but she also had an exquisite artistic sense and a love of beauty, which you can see in the silk quilt and bed curtains in her room, which enhance the only known example of a Philadelphia Queen Anne high post bed.

Susanna Wright was interested in establishing a silk industry in Pennsylvania and had more than fifteen hundred silk worms. The quality of the silk she produced was so good that Queen Charlotte of England wore a dress made from Susquehanna silk, presented to her by Benjamin Franklin, to George III's birthday celebration.

Wright's Ferry Mansion is a special place that reflects a special lady. When you visit, you will come away with a new appreciation for a woman who few remember today but who was a generation ahead of her time. Wright's Ferry Mansion is open May through October on Tuesday, Wednesday, Friday, and Saturday from 10:00 A.M. to 3:00 P.M. Admission is charged.

Directions: From I-76, the Pennsylvania Turnpike, take Exit 21. Travel south on Route 222 to Lancaster, then proceed west on Route 30 to Columbia. Take Route 441, N. Third Street, into Columbia. Turn left at Poplar Street, continue down to Second Street, and proceed to 38 Second Street. You will see the restored home on your right.

Delaware

John Dickinson Mansion

How strange that the man known to this day as "the Penman of the Revolution" because of the many articulate papers he wrote listing the colonists' rights and complaints and opposing the Stamp Act and the Townshend Acts would refuse to sign the one document that enumerated all of the colonial grievances against the British crown. John Dickinson lost a great deal of his popularity after he refused to sign the Declaration of Independence and left the Second Continental Congress arguing for delay in hopes that England would even yet modify her stand. Some even accused him of turning Loyalist, a rumor quickly scotched when he served in the Continental Army, reaching the rank of brigadier general.

Although he was the author of the Articles of Confederation and one of the framers of the US Constitution, he never achieved prominence outside of Pennsylvania and Delaware. John Dickinson's popularity in these two states remained undiminished. He served as chief executive of Delaware from 1781 to 1782, then that same year (1782) was elected governor of Pennsylvania, serving until 1785—a governmental transition unequaled.

You can tour John Dickinson's boyhood home, which was built by his father in 1740, when John was eight years old. This Georgian plantation house outside Dover overlooks the St. Jones River and provides an excellent sample of plantation architecture in Delaware. When John was eighteen, after years of classical study with a tutor, he moved to Philadelphia to begin legal training under John Moland, the king's attorney. In 1753, John Dickinson began four years of study at the Inns of Court in London, after which he returned and practiced law in Philadelphia, where he took an active part in the colonies' defense against intruding English laws.

The house you can see today was damaged by a fire in 1804, which did considerable damage to the interior, and some early Dickinson family pieces were lost. But the house has been carefully restored, and some of the furnishings are original. The house is listed in the National Register of Historic Places.

The **John Dickinson Mansion** and outbuildings are open Tuesday through Saturday from 10:00 A.M. to 3:30 P.M. and on Sunday from 1:30 to 4:30 P.M. The house is closed on Mondays, holidays and on Sunday in January and February. There is no admission charge.

Directions: Take Washington Beltway Exit 19 (Route 50) over the Bay Bridge; continue north on Route 301 when it splits from Route 50. Make a right on Route 301 and another right on Route 44 to Dover. From Dover go south on Route 113 to Route 68 and Kitts Hummuck Road, which will lead directly to the John Dickinson Mansion.

George Washington and the Washington Family Homes

George Washington, always larger than life, actually towered over his contemporaries. It is hard for us to imagine the "Father of our Country" as an awkward young man, but ladies once laughed behind their fans and were reluctant to dance with him because of his oversized feet. And he had virtually no talent for small talk. The few girls he fell in love with were totally uninterested in his proposals.

One of the true loves of his life was Sally Fairfax, the wife of a good friend and neighbor. Their relationship was always honorable and never evoked the usual neighborhood gossip. Sally helped George overcome his shy, inarticulate manner. Though thwarted in his attempts to wed until the rather late age of twenty-three, family was always important to Washington.

Born at Pope's Creek Plantation on February 22, 1732, to Augustine and Mary Ball Washington, George was named not after the English king, but his mother's guardian. By the age of six, he had a sister, Betty, and three brothers: Sam, John, and Charlie. He also had two half brothers, Lawrence and Augustine, who were studying in England.

When George was eleven, his father died suddenly of a severe gout attack. His half brothers each inherited one of the Washington family homes. The eldest son, Lawrence, inherited Eppewasson, renaming it Mount Vernon in honor of his commanding officer Admiral Vernon. Augustine settled at Pope's Creek, which his son would later rename Wakefield. George was left Ferry Farm, on the Rappahannock River near Fredericksburg. His mother and the younger children also lived there.

Young Washington enjoyed exploring Fredericksburg, which was his first experience with town life. A chance observance of some surveying work being done outside town sparked the idea of pursuing that line of work. He found some rusting equipment that his father had stored away, and in 1747, at the age of fifteen and a half, he was paid for his first job.

A fortuitous opportunity presented itself when young George was given the chance to help survey Lord Thomas Fairfax's fifteen thousand acres beyond the Blue Ridge Mountains. This foray into Native American territory was an exciting adventure for the sixteen-year-old Washington. He often talked of watching warriors dance around the camp bonfire. Washington's career as a surveyor was off to a good start. In three years he was made the official surveyor of Culpeper County.

But family matters did not go as well. His favorite brother, Lawrence, was suffering from a series of debilitating illnesses. Although Washington abandoned his own responsibilities to accompany his brother to the Caribbean in hopes of improving his failing health, it was to no avail. They returned to Virginia, where Lawrence died at the age of thirty-four. Less than a month later, Lawrence's infant daughter also died. These double tragedies meant that George acquired the family home, Mount Vernon. Before dying Lawrence insured that his brother would follow his lead, taking his place in the Ohio Company, the Virginia House of Burgesses, and the Virginia Militia.

During the French and Indian War, Maj. George Washington served as aide-de-camp to General Braddock. His heroic action in the Battle of Fort Duquesne began the Washington legends.

Washington, his clothes bullet ridden, with three horses shot from beneath him, and so feverish he could barely remain in the saddle, continued to regroup the British forces in the face of the advancing French. When General Braddock was shot and the troops were in full flight, Washington was one of the three officers who carried the dying general back behind the lines. Still not giving in to his own condition, Washington returned to the battlefield, riding all night to get the wounded to wagons and safety. Though the British lost the battle, Washington's actions were so noble that the public cheered. Having a new hero salved the sting of defeat. His conduct during this crisis was a major factor in his later appointment as commander of the American Revolutionary forces.

Washington, having experienced success on the battlefield, was also to finally succeed in winning a wife. He married the wealthy widow Martha Custis on January 6, 1759. He unofficially adopted her two young children, Jack Parke Custis, age four, and Patsy, age two. It is ironic that Washington, paterfamilias to a whole country, never realized his own deep wish to have a child of his own.

The next fifteen years were probably the happiest of Washington's life. He had his new family and was able to supervise the growth of his beloved Mount Vernon. He bought four additional farms in the area, increasing his acreage from 2,126 to 8,000 acres. His interest in the details of the estate overwhelmed his overseer.

As relations between England and the colonies disintegrated, Washington was forced to leave Mount Vernon. He attended the Second Continental Congress in Philadelphia. His absence was greatly extended when he was appointed commander-in-chief of the colonial forces. For six long years Washington struggled against the British. He had to fight the Continental Congress as well for supplies, munitions, and pay for his troops. In October 1781, the British finally surrendered at Yorktown.

Family misfortune conspired to blight what would otherwise have been a jubilant victory. His twenty-four-year-old stepson, Jack, ill from exposure and fatigue, died immediately after the Battle of Yorktown. He requested his father take care of his family.

Washington again unofficially adopted Jack's two youngest children, George Washington Parke Custis and Eleanor (Nellie) Custis. He returned to Mount Vernon for Christmas with his new young family.

Every time Washington relaxed and began to enjoy the life of a gentleman farmer, he was interrupted by his country's call to service. This time he learned that Congress had unanimously elected him president of the United States.

Though Washington was inaugurated in New York, Congress moved to Philadelphia while the new capitol was constructed. The new Federal City, situated between the north and the south, was laid out across the Potomac from Alexandria. In his honor the ten-mile square city was named Washington, but he always referred to it as the Federal city.

After two terms Washington relinquished the presidency to John Adams and returned for the last time to Mount Vernon. Three years after his final homecoming, on Saturday, December 14, 1799, Washington died. His final wishes were followed, and he was buried on the Mount Vernon grounds.

Six houses of the Washington family survive and are restored to permit visitors a glimpse of the lifestyle of the different generations of our country's first First Family. The houses are open to the public and easily accessible, none being more than two hours from the Washington Beltway.

Arlington House

The story of George Washington throwing a silver dollar across the Potomac River has become an accepted part of American folklore. As in the children's game Rumor, each retelling of the original incident brought changes: The Rappahannock became the Potomac, the Spanish doubloon became a dollar, and the story became suspect. But it was included in the book, *Young Washington,* that George Washington Parke Custis wrote about his stepgrandfather after Washington's death.

George Washington raised Custis after his father, Washington's stepson John Parke Custis, died of fever following the Battle of Yorktown at the end of the American Revolution. After George Washington's death, as the principal male heir, Custis inherited the Mount Vernon portraits, china, silver, and many other valuable pieces. He began building **Arlington House** in 1802 with the idea of making it a "treasury of Washington heirlooms." It was designed by British architect George Hadfield, who had come to the Washington area to help design the US Capitol.

In 1804 Custis married Mary Lee Fitzhugh. Many of the notable figures of the time came to Arlington House to pay tribute to the Washington legend. A frequent guest was the young Robert E. Lee. After graduating from West Point, Lee married Mary Anna Randolph Custis, the only surviving Custis child. The marriage, on June 30, 1831, was celebrated in the family parlor at Arlington House.

Mary Anna stayed in her girlhood home and raised their seven children. Lee's military career left him little time to spend with her. When Lee left to serve in the war, he never saw Arlington House again. Mrs. Lee and the children moved to Richmond, and the house was occupied by Federal troops. The grounds became part of the capital defenses. After the Civil War the eleven-hundred-acre estate was confiscated by the federal government, and the Washington family possessions scattered. A Supreme Court decision in 1882 returned the house to Robert E. Lee's son, but in 1883 he sold it back to the federal government for $150,000. In 1925, the house was restored to its appearance during the Lee years. George Washington Parke Custis links two great American families, the Washingtons and the Lees, and through them, two epic periods of United States history. Arlington House symbolizes that link.

The house, part of **Arlington National Cemetery**, is open to the public without charge from 9:30 A.M. to 4:00 P.M. during the winter months and until 6:00 P.M. the rest of the year. Maps of the house, with details of the rooms and furnishings, permit visitors to explore at their own pace. Many of the pieces exhibited are copies of originals, though others are Lee family pieces and a few Custis furnishings. The grand Greek Revival exterior with its eight massive pillars is in counterpoint with the simple and hospitable interior. The view from the portico of the Lincoln Memorial across the river is riveting.

Directions: Take I-95 to the perimeter of Washington; at the intersection with the Beltway (I-495/95) and I-395, take the latter and head toward the city. Then exit at Memorial Bridge/Rosslyn onto Route 110 north. From Route 110 exit at Memorial Bridge/Washington. At the top of the exit turn left onto Memorial Drive, which goes directly to the entrance of Arlington National Cemetery and Arlington House.

George Washington Birthplace National Monument

On the western shore of the Chesapeake Bay lies Virginia's Northern Neck, first charted in 1608 by that intrepid explorer, John Smith. During the colonial period it was the port of call for many trading ships on their way to the West Indies and England.

The patriarch of one of America's first families arrived on one of those early trading ships. John Washington, great-grandfather of George, was a mate on an English ship that was trading for tobacco in 1657. It ran aground near Mattox Creek while sailing down the Potomac River on its voyage home. John Washington was so impressed with the land, the southern hospitality, and the daughter of his host, Col. Nathanial Pope, that he decided to remain. When he and Anne Pope were married, they were given seven hundred acres of choice land on Mattox Creek. He purchased additional land on Popes Creek, and an American dynasty was begun.

It was here at Popes Creek Plantation that George Washington was born on February 22, 1732. The site is now the **George Washington Birthplace National Monument**. Because both progress and wars have bypassed this region, the grounds of the Washington plantation and the surrounding countryside look much as they did in the eighteenth century.

The natural beauty of the meandering Popes Creek, the broad views of the Potomac River, and the gently rolling fields all can be enjoyed as you stroll along the park's trails. The land's historical significance is captured in the evocative film *A Childhood Place*, shown at the visitors center. Fall leaves and migratory birds, snowy farmland, spring planting, and summer wildflowers speak quietly and eloquently of the same seasonal shifts that influenced young George Washington. These natural rhythms form a bond between those who visit and those who once lived here.

George Washington lived on this family plantation until he was three and a half years old, when the family moved to Little Hunting Creek Plantation, now known as Mount Vernon. After his father's death when he was eleven, George often returned to his early childhood home, inherited by his half brother Augustine.

The family home was destroyed by fire on Christmas Day 1779, while George was commander of the revolutionary army. Oyster shells now delineate the foundations of the original home. A memorial house, erected in 1930 through 1931, represents a house typical of the kind the moderately wealthy Washingtons could afford. Although most of the furniture is over 200 years old, only a small tea table and an excavated wine bottle are from the original house.

Both birth and death are remembered here. As you enter the grounds, you'll see the miniature Washington monument, a single granite shaft erected in memory of George Washington in 1896. Nearby is the family burial grounds where George's father, grandfather, and great-grandfather are all buried.

But it is the rebirth of nature that brings the long-ago days to life. George Washington in his later years remembered fishing along Popes Creek. You can easily imagine the young boy making his way to the river and perhaps glimpsing an oceangoing trading ship from the shore. Today the National Park Service owns 538 acres of preserved shoreline, woods, and pasture at Popes Creek Plantation. Fields are still planted and tilled by eighteenth-century methods. During the summer months, special demonstrations are given on sheep shearing, tobacco planting, harvesting and curing, soapmaking, candlemaking, dyeing, and weaving. Colonial music programs feature the spinet and other instruments.

The George Washington Birthplace National Monument is open daily from 9:00 A.M. to 5:00 P.M. except Christmas and New Year's Day. A nominal admission is charged. A picturesque picnic area overlooks Popes Creek. You also can picnic at nearby Westmoreland State Park. While at the park, you may want to take advantage of the Olympic-size pool or even spend a relaxing hour on the beach.

Also nearby (north off Route 3/301 on Route 218, just across the Potomac River bridge from Maryland) is **Caledon Natural Area**, a designated National Natural Landmark because of its bald eagle habitat. The hiking trails in this 2,579-acre natural area provide a chance to see one of the largest concentrations of bald eagles on the East Coast. Staff-led interpretive tours of their habitat are given from mid-June to Labor Day (reservations are recommended). There are five hiking trails at Caledon, ranging from 0.7 mile to two trails of 1.1 miles. Exhibits on the bald eagle are on display at the visitor center in the Smoot House. For information on programs at Caledon Natural Area call (540) 663-3861.

Directions: From I-95 take Route 3 east to Route 204. The George Washington Birthplace National Monument is 1.7 miles off Route 3 on Route 204.

Kenmore Plantation and Gardens and Mary Washington House

Like mother, like daughter—if Mary Ball Washington and her daughter Betty Washington Lewis were not completely alike, they were at least very similar. Both were widowed, both lived in Fredericksburg, and both had households supported in part, if not entirely, by George Washington.

Betty's husband, Fielding Lewis, was a wealthy landowner, businessman, court justice, and member of the Virginia House of Burgesses. Lewis spared no expense building a luxurious Georgian mansion shortly after marrying Betty in 1750. **Kenmore** was one of the earliest colonial mansions to have plastered rather than paneled walls. The ornate plasterwork on walls and ceilings is considered the finest example of the art in the United States. The drawing room ceiling is a masterpiece and deservedly was included in Helen Comstock's *100 Most Beautiful Rooms in America* (now unfortunately out of print).

It is well that Fielding Lewis did not wait to build his bride a home; his efforts to support the Continental army bankrupted him. He used his substantial fortune to found the Fredericksburg Gunnery, which manufactured and repaired munitions for the army. He also outfitted ships. His death just two months after the Battle of Yorktown gave him no opportunity to recoup his losses, thus it fell to Betty's brother George to help support her household.

The furnishings you will see on your tour match the inventory taken after Colonel Lewis's death in December 1781, with additional items reflecting the belongings sold after Betty's death in 1797. One family piece is Betty's portrait in the dining room. She looked like her brother. According to one account, "It was a matter of frolic to throw a cloak around her and, placing a military hat on her head, such was her amazing resemblance that battalions would have presented arms..."

The path to the kitchen leads through the eighteenth-century formal boxwood gardens; spend some time exploring this re-created haven with its flanking gazebos. The brick path once led to the **Mary Washington House**, just two blocks away. It is said that when Lafayette visited Fredericksburg, he, too, used this garden path and came upon the commander-in-chief's mother working in her boxwood garden in her apron.

George purchased this town house for his mother on September 18, 1772. As he explained to his friend Benjamin Harrison, "Before I left Virginia (to make her more comfortable and free from care) I did

In 1772, before setting out to take command of the colonial troops, George Washington persuaded his widowed mother, Mary, to leave her Rappahannock River farm and move to this house in Fredericksburg. Washington's last visit with his mother was on March 11, 1789, just before he departed for New York to be inaugurated as the country's first president.

at her request, but at my own expense, purchase a commodious house, garden and Lotts (of her own choosing) in Fredericksburg that she might be near my sister Lewis, her own daughter . . ." Although she suggested the move, Mary Washington often complained of the city noises and water. According to local legend, she sent a slave back to Ferry Farm, her former rural residence, each day for fresh well water.

This was not the only complaint she made. When she moved from her four-hundred-acre farm in 1772, George made arrangements to pay its rent. According to his own records, he often got involved in the country's business and neglected to pay her rent in a timely manner.

Like Kenmore, the town house is furnished to reflect items in the wills of Augustine and Mary Washington. Eighteenth-century pieces fill the rooms; only a few, like the looking glass, engravings, and *Book of Meditations,* belonged to Mary Washington.

Mary Ball Washington lived for the last seventeen years of her life in this house. She died four months after George Washington's inauguration on August 25, 1789. At her request she is buried on land that was once part of Kenmore near Mediation Rock.

Kenmore Plantation and Gardens is open March through December, 10:00 A.M. to 5:00 P.M.; on Sunday it opens at noon. In January and February it is open Monday through Friday by reservation only; Saturday and President's Day, 10:00 A.M. to 4:00 P.M.; and Sunday noon to 4:00 P.M. It is closed on major holidays. Tickets are purchased in Kenmore's Museum Shop. Hours at the Mary Washington House are 9:00 A.M. to 5:00 P.M., March through November and 10:00 A.M. to 4:00 P.M., December through February. Both charge admission.

Directions: From I-95 take the Fredericksburg exit and follow Route 3 east, which becomes William Street. Make a left on Washington Avenue for Kenmore. For the Mary Washington House, continue down William Street to Charles and turn left. The house is at 1200 Charles Street.

Mount Vernon

George Washington's great-grandfather acquired the land on which Mount Vernon stands in 1674. George Washington's father obtained Little Hunting Creek Plantation, as it was first called, in 1726. At his death George's elder half brother, Lawrence, inherited it. Lawrence renamed the estate Mount Vernon in honor of his commanding officer Admiral Vernon.

At Lawrence's death, George first leased Mount Vernon from his brother's widow, then inherited the family estate. On January 6, 1759, George married the wealthy widow Martha Dandridge Custis, whose worth by today's standards has been calculated by some historians (who may exaggerate as these figures are difficult to substantiate) as approaching six million dollars, not counting the vast acres of land she owned. Before he moved his bride and her two children to Mount Vernon, Washington enlarged the main house to two and a half stories.

George Washington continued to enlarge, ornament, and plan the grounds of his Virginia plantation throughout the long years of his military and political service. He managed the day-to-day activities of his estate amid the turmoil of war and the travail of establishing a new government. Take, for example, his letter in 1776 to his cousin, Lund Washington, Mount Vernon's wartime manager. The letter mixes disturbing wartime news with directions for the building of the two-story dining room addition. Washington advises: "The chimney of the new room should be exactly in the middle of it—the doors and everything else to be exactly answerable and uniform—in short I would have the whole executed in a masterly manner."

Or consider the letter he wrote on June 6, 1796: "Tell the Gardener I shall expect everything that a Garden ought to produce, in the most ample manner." Washington also wrote: "My agricultural pursuits and rural amusements... (have) been the most pleasing occupation of my life, and the most congenial to my temper."

No detail was too small for him. There are thirty-seven volumes of Washington's writings, plus letters and weekly garden reports. These precise records and a long detailed inventory left by his executors helped the Mount Vernon Ladies' Association in restoring Washington's home to its appearance at the time of his death, on December 14, 1799, as did a room-by-room inventory.

Bushrod Washington and John Augustine Washington, inheritors of Mount Vernon, worked hard to keep up the estate, but they were not farmers by trade, and it was difficult to maintain. Their concern that it be preserved as a shrine led them to approach the federal government and the Commonwealth of Virginia about selling Mount Vernon; but neither accepted the offer.

Mount Vernon's journey back to its days of glory began on a moonlit night in 1853 when Mrs. Robert Cunningham, cruising the Potomac River, saw the rundown house on the hilltop. She wrote her daughter, "I was painfully distressed at the ruin and desolation of the home of Washington." She further related, "The thought passed through my mind: why was it that the women of his country did not try to keep it in repair, if the men could not do it? It does seem such a blot on our country."

The recipient of this letter, Ann Pamela Cunningham, realized her mother's hopes by founding the Mount Vernon Ladies' Association. After both state and federal governments had refused to purchase Washington's home, her group raised the funds necessary to purchase the estate in 1858 for two hundred thousand dollars. Over the years, nineteenth-century additions were removed, furniture was restored, and the atmosphere of the original plantation that Washington so enjoyed was recaptured. Visitors to the estate today can imagine the great man strolling the home he once called "a well resorted tavern." It was always the home of a gentlemen farmer. The presence of George Washington can be sensed at Mount Vernon, and this is perhaps the greatest legacy the Mount Vernon Ladies' Association offers to succeeding generations.

Mount Vernon provides a variety of programs and events year-

Mount Vernon Plantation, home and final resting place of George Washington, overlooks the Potomac River in Virginia. Here, the first president of the United States lived the life he loved best—that of a prosperous country squire. The gardens and grounds remain largely as Washington designed and planned them.

round. From April through October, the estate offers "Slave Life at Mount Vernon" and garden and landscape walking tours. The slave life tour and other programs and events provide a glimpse of the 316 former residents that have until recently been ignored on most tours. "Slave Life at Mount Vernon," a half-hour walking tour, focuses on the slaves who built and operated the estate. The tours, led by historical interpreters, are offered at no extra charge; call (703) 780-2000 for a current schedule. George Washington inherited slaves from his father when he was eleven. Although slavery was considered a necessity in colonial Virginia, after the American Revolution, Washington resolved never to buy or sell another slave. By 1797 his view was even more extreme; he wrote, "I wish from my soul that the Legislature of this State could see the policy of a gradual Abolition of Slavery." Washington freed his slaves in his will.

Visitors who take this tour discover that the operation of the plantation depended on slave labor not only for field and housework. Slaves were also blacksmiths, gardeners, carpenters, spinners, and animal caretakers. The workday began at sunrise and lasted until dark, which was up to fourteen hours in the summer. Women did much of the fieldwork—they plowed, hoed, and planted. The tour encompasses both living and work space. Many of the details presented on this tour come from Washington's diaries, though family histories of former slaves also provided information.

Mount Vernon is open 9:00 A.M. to 4:00 P.M., November through February; 9:00 A.M. to 5:00 P.M., March, September, and October; and 8:00 A.M. to 5:00 P.M., April to August. Admission is charged. During the summer months special children's programs offer hands-on-history lessons that re-create the atmosphere of a busy plantation. A recent addition is the George Washington: Pioneer Farmer site where visitors can watch authentically clad workers tilling the fields and caring for the animals. There are hands-on activities and a dramatic surround-sound video program. If time permits you also can explore the Mount Vernon Historic Trail. Annual events include a wine tasting festival in May, the September eighteenth-century crafts fair, candlelight tours in December, the February George Washington's birthday celebrations, and a hands-on-history tent on the grounds during the summer months.

The Mount Vernon Museum has been completely renovated. The Shops at Mount Vernon offer an enticing array of items, and if you are touring around lunchtime or want to enjoy an elegant dinner, be sure to stop at the Mount Vernon Inn restaurant. For additional information you can visit Mount Vernon's Web site at www.mountvernon.org.

Directions: From I-95 south of Alexandria, take Exit 54, US 1. Take US 1 north to Route 235, the Old Mount Vernon Highway. Make a right turn on Route 235, which will take you directly to the traffic circle in front of Mount Vernon. You also can take the George Washington Memorial Parkway from Alexandria to the estate.

Woodlawn

George Washington's last birthday, February 22, 1799, was a happy one. There was a family wedding at Mount Vernon on that date, uniting his foster daughter, Eleanor (Nelly) Parke Custis, and his sister Betty's son, Maj. Lawrence Lewis. The delighted Washington, noted for buying land, rather than giving it away, made the newlyweds a present of a portion of his beloved Mount Vernon estate. He said the two thousand acres would be a "most beautiful site for a gentleman's seat."

Dr. William Thornton, first architect of the US Capitol, designed a stately mansion for the crest of the highest hill on the Lewises' property. While their house was being built, they lived at Mount Vernon, comforting the grief-stricken Martha Washington, who was widowed on December 14, 1799. In 1802, at Martha's death, the Lewises and their two young children moved into the completed wing areas of **Woodlawn**. The center portion wasn't finished until 1805.

Visiting Woodlawn gives you a sense of the deep grief Nelly felt at the death of the only father she ever knew. She placed his bust on a pedestal as high as Washington's own considerable height. A swath was cut through the trees so that she could see Mount Vernon, her girlhood home, from Woodlawn's river entrance.

In the music room you see Nelly's music on a pianoforte similar to one she once played. Her husband was more interested in hunting than harmonics. He imported thoroughbred horses and the first merino sheep in North America. When Lawrence Lewis died in 1839, his widow moved to Clarke County to live with her son and his family at Audley Plantation.

The Garden Club of Virginia has re-created the formal gardens. An unexpected addition to this nineteenth-century plantation is the twentieth-century Usonian **Pope-Leighey House**. Designed by Frank Lloyd Wright, the house is built of cypress, not of concrete like many of his later models.

The house, named after its two owners, was in Falls Church, Virginia, in the early 1940s and moved to the current Woodlawn site to avoid destruction by the impending path of I-66. The Usonian Houses were designed and built to "meet the housing needs of Middle Class America." Pope-Leighey embodies a simple lifestyle. In keeping with the projected owners, the architectural design does not call attention to itself, but rather becomes an integral part of its surroundings. Complete with its original furnishings, also Wright-designed, it was ahead of its time. It was seen as "futuristic," with its radiant-heated floors, carport, and recessed lighting. It fits beautifully in today's world.

The high-ceilinged dining room was the center of hospitality at Woodlawn Plantation, the hilltop estate of George Washington's foster daughter Nelly Custis and nephew Lawrence Lewis. The property, once part of Mount Vernon, was Washington's gift to the couple after their marriage in 1799.

A unique opportunity exists at this site, which allows the visitor to compare two different time periods, houses, lifestyles, and famous architects. Woodlawn and the Pope-Leighey House are museum properties of the National Trust for Historic Preservation. They are open daily from 9:30 A.M. to 4:30 P.M. from March through December and on weekends in January and February from 9:30 A.M. to 4:30 P.M. The houses are closed on Thanksgiving, Christmas, and New

Year's Day. Many special events are scheduled throughout the year.

Directions: From I-495/95, take Exit 1, US 1 south to Fort Belvoir. Woodlawn is located on Route 1 and Virginia Route 235 in Mount Vernon.

Colonial Towns

If the goal of all new settlers was to farm their own land, what caused the development of towns? Simply, they were necessary. As settlements grew, towns developed as centers of trade, which supplied the necessities farmers could not grow or produce for themselves. Since many of these items came from Europe, towns generally grew around ports and served as centers for shipping.

By the time of the American Revolution, the largest colonial towns were already over a hundred years old. Philadelphia, with forty thousand inhabitants, was second only to London as the largest English-speaking city in the world. Also in the top five were New York with twenty-five thousand people, Boston with sixteen thousand, Charleston with twelve thousand, and Newport with eleven thousand.

Only Philadelphia and Charleston were laid out by city planners. The others just grew from irregular roadways. Of these two, Philadelphia was the most advanced. It was one of the first towns to pave its roads. Boston's method of putting gutters on the side of the street rather than having a shallow trench run down the middle was also rapidly incorporated. This latter method was often disastrous for poor drivers, who were constantly getting their wagon wheels stuck in the trench. Charleston, on the other hand, had dirt roads long after the Revolution.

Baltimore is a good example of the growth of one of the smaller colonial towns. It developed because in 1729, planters north of Annapolis wanted a convenient tobacco-inspection site. The town consisted originally of sixty one-acre lots. By 1752, the population of the entire city of Baltimore was still only 250. There were twenty-five homes, two taverns, and one church. Baltimore was noteworthy because it was America's only walled city. It is uncertain whether the city dwellers were trying to protect themselves from marauding Native Americans or the foraging of pigs and geese from the surrounding pastures.

The towns were the hotbeds of the Revolution. The merchants and lawyers would frequently meet in the taverns and exchange complaints. The harsh restrictions imposed by George III hit them the hardest of all the colonists. These articulate colonials were able to express the anger felt not only by them, but also by the more isolated farmers.

Though many of the colonial lawyers were trained in England, they also were the ones who wrote the script of the Revolution. However, the architect of the Declaration of Independence, Thomas Jefferson, received his legal training with George Wythe in Williamsburg, Virginia.

Communication between the colonies was made easier by the improvement of inland roads. By 1732, there was enough travel to warrant the publication of a small book giving the mileage between major colonial towns.

The mail service was the main beneficiary of the improved roads. By 1692, post riders were traveling from one colony to another. In 1763, a road linked not only the British colonies, but also extended all the way down to Spanish St. Augustine in Florida.

Improved communication helped the patriot cause. Committees of Correspondence insured that British actions against the citizens in one area were known by all. Thus were formed the links that would forge a nation.

Maryland

Hammond-Harwood House

William Buckland built Georgian homes for two Annapolis residents; neither were able to enjoy their beautiful mansions. Samuel Chase's (see Chase-Lloyd House selection) dreams foundered for financial reasons. Mathias Hammond's foundered on the shoals of the revolution brewing in the colonies, and the end of his legislative career.

William Buckland's splendidly ornamented **Hammond-Harwood House** was his last creation; he died before the house was finished. But it was also the first and only house he both designed and built; it stands as a testament to Buckland's singular talent. Thomas Jefferson so admired the house that he sketched it, perhaps looking for inspiration for an addition to Monticello.

The house is a classic, five-part Georgian mansion, considered by some experts the finest example of the style in America. Ionic pilasters, like those Buckland used in the interior of the Chase-Lloyd House, flank the front door. The columns support an elaborately carved pediment and frieze.

Inside, a wealth of details embellish the formal rooms. The dining room and drawing room are particularly fine examples of Buckland's work, and they reflect the culmination of years of craftsmanship. The Hammond-Harwood House is not a mere decorative shell, either. The house is exquisitely furnished with pieces from the Chippendale, Federal, and even the earlier Queen Ann periods. Maryland craftsmen are well represented, and there are several portraits by Charles Willson Peale. Appropriately, there is a copy of his portrait of William Buckland, which shows in the background the drawings for this very house. There is also an original Peale portrait of Buckland's daughter.

The house came to be known as the Hammond-Harwood House after 1834, when it was given to the daughter of its second owner and her husband. The man she married was William Harwood, the great-grandson of William Buckland, the man whose vision and artistry had given birth to the beautiful house.

The Hammond-Harwood House is open for guided tours Monday through Saturday from 10:00 A.M. to 4:00 P.M.; on Sunday it opens at noon. The last tour begins promptly at 3:00 P.M. It is closed on Thanksgiving, Christmas, and New Year's Day. Admission is charged.

Directions: From Baltimore, take Route 97 to Route 50 east. Take Route 50 to Rowe Boulevard exit. Follow to College Avenue and turn left onto College Avenue; then right at the first light onto King George Street. Proceed on King George Street one block to Maryland Avenue. The Hammond-Harwood House is on the corner of King George Street and Maryland Avenue.

Mount Clare Mansion

The ten acres on which Mount Clare Station was built were virtually given to the B&O Railroad by James MacCubbin Carroll for the bargain price of one dollar. It was here that the story of the American railroad began (see B&O Railroad Museum selection). Carroll's nearby family home, **Mount Clare Mansion**, is also open for tours.

This pre-Revolutionary Georgian estate is the oldest in Baltimore, circa 1760, and one of the oldest house museums in the state. It was the center of Charles Carroll's eight-hundred-acre Patapsco River plantation. Carroll, the barrister, helped write the Declaration of Rights for Maryland and the Maryland State Constitution. Carroll's first wife, Margaret Tilghman Carroll, who was Mount Clare's longest resident, was responsible for much of its expansion. The estate's greenhouse, which has been excavated, was the model for the greenhouse at George Washington's Mount Vernon estate.

Approximately 80% of the more than one thousand objects and furnishings in the house are Carroll family pieces. Rare furnishings include the Louis XV painted and gilded sofa and ten sidechairs, ordered from England by Mrs. Carroll between 1780 and 1790. In the dining room, silver ordered by Charles Carroll is complemented by his eighteenth-century wine cooler, Chippendale serving table, and copper plate warmer. Mrs. Carroll's eighteenth-century firescreen sits by the parlor fireplace. Michael Trostel, a noted Baltimore architect and author, claims that "Mount Clare is the only eighteenth-century museum house in Maryland to contain so many of the daily artifacts of life belonging to the builder of the house and used by his family."

Mount Clare is noted for its portrait collection, which includes portraits of Charles Carroll, the barrister, and Margaret Tilghman Carroll, which are among the finest works by Charles Wilson Peale. Other noted portraits are done by Robert Feke, Robert Edge Pine, John Wesley Jarvis, William James Hubard, and John Hesselius. You can tour the house Tuesday through Friday at 11:00 A.M., noon, 1:00, 2:00, and 3:00 P.M. and on weekends at 1:00, 2:00, and 3:00 P.M. It is closed on Mondays and holidays. For more information, call (410) 837-3262.

Directions: From the Baltimore Beltway, I-695, take Exit 11A to get to I-95 north. From I-95 north, take Exit 51, Washington Boulevard, and turn left at the bottom of the exit onto Washington Boulevard. Turn into Carroll park at the fourth traffic light, the intersection of Bush Street and Washington Boulevard. Proceed to Mount Clare at the top of the hill. From I-95 south, proceed through the Fort McHenry Tunnel; then take the first right, Exit 53. Follow I-395 to Martin Luther King, Jr. Boulevard and make a left onto Washington Boulevard. Proceed to the seventh traffic light and turn into Carroll Park on the right. From the Inner Harbor, proceed west on Lombard Street and turn left on Martin Luther King, Jr. Boulevard. Go two blocks and turn right at Washington Boulevard. Proceed to the seventh traffic light and turn into Carroll Park on the right.

Virginia

Adam Thoroughgood House

On the shore at Virginia Beach, **First Landing Cross** commemorates the spot where the Jamestown settlers touched the shore of the New World on April 26,1607. Easter sunrise service is held here each year, and on the April Sunday closest to the landing date, the Order of Cape Henry makes a pilgrimage to this National Historic Landmark.

Two brick homes in Virginia Beach have survived from the colonial period. The **Adam Thoroughgood House**, circa 1680, is one of the oldest standing brick houses in America built by early English settlers. The house was named for a young indentured servant who arrived in Virginia in 1621. After completing his servitude, he married a lady from a well-to-do family and used her dowry to pay the passage for 105 indentured servants to come to Virginia. In return for providing passage for these settlers, Thoroughgood was granted 5,350 acres of land.

It is on this land that his grandson built the one and one-half story house of local brick and oyster shell mortar. Built on the east, north, and south sides in English bond and on the west side in Flemish bond, it has glazed header at the gable ends on the west side. The leaded glass casement windows are in seventeenth-century style, and the furnishings are seventeenth- and eighteenth-century antiques and several ornately carved and inlaid court cupboards. A collection of unusual lighting devices includes rush and betty lamps. Guides in period attire give tours on Saturday from 10:00 A.M. to 5:00 P.M. and Sunday, 1:00 to 5:00 P.M. It is closed on major holidays and on Mondays. Admission is charged. Because the Adam Thoroughgood House is owned by Norfolk, it is included on the Norfolk Automobile Tour, but is located in Virginia Beach.

Lynnhaven House, built between 1725 and 1730, is very much like the Adam Thoroughgood House, but the crafts and furniture represent the eighteenth century. It is open for a nominal admission, Tuesday through Sunday from noon to 4:00 P.M. from June through September, and weekends from noon to 4:00 P.M. in May and October.

Directions: From I-95 in the Richmond area, take I-295 and head east on I-64 to the Virginia Beach-Norfolk Expressway, Route 44. Take the expressway east to Virginia Beach. The Adam Thoroughgood House can be reached via Route 255, Independence Boulevard, off the Virginia Beach-Norfolk Expressway, Route 44, or off Northampton Boulevard, Route 13, to Pleasure House Road. Lynnhaven House is just off Route 225, at Independence Boulevard and Wishart Road.

Moses Myers House

People are always curious about millionaires and especially so about the lifestyle of the extremely rich, which is why it is interesting to see the eighteenth-century home built by one of Norfolk's "merchant princes."

When Eliza Abraham and Moses Myers were married in 1787, they chartered a boat and moved from New York to Norfolk. Myers was the first Jewish settler in Norfolk. Within four years, he had established a five-vessel fleet for his import-export business and built a classic Georgian town house.

The oldest four-square portion of the house was constructed of eighteenth-century English ballast bricks. In 1796, the **Moses Myers House** was expanded from ten to thirteen rooms. From the outside, you can clearly see the difference between the English and American bricks. Five generations of Myers lived here, and 70% of the furniture is original. Moses Myers was a community leader, and his home reflects his successful lifestyle.

Myers was president of the common council, major in the Virginia militia, Dutch and Danish consul, mercantile agent for France, the Netherlands, and Denmark, president of the Assembly Ball, superintendent of the Bank of Richmond, and collector of customs.

From the moment you pull the old English bell to gain entrance, you'll be intrigued by this remarkably well-preserved city mansion. The Myers did not carry door keys; servants were always on hand with a massive one pound key to unfasten the English triple-box lock. The entrance hall still has the original four-inch native heart pine floorboards and a decorative snowflake-pattern plaster ceiling.

In the drawing room you'll see Gilbert Stuart's portraits of Moses Myers when he was in his early fifties and of Mrs. Myers when she was in her early forties. The parlor's Portuguese tole chandelier is a curiosity—the light prongs surrounding the eternal flame bear the supposed likeness of Christopher Columbus. The mantle decoration around the parlor fireplace also reveals the visage of an important historical figure. George Washington gazes out from the rosettes flanking the fireplace on this unique mantle.

The dining room is regarded as one of the most beautiful in the South. Here the Myers entertained President James Monroe, Daniel Webster, Stephen Decatur, Henry Clay, and Gen. Winfield Scott. In the china cabinet, you'll see Mrs. Myers's apricot Spode tea and coffee set. The white, blue, and silver decor combines with the black and white patterned canvas floor cloth to create a surprisingly modern look.

The Myers were musical, and their music room has a harp and the original pianoforte and grand harmonican. The family reputedly had the largest collection of sheet music in early America, with George Washington's family a distant second. The three Myers daughters copied musical scores in quite a number of books. Displayed in the upstairs hallway is the dueling pistol possibly used in the 1820 Barron-Decatur duel. Another room has a seven-lock iron strongbox that Myers anchored to the floor with iron bolts.

Over the Myers's bed is a carved acorn, symbol of fertility. It obviously was effective; they had twelve children. In Mrs. Myers's bedroom, you'll see her oriental worktable. The back bedroom had a six-foot modified sleigh bed. Before ending your tour, be sure to visit the outside kitchen and the garden.

The mansion is open from April through December, 10:00 A.M. to 5:00 P.M., Tuesday through Saturday. On Sunday, it opens at 1:00 P.M. From January through March, the house is open noon to 5:00 P.M., Tuesday through Saturday, and closed on Sundays, Mondays, and major holidays. This is one of the few historic homes in which Hanukkah, the Jewish Festival of Lights, which occurs in December, is celebrated. Candles are lit in a brass menorah for each of the festival's eight days. Admission is charged.

Directions: From I-95 in the Richmond area, take I-64 east to Norfolk; then follow I-264 east to the Waterside Drive Exit. Take Waterside Drive to St. Paul's Boulevard; then turn left on Charlotte Street and left onto Bank Street. The Moses Myers House is at the corner of Freemason and Bank Streets.

Peyton Randolph House and the Brush-Everard House

The sights of Williamsburg include more than eighty-eight original buildings and an additional four hundred reconstructions. You can get a real feel of what it was like to live in this town by visiting two private homes: the Peyton Randolph House and the Brush-Everard House.

The original owner of the **Peyton Randolph House** was Sir John Randolph, the only colonial Virginian to be knighted. He was first clerk of the Virginia House of Burgesses, then the member representing the College of William and Mary, and, finally, Speaker of the House of Burgesses. When Sir John died in 1737, his wife inherited his Williamsburg home. On her death, it passed to his son, Peyton, for whom it is named.

Peyton Randolph's career paralleled his father's. He, too, studied law in London after attending William and Mary. He, too, was sent to England on behalf of the colony. He was elected to the House of Burgesses in 1748, and in 1766 he, too, was chosen Speaker. It was up to him to guide the Assembly through the tumultuous debates that led to the Revolution.

The Randolph's home is sectional. The western-most section of the house, built in 1715, was Sir John's home. He also purchased the house on the adjoining lot. Later, the two homes were connected to make one large residence. The furnishings are stylish yet comfortable; it is definitely a home, not a museum. The paneled rooms exude a warmth that was enjoyed by two French guests. Count de Rochambeau used this house as his headquarters during the siege of Yorktown. When Lafayette returned to America fifty years after the Revolution, he, too, stayed here.

After Peyton Randolph's death, Thomas Jefferson purchased his library. When the federal collection in Washington, D.C., was burned by the British during the War of 1812, Jefferson donated his extensive collection of books to the Library of Congress. Thus, the combined libraries of Jefferson and Randolph became the nucleus of the national collection.

Like the books at the Randolph house, those at the **Brush-Everard House** also have a Jeffersonian connection, though not direct. This library was compiled from a list of three hundred basic books that Jefferson had recommended to a Virginia planter. The Brush-Everard House represents the eighteenth-century middle-class lifestyle. A modest frame house, it was built in 1717 by John Brush, gunsmith, armorer, and the first keeper of the colony's magazine. After passing through the hands of several owners, the house was purchased by Thomas Everard, who was mayor of Williamsburg in 1766 and again in 1771. Everard enlarged the house, embellished the interior, and added a small pond.

To see how John Brush would have practiced his craft, visit the gunsmith shop near the Capitol. It is just one of many colonial crafts you can see demonstrated. There is a milliner, printer, bookbinder, blacksmith, cooper, boot maker, wheelwright, harness maker, cabinet maker, wig maker, and musical instrument maker.

For a look at Williamsburg from a different perspective, sign up for "The Other Half" tour. Half of the city's population were African Americans, and this two-hour walking tour tells you about their lives. The tour, which begins at the Greenhow Ticket Office, focuses on slave culture, racial interaction, African American music, and the differences between plantation and town life.

Admission to all the homes and shops mentioned here is included in the basic ticket, which is sold at the visitor center. All are generally open from 9:00 A.M. to 5:00 P.M. The days and times do change depending on the season.

Directions: From I-95 in the Richmond area, take Exit 238, I-64 east, to Colonial Williamsburg and follow the signs to the visitor center.

Ramsay House and Carlyle House

Both the **Ramsay House** and **Carlyle House**, just five doors apart on Fairfax Street, reveal Scottish influences. The Ramsay House was built about twenty-four years before Alexandria was founded. Its gambrel roof makes it an unusual structure on the city's skyline. Historians believe that in 1749, William Ramsay's house was barged up the Potomac River from the Scottish settlement at Dumfries. It was the first residence placed on the newly auctioned Alexandria lots.

Over the years, the house has been substantially altered, and little of the original structure remains. Scottish merchant John Carlyle built his grand mansion three years later, in 1752. It was inspired by an elaborate Scottish country house in a popular architectural pattern book. Its manor house design, like the Ramsay House design, was unique to Alexandria.

William Ramsay and John Carlyle made more than architectural history in the newly developing town. Ramsay served his community as town trustee, census taker, postmaster, member of the Committee of Safety, colonel of the Militia Regiment, and honorary lord mayor. One of his eight children would later be elected mayor of Alexandria. His wife, Anne, raised over seventy-five thousand dollars for the cause of American independence. At William Ramsay's funeral in 1785, George Washington, his close friend, joined the funeral procession.

The Carlyle House found its place in history just three years after it was built, when Gen. Edward Braddock chose it as his headquarters. Braddock summoned the colonial governors (five attended) to a meeting that John Carlyle called "the Grandest Congress ... ever known on the Continent." The idea of taxing the colonies to support British expenditures in the New World was first proposed at this meeting as a means of financing the French and Indian War. This concept of taxation without representation was one that the colonists would bitterly reject. When it was imposed ten years later by the Stamp Act, it became a leading cause of the American Revolution.

John Carlyle, like William Ramsay, was a merchant. His marriage to Sarah Fairfax linked him with one of the most powerful families in Virginia. He was a partner in a number of merchant firms and acquired great wealth.

The Carlyle House is furnished to suggest the elegant lifestyle of the Carlyles. One room, however, has been left unfurnished and serves as an architectural exhibit room. It clearly reveals even to the untrained eye how the eighteenth-century work was changed in the nineteenth century, then returned to its original appearance in the twentieth century. Carlyle House can be visited from 10:00 A.M. to

4:30 P.M., Tuesday through Saturday, and noon to 4:30 P.M. on Sunday. Admission is charged.

Although the Ramsay tartan hangs on the front door, the Ramsay House is not interpreted as a private residence, but as a visitor center. It is the ideal first stop for anyone exploring Alexandria. You can obtain maps, brochures, and up-to-date information on special events, museums, shops, restaurants, and hotels—plus parking passes for nonresidents. There is a free orientation video and a gift shop. Ramsay House is open daily, 9:00 A.M. to 5:00 P.M. It is closed Thanksgiving, Christmas, and New Year's Day.

Directions: From I-495/95, take Exit 1, US 1 north into Alexandria. Continue down US 1 to King Street and turn right. The Ramsay House is at the corner of King and Fairfax streets. The Carlyle House is at 121 North Fairfax Street.

Willoughby-Baylor House

William Willoughby's family roots extended back to the earliest days of the Virginia colony. His great-great-great-grandfather, Thomas Willoughby, had arrived here in 1610 at age nine. By 1636, Thomas had obtained a patent for two hundred acres of Tidewater land, on which Norfolk was later built. Thomas already owned the five-hundred-acre Willoughby Plantation that is now Ocean View.

When William, prominent retail merchant and contractor, repurchased the old family acreage, Norfolk was struggling to recover from the massive fire damage caused by Lord Dunmore's bombardment in 1776. In 1794, Willoughby built one of the first twenty brick town houses in Norfolk. The town house reflected Federal and Georgian design. The furnishings you will see are in keeping with the 1803 probate inventory filed at William's death. The original furnishings had dispersed long ago.

In the front parlor you'll notice that the handkerchief table, card table, and tilt-top table all fold up. Furniture in the eighteenth century had to be versatile and movable to allow maximum use of space. The pair of Queen Anne mirrors that hang opposite each other, one in the front parlor and the other in the adjoining back parlor, were designed to reflect candlelight, not images; called glasses when used downstairs, they were listed on inventories as looking glasses when used upstairs. The dining room table was once owned by James Madison's mother and was used in the White House during the Madison administration. The second floor is currently unfurnished. It is used for educational programs.

The Willoughby-Baylor house is open April through December by appointment only; call (757) 664-6283. It is closed on Mondays and major holidays. Admission is charged.

Directions: From I-95 in the Richmond area, take I-64 east to Norfolk; then I-264 east. Exit on Waterside Drive and take an immediate right at St. Paul's Boulevard. Take a left onto Charlotte Street; then the next right onto Bank Street; and then left onto Freemason Street. The house is at the corner of Cumberland and Freemason Streets.

District of Columbia

The Old Stone House

The **Old Stone House** is the only pre-Revolutionary building in the District of Columbia and reflects the dual nature of Georgetown, both then and now—it was used as a home and a business.

The sixty acres composing Georgetown (so named for George III) were divided into eighty lots. Christopher Layman's lot was on the main street. He started this stone house in 1764, living above the ground-floor carpentry shop. Layman sold not only his own work, but also that of enterprising carpenters who wanted to display their work in this growing port city. Layman's death in 1765 left the burden of finishing the house on his wife. She remarried and sold the house to Cassandra Chew, a prosperous businesswoman who added to the north wing.

The shop has been restored, as have five family rooms, providing a glimpse of middle-class life in Georgetown in the 1700s. On the ground floor, in addition to the shop, is the kitchen. On the second floor are the dining area, family parlor, and one bedroom. On the third floor are the family bedrooms. The small yard has a seasonal garden.

The Old Stone House is open Wednesday through Sunday from noon to 5:00 P.M. It is closed on federal holidays.

Directions: The Old Stone House is located at 3051 M Street, N.W., in Washington, D.C.

Pennsylvania

Betsy Ross House

Did Betsy Ross really live in this Philadelphia town house? Did she make the first American flag? The Philadelphia Historical Commission disputes both of these claims. This legendary figure may be legendary indeed, since the historical verification of Betsy Ross's contribution is weak.

There is some evidence to support the legends that surround Betsy Ross. She was born Elizabeth Griscom in 1752. In 1773, she married John Ross, a young upholsterer. Both John and Betsy were supporters of American independence, but John Ross died in 1776, and she was left to carry on alone. She did upholstery work for Independence Hall and for various civic leaders, including Benjamin Franklin. She did undoubtedly make flags for the Pennsylvania navy. Many believe that Betsy Ross did make the first American flag.

Betsy outlived three husbands, raised her own five daughters and several orphaned nieces, and carried on her flag-making business. She died in 1836 and is buried in the Atwater Kent Cemetery, which is located near the Betsy Ross House. For almost a century, the story of Betsy Ross making the first Stars and Stripes was simply preserved as a family tradition. But in 1870, one of Betsy Ross's grandsons told her story in public, and it swept the nation. More than two million people contributed to the preservation of the Betsy Ross House, and she became one of the best-known women in American history.

The house on Arch Street that bears her name has a restored upholstery shop, where colonial methods and equipment are demonstrated. Even if Betsy Ross never lived in this house, it would be worth a visit. It is an excellent example of in-town living, with a basement kitchen and typical winding staircase. The house is furnished with many pieces that belonged to Betsy Ross.

The Betsy Ross House, 239 Arch Street, is open at no charge from 10:00 A.M. to 5:00 P.M., Tuesday through Sunday and on Monday holidays.

Directions: From I-95 southbound (from points north) take Exit 17. Using the right-hand lanes of the exit, follow the signs for Callowhill Street/Independence Hall. At the bottom of the exit ramp, follow 2nd Street straight ahead to Chestnut Street. Continue a half block past Chestnut Street for the Historic Area Parking Garage on the left. It is best to park your car and walk to all the sites in the Historic District. Start at the Independence National Historical Park Visitors Center, one block away, at 3rd and Chestnut Streets, where you can pick up an easy-to-follow map of the district and a park schedule. If you are traveling northbound on I-95 (from points south), you will also take Exit 17. Stay in the left lane because you will exit on the left side of I-95. At the exit, stay in the right-hand lane and follow the signs for Independence Hall/Historic Area. Turn left at 6th Street to Chestnut and drive through the heart of the Historic District to 2nd Street. Turn right on 2nd Street. The entrance to the Historic Area Parking Garage is on the left. The Betsy Ross House, at 239 Arch Street, is within walking distance of the garage.

Cliveden

A painting by E. L. Henry of the Battle of Germantown hangs at Cliveden on the same walls that still bear traces of the perilous moments in 1777 when the Americans tried valiantly to breach the sturdy stones and defeat the British. You will see reminders of this October 4 confrontation when you tour **Cliveden** (pronounced cliv-den).

Benjamin Chew, who built and owned Cliveden, was being held under arrest in New Jersey because of his suspected British sympathies. As chief justice of Pennsylvania, he had scrupulously endeavored to uphold the British law, which led to his arrest in the summer of 1777. He did not see his war-ravaged house until the following spring. It was "an absolute wreck, and materials not to be had to keep out the weather." Chew's despair was keenly felt because he had helped design his countryseat in 1767. It took four years to build the mid-Georgian, two-and-a-half-story house. Particularly pleasing to Chew were the five urns that adorn the roof, each on its own ornamental pedestal. These fortunately survived the colonial confrontation.

Another Henry painting you will see when you tour Cliveden is of the "Lafayette Reception," held in 1825 when the Marquis de Lafayette returned to America to celebrate the Revolutionary victories. The painting hangs in the front entrance hall and replicates the two portraits and the Tuscan columns that are still there.

In Mrs. Chew's sitting room, there is a silhouette of Benjamin Chew. A portrait was painted later from this likeness, and it hangs in the front hall. While observing the lavish furnishings, look for the names of earlier guests inscribed on the window panes with a diamond-point stylus. The ornate parlor mirrors may have been used to decorate the tent walls when General Howe's junior officers threw an elaborate party, or fête champêtre, in his honor before his return to England.

As you move to the second floor, you will pass the window that once looked out on the rear court. An 1867–68 addition to the main house has been artistically camouflaged so that visitors do not lose the original ambience. Upstairs, the thirteen-foot ceilings are reminders of the lavish construction associated with this early era.

Antique lovers and history buffs will appreciate the many fine family heirlooms. Cliveden, with the exception of an eighteen-year period after the Revolution during which it was owned by a wealthy Irish-American merchant, has always belonged to the Chew family. It was acquired by the National Trust for Historic Preservation from the Chew family in 1972.

You can visit the six-acre Cliveden estate at 6401 Germantown Avenue from April through December on Thursday through Sunday from noon to 4:00 P.M. It is closed on major holidays. Admission is charged.

Directions: From I-95 in the Philadelphia area, take the exit for I-76 west, the Schuylkill Expressway. Take the Expressway to exit 32, Lincoln Drive (it is also marked Germantown-Wissahickon Park). Take Lincoln Drive to Johnson Street. Turn right onto Johnson; go to the fourth traffic light, which is Germantown Avenue. Turn left onto Germantown; go one block and turn right onto Cliveden Street. Street parking for Cliveden is available at the end of the first block on Cliveden Street.

Historic Bartram's Garden

There's a tendency to imagine that during the arduous task of establishing a new country, the arts and sciences were ignored in America. But, while they didn't flourish, they did exist.

In 1728, Quaker farmer John Bartram purchased a 102-acre farm with a small stone house. From a young age, Bartram was fascinated by plants. Although he had little formal education, Bartram diligently studied botany to further his pursuit of American plant specimens. He taught himself Latin so that he could read the horticultural books that Benjamin Franklin, James Logan, and others gave him.

Bartram's interest in American plants was shared by English botanical enthusiasts. Peter Collinson, a prosperous London wool merchant, arranged for John Bartram to provide him an assortment of plants from America. They never met, but Bartram and Collinson corresponded for thirty-five years. Their letters provide a record of Bartram's expeditions throughout the American wilderness. On his plant quests, Bartram went north as far as New York, south to Florida and west to the Ohio River. Bartram's contacts with English and European botanists were reciprocal; plants were sent both ways. Bartram was responsible for introducing two hundred North American species into cultivation here.

Bartram returned from each trip to his Philadelphia farm and planted the seeds, roots, and cuttings he gathered. As his collection grew, so did his fame, and in 1765, George III appointed him "Royal Botanist." The noted Swedish botanist, Carl Linnaeus, who developed a system for classifying plants, called Bartram "the greatest natural botanist in the world."

Following in his father's footsteps, quite literally, was William, who Bartram called "my little botanist." William accompanied his father on many of his plant exploration forays. In 1765, they went to Florida together. William's interest was intense, and he later returned alone and spent four years traveling in the Deep South. He wrote of this experience in *Travels,* published in 1791.

William returned to the Schuylkill farm and spent the rest of his life writing and maintaining America's first botanic garden. Another of Bartram's nine children, John, Jr., organized the garden into a nursery at his father's death. He completed the first sales catalog of American plants.

Purchased as a city park in 1891, Bartram's garden survives as **Historic Bartram's Garden**. Growing here today are descendants of the plants that made horticultural history. One such plant, now extinct in the wild, is the *Franklinia alatamaha,* named after Bartram's famous friend. When you walk the garden paths, you follow in the footsteps of George Washington, Thomas Jefferson, and numerous noted North American scientists who have visited and admired Bartram's collection.

You can also tour the eighteenth-century stone house that John Bartram built around the original portion he acquired with the farm. He labored on the house himself. Above an attic window, a date stone reads, "John—Ann Bartram 1731." His stone work can be observed on a water trough and on the cider mill at the river's edge.

The grounds, at 54th Street and Lindbergh Boulevard, are open daily at no charge during daylight hours year-round. Keep in mind that this is a rustic, eighteenth-century, native plant garden and not a display garden. There is a nominal fee to tour the house, which is open May through October on Wednesday through Sunday from noon to 4:00 P.M. The house is closed on weekends from November through March.

Directions: From I-76, the Pennsylvania Turnpike, take the Schuylkill Expressway east through the center of Philadelphia. Get off the Expressway at Gray's Ferry, Exit 41. Bear left through the exit light and go over the bridge. Turn right at the next light onto Gray's Ferry Avenue (Marshall Lab/Dupont will be on the right corner). Go over another bridge and turn left onto Paschall Avenue; then turn left at the next light onto 49th Street and follow the trolley tracks. The street name changes to Gray's Avenue and Lindbergh Boulevard. Continue past the sign for 54th Street. Make a sharp left turn into Bartram's Garden just beyond the gas station. The entrance is not visible until after the turn.

Stenton

The stately brick countryseat begun in 1723 by James Logan, William Penn's secretary, hardly looks like an economic move to modern visitors. But that is indeed what it was. Logan suffered a series of business failures in the early 1720s, and he decided to retire to the country while he still had enough capital to establish a workable plantation for his family.

Logan began acquiring land in old Germantown in 1714, while managing the affairs of the colony in Penn's absence. He eventually had 511 acres and planned to build an inexpensive stone house. In keeping with his run of bad luck, the quarries failed. During the next two years, Logan was unable to find any reasonable source of native stones. In 1717, he decided to begin building his home using bricks. **Stenton**, named after Logan's father's Scottish village, was finished in 1730.

Although James Logan's economic fortunes suffered, his political fortunes did not. Logan was secretary of the province, commissioner of property and receiver general, and clerk. Later, he was president of the Pennsylvania Provincial Council, chief justice for the colony, and William Penn's Indian agent.

The brick floor you see in the entrance hall at Stenton was a practical accommodation to the large number of visitors who called on James Logan. Frequently, the Lanapes camped at Stenton while traveling back and forth from Philadelphia.

The elements of Logan's Quaker beliefs are seen in the simplicity of Stenton's design and its furnishings. The room interpreted as Logan's study does not display the one extravagance that Logan enjoyed—his three-thousand-book library, which became the nucleus for the Library Company of Philadelphia. Logan was a genuine scholar; in addition to being fluent in seven languages, including Native American dialects, he conducted astronomy and agronomy experiments.

James Logan's son, William, followed in his father's footsteps. He acted as attorney for the Penn family and served on the Provincial Council from 1747 to 1776. He, too, made his mark on Stenton. William added the "old" kitchen and the piazza. His family also contributed some of the finer pieces of furniture. Each room reflects and interprets one of the three generations to live at Stenton from 1730 to 1780, ending with George Logan.

The stone bank barn was added by George Logan, who was intensely interested in agriculture. He turned Stenton into a model farm. His wife, Deborah Norris Logan, transcribed the correspondence of James Logan and William Penn and gained the distinction of being the first woman member of the Historical Society of Pennsylvania.

Stenton is open for tours April into November, Tuesday through Saturday from 1:00 to 4:00 P.M. There is a nominal admission charge.

Directions: From I-95 in the Philadelphia area, take Schuylkill Expressway, Route 76 north, to Roosevelt Boulevard, Route 1 north, and proceed to second exit on right. Follow exit, bearing left to the third traffic light. Beyond this light, the road bears left, becoming Old Stenton Avenue.

Wyck

Old roses and Old World charm are found in abundance at Wyck, home to one Quaker family from 1689 to 1973. The history of **Wyck** dates to 1689, when Hans Millan, a German Mennonite, acquired land on which he built a small house in 1690. After his daughter Catherine married Dirck Jansen, a second house, in front of the first, was built in 1736. In 1771, the 1690 house was torn down and a new, large stone house was built. In 1777, when the house was used as a field hospital during the Battle of Germantown, it appeared as a long stone structure made of different stone work. In 1799, Caspar Wistar Haines visually united the stone sections into one manor house by applying a coat of white stucco.

Not only is Wyck a National Historic Landmark but it is also a comfortable old home. Nine generations of families, primarily the Wistars and Haines, enjoyed life at Wyck. The original furnishings and decorative pieces are blended in style and period. More than ten thousand objects and a hundred thousand family documents illustrate the continued family life from the eighteenth century to 1973.

In 1824, Wyck's interior underwent major renovation when Reuben Haines III asked his friend, architect William Strickland, to assist in repairs to the house. He created a suite of sunlit rooms in the

Greek Revival style overlooking the south lawn and formal gardens. This series of rooms is beautifully decorated in a comfortable and cheerful style.

A visit to Wyck in late May through mid-June coincides with the peak blooming season of Wyck's historic old roses, planted according to the original garden plan dating from the 1820s. Their form, beauty, and especially their fragrance set them apart from the modern hybrid tea roses. A total of thirty-five different roses flourish in Wyck's box-bordered rose garden. The estate's two-and-a-half acre grounds also include early outbuildings: a coach house, smokehouse, icehouse, and greenhouse.

Wyck, at 6026 Germantown Avenue at the corner of Walnut Lane, is open April through December 15 on Tuesday, Thursday, and Saturday from 1:00 to 4:00 P.M. and year-round by appointment. To arrange a tour call (215) 848-1690. Admission is charged.

Directions: From I-95, take the Vine Street Expressway exit, Route 676. Follow Route 676 until it joins with Route 76 west, the Schuylkill Expressway. Take the Lincoln Drive exit and follow Lincoln Drive to the first traffic light. Turn right onto Rittenhouse Street. Turn left at the second light onto Wissahickon Avenue. Turn right at the first light onto Walnut Lane and follow for approximately five blocks up to Germantown Avenue. Wyck is behind a gray fence on your right. Parking is available in a small lot off Walnut Lane or along Germantown Avenue.

Delaware

Corbit-Sharp House

The guides at the **Corbit-Sharp House** used to tell a story about the mistress of the Corbit home. They said she certainly would have preferred the Brick Hotel, which was just across the street from her home, in its present incarnation as an art museum. Back in 1860 when Mrs. Corbit lived in Odessa, Delaware, there frequently was rowdy behavior at the hotel. So incensed was the Quaker matron at this unruly behavior, she began a campaign that resulted in the hotel losing its liquor license.

The Corbit-Sharp House was built between 1772 and 1774 by William Corbit, and it has been faithfully restored using inventories kept since the eighteenth century by various family members. The family also has contributed to the present decor. There are small

The Corbit-Sharp House, in Odessa, Delaware, is named for its builder, William Corbit, and its restorer, H. Rodney Sharp. Built between 1772 and 1774, it was sold to Sharp in 1938.
WINTERTHUR MUSEUM AND GARDENS

samplers done by William Corbit's granddaughter in the 1820s.

Much of the furniture is original to the house. The grandfather clock was listed in Corbit's records as costing sixty dollars in 1772. It was made by Duncan Beard, a Scotchman who settled one mile outside Odessa in 1767. The dining room also has a desk made by Delaware valley craftsmen between 1775 and 1790.

When the house was restored in 1938, an old-fashioned boxwood parterre garden was added. Also on the grounds is a smokehouse, the only outbuilding remaining from the eighteenth century.

The Corbit-Sharp House is open Tuesday through Saturday from 10:00 A.M. to 4:00 P.M. and Sunday from 1:00 to 4:00 P.M. It is closed on Mondays and holidays. Admission is charged.

Directions: Take Washington Beltway (I-495/95) Exit 19 (Route 50-301). After crossing the Bay Bridge, follow Route 301 to Odessa, Delaware. The Corbit-Sharp House is on Main Street.

Wilson-Warner House

It may seem unusual to name an American town after a Ukrainian city. In the case of Odessa, Delaware, it was not because the townspeople were immigrants, but rather due to the similar functions of the two towns. Odessa was the great grain port of Russia, and this town in Delaware was the principal grain market of the region. Six large granaries stored the harvests from 1820 until 1840. The town shipped four hundred thousand bushels of grain annually.

One of the town's prosperous merchants was David Wilson, brother-in-law of William Corbit. Wilson built his home in Odessa in 1769. He had a general store on Main Street. Older, smaller, and simpler than the Corbit House, the **Wilson-Warner House** is more typical of Delaware architecture. Like the Corbit House, it also is painstakingly decorated with period pieces from the colonial era.

On the grounds is a "skinning shack" built in the early eighteenth century and moved here during restoration. Also, a stone stable built by David Wilson in the late 1700s or early 1800s still stands.

The Wilson-Warner House is open Tuesday through Saturday from 10:00 A.M. until 4:00 P.M. and on Sunday from 1:00 until 4:00 P.M.; it is closed on Mondays and holidays. Admission is charged.

Directions: Take Washington Beltway (I-495/95) Exit 19 (Route 50-301); after crossing the Bay Bridge, follow Route 301 to Odessa, Delaware. The Wilson-Warner House is on Main Street in Odessa.

Colonial Churches

Two colonies—Maryland and Pennsylvania—were founded by proprietors who placed the right to worship in the church of their choice above all else. Most settlers came to America to improve their economic lot rather than to practice religious freedom. It is estimated that in the years before the Revolution, only about one out of eight persons in the New England area, one out of seventeen in the middle colonies, and one out of twenty in the South belonged to a church.

These figures do not mean that most were unbelievers, but instead reflect other factors. Citizens of isolated settlements were often too far from a church to attend services. Many others considered formal church affiliation unnecessary; they felt it was sufficient to read the Bible within their own home.

A widespread policy of religious toleration eliminated much of the political element of church attendance—it was less vital to have the protection of the group. Religious troubles did still occur, however, as evidenced by the disruption of the government in Maryland as Protestants vied with Catholics for control.

Religion in the colonies, as elsewhere during this period, contained a strong superstitious element. The unsettling wilderness, importation of black slave labor, and hostile Native Americans confirmed for some the impression that this was a place in which God would do battle with the devil.

Many colonists believed in the direct intervention of God. This personal God was accepted by those of all social classes, regardless of the degree of education. Supernatural intervention was held accountable for unusual weather phenomena; hurricanes, drought, comets, earthquakes, and floods were all assumed to be direct warnings from God. On the other hand, good crops, success in battle, and good health were seen as signs of God's favor.

Of the organized churches in colonial America, the oldest was the Anglican, or the Church of England. Begun in Jamestown, it was strongest in the South, where, prior to the Revolution, more than half of the 480 churches were Anglican. The philosophy of these worldly parishioners can be summed up in this 1676 epitaph for William Sherwood of Jamestown:

A Great Sinner
Waiting for
A Joyful Resurrection

Anglicans had confidence that God would forgive their sins and they would be saved. The Southern colonists enjoyed drinking, singing, dancing, horse racing, cock fighting, and rich apparel. Sunday was not a day of penance but of service and sociability.

The largest denomination in colonial America was composed of the New England–based Congregationalists, who were descendants of the early Puritan settlers. Second were the Presbyterians, located mainly in the middle colonies; third were the Baptists, who had founded Rhode Island and expanded from there. The Church of England was fourth largest, with the Methodists fifth, and the sixth and least numerous of the major sects were the Quakers.

Despite the fact that Maryland was established by the Calverts to offer persecuted Catholics a refuge, there were only fifty Catholic churches in America at the time of the Revolution, almost all of which were located in Maryland.

Although ministers, or priests in Maryland, were the first professional men in the colonies, their position of leadership and influence soon declined. By the 1700s, many pastors had to sue their congregations for their pay. In the southern Anglican area, since clergy had to travel to London to be ordained, positions were filled primarily by English pastors who had not succeeded in England. Conditions deteriorated so that in 1624 the Virginia legislature passed laws forbidding the clergy to drink excessively, to gamble, or to engage in other excesses.

Things were equally bad in Maryland, where, in June 1747, a woman in Patapsco was fined only a penny for flogging the minister, since the court decided he deserved it.

The Great Awakening of the 1740s brought a religious revival. The nondenominational character of this five-year revival led to a great many conversions. It also increased the respectability of the clergy.

Ultimately, the colonial religious experience led those who would write the laws of the new country to establish freedom of religious worship.

Virginia

Bruton Parish Church

Philadelphia was not the only town with a Liberty Bell. Williamsburg also had one, which was presented to Bruton Parish Church in 1761. It too rang out to celebrate momentous events in colonial history.

On June 1, 1774, when it became known that Parliament had closed the port of Boston, the bell called members of the parish and House of Burgesses to a day of fasting, humiliation, and prayer. From that day's events came the call to the First Virginia Convention.

The bell rang once again to announce the repeal of the Stamp Act. On May 15, 1776, it rang out for Virginia's first act of sovereignty, six weeks before the Liberty Bell in Philadelphia would peel out a similar message.

Construction on Bruton Parish Church was begun in 1711, when it became obvious that the small church that had served the middle plantation area would not accommodate the congregation of Virginia's new capital.

This church has been in continuous use from 1715 to the present. It was quite fashionable to attend Bruton Parish Church during colonial times. Plantation owners and their wives from the large estates along the York and James Rivers came into town by coach for services.

Prominent political figures often served as vestrymen, including George Washington, Henry Tyler, and America's first professor of law, George Wythe. In the galleries set aside for college students sat Thomas Jefferson, James Monroe, John Tyler, Edmond Randolph, John Marshall, and Winfield Scott. Although the interior of the church was simple, it did have a special box in front of the pulpit for the royal governor.

It was a rector of Bruton Parish Church, the Reverend W. A. R. Goodwin, who in 1905 began the crusade to restore the city of Williamsburg to its colonial glory. He interested John D. Rockefeller, Jr., in this project, and the rest is history. Visitors leaving the church will see his grave along with those of two royal governors and numerous important figures of colonial days.

Bruton Parish Church is open daily at no charge. Special candlelit organ concerts are held here; check Colonial Williamsburg Visitor Center for times.

Directions: Take Washington Beltway Exit 4 (I-95) to the Richmond Bypass, Route 295. Follow this to Route 64 east, which will lead into Williamsburg. Bruton Parish Church is on the corner of Duke of Gloucester Street and Palace Green.

Christ Church

In 1767, the Georgian style **Christ Church** was under construction; work continued until 1773. Col. James Wren, who according to some was a relative of the noted British architect Sir Christopher Wren, made the architectural drawings and specifications for the building, but James Parson and John Carlyle oversaw the actual work of construction. George Washington was among the first members of the congregation to purchase a pew. A silver plate marks the pew he bought for thirty-six pounds and twenty shillings (approximately twenty dollars). His pew is the only one preserved in its original configuration.

The interior has been restored to its appearance in the 1890s. The Palladian chancel window was an unusual feature for a church of this period. The hand-lettered tablets were painted by James Wren. The galleries were added in 1787, when attendance outgrew the seating in the pews on the main level. The bell tower provided the stairway to the galleries and then was extended in 1820.

When the widowed Martha Washington died, her grandson, George Washington Parke Custis, gave the Washington family bible to Christ Church. Another prominent American family, the Lees, considered this their family church. Robert E. Lee and two of his daughters were confirmed at Christ Church on July 17, 1853. A silver plaque on the chancel rail marks where the confirmation occurred. The wedding of Robert E. Lee to Washington's stepgreat-granddaughter, Mary Custis, linked the two families. During the Civil War, the church was taken over by the Union soldiers as their chapel. The Union soldiers occupied the area to protect the nearby capital.

Christ Church is open daily from 9:00 A.M. to 4:00 P.M. and Sunday from 2:00 to 4:40 P.M. Guided tours are available. There are regularly scheduled services every Sunday. Nearly all of America's presidents have attended service here on the Sunday closest to George Washington's birthday. The gift shop is open Tuesday through Saturday from 10:00 A.M. to 4:00 P.M.

Directions: From I-495/95, take Exit 1, US 1 north into Alexandria. Continue down US 1; the entrance to Christ Church is on Columbus Street.

Old Blandford Church

Memorial Day observances began at **Old Blandford Church** on Well's Hill in Petersburg, Virginia, on June 9, 1865, and not on the last weekend in May as it is observed today. It was the following year that Mary Cunningham Logan, wife of Gen. John A. Logan, saw young schoolgirls placing flowers on the graves of slain Confederate soldiers on May 26th, the day set aside by Mississippi to commemorate the fallen. When Mrs. Logan learned from the girls' headmistress, Nora

Davidson, that they intended to hold a "Decoration Day" every year, she urged her husband to propose extending the gesture nationwide. As commander-in-chief of the Grand Army of the Republic, General Logan spearheaded the work for the establishment of an official Memorial Day. His objective was achieved when, by act of Congress, the occasion was first celebrated across the country on May 30, 1868.

The history of Old Blandford Church does not start with the War between the States. The church, the oldest building in Petersburg, was built in 1735.The earliest date on a gravestone, 1702, marks the grave of Richard Yarbrough, who died at the age of eighty-seven. When the British lost the Revolutionary War, the Church of England, or Protestant Episcopal Church as it was renamed in 1784, lost members. In 1799, only six services were held at Blandford Church, one a memorial service for George Washington. The church was abandoned entirely by 1806.

The City of Petersburg added a new roof to the deteriorating building in 1882. But it was not until 1901 that the Ladies Memorial Association of Petersburg undertook its restoration. During the Siege of Petersburg, Blandford Church served as a hospital for wounded Confederate soldiers. More than thirty thousand Confederate dead were laid to rest in the cemetery in the decades following the end of the Civil War. To honor these sons of the South, the Ladies Association of Petersburg commissioned Louis Comfort Tiffany to design windows for the restored church, one for each of the southern states plus the three border states of Maryland, Missouri, and Kentucky. Each state had to raise the money (about four hundred dollars) for its window.

Louisiana's window, commissioned and paid for by the Washington Artillery of New Orleans, was the only regiment represented. All the states paid except divided Kentucky, which had already arranged its own memorial. Tiffany donated the fifteenth window, the "Cross of Jewels." This window, even more than his other works, has the iridescence of jewels. Tiffany developed a unique technique for adding crushed copper, gold, and cobalt for special depth and luster. No one has ever been able to duplicate Tiffany's artistic creations. Legend claims that on the morning after his death, at his direction, his formula and notes were destroyed.

The church contains several memorial plaques. One honors the men who lost their lives in the Battle of the Crater. Their gallant commander, Gen. William Mahone, who led the crater charge, is, at his request, buried in Memorial Hall. A plaque on the church wall has a poem attributed to the Irish actor Tyrone Power, grandfather of the Hollywood star, written before the restoration when the church was still in ruins.

Thou art crumbling to the dust, old pile,
Thou art hastening to thy fall,
And 'round thee in thy loneliness
    Clings the ivy to thy wall
The worshipers are scattered now
Who knelt before thy shrine,
And silence reigns where anthems rose,
In days of "Auld Lang Syne."

The historic graveyard has been the scene of more than one duel. On one notable occasion, two suitors, R.C. Adams and James B. Boisseau, fought for the affections of Ellen Stimson and were both mortally wounded. Dr. Ira Ellis Smith, who was called to their sides, failed to save his patients, but he saved Miss Stimson by marrying her.

You can visit daily from 10:00 A.M. to 5:00 P.M. Admission is charged.

Directions: Take I-95 to Petersburg. Take the Wythe Street Exit and go east on Wythe Street for one block; then turn right on Crater Road, Route 301-460. Blandford Church is located on Crater Road at Rochelle Lane.

Pohick Church

If you've visited Christ Church in Alexandria (see selection), you will easily recognize **Pohick Church**. They were both designed by Col. James Wren. Pohick, a Native American word for hickory, was built between 1769 and 1774. George Washington and neighbor George Mason (see Gunston Hall selection) were on the building committee; Mason supervised the construction. Unlike Christ Church, this church has no steeple because the congregation did not live close enough to hear church bells. The interior was badly damaged during the Civil War. It has been restored, and you can see the box pews belonging to Washington and Mason.

This is the only church remaining from the colonial Truro Parish, which was divided in 1765 to found the Fairfax Parish.

Directions: From I-495/95, the Washington Beltway, take Exit 1, US 1 south seven miles. For Pohick Church, continue south past Woodlawn Plantation on Route 1, and the church will be on your right.

St. John's Church and St. Paul's Church

Necessity often forced the Founding Fathers to mix church and state. On one historic occasion in 1775, the Second Virginia Convention chose **St. John's Church** as their meeting place because it was the largest public gathering place in Richmond. On the fourth day of their week long convention, Patrick Henry delivered his famous "Liberty or Death" speech (see Scotchtown and Red Hill selections).

This historic occasion is re-enacted on summer Sundays at 2:00 P.M. from the last weekend in May through the first Sunday in September and on the Sunday closest to March 23, the day on which Henry delivered his impassioned plea. Join costumed actors portraying Henry, Washington, Jefferson, and other Virginia delegates as they debate the future of the American colonies. You are indeed where history happened. Later during the Revolutionary War, Benedict Arnold quartered his troops in St. John's while occupying Richmond.

St. John's, thirty-five years old when the Revolution began, is the oldest church in Richmond and one of the oldest surviving wooden buildings in the city. It was built in 1741 on land given to Henrico Parish by William Byrd II. Although the church has been largely restored since colonial days, the high pulpit, flooring, transept, and many of the pews are original.

Guided tours of the church are given for a nominal admission, Monday through Saturday from 10:00 A.M. to 4:00 P.M. and Sunday from 1:00 to 4:00 P.M. The last tour starts at 3:30 P.M. St. John's is closed on major holidays. Sunday Episcopal worship services are held at 8:30 and 11:00 A.M. with a noon coffee hour and reception. During hours when tours are conducted, the Chapel Gift Shop is open in the old Victorian Gothic keeper's house.

Also historically significant is **St. Paul's Church** at 815 East Grace Street. You can attend services at noon Monday through Friday and 11:00 A.M. on Sunday at this church where both Robert E. Lee and Jefferson Davis worshiped. The president of the Confederacy was attending service on Sunday, April 2, 1865, when he received word that Petersburg had fallen and the Union army was marching on Richmond. The fear that spread through the congregation was quickly confirmed by Davis's order to evacuate the city. St. Paul's Church is open Monday through Saturday from 10:00 A.M. to 4:00 P.M. and Sunday 1:00 to 4:00 P.M.

Directions: Take Exit 10 from I-95 in Richmond. St. John's is located at 2401 East Broad Street, down from the Richmond National Battlefield Park. (You can follow the battlefield signs.) For St. Paul's Church, take Broad Street to 8th Street and turn left. Make a right on Grace Street.

Pennsylvania

Ephrata Cloister

Visit **Ephrata Cloister** and enter another era and another continent. The eleven surviving cloister buildings are European in origin. More than 250 years after the community was founded, it still retains an aura of harmony and otherworldliness. At dusk, or on a cold, gray day, the atmosphere of austerity and simplicity is most keenly felt.

Life in the colonies was hard for all newcomers, but the members of Conrad Beissel's Ephrata sect were not content to merely suffer the normal hardships of settlement in William Penn's tolerant colony. Beissel's society strove to discipline themselves still more. The sparse nature of their furnishings attests to their philosophy of self-denial. As you tour the Saron, or Sisters' House, notice the narrow corridors, which reminded the community of the "straight and narrow path of virtue and humility." The low doors were constant reminders to members of their vows of humility. Wooden benches with wooden "pillows" kept the notion of self-denial in their mind even as they slept. Members went to bed at 9:00 P.M., then were awakened at midnight for nightly prayers.

The Brothers' quarters, Bethania, was torn down in 1908. A group of married Householders were also part of the sect. At its height, the community numbered about three hundred.

Members toiled in the fields, growing the food necessary for their survival. Eating, like sleeping, was carefully governed by this religious group. Special dietary restrictions were imposed so that the members could purify their voices and perform the hymns written by Beissel in the proper fashion.

Conrad Beissel was one of America's first composers. He wrote a number of hymns extolling the tenets of ascetic self-denial. Using the calligraphic art of Frakturschriften, the sisterhood created hand-illuminated songbooks. The calligraphy on display at the visitor center is as elaborate as today's laser prints. Illuminated books were a special art form practiced at the cloister.

A slide show at the visitor center reveals the daily life of this otherworldly sect. After your orientation, guides wearing the white garb of Ephrata members escort you through the Sisters' House, the austere chapel and the Householder's modest dwelling. After these stops, you are on your own to explore the alms and bake house, Beissel's log cabin, the print and weaver's shop, a solitary cabin, and the old graveyard, where many of the original members of the society are buried.

Ephrata Cloister is open Monday through Saturday from 9:00 A.M. to 5:00 P.M.; on Sunday it opens at noon. Admission is charged.

Directions: From I-76, the Pennsylvania Turnpike, take Exit 21, the Reading Interchange. Go south on Route 322 to Ephrata Exit. Travel west on Route 322 for about three miles. Ephrata Cloister is on the left, at 632 West Main Street in Ephrata.

Hans Herr House

The **Hans Herr House** is the earliest surviving dwelling in Lancaster County and the oldest Mennonite meetinghouse in America. Hans Herr and a small group of Mennonites came to Pennsylvania in 1710 in response to William Penn's call for settlers. Herr was seventy-one years old at the time, yet he undertook the ardors of the journey to escape religious persecution in the Palatinate (a southwest German district that was part of Bavaria).

The medieval-looking sandstone house you see was built by Hans Herr's son Christian. The date of construction, 1719, can be clearly seen on the door lintel along with Christian's initials, CHHR. This two-story house has a cellar that extends beneath one-third of the house. The windows of the underground room open to the outside to allow some air circulation in this cold-storage area.

The Herr House is laid out according to a standard Germanic floor plan. The furniture is sparse and plain and represents items found listed on Christian Herr's 1749 inventory. It is interesting to see the way in which the huge "schrank," or wardrobe, can be taken apart almost like a tinker toy. The house has a masonry heating stove and a cellar door that closes by itself, which prevented small children from falling down the steep stairway.

Before you explore the house, stop at the visitor center, where exhibits provide background information on the Mennonites and the Herr family. There is also a shed with an exhibit on Mennonite rural life, a blacksmith's shop, and period Pennsylvania German raised bed gardens.

The Hans Herr House is open April through November, Monday through Saturday, from 9:00 A.M. to 4:00 P.M. It is closed on Sundays. You can visit by appointment only December through March; call (717) 464-4438. The first Saturday in August is Hans Herr House Heritage Day, with demonstrations of eighteenth- and nineteenth-century crafts. The first Saturday in October is the Apple Harvest Festival called Snitz Fest; Christmas Candlelight Tours are held the first Friday and Saturday evenings in December.

119

The Hans Herr House, built in 1719, is the oldest surviving structure in Lancaster, Pennsylvania. This outstanding example of early Germanic architecture was used as a Mennonite meeting house.
1990 PA DUTCH CONVENTION & VISITORS BUREAU

Directions: From I-76, the Pennsylvania Turnpike, take Exit 21, Route 222 through Lancaster. Five miles south of Lancaster's center, near the town of Willow Street, turn right off of Route 222 onto Hans Herr Drive. Travel 0.75 mile on Hans Herr Drive to the museum entrance on the left.

Colonial Business

Colonial America proved to be a land of opportunity. Many of those who came as indentured servants or who worked as apprentices went on to enjoy success and even fame. There was no stigma attached to humble beginnings. Three of the signers of the Declaration of Independence worked as apprentices. While a young man, Benjamin Franklin was a printer's apprentice. Roger Sherman of Connecticut worked for a shoemaker, and George Walton of Georgia was a carpenter. The "taste maker" of the colonies, William Buckland, came to Virginia as George Mason's indentured servant. He went on to become America's most noted architect.

The men who first came to America performed all tasks: They planted, built, panned for gold, fought the Native Americans, and explored the wilderness. But as time passed, towns grew and specialization began.

New towns created new jobs—lamplighters, town criers, bell ringers, chimney sweeps, and inspectors. The inspectors were respected community members who ensured that certain standards were maintained in agricultural produce and in building safety. One of the most important inspectors checked the tobacco harvest to be sure that it was of high quality.

These men were often called viewers. The gutter viewer made sure roof gutters did not spill rain or snow on pedestrians. The egg viewer checked for bad merchandise. There was also a chimney viewer, weight viewer, tide viewer, fence viewer, and a scrutineer, now called election judge.

Public service functions were filled by policemen, called leatherheads; street cleaners, who were known as whitewings because of their white uniforms; and volunteer fire fighters.

The most respected colonial professionals were the landed gentry, with their large plantations, and the lawyers and merchants. Many distinguished colonists also were inn or tavern keepers. John Adams, the second president, owned an inn, and George Washington's youngest brother, Charles, had a tavern in Fredericksburg, Virginia.

On the plantations, most of the necessary work was done on the estate; but in towns, small enterprises served the general population. The term "maker" was added to any number of jobs—candlemaker, wigmaker, clockmaker, sleighbellmaker—and even to such short-lived jobs as the paper collar maker and mantuamaker.

Another job suffix was "wright," which meant skilled workman. There were millwrights, plowwrights, tilewrights, timberwrights, bookwrights, and, of course, playwrights.

The traders and peddlers were "mongers." There were cheese-mongers, fishmongers, coalmongers, poultrymongers, and fellmongers, who sold animal pelts.

There were a great deal of "smiths," a word indicating all those who worked with metal: brasssmith, silversmith, goldsmith, scissor-smith, toolsmith, coachsmith, and swordsmith.

Finally "man" and "woman" were added to a long list of jobs: clipperman, codman, stallman, and cat food man. The latter fed city cats in areas where they were needed to catch mice and rats. There was even a secondhand meat man, who sold restaurant table scraps. There were applewomen, herdswomen, woodswomen, shopwomen, leechwomen, lacewomen, and many more.

Most of the jobs in the colonies were individual trades, but there were a few early American industries: iron ore smelting, charcoal burning to produce carbon blocks, and glassmaking. There were also paper mills and those jobs connected with transportation, such as building the roads and bridges that would connect the diverse colonies.

Virginia

George Washington's Gristmill Historical State Park

For three decades George Washington hired a miller to run the gristmill on his Mount Vernon estate. The first miller he hired became so fond of the liquor made at the mill distillery that, despite his family of seven children, Washington was compelled to dismiss him.

The gristmill at Mount Vernon was the second mill Washington owned. There was a mill at Mount Vernon when Washington acquired the estate from his sister-in-law, but it was not operating efficiently. In 1770, Washington had the three-and-half story stone millhouse you see today constructed. Associated with the mill was the distillery that so tempted the first miller, a cooper's shop, and a stable.

All of these activities are represented at **George Washington's Gristmill Historical State Park**. There is much to see, and the displays offer an insightful look at the ingenuity of our forebears. A taped message from the miller's wife explains what happened when grain was brought by customers to be ground. The "merchant trade" had wheat ground into flour, while the "country trade" relied more on ground corn. Each customer's grain was tagged and ground separately, for each wanted to be sure he received his own batch. You can see the machinery used for this colonial operation.

An intriguing feature of the mill is that the three floors above the ground level permit a number of perspectives from which to view the large waterwheel. On the ground floor there is a "cog pit," where the wheel can be seen head on. From the upper levels, you can look down on the massive wheel.

The cooper's art is represented in exhibits and diagrams. Once wheat was ground into flour, it was stored in barrels, which is why coopers were so often found operating in the vicinity of mills. On the top floor of the mill, a display of early American tools includes a mallet, axe, froe club, sashsaw, and hand adze.

In 1799, George Washington rented his mill to his nephew Lawrence Lewis, but he still kept an eye on its operation. This mill was the last place Washington visited before his death. It was a snowy day, and he caught a cold from which he never recovered.

The George Washington Gristmill Historical State Park is open weekends only, Memorial Day to Labor Day from 10:00 A.M. to 6:00 P.M. A reconstruction project, under the auspices of the Mount Vernon Ladies Association, who will be taking over the mill from the Virginia Department of Conservation and Recreation, was completed in the fall of 1999. There is a nominal admission.

Directions: From I-495/95, the Washington Beltway, take Exit 1, US 1 south, seven miles. Near the Woodlawn Plantation entrance (see selection), turn left on the Mount Vernon Memorial Parkway, Route 235. The mill is about 0.25 mile on the left.

Hugh Mercer Apothecary Shop

Anyone who has ever left either their home or shop with others in charge for just a few days can appreciate the significance of the absolute fidelity of the **Hugh Mercer Apothecary Shop**. The apothecary shop looks as it did the day in 1776 when Mercer left Fredericksburg to serve in the Continental army. Mercer, a brigadier general, was killed at the Battle of Princeton. His shop, though filled with few original items, does authentically reflect the colonial practice of both diagnosing ailments and preparing medications. (Of note: Gen. George S. Patton of World War II fame was Hugh Mercer's great-great-great-grandson.)

Dr. Mercer obtained his medical degree in Scotland at the University of Aberdeen. He served as assistant surgeon to the Army of the

Pretender, Charles Edward Stuart, and provided medical assistance at the Battle of Culloden. Mercer's support for a losing cause forced his emigration to Philadelphia in 1746. Later, when he moved to Fredericksburg, he entered into practice with Dr. Ewen Clements. They placed the following ad in an issue of the *Virginia Gazette* in 1771: "... This day became Partners in the Practice of Physick and Surgery, and have opened Shop on Main Street, furnished with a large assortment of Drugs and Medicines just imported from London."

Dr. Mercer had become friends with several Virginians while serving in the French and Indian War. One of his closest friends was George Washington. Since Washington's mother, brother, and sister lived in Fredericksburg, and all but his sister were patients of Dr. Mercer (see Kenmore Plantation and Mary Washington House selection), the two men were able to maintain close ties. It is likely that many Virginia patriots gathered with these two experienced soldiers in the candle-lit office library to discuss British intransigence.

The Hugh Mercer Apothecary Shop at 1020 Caroline Street is open daily, 9:00 A.M. to 5:00 P.M. A nominal admission is charged.

James Mercer (not, as you might expect, related to Hugh Mercer), a lawyer who moved to Fredericksburg in 1768, was also a friend of the Washington family. He wrote the will of Mary Ball Washington (George's mother) in 1788. Mercer purchased ten lots in a new part of Fredericksburg created by Fielding Lewis (the husband of George Washington's sister, see Kenmore selection).

Mercer called his small gambrel-roofed house **St. James House** in remembrance of the Dublin, Ireland, street where his family's home was located. Mercer was politically active, serving in 1779 as one of Virginia's delegates to the Continental Congress and ending his career by serving as a judge on the Virginia Court of Appeals.

The house, filled with elegant English and American antiques as well as outstanding eighteenth-century porcelain and glass, is now owned by the Association for the Preservation of Virginia Antiquities. It is open during Historic Garden Week and the first week in October, and other times by appointment; call (540) 373-0776.

Directions: From I-95, take the Fredericksburg exit, Route 3. Take Route 3 to William Street; then follow the blue visitor signs and turn right on Princess Ann Street. Then turn left on Charlotte Street. Continue following blue signs to the Fredericksburg Visitor Center on Caroline Street. You can obtain maps and brochures on all the city attractions. The Hugh Mercer Apothecary Shop is at 1020 Caroline Street, and St. James House is at 1300 Charles Street.

Stabler-Leadbeater Apothecary Shop

In 1792, a new shop opened in Alexandria, the **Stabler-Leadbeater Apothecary Shop**. It is the second oldest drugstore in the United States, predated only by a shop in Bethlehem, Pennsylvania.

Although it is often called George Washington's drugstore, there is no documentation of any personal visits from him. A note from Martha dated April 22, 1802, reads: "Mrs. Washington desires Mr. Stabler will send by the bearer a quart bottle of his best castor oil."

The Alexandria lot on which the store stands was originally purchased in 1752 by Washington's neighbor, George Mason of Gunston Hall. It was purchased later in 1774 for seventeen dollars by Philip Dawe, who built the three-story brick building that still stands. He leased it to Edward Stabler, who ran an apothecary shop until 1852. At that time his son-in-law, John Leadbeater, took over the shop. This drugstore served the community for 141 years until it closed in 1933, a victim of the Great Depression.

The shop has the largest and most valuable collection of medicinal glass in North America. Long wooden shelves border the narrow store. Since many customers were unable to read, color was used to convey warnings. Poison was always put in blue bottles that had been deliberately roughened so that even in the dark their message could be read by touch. Another warning was conveyed by the large apothecary jars in the shop window; when they were filled with red liquid, it meant danger—an epidemic in town. Green liquid meant "all clear." Many of the containers of this repository of the past still hold their original potions.

According to local lore, Robert E. Lee was making a purchase at the Stabler-Leadbeater Shop on October 17, 1859, when Lt. Jeb Stuart hurried in to bring orders that would take both him and Lee, two young Marines, to Harpers Ferry to quell John Brown. The two Southerners ultimately resigned their commissions to fight in the Confederate army. You can visit this shop at 105 S. Fairfax Street from 10:00 A.M. to 4:30 P.M. Monday through Saturday. Entrance is through the adjoining antique shop. Admission is charged.

Directions: From the Washington Beltway, I-495/95, take Exit 1, US 1, north into Alexandria. Turn right on Franklin Street; left on Washington Street; then right onto King Street. For the Stabler-Leadbeater Apothecary Shop, continue down King Street to South Fairfax Street and turn right. The shop museum is at 107 S. Fairfax Street.

Maryland

Victualling Warehouse and the Tobacco Prise House

The eighteenth-century **Victualling Warehouse** brings back the days when Annapolis was a bustling commercial center, the principal seaport of the upper Chesapeake Bay as well as one of Maryland's tobacco inspection centers. This warehouse, at 77 Main Street, like others that once existed along the waterfront, was likely used as a victualling warehouse. Victualling (pronounced vit-alling) simply means provisioning. The term first referred to stocking up with victuals, or food, but later encompassed the supplies, sails, cordage, and other equipment necessary for sailing. Annapolis was highly regarded for the quantity and quality of its ship chandlery, or provisioners.

The building currently houses Historic Annapolis Foundation's Museum Store, where, in addition to antique reproductions and books on Maryland history, visitors will find a model of the Annapolis waterfront as it would have looked during the Golden Age of the 1750s and 1760s. It is open Monday through Saturday from 10:00 A.M. to 5:00 P.M. and Sunday, noon to 5:00 P.M.

Another building of this era is the **Tobacco Prise House**, located on Pinkney Street, across City Dock from the Victualling Warehouse. This warehouse is far smaller and possibly was used to pack and store inspected tobacco. Small farmers close to town would have brought their tobacco already packed in hogsheads to such a warehouse for inspection. These hogsheads (or large barrels) were unpacked by the appointed inspectors, who then assigned the tobacco a particular value. Slaves or laborers hired for the occasion would then repack the tobacco using a prise. At the side of the warehouse you'll see a prise, or wooden lever, that was used to compress the tobacco into the hogshead. These hogshead, weighing between 750 and 1,200 pounds, would then be stored at the warehouse until a ship could be arranged to carry the tobacco to a buyer. This building is open on special occasions.

Just up Pinkney Street from the Tobacco Prise House is one of the oldest surviving houses in Annapolis. The **Shiplap House**, named for the type of board siding that is on the rear of the building as well as the side addition, was built in 1715 by Edward Smith. Smith operated an ordinary, or tavern, on the property. When the building is open, visitors will find a re-creation of Smith's Tavern in one of the downstairs rooms. Smith died in 1723, and the house subsequently had many owners and tenants. Just prior to the Revolution, Nathan Hammond owned this house and operated a small merchant's shop here. Town residents could purchase nails, sugar, cloth, and other necessities at Hammond's store. During the latter half of the nineteenth century, this house became the residence of noted artist Francis Blackwell Mayer. The building currently houses the headquarters of Historic Annapolis Foundation. The museum floor is open on some afternoons—check the sign on the door. No admission is charged.

A bit farther up the street at 43 Pinkney Street is a mid-eighteenth-century, gambrel-roofed house. Known as the **Barracks**, this carpenter's house was typical of the many small homes leased to the state for use as Continental soldier barracks during the American Revolution. Housing was so scarce that even such small dwellings were pressed into service. Records from that period indicate that neither side was happy with the enforced troop quartering. The soldiers complained of the meagerly furnished rooms and lack of firewood. They retaliated by burning what furniture there was as well as structural portions of the houses—to the dismay of their landlords. The first floor of this building is open on special occasions. For more information, you can call (410) 267-7619.

Directions: From Baltimore, take I-97 south to Route 50 east. Take Exit 24 (Rowe Boulevard) off of Route 50 into historic downtown Annapolis.

Pennsylvania

Bethlehem Historic District

Each year pilgrims from around the world flock to Bethlehem during the Christmas season. That might seem like an impossible destination for a one-day trip, but not if you head north of Philadelphia to Bethlehem, Pennsylvania. This is a town that was named on Christmas Eve back in 1741 when the newly arrived Moravian settlers held their religious services in their Gemein Haus. This community log structure housed both the settlers and their animals (in an adjoining stable). As they sang "Not Jerusalem-lowly Bethlehem 'twas that gave us Christ," their leader, Count Zinzendorf, patron of the Moravian Church, suggested that they christen their new town Bethlehem.

The town even has its own Star of Bethlehem, sparkling high above the city from atop South Mountain. The nearly one-hundred-foot-high star can be seen for miles. You will see smaller Moravian stars displayed throughout the entire town during the month of December, while candles flicker from the windows of houses and public buildings. Special Lanternlight Walking tours are conducted. As you near the old Moravian settlement, you will see one of the largest decorated community trees in the country.

By planning at least three weeks ahead, you can make the necessary reservations for the hour-long Night Light bus tour, the Old Town Walking tour, or the Bethlehem by Day tour. These popular annual tours are led by guides dressed in Moravian attire. In the Night Light bus tour, you not only see the sights of this Christmas-bedecked town, you also ride to the top of South Mountain for a view of the valley's twinkling lights. To find out more about these tours, call (215) 868-1513.

The city also hosts a Yuletide market fair, Christkindlmarkt, offering more than two weeks of holiday fun. More than fifty juried craftspeople and scores of other retailers sell their unique wares just like they have for centuries in such German towns as Munich, Rothenburg, and Nurnberg. Entertainment and a wide variety of food vendors will add to the occasion.

In the Christian Education Building of the Central Moravian Church, there is a Moravian *putz*, German for "decoration," which has come to be used for Nativity scenes. The *putz* is composed of hand-carved wooden figures, many originally from Germany. Combining these wooden figures with music and narration, the story of the Nativity is told. The story of the Bethlehem settlement also is told.

December, with its special Christmas glow, is the best time to visit this historic town. But it is by no means the only time, as each season has its own appeal. If you prefer warm-weather excursions, you can wait until August for Musikfest with its Moravian crafts, music, and food.

Bethlehem, spanning three centuries of history, really does not require any special event to warrant a visit. In fact, you might prefer to plan your first trip at an off-time so that you can take in the many attractions of this old town without fighting the additional crowds that predictably accompany the popular annual programs. Whenever you arrive in Bethlehem, start your visit at the visitor center and pick up a schedule of daily activities and a self-guided walking tour map. Try to see the half-hour orientation film, *City in the Wilderness*, as well as *Mission Bethlehem*, a twenty-minute multimedia presentation on the founding of Bethlehem. Guides costumed in old Moravian dress lead group tours (minimum of five people) through the Moravian community. Call (215) 867-0173 or 868-1513 for information.

The walking tour encompasses twenty-six sites—probably more

than you'll have time to see on a single visit. One stop you won't want to miss is the **Gemein Haus,** the five-story log cabin built in 1741. Constructed without nails from wood and mud plaster, this is the largest log dwelling still standing in the United States. It not only served as a place of worship, but also as a dormitory and craft workshop. Today, this community house serves as the Moravian Museum, where you can see examples of early Moravian furniture, needlework, musical instruments, dolls, and religious art, plus a typical kitchen and schoolroom. There is also a room furnished as it would have been when Count Zinzendorf stayed at the Gemein Haus. The Gemein Haus, at 66 West Church Street, is open Tuesday through Saturday from 1:00 to 4:00 P.M. and, like many of Bethlehem's attractions, is closed in January.

Probably the second most significant site to be explored is the eighteenth-century **Moravian Industrial Quarter,** located along the Monocacy Creek, an easy walk from Main Street. In addition to Bethlehem's Christmas connection, the town is associated with one of the country's largest steel corporations—Bethlehem Steel. The town's industrial heritage goes back to the early settlers, who developed an industrial complex of thirty-two craft and trade shops on the banks of Monocacy Creek.

In the **1761 Tannery,** you can watch authentically dressed workers demonstrate the art of leather crafting. In its heyday roughly three thousand hides were tanned annually at this massive plant. You will hear a step-by-step description of the tanning operation while gazing down from wooden walkways into the huge vats where the animal hides were soaked. Other early industries are also demonstrated; there is a working model of the 1765 oil mill and the 1762 waterworks. After viewing the small-scale models, you can visit the reconstructed operating mechanisms of the original waterworks, considered the first municipal works in the American colonies.

The tannery also has a children's discovery room. Youngsters can get in touch with history by trying on old-fashioned costumes, by attempting to communicate using Native American sign language, and by guessing the use for various unusual tools. This educational area is open weekends, April through December, and Tuesday through Sunday during the summer months.

In addition to these pivotal spots, you can visit the Sun Inn, circa 1758; the 1810 Federal-style Goundie House; the Kemerer Museum of Decorative Arts, a town house filled with the results of a lifetime search for beauty; and the Apothecary Museum, a repository of old medicinal equipment. The latter is open by appointment only. For a glimpse of the Moravians' agricultural practices, visit Burnside Plan-

129

tation, just off Schoenersville Road. The 1749 farmhouse is being restored, and living history makes pre-industrial farm life come alive. Tours are by appointment; call (215) 868-5044.

Directions: From the Northeast Extension of the Pennsylvania Turnpike (I-76), take the Lehigh Valley exit and travel east on Route 22. At the intersection with Route 378, go south to Center City Bethlehem (Historic District) Exit 3 and follow the signs. The visitors center is located at 509 Main Street.

Historic Yellow Springs

History, health, art, and nature all merge in the tiny village of Yellow Springs. The Lenni Lenape and Susquehanna Indians were aware of the medicinal properties of the yellow water that bubbled up from beneath the ground, changing the color of the creek banks. Before long the European settlers in nearby Pikeland became aware of the healing qualities of the springs.

By 1721, Philadelphia physicians were sending patients out of the city to Pikeland to "take of the mineral springs." By 1750, the area was a health spa, with roads constructed to carry travelers to the east bank of Pickering Creek, where the springs were most active. The first of many taverns, Prichard's Publick House of Entertainment, opened in 1762. The fame of the springs was by this time attracting visitors from as far as the West Indies. As Yellow Springs became more fashionable, the comfortable bathhouses added drawing rooms and fireplaces. Physician Benjamin Rush, who signed the Declaration of Independence for Pennsylvania, promoted the healing properties of the bubbling springs.

In the spring of 1774, Dr. Samuel Kennedy purchased the springs. He served under Gen. Anthony Wayne, whose estate, Waynesborough, was not far away. Kennedy loaned part of his land to Congress as a hospital for Continental soldiers during the Revolutionary War. The proximity of Yellow Springs was one of the factors that convinced General Washington to make his winter encampment at Valley Forge. In fact, Washington established temporary headquarters at the Yellow Springs Inn in September of 1778 after the Battle of Brandywine and the Battle of the Clouds in Malvern.

When you visit **Historic Yellow Springs**, you will see the restored ruins of "Washington Hall," the only official Revolutionary War hospital constructed with the authorization of the Continental Congress. Erected in the winter of 1777–78, the hospital remained in use until

1781. Concerned that his men were contracting smallpox, General Washington took the progressive step of ordering the men under his command to be vaccinated and soldiers with contagious diseases to be removed to the Yellow Springs Hospital. To reassure the men that the procedure was safe, Washington received one of the first shots administered by Dr. Otto, the director and chief surgeon of the hospital. The unmarked graves around the hospital site are mute testimony to the overwhelming struggle against disease, hunger, and the elements fought by the army at Valley Forge.

After the hospital closed, the village and its spas were restored to their prewar condition, and travelers returned to the healing waters. New buildings were added around 1820. Several still stand, including the George Washington Building, now the Inn at Yellow Springs, a popular and picturesque restaurant. The Lincoln Building is connected to the inn by a wooden piazza. Once called "The Cottage," it now serves as exhibit space for Historic Yellow Springs and other village organizations. The Chester Springs Library, a branch of the Chester County Library system, is located here as well as the offices of Historic Yellow Springs.

The iron springs were the first to be used, but over the years, a sulphur and a magnesium spring were discovered. New bathhouses were added to serve the growing need. Notable figures joined the crowd seeking the healing waters. Presidents Madison and Monroe visited Yellow Springs as did Henry Clay, Daniel Webster, and DeWitt Clinton. Popular entertainers performed at the inn; Jenny Lind even had one of the springs named after her. (In a later era, Steve McQueen lived at the inn while filming *The Blob* on location in Chester Springs.)

After the Civil War, the state acquired the spa as an orphanage for the children of soldiers who became indigent as a result of the war. In 1902, the hospital, which was being used as a classroom building, was destroyed by fire. It was rebuilt, but burned again in 1962. Today, the restored fieldstone foundations and an authentic eighteenth-century herb garden occupy the site.

In 1916, the Pennsylvania Academy of the Fine Arts purchased the facilities of Yellow Springs to use as a residential, summer landscape school. To enhance the scenery for the school's art students, the Academy hired an English landscape gardener to create an oriental bog garden around the springs.

After Good New Productions purchased the buildings in 1952, they made several science-fiction films here, including the cult classics *The Blob* and *4-D Man*. The company also made hundreds of religious and educational films for television and the cinema.

In 1965, the Yellow Springs Association began to bring artistic and cultural programs to the area. When the Yellow Springs property was put on the market in 1973, this small grassroots organization formed the Yellow Springs Foundation, which purchased the property in 1974. The two groups then joined to form Historic Yellow Springs, Inc., which has restored the historic buildings and conserved the unique landscape. Today, this charming village offers workshops, exhibits, programs, and performances. The village, listed on the National Register of Historic Places, is also home to the Chester Springs Studio. A restoration of the water gardens and wetland was completed in 1994. A path through the water gardens takes you to the sulfur and magnesium springs, where you can peak into the historic spa buildings where the hopeful "took the cure."

The best time to visit the village is during one of the four annual events: the art show, frolics, antiques show, and craft festival. Call (610) 827-7414 for details and dates. If you visit in the fall, you are apt to see members of the Pickering Hunt in their scarlet coats following the hounds on their traditional fox hunts.

Directions: From I-76, the Pennsylvania Turnpike west, take Exit 23 to Route 100 south; continue and turn left onto Route 113 north to Chester Springs. Turn left on Yellow Springs Road for the village of Yellow Springs.

Delaware

Historic Batsto Village

What's a "batsto?" Many of the settlers in this part of New Jersey were Scandinavian, and when they saw the steam rising from the hot iron, they called it *batstu*, which actually meant "bathing place."

In 1766, Charles Read built the Batsto Iron Works near the mouth of the Batsto River. It was the first known bog iron furnace in the area, which in the next decade became the site of a bog iron and glassmaking industrial center. Batsto supplied iron to the Continental army during the American Revolution. The Batsto Furnace was almost captured by the British in 1778 but was saved by Pulaski's Legion.

In 1784, William Richards purchased Batsto Iron Works. His family maintained ownership of the property for ninety-two years. When the iron industry began to fail in the early nineteenth century, Batsto became known for its production of window glass. Eventually, the glassmaking industry declined, and Batsto fell into receivership. In 1876, it was purchased by Joseph Wharton, who embarked on numerous agricultural pursuits as well as manufacturing forest products. Wharton also transformed the mansion and village into a "gentleman's farm."

Historic Batsto Village brings to life the early and late nineteenth century with thirty-three historic buildings, including a thirty-five-room mansion, general store, sawmill, gristmill, village houses, and assorted barns. There is also an environmental interpretive center. This state historic site is located in the Wharton State Forest, part of the Pinelands National Reserve, established by Congress in 1978 to protect the unique natural and cultural resources in the Pinelands.

The village is open daily from 9:00 A.M. to 4:00 P.M. between Memorial Day and Labor Day. The rest of the year, it is open Wednesday through Sunday. The grounds are open from dawn to dusk at no charge. There is a nominal fee for a guided tour of the mansion. Additional information can be obtained by calling (609) 561-3262.

Directions: Take I-95 north to the New Jersey Turnpike; then head north to the Atlantic City Expressway. Take that east to the Garden State Parkway; then head north on that to Exit 50, New Gretna. Take Route 9 north until you see a Gulf gas station; turn left on Route 542 and go approximately ten miles. The village is on the right, with the entrance marked by two flags.

Colonial Taverns

Talk about paying for your drink with bits and pieces—that was literally the preferred currency during the colonial period, referring as it did to pieces of the gold doubloon. The doubloon was the Spanish dollar, available throughout the English colonies as a result of extensive Spanish trading for British goods. Gold pieces were routinely divided into eight sections, or pieces of eight. Each piece was called a "bit" and was worth twelve and a half cents—hence the expression, "two bits, four bits, six bits, a dollar." A tankard of ale cost half a bit, or six and a half cents; if the patron had two tankards, it would cost a whole bit, and the piece would not have to be broken. It would take a thirsty customer to drink two tankards.

Another method of payment was the barter technique. Drinks could be purchased with farm goods. A quart of rum was worth one and a half pounds of butter. Tobacco notes also were accepted by tavern keepers.

Of course, since Americans were then English colonists, English currency—the pence, shilling, and pound—also was used. With inflation creating a constant fluctuation of monetary values, it can only be roughly estimated that in the 1740s, a pence was worth a penny. There were twelve pence, or cents, to a shilling and twenty shillings to a pound.

The menu prices charged by inns and taverns were set by the court. For example, in 1791, the court of Bath County, Virginia, established the following prices: 6 pence for a night's lodging, 4 pence for a gallon of corn whiskey, 4 shillings for a quart of rum, 12.5 pence for a cold supper, and 21 pence for a hot dinner.

Taverns were the social and civic centers of most towns. From 1619, taverns operated in America, providing food, shelter, lodging, and a meeting place for the community. Jamestown had a lively tavern during the ninety-two years that city served as Virginia's capital. Popular taverns, like the Raleigh in Williamsburg, City Tavern in Philadelphia, the Rising Sun in Fredericksburg, and Gadsby's Tavern in Alexandria, were centers of patriot activity.

Taverns played a considerable role in events leading up to the Revolution, serving as a patriot "underground." George Washington made his headquarters in a tavern while fighting the British in New York. He later appointed Samuel Fraunces, the tavern keeper, to be his household steward during his terms as president. The second president, John Adams, owned a tavern during the 1780s. It was quite a respectable colonial occupation.

In the country, taverns were much simpler, many even crude. Often they were called "ordinaries" because the food would likely be similar to a family's ordinary fare. Travelers needed these rest stops, although gentlemen usually were able to find a nearby plantation to whose owners they were either related, acquainted, or carried letters of introduction. The ferry taverns sometimes slept as many as thirteen in one room. It was quite common, even in city taverns like the Raleigh, to find yourself sharing a bed with one or more strangers.

Virginia

Gadsby's Tavern

Even the patronage of such illustrious colonial gentlemen as George Washington, George Mason, and the Lees did not preclude an evening that would, by today's standards, be considered unruly. At

Revolutionary troops fire muskets in front of Gadsby's Tavern during a re-enactment of Washington's Review of the Troops. In the eighteenth century, this tavern was the center of Alexandria's political, social, and cultural life.

eighteenth-century dinner parties, such as those held at **Gadsby's Tavern** in Alexandria, breakage was typically figured in the cost of the evening.

A tavern bill from a 1778 party for 270 gentlemen included a charge for breakage of ninety-six wine glasses, twenty-nine jelly glasses, nine glass dessert plates, eleven china plates, three china dishes, five decanters, and a large inkstand! This excessive damage is perhaps explained by reading the listing of alcoholic beverages consumed by yet another party of fifty-five at a 1787 dinner party. The fifty-five revelers were charged for twenty-two bottles of Porter, fifty-four of Madeira, sixty of claret, eight of Old Stock, eight of cider, eight of beer, and seven large bowls of punch.

They don't have parties like that any more. They do, however, still serve lunch, dinner, and Sunday brunch at Gadsby's Tavern Restaurant, the "finest publick house in America." The eighteenth century is evoked by the menu, service, and surroundings in the three restored tavern rooms.

Even if you don't stop by for a taste of the past, you should stop for a tour of Gadsby's Tavern Museum. The tavern consists of two buildings: the 1770 tavern and the 1792 City Hotel, acquired by John Gadsby in 1796. Gadsby's Tavern was the center of Alexandria's political, social, and cultural life. Here, the colonial leaders met both before and after the Revolution. One of the grand events of the year was George Washington's birth night ball, first held in 1789 and still a popular Alexandria event. The tavern tour includes the restored ballroom where Washington enjoyed dancing. There are also restored bedrooms to give you an idea of tavern accommodations. Guided tours of Gadsby's Tavern Museum are given daily at quarter of and quarter after the hour from 10:00 A.M. to 4:15 P.M. and on Sunday, 1:00 to 5:00 P.M., from April through September. Winter hours are Tuesday through Saturday, 11:00 A.M. to 4:00 P.M., and on Sunday, 1:00 to 4:00 P.M. For information regarding museum tours and programs, you can call (703) 838-4242. For lunch and dinner reservations, call (703) 548-1288.

Directions: From the Washington Beltway, I-495/95, take Exit 1, US 1 north into Alexandria. Turn right on Franklin Street; left on Washington Street; then right onto King Street to Royal. Gadsby's Tavern is one block to the left at 134 North Royal Street.

Michie Tavern, ca. 1784

Michie Tavern, ca. 1784 is one of the oldest homesteads remaining in Virginia. It was originally located on a well-traveled stagecoach route some seventeen miles northwest of the present site. To accommodate the many travelers seeking food and shelter at his home, William Michie opened his dwelling as an "ordinary" in 1784.

Michie (pronounced Micky) Tavern's museum hostess will tell you about young William. His father, "Scotch John" Michie, was deported to Virginia in 1716 after taking part in the Scottish Jacobite Rising. When John arrived in Virginia, he began acquiring land; ultimately, he handled more than 11,500 acres. The land on which his son would eventually build Michie Tavern was acquired from Maj. John Henry, father of Patrick, another rebel against England.

William Michie also played a role in the struggle against England. He was part of the Continental army that wintered with Washington at Valley Forge. He signed the Albemarle Declaration of Independence in 1779. It was after the Revolutionary War that William Michie obtained a license to operate his ordinary.

After the guide's introduction, you will make your way through the tavern. Each room has a recorded narration, and guides quite often offer living-history interpretation. The tavern has about fifty items that once belonged to the Michie family. The first room on the tour is the gentlemen's parlor with its adjoining taproom. The tap bar is a very small enclosure, so built as to bar the public from its access. The tavern keeper became known as the bartender—a term still widely used.

From the gentlemen's parlor, you'll move across the hall to the ladies' parlor. After the Revolutionary War, road conditions and travel by coach improved. Female travelers were no longer an oddity, and it was in the proprietor's best interest to set aside a special room for women. The woodwork and furnishings are more elaborate here.

The upstairs ballroom served many functions, including additional sleeping space, a place for church worship, dancing lessons, and school. Entertainers and traveling doctors and dentists set up shop in this room. It is the thought of so many long-ago balls, however, that strikes the most romantic chord. It was here, legend proclaims, that the first waltz was danced in the colonies. Although no surviving account can document this story, old-timers claim the event was recorded in the margins of the tavern log book, which mysteriously disappeared in the 1950s. The story claims that one of Jefferson's daughters had just returned from France, where she had learned a "radical" new dance step. She danced it gaily in the arms of a dashing officer. Onlookers were shocked, and her chaperone quickly escorted her from the floor. According to reports, she was harshly scolded.

Back downstairs, you will see the keeping hall, where food was kept warm before serving. This room holds a fine selection of spinning equipment. One special piece is a yarn winder, which was invented to count thread. A small wooden peg (known as the weasel) pops loudly after each revolution of the wheel (known as the monkey). The "monkey" chases the "weasel" as in the nursery rhyme *Pop Goes the Weasel*. Other handy kitchen items include the hand-carved cheese press, apple peeler, coleslaw shredder, and french-fried potato cutter.

The narration continues as you tour the dependencies—kitchen, necessary, spring house, well house, and smokehouse. If you have problems with steps, you may want to skip these buildings. Your tour ends beneath the tavern in the wine cellar that now houses the **Virginia Wine Museum**. After your tour, you may continue to the ordinary and enjoy a colonial buffet. Michie's hospitality didn't end with the eighteenth century. The ordinary still serves fried chicken, black-eyed peas, stewed tomatoes, coleslaw, southern beets, green bean salad, potato salad, corn bread, biscuits, and apple cobbler. Lunch is available from 11:30 A.M. to 3:00 P.M. daily in four dining rooms and an outdoor courtyard.

The thread of preservation continues with the **Sowell** (pronounced Soul) **House**, an early nineteenth-century structure that was reconstructed on the Michie Tavern site. Tours of this house focus on the architectural development of the house and the way that it reflects events in the life of the Sowell family—both personal and national. Before leaving you should also tour the **Meadow Run Grist Mill**, which houses the General Store. The mill was moved fifty miles to this new location. It is an appropriate addition because the Michie family owned and operated a mill and general store. Their family history is further preserved through the interpretation. The tavern was relocated to this site in the 1920s, and the move itself became a historic event. The Michie Tavern is significant as an example of the early preservation movement.

Michie Tavern is open 9:00 A.M. to 5:00 P.M., with the last tour beginning at 4:20 P.M. Admission is charged and includes both the tavern and gristmill.

Directions: From I-95 in the Richmond area, take I-64 west to the Charlottesville area. From I-64, take Exit 121A, Route 20 south. Just past the Thomas Jefferson Visitors Bureau, turn left on Route 53. Michie Tavern is on the right just before the entrance to Monticello; both are well marked.

Rising Sun Tavern

One of the most popular colonial meeting spots in Fredericksburg was the **Rising Sun Tavern**. Built in 1760 for Charles Washington, George's younger brother, it was his home and not a tavern. Later in the century, it became a tavern, where entertainment was provided by traveling players. Balls and many meetings took place as well. The tavern also served as the stagecoach stop and post office.

Visitors to Rising Sun Tavern see the original tavern; although it has been extensively restored and refurnished, it has never been structurally altered. It is a simple, colonial, story-and-a-half frame house that looks more residential than commercial. The hand-beveled clapboard, steep gabled roof, and narrow dormer windows look quite homey.

During renovations, the original bar railing was found, which made it possible to rebuild the bar to its eighteenth-century specifications. The tap room has an impressive collection of English and American pewter. There are also gaming tables, reflecting the sporting nature of the tavern.

Guided tours of the Rising Sun Tavern are given daily, April through November, from 9:00 A.M. to 5:00 P.M. From December through March, hours are 10:00 A.M. to 4:00 P.M. The tavern is closed on major holidays. Admission is charged.

Directions: From I-95, take the Fredericksburg exit, Route 3. Take Route 3 to William Street; then follow the blue visitor signs and turn right on Princess Ann Street. Then turn left on Caroline Street. Continue following blue signs to the Fredericksburg Visitor Center on Caroline Street. You can obtain maps and brochures on all the city attractions. Rising Sun Tavern is at 1304 Caroline Street.

Colonial Williamsburg's Taverns

During the eighteenth century there were forty taverns in the Virginia capital of Williamsburg. Today, there are seven, offering a variety of tavern experiences. Lodging is available in the historic area at Brick House and Market Square Taverns. Guided tours are given of Raleigh and Wetherburn's Taverns. You can dine at King's Arm, Christiana Campbell's, Shields, or Chowning's Tavern and take in evening "gambols" at the latter.

Raleigh Tavern, which opened in 1932, was the first Colonial Williamsburg reconstruction. The colonial capital was the focal spot of rebellion in Virginia, and a great deal of the action took place at the Raleigh Tavern. When the royal governor dissolved the House of Burgesses, the members resumed their meetings at the Raleigh Tavern. Often merchants and medical practitioners arranged their schedules so that they stayed at the Raleigh while the Burgesses met.

The most expensive piece of tavern equipment was the billiard table in the gaming room, where ladies never ventured. You will see one of these old playing tables with ivory balls and hand-carved cues.

Ladies could attend the balls and formal functions given in the Apollo Room. Thomas Jefferson, in his diary, notes that he danced here with Rebecca Burwell, his "fair Belinda." The residents of

Williamsburg gathered in the Apollo Room to celebrate the Treaty of Paris, officially ending the American Revolution. Some years later, in 1824, Lafayette attended a party at the Raleigh celebrating the American victory at Yorktown. The tavern is open daily from 9:00 A.M. to 5:00 P.M. and is included in all Colonial Williamsburg tickets. Behind Raleigh Tavern is the bake shop, which still employs two-hundred-year-old techniques to prepare gingerbread cookies and other delicacies for its customers.

Across Duke of Gloucester Street and down about half a block is **Wetherburn's Tavern**, which is also open on a schedule that varies with the seasons. The archeological on-site dig helped ensure the authenticity of this restoration. Pottery shards and tavern equipment unearthed in dry wells, the garbage dumps of the eighteenth century, enabled the Colonial Williamsburg Foundation to furnish the tavern according to the inventory left by Mr. Wetherburn. Like many of his colonial contemporaries, Mr. Wetherburn had two wives. He mourned eleven days before marrying the widow of a fellow tavern keeper, thus securing her inherited goods, including a good bit of silver.

As you will readily observe at both Raleigh and Wetherburn's, taverns in the eighteenth century were a combination hotel, restaurant, bar, and community center. Unless he paid dearly for a private room, a guest was apt to sleep with three or four strangers—not just in the same room, but in the same bed! From this practice comes the expression "sleep tight." The ropes supporting the mattress were tightened each night; otherwise all the occupants would roll into the center of the bed. Slaves traveling with their masters slept either on the floor or in one of the dependencies.

Dining in the taverns of Williamsburg today is far different from what it was during the colonial period. The smaller taverns in the eighteenth century prepared only one meal; few had the luxury of a menu. Now, at four taverns you can have a choice of colonial and traditional fare for lunch and dinner. The fare at **King's Arm Tavern**, the most elegant of the four, features a dinner menu of game pie, oyster pie, Cornish game hen, and beef with Sally Lunn bread, Indian corn muffins, assorted relishes, vegetables, and old-fashioned desserts to complement the meal. At **Christiana Campbell's**, dinner selections include clam chowder, Virginia ham, backfin crab imperial, and southern fried chicken. **Josiah Chowning's** features Brunswick stew, barbecued ribs, or pork barbecue; Welsh rabbit is a lunchtime favorite. The newest kid on these very old blocks is **Shields Tavern**, which opened in 1989. Featuring the food enjoyed by the lesser gentry and upper middling ranks of locals and travelers, the menu includes spit-roasted chicken, Chesapeake Bay poached seafood, and a delightful greengage plum ice cream. The most accurate replication of eighteenth-century food offered at any of the Williamsburg taverns is the appetizer assortment "Shields Sampler: A Tasting of 1750s Foods." Reservations are a must for these colonial dining experiences and should be made well before your visit (as much as two months during the peak season) by calling (800) HISTORY. Be sure to confirm your reservation when you arrive. If you stay over in Williamsburg, you might want to drop in on the nightly "gambol" at Chowning's. These evenings of tavern games are very popular. You can play backgammon, checkers, chess, cards, or learn such new "old" board games as "The Royal and Most Pleasant Game of Goose," "Bowles' Royal Pastime of Cupid," and "Entertaining Game of Snake."

The **Brick House Tavern** has been advertising "12 or 14 very good lodging rooms" since 1770. Unlike many taverns of the day, it welcomed women guests. Today, eighteen rooms are available for any Williamsburg visitor who can get reservations.

Just two blocks away up Duke of Gloucester Street is **Market Square Tavern and Kitchen**, where visitors have found accommodations for three centuries. The eighteen-year-old apprentice law student, Thomas Jefferson, rented rooms here while he studied with George Wythe.

Tavern rooms are available though the Colonial House program at Williamsburg Inn. In all, there are twenty-three guest houses, each enhanced by period furnishings, and three taverns that offer lodging. For information or reservations, call (800) HISTORY.

Directions: From I-95 in the Richmond area, take Exit 238, I-64 east to Williamsburg. Use Exit 56 onto Route 143 (you will bear right off I-64). This is quickly followed by a right onto Route 132. You'll turn left onto feeder Route 132Y into the Colonial Williamsburg Visitor Center.

Maryland

London Town Publik House and Gardens

Doors as enormous as those at the **William Brown House**, part of Edgewater's **London Town Publik House and Gardens**, seem built to accommodate giants. Fittingly, some historic giants did pass through these portals. George Washington, Thomas Jefferson, and Francis Scott Key were among the well-known figures who noted in their diaries crossing on the ferry at London Town.

London Town was a bustling colonial ferry stop on the South River for travelers between Williamsburg and Philadelphia. The William Brown House, which served as an inn, is the only town building that has survived.

This once-bustling town on the South River was one of the major ferry stops for travelers between Williamsburg and Philadelphia. It was also a point of departure for Europe and, after 1683, the port of entry for tall-masted ships carrying cargoes of European and East Indian goods to the colonies and taking tobacco back to England.

A log tobacco barn, built in 1790 on a Maryland plantation, has been moved to the grounds at London Town, but the William Brown House, now a National Historic Landmark, is the only town building to survive. Its extra thick walls were built to last. The bricks were laid in an all-header pattern, which you'll see on a number of colonial houses in nearby Annapolis. This pattern was costly, requiring far

142

more bricks than the more traditional lengthwise pattern. The all-header pattern ensured greater depth and thus improved insulation. The publik house sits on a bluff overlooking the river, so it needed protection from the elements. As an additional deterrent to drafts, each room was raised one step. All of the exterior doors, woodwork, hardware, and even some windows are original. The sturdy furniture has been collected to reflect eighteenth-century styles.

According to records, the inn was built on land deeded to Col. William Burgess by Lord Baltimore in 1651.The publik house served as both an inn and post house. It was to the inn that town folk flocked for news. The innkeeper frequently had more than one job. From 1764 to 1781, William Brown ran the publik house, operated a cabinetmaking business, served as ferry keeper, and owned farm land nearby.

The trees and flowers of the London Town Gardens entice visitors to return to enjoy the site in different seasons. Spring is a particularly popular time to explore the eight-acre woodland gardens. A spring walk features bleeding heart, Lenten rose, primrose, may apple, and phlox, with a separate area for azaleas and viburnums. The wild flower walk is also at its best in the spring. The garden has one of the largest magnolia collections in the east.

During the summer months, the daylilies provide the main attraction, but see the herb garden as well. Waterfowl, which can be seen at London Town's pond year-round, are abundant during their autumn migration. The winter garden features dwarf conifers.

London Town Publik House and Gardens hours are 10:00 A.M. to 4:00 P.M., Monday through Saturday, and noon to 4:00 P.M. on Sunday, year-round. Admission is charged.

Directions: From Baltimore take I-97 south to the Annapolis area. Go west on US 50/301 to Parole and exit, following Route 2 south. At the second traffic signal past the South River (Veterans Memorial) Bridge, turn left on Mayo Road, Route 253. Take Mayo Road for one mile and then turn left onto Londontown Road, which leads to the grounds of the London Town Publik House.

Pennsylvania

City Tavern

If billboards and commercials had been part of eighteenth-century life, then **City Tavern** would certainly have promoted John Adams's testimonial that this tavern was "the most genteel one in America."

From its opening in 1774 through the next eighty tumultuous years as America found its place in the world, this tavern served the men who made the nation. It was a favorite meeting spot for revolutionaries and businessmen. Paul Revere brought news to tavern patrons on May 20, 1774, that the port of Boston was closed. A large group gathered at City Tavern and agreed to send a message of sympathy to the people of Boston.

During the American Revolution, the tavern was used by General Washington as his headquarters. Colonial officers lodged here, including Horatio Gates, Benedict Arnold, and the Marquis de Lafayette. The British enjoyed the hospitality of City Tavern during their occupation of Philadelphia. Many Tory balls were held here during 1777 and 1778.

This is a reconstruction of the original City Tavern, and it is part of Independence National Historical Park. The first innkeeper, Daniel Smith, was an Englishman who wanted his tavern to resemble those in London. The menu reflects not only colonial but modern tastes.

Directions: From I-95 southbound (from points north), take Exit17. Using the right-hand lanes of the exit, follow the signs for Callowhill Street/Independence Hall. At the bottom of the exit ramp, follow 2nd Street straight ahead to Chestnut Street. Continue a half block past Chestnut Street for the Historic Area Parking Garage on the left. It is best to park your car and walk to all the sites in the Historic District. Start at the Independence National Historical Park Visitors Center, one block away, at 3rd and Chestnut Streets, where you can pick up an easy-to-follow map of the district and a park schedule. If you are traveling northbound on I-95 (from points south), you will also take Exit 17. Stay in the left lane because you will exit on the left side of I-95. At the exit, stay in the right-hand lane and follow the signs for Independence Hall/Historic Area. Turn left at 6th Street to Chestnut, which will take you through the heart of the Historic District to 2nd Street. Turn right on 2nd Street. The entrance to the Historic Area Parking Garage is on the left.

Golden Plough Tavern

The Golden Plough Tavern is the oldest building in York. In 1741, Thomas Cookson surveyed and laid out the new town of York. There were more than 500 lots, and Martin Eichelberger purchased Lot 120. A condition of purchase was that a house had to be built on the land within a specified amount of time. A building, suggesting the build-

The 1741 Golden Plough Tavern is probably the oldest surviving structure in York, Pennsylvania. This Germanic, half-timber building contains a fine collection of furnishings reflecting the William and Mary period.

ings of Eichelberger's early home in Germany's Black Forest, probably stood on this property by 1744 or 1745. In fact, Eichelberger's building is one of the few in the United States done in a medieval style. The building is half brick and half large, hand-hewn timber with a pitched roof.

It is not clear from historical records whether Eichelberger operated a tavern in this building. Eichelberger applied for a tavern license in July 1753, but by that time, he no longer owned this property. Joseph Chambers, who bought Lot 120 in 1751, held a tavern license from 1752 to 1771, so it is quite likely he operated the tavern here. It was Chambers who built the house that is now known as the General Gates House (see York Historic District selection).

The Golden Plough Tavern is only one of a number of restored buildings in Historic York. Other restorations and museum exhibits in the area depict the Center Square as it was in the 1830s. The Gold-

145

en Plough Tavern is attached to the home of the Revolutionary general Horatio Gates.

The Golden Plough Tavern is open Monday through Saturday from 10:00 A.M. to 4:00 P.M. and Sundays from 1:00 to 4:00 P.M., March through December.

Directions: From the Washington Beltway, I-495/95 take Exit 27, I-95 north. Then take the Baltimore Beltway west to Route 83 for York. The Golden Plough Tavern is on West Market Street in York.

Colonial Government

There are a great many myths and fallacies in the standard portrayal of America's past. It is a common belief that the first democratic representative legislature met in Jamestown, Virginia, in 1619. This belief is far from accurate. Democratic representation was not the colonists' objective; they were Englishmen, and there was nothing democratic about the English system of government at that time. What the colonists really wanted were the rights of free Englishmen under British common law.

The London Company kept Jamestown under martial law for the first five years. There was a communal economy with no individual rights of property. By 1618, company directors had decided that this system was not feasible and had made substantial reforms. The colonists were given common law rights as well as the power to elect two burgesses from each plantation to a legislative body that would make laws for the colony. This legislative body, composed of twenty-two leading planters from eleven boroughs, or plantations, met with the governor and council for the first time from July 30 to August 4, 1619, in the Memorial Church at Jamestown (see Jamestown Colonial Historical Park).

From 1624, when the London Company broke its colonial connections, to 1638, the burgesses were left with no legal status. Royal governors called them to meetings at their whim. Colonists made numerous attempts to have the king establish the right of the colony to an elected assembly that met regularly, which King Charles I did in 1638, marking a victory for limited self-government in the colonies.

This new legislature was hardly representative since it served only the wealthy tobacco planters and the merchants. Just how the wealthy used their power is illustrated by the manner in which taxes were levied by the Assembly.The poll tax passed in 1629 required everyone to pay five pounds of tobacco. The farmer with only a few acres paid as much as the plantation owner with thousands of acres.

The outcry against this tax was loud and long. In 1645, the tax was changed to reflect the amount of property and number of servants a person owned. This democratic shift was short-lived. It was repealed, and in 1648, the poll tax again benefited the large plantation class. From this, the Assembly gained the name "planter's parliament."

Events in England were leading to a more active interest and involvement in colonial trade. At the same time, the colonists were anxious for self-determination. The years from 1677 to 1698 were a time of expanding royal control. The royal governor kept the House of Burgesses on a tight rein, disbanding them whenever he was displeased with their actions.

Dissatisfaction with autocratic King James was spreading not only in the colonies but also in England. In the late 1680s the Glorious Revolution removed King James from the throne. The change brought reforms to the relationship between the mother country and the colonies. The right of the colonial legislative bodies to issue laws was affirmed, and they were assured of permanent status; no longer were they to be disbanded at the whim of royal governors. Finally, they were, henceforth, to be bicameral bodies.

Charles I granted Maryland as a royal proprietoryship to Cecilius Calvert, who held the hereditary title of Lord Baltimore. The Maryland colony was established to provide religious freedom. So, unlike Virginia, which belonged to a company of merchants (the London Company), Maryland belonged to a family (the Calverts). As royal proprietors, the Calverts were empowered to govern the inhabitants on their land—a return to feudal, Middle Age practices, when the landowners had sole power over their serfs.

On February 26, 1635, the first General Assembly, composed of all free adult males, met in St. Mary's to pass laws for the Maryland colony. When these measures were forwarded to London, Lord Baltimore refused to acknowledge their right to make laws. He reminded the colonists that under the terms of the royal charter only he or his representative, the governor, could make laws. The governor could convene an assembly if he so desired, but merely to approve his laws. A meeting was not held again until 1638.

The Puritan revolt in England caused problems in Maryland. Governor Calvert fled the colony, and Maryland had no effective government for two years. In 1646, Calvert, aided by the governor of

Virginia, regained control. At his death the following year, a Protestant governor was chosen in an effort to appease the Protestant settlers and enable the Calvert family to retain the royal charter. It was at this time, in 1649, that Lord Baltimore issued the Toleration Act, giving complete religious freedom to all Christians.

From 1649 to 1661, Maryland suffered turbulent times with one religious group or another vying for political control. Government chaos was the result. At the request of the Protestant settlers, Maryland became a royal province in 1649. Thus the king, rather than the Calverts, as proprietors, controlled its administration.

Virginia

Capitol in Williamsburg

The idea of legislators being fired up over an issue is not unusual; but the Jamestown legislators carried it too far. The State House in Jamestown was burnt to the ground on two separate occasions. After the second experience the legislators decided it was time to move. The capital was shifted inland to a small village outside the College of William and Mary.

The burned-out burgesses were so determined to prevent this disaster from occurring in their new chamber that the new capitol was built without chimneys. The use of fire, candles, or tobacco was forbidden. The building eventually became so cold and damp that the papers actually began to mildew.

In 1723, the needed chimneys were added. Candles also were permitted, and the burgesses allowed to smoke their "noxious weed." It looked like they just couldn't win. On January 30, 1747, the Virginia legislature was again burned out of business when the building was completely gutted by fire. It was rebuilt, but after the government moved to Richmond, the legislative building was a victim of fire for the fourth time in 1832.

The first **Capitol** has been reconstructed at Colonial Williamsburg. The original design, begun in 1701, was supervised by Henry Cary. He erected a Renaissance building, without the elaborate facade it would have had in England. The H-shaped building was well planned to serve the needs of the Virginia government. One wing was for the House of Burgesses and the other for the General Court. The second floor held the Council Chamber as well as committee rooms for the burgesses. The Conference Room on the second floor linked the two wings, and both burgesses and councilors met there for morning prayer.

Almost every Virginian of note would meet within these walls in the eighteenth century. A great deal of American history took place here. George Washington was lauded for his heroic action in the French and Indian War. Patrick Henry made his famous Caesar-Brutus speech and was accused by some of treason. The Virginia Declaration of Rights by George Mason was passed in 1776, and Patrick Henry was elected first governor of the Commonwealth of Virginia.

Colonial Williamsburg is open year-round, with many special events occurring in the evening. There are Candlelight Tours of the Capitol. Admission is charged to tour exhibit buildings and program areas and for evening programs. Hours are 9:00 A.M. to 5:00 P.M. daily.

Directions: Take the Washington Beltway (I-495/95) Exit 4, I-95 to the Richmond Bypass, Route 295. Follow this to Route 64 east, which will lead into Williamsburg. Maps of Colonial Williamsburg and information on tours and special programs can be obtained at the visitor center.

Governor's Palace

A man's home may be his castle, but few want to pay the cost of building a castle, or a palace, for someone else. The problem of spiraling costs for government buildings is not new. In 1706, the Virginia House of Burgesses s et aside three thousand pounds to build a home for the royal governor in the new capital at Williamsburg. A popular story concerning this "home" is that, when it was finished in 1720, it had cost so much more to build than originally allotted that the public protested loudly. The people complained that they had ended up building a palace, and that is what it has been called ever since—the **Governor's Palace**.

The first of the seven governors who would live in this palace was Alexander Spotswood, who spent a considerable amount of his own fortune embellishing his new home. The castellated walls of this Georgian mansion provide the formality thought appropriate for the king's representative. The gardens, too, reflect European formal tradition; but the outbuildings are distinctly Virginia plantation style.

At the Governor's Palace in Colonial Williamsburg, the passive spectator has been changed into an active participant. Visitors are part of living history, and their roles change as they move through the rooms. Roles shift from that of being a tradesman petitioning the governor to servant, to invited guest, and even to a relative of the distinguished representative of the king. The illusion of the past comes to life and is appreciated more fully because it is personalized.

The gardens re-create many of the intricate details of English gardens of the time. A holly maze copies Hampton Court. The twelve yaupons, a fast growing holly of this area, were called the "Twelve Apostles" and could be found on many English estates. Geometrically designed hedges, topiary work, and a greensward open enough for a garden game also remind visitors of England.

The last royal governor, the Earl of Dunmore, fled the Palace one June morning in 1775. He recognized the beginnings of the colonial revolt, which was the beginning of the end of English rule in Virginia. The first two elected governors of Virginia, Patrick Henry and Thomas Jefferson, would also live in the Palace.

Colonial Williamsburg is open daily from 9:00 A.M. to 5:00 P.M.

Directions: Take the Washington Beltway (I-495/95) Exit 4, I-95 to the Richmond Bypass, Route 295. Follow this to Route 64 east, which will lead into Williamsburg. Signs will provide directions to the visitor center, where maps of Colonial Williamsburg can be obtained, as well as information on tours and special programs.

Public Hospital—Williamsburg

The last of the reconstructed eighteenth-century Williamsburg public buildings, the **Public Hospital**, opened in 1985, a full century after it was destroyed by fire. When the hospital originally opened in 1773, it was the first institution in America devoted solely, as the law stated, "for the Support and Maintenance of Ideots, Lunatics, and other Persons of unsound mind."

During the first year, only twelve patients endured the harsh conditions you will become aware of as you tour the Public Hospital. A reconstruction of one of the original twenty-four primitive cells illustrates conditions prevalent during the Age of Restraint, which lasted from 1773 until 1835. The cell contains only a straw mattress and chamber pot. Patients were manacled. The windows were barred, and the doors padlocked. A taped vignette helps re-create the lot of these early victims of mental illness, who were treated by cold water plunge baths and harsh drugs.

The opposite side of the viewing room at the Public Hospital has a nineteenth-century apartment representing the period of Moral Management from 1836 to 1862. This approach was based on the realization that the patient suffered emotional problems, needed kindly and respectful treatment, plus work and recreational activities to fill their time in confinement. The room contains a quilt-covered bed, table, chairs, rug, and even a violin and newspaper.

Many of the "tools" of the mental health trade were recovered from on-site excavations. The museum section of the hospital contains a strait jacket, Utica crib (a wire cage-like bed for violent patients), a tranquilizer chair, and more benign objects like the sports equipment and games used in later years.

This Colonial Williamsburg exhibit certainly runs the gamut of "pain and pleasure," because after the horrors of the mental ward come the delights in the adjoining **DeWitt Wallace Gallery**, built with funds contributed by DeWitt and Lila Wallace, cofounders of the Reader's Digest Association. The gallery is reached by elevator or stairs from the hospital lobby. On entering this bilevel museum, you go through an introductory gallery that suggests the scope of this incredible collection. More than half of the eight thousand items on display have never, or only rarely, been shown, so it is indeed a new look at some very old items from the seventeenth, eighteenth, and early nineteenth centuries.

Around an attractive central court, you'll see the master works exhibit, with selected pieces from the diverse small study galleries, which branch off this core area. The prize pieces are the matched portraits of George III and George Washington that flank a throne-like ceremonial chair. Painted in the same pose, the two pivotal figures present a study in contrasts; the king, with his full figure outfitted in elegant finery, and the uniformed Washington, with his military bearing and piercing gaze.

Study galleries at the museum include textiles, ceramics, glass, metals, prints, paintings, and maps, plus special rotating exhibits. A major collection of early-eighteenth-century furniture and accessories was donated to the gallery by Miodrag and Elizabeth Ridgely Blagojevich. This important collection contains items too splendid for the modest means of the eighteenth-century Williamsburg residents.

The museum is open daily, 10:00 A.M. to 6:00 P.M. Admission is by Colonial Williamsburg Good Neighbor Card, Patriot's Pass, Museums Ticket, or Annual Museums Ticket, available at the visitor center.

The Public Hospital and DeWitt Wallace Gallery are at 325 Francis Street, between South Henry and Nassau Streets. Parking is available at a lot on Nassau Street. A cafe at the gallery is ideal for lunch, tea, or snacks.

Directions: From I-95 in the Richmond area, take Exit 238, I-64 east to Colonial Williamsburg, following the signs to the historic area.

Maryland

Maryland State House and Old Treasury Building

When Francis Nicholson replaced Sir Lionel Copley as royal governor of Maryland in 1694, he immediately took steps to move the capital from St. Mary's City to Arundel Towne (it was renamed Annapolis to honor Queen Anne) on the Severn River at Todds (now Spa) Creek. The town's designation as the provincial seat of government prompted Nicholson to choose a Baroque town plan, with streets radiating from two major circles, rather than the more common grid plan. The highest point of land was selected for Public Circle, now called State Circle, following Nicholson's directions to "survey and lay out in the most comodius [sic] and convenient part and place of the said town six acres of Land intire [sic] for the erecting of a Court House and other buildings as shall be thought necessary and convenient."

State Circle was never quite the six acres Nicholson ordered, but it did become the visual and actual hub of the new town. The first **Maryland State House** was built between 1696 and 1698. When fire destroyed all but sections of the brick walls and foundations in 1704, it was rebuilt from the standing remains. The second State House, completed in 1707, was by 1772 so derelict that it was described as an "emblem of public poverty."

The cornerstone of the third State House was laid in March 1772. Work was slow because of the Revolutionary War. When George Washington came to Annapolis in December 1783 for the Continental Congress, it was still unfinished. The state legislature had been meeting in the half-built edifice since 1779. It was eventually completed, and the marble addition you see today was added between 1902 and 1905.

Annapolis was the first peacetime capital of the United States from November 26, 1783, until June 3, 1784. It is the oldest State House in continuing legislative use in the country.

In the last weeks of 1783, George Washington bade farewell to his Continental army officer in New York and traveled to Annapolis to resign his commission before the Continental Congress. The evening prior to the ceremony, December 22, a lavish dinner was held for two hundred guests. After thirteen convivial toasts were drunk, the guests moved to the State House to dance by the light of eight pounds worth of candles, an expensive indulgence. It is said Washington danced with every lady present.

The next morning, in full military uniform, General Washington walked to the State House. In the Old Senate Chamber, he emotionally resigned the commission issued by the Congress on June 15, 1775. A mannequin now stands where he is thought to have stood for this dramatic leave-taking. A painting, hanging over the governor stairway, purporting to capture this moment, shows Martha Washington watching from the Senate floor. Actually, women were not permitted on the floor, and Martha had remained at Mount Vernon. Washington left immediately to join her for the Christmas holiday.

Another moment of history at the State House was the January 14, 1784, ratification of the Treaty of Paris by the Continental Congress. This treaty officially ended the American Revolution. In this, America's first peace treaty, Great Britain formally recognized the independence of her former colonies, which is worth remembering when you view the copy of the Declaration of Independence in the Silver Room. Portraits of the Maryland signers grace the walls. Here, too, is the Edwin White painting of Washington's resignation. On May 7, 1784, Thomas Jefferson was appointed as the first United States minister to a foreign government.

The State House is open daily, 9:00 A.M. to 5:00 P.M., and closed Christmas. Twenty-minute guided tours are given daily at 11: 00 A.M. and 3: 00 P.M.

You may also want to stop by another of Annapolis's historic buildings on State Circle, the **Old Treasury**, which is the city's oldest surviving public building, erected between 1735 and 1737. Local designer Patrick Creagh planned the building to offer security for the money it held in trust. There were iron bars on the windows, thick brick walls, and even brick floors to reduce the risk of fire. Today, the Old Treasury houses the Research Center of Historic Annapolis Foundation and is open by appointment; call (410) 267-7619.

The State House Visitors Center on the first floor of the State House is an excellent spot to pick up brochures on Annapolis and Maryland attractions and information on the state.

Directions: From Baltimore, take I-97 south to the Annapolis area. Then take Route 50 east to Exit 24 and follow signs to Rowe Boulevard. Proceed into Historic Annapolis to Church Circle, then around to State Circle via School Street.

Pennsylvania

Carpenters' Hall

A political statement was made in 1774 when the First Continental Congress voted to meet in **Carpenters' Hall** instead of the State House, which was just two blocks up the street.

The moderates wanted to meet in the formal, official government offices of the colony. They hoped to exert more influence at the State House. Joseph Galloway, Speaker of the Pennsylvania Assembly, had aspirations of leading the Congress. These plans were circumvented when the delegates met at City Tavern on September 5, 1774, and headed as a group to inspect Carpenters' Hall.

On that September day, the carpenter's guild was in the final stages of construction on Carpenters' Hall. It was a handsomely proportioned two-story building. On the ground floor two meeting rooms were divided by a long hall. The delegates to the First Continental Congress inspected the East Room, which was a small, bright chamber with rows of commodious hickory armchairs.

The delegates were well pleased and voted, with the moderates objecting, to meet for their deliberations in this room. Peyton Randolph was then chosen to chair the meeting.

The next major point of dispute was how to count the delegates' vote: by colony, one vote for each; or by poll, counting heads with a majority winning. There was no real correlation between population of the colony and the number of delegates. Massachusetts, with a large population, had four members; New Jersey had far fewer residents but one more delegate. Virginia had seven delegates, and there were fears that Pennsylvania and Maryland would send additional members to vote on major issues. John Jay of New York proposed that the Congress give each colony one vote as a temporary working arrangement but not as a precedent. These events are brought to mind when exploring Carpenters' Hall.

The hall contains exhibits about the First Continental Congress and modern exhibits of the carpenter's guild, which is the oldest trade organization in the United States.

Carpenters' Hall is part of Independence National Historical Park in Philadelphia. The hall is open daily.

Directions: From I-95 southbound (from points north), take Exit 17. Using the right-hand lanes of the exit, follow signs for Callowhill Street/Independence Hall. At the bottom of the exit ramp, follow 2nd Street straight ahead to Chestnut Street. Continue a half block past

Chestnut Street for the Historic Area Parking Garage on the left. It is best to park your car and walk to all the sites in the Historic District. Start at the Independence National Historical Park Visitors Center, one block away, at 3rd and Chestnut Streets, where you can pick up an easy-to-follow map of the district and a park schedule. If you are traveling northbound on I-95 (from points south), you will also take Exit 17. Stay in the left lane because you will exit on the left side of I-95. At the exit, stay in the right-hand lane and follow signs for Independence Hall/Historic Area. Turn left at 6th Street to Chestnut, which will take you through the heart of the Historic District to 2nd Street. Turn right on 2nd Street. The entrance to the Historic Area Parking Garage is on the left.

Independence Hall and the Liberty Bell Pavilion

Many historians consider Independence Hall's Assembly Room to be the single-most historic room in the United States. In this room delegates met to debate and sign the Declaration of Independence and to write the Constitution of the United States.

Funds were appropriated for a State House in 1729, but it was nineteen years later that Alexander Hamilton's designs were finally realized. The State House, later called **Independence Hall**, served as government meeting rooms for the Pennsylvania colony. The ground floor had a large Assembly Room.

The Assembly Room has been restored to look as it did at the last quarter of the eighteenth century. The individual tables that served each colonial delegation during the Second Continental Congress are placed in a semicircle before the table where the Declaration of Independence was signed. Few pieces in the room are original. Thomas Jefferson's walking stick has been placed on a table that is believed to have belonged to the Virginia delegation. (The original inkstand used by the delegates to sign the Declaration, once displayed on the Speaker's stand, is now in an exhibit in the West Wing of Independence Hall.) After Lord Cornwall surrendered to Washington at Yorktown, the captured colors of the British army were brought to Philadelphia and presented in this room to the state delegations on November 3, 1781. The Rising Sun Chair, used by George Washington as the presiding officer of the Constitutional Convention, was purchased for this room in 1778.

A chamber on the first floor was used by the Supreme Court of the Province. The courtroom was in the English tradition and,

155

A cherished shrine of liberty, Independence Hall in Philadelphia saw the adoption of the Declaration of Independence and the Constitution of the United States. Here, also, the new nation was governed during the formative years between 1774 and 1800. NATIONAL PARK SERVICE PHOTO BY RICHARD FREAR according to colorful tales about this era, illustrates the term "standing trial." According to local lore, the defendant was forced to stand throughout the trial in a spiked, cage-like dock (although the dock has not had spikes on it for many years). If dangerous, the defendant would be placed in handcuffs by a blacksmith. Should the defendant be declared innocent, he would have to pay to have the iron cuffs sawed off. Trials were enjoyed by town residents, who watched the proceedings, groaning or applauding at each decision.

Upstairs is the Long Gallery, one of the largest rooms in colonial Pennsylvania. This was the scene of many balls and banquets. On September 16, 1774, the members of the First Continental Congress gathered here for a sit-down dinner. The legislature of Pennsylvania conducted sessions in part of the Long Gallery, while the Continental Congress met in the Assembly Room below.

The State House was given the name Independence Hall in 1824, when Lafayette was in Philadelphia celebrating the American Revolution victory. While touring the State House, Lafayette said, "That is the hall of independence," and so it has been called ever since.

One of the landmarks of the hall has been moved. The one ton **Liberty Bell** is now in a pavilion directly opposite the hall. For many years, it was thought (and recorded in the history books) that the bell was made in England in 1752. There was a bell ordered from England that arrived broken, or broke on arrival. That bell was used as a source of metal by Pass and Stow, local artisans, to create the bell that we today call the Liberty Bell. Since the original English bell was never called the Liberty Bell and never tolled from the tower, the Liberty bell was in fact colonial-made from English material. The Pass and Stow bell hung in the State House steeple for many years.

In 1835, John Marshall, chief justice of the Supreme Court, died while visiting Philadelphia. The bell was rung for thirty-six continuous hours, but, contrary to legend, it did not crack. It was in use until the George Washington Birthday celebration of 1846. The actual date of the crack is unknown. From that time on, the bell was only a symbol. The term Liberty Bell stems from the early use of the bell by the Abolitionist movement starting in the early nineteenth century. To discover more about the bell's history, read *Venerable Relic: The Story of the Liberty Bell*, by David Kimball.

The wonderful thing about the Liberty Bell is that visitors are able to get close to this tangible reminder of the turbulent events of our country's past. It is touching to watch the crowds slowly walk past this historic memento.

Before touring Independence Hall, visitors should stop at the **Independence National Historical Park** Visitor Center, where a twenty-eight-minute film directed by John Huston literally introduces the great leaders who met in Philadelphia in 1774 and 1776. Actors portraying these giants explain the events that took place here. In the fall of 2000, a new visitor center at 6th and Market Streets will provide additional information and exhibits.

The park's historic buildings are open daily from 9:00 A.M. to 5:00 P.M., with different buildings open on different days. To check operational hours when not in town, log on to the park Web site at www.nps.gov/inde for current schedules. There are charges for some of the buildings, and others have a timed ticket system to control the stream of visitors.

Directions: From I-95 southbound (from points north), take Exit 17. Using the right-hand lanes of the exit, follow the signs for Callowhill Street/Independence Hall. At the bottom of the exit ramp, follow 2nd Street straight ahead to Chestnut Street. Continue a half block past Chestnut Street for the Historic Parking Garage on the left. It is best to park your car and walk to all the sites in the Historic District. Start at the Independence National Historical Park Visitors Center, one block away, at 3rd and Chestnut Streets, where you can pick up an easy-to-follow map of the district and a park schedule. If you are traveling northbound on I-95 (from points south), you will also take Exit 17. Stay in the left lane because you will exit on the left side of I-95. At the exit, stay in the right-hand lane and follow the signs for Independence Hall/Historic Area. Turn left at 6th Street to Chestnut, which will take you through the heart of the Historic District to 2nd Street. Turn right on 2nd Street. The entrance to the Historic Area Parking Garage is on the left.

York County Colonial Court House

When the British captured Philadelphia in 1777, Congress was forced to flee the city. They traveled eighty-eight miles to York, prudently putting the Susquehanna River between themselves and the British. Congress reconvened in the York courthouse and drafted the Articles of Confederation, which, when adopted, served as the nation's first constitution.

History comes alive at the **York County Colonial Court House** with a three-dimensional dramatic narrative. Actors give voice to the words of John Adams, John Hancock, Thomas Paine, Samuel Adams, Philip Livingston, Francis Lightfoot Lee, Charles Carroll, Gouverneur Morris, and many other significant figures of the day. The courthouse has been restored to look as it did when the Continental Congress met here from September 30, 1777, to June 27, 1778. Time appears to stand still when you look at the rare, tall case clock that marked the course of time for these patriots who proclaimed the formation of the United States of America. Copies of the documents associated with American liberties—the Articles of Confederation, Declaration of Independence, and the Constitution—are on display. The courthouse is located at 205 West Market Street.

It was also in York that George Washington came perilously close to losing the command of the Continental army. Gen. Horatio Gates, hero of the Battle of Saratoga, was headquartered in York during 1778, while Washington stayed with the army at Valley Forge. Congress, either because of proximity or the spell of Saratoga, appointed Gates to the position of president of the War Board. Gen. Thomas Conway, who bore a grudge against Washington because he was only commissioned a brigadier general (although, with the help of influential friends in Congress, he was promoted to major general over Washington's objections), attempted to secure the command of the Continental army for Gates. The "Conway Cabal" was thwarted by the Marquis de Lafayette, who realized that a plot was afoot while attending a dinner party at the Gates house. His timely toast to Washington, "… May he remain at the head of the Army until independence is won," is credited with scotching the plot. If Lafayette had not spoken out so strongly for Washington, it is quite possible he would have been replaced by Gates.

The **Gates House**, at 157 West Market Street, is across Pershing Avenue from the Colonial Courthouse. It contains period pieces representing the furnishings popular in this south-central Pennsylvania region in the eighteenth century. Attached to this historic old home is the **Golden Plough Tavern** (see selection). This half-timbered tavern with a pitched roof is worth visiting, as it is one of the few buildings in the country constructed in a medieval style. Behind the tavern you'll see the **Barnett Bob Log House**, circa 1812, typical of the homes of German settlers who frequented the tavern after it was built in 1741.

The **Historical Society of York County Museum** at 250 East Market Street has re-created a life-size village square. You can stroll down the "Street of Shops" and look into store windows replete with toys, apothecary jars, and other necessities of a bygone era. Costumed mannequins also add to the sense of "history come alive." In addition, the museum has a Revolutionary War collection plus weapons and uniforms from the country's Second War of Independence in 1812.

The attractions of the Historical Society of York County are open Tuesday through Saturday from 9:00 A.M. to 5:00 P.M.

Directions: From I-76, the Pennsylvania Turnpike, take I-83 exit. Travel south on I-83 to York. Take the Market Street exit for the historic attractions.

The French & Indian War and Pontiac's Rebellion

A s the French moved south from Canada in the mid-eighteenth century, seeking new settlements in the vast Ohio Valley, Great Britain began to resist encroachment into regions its leaders long claimed. Taking action in 1753, Virginia Governor Robert Dinwiddie placed a letter into the hands of his young surveyor, George Washington, telling him to deliver it to the commander of Fort LeBoeuf (in present-day Waterford, Erie County, PA).

"By whose authority," it read, "(have the French) invaded the King of Great Britain's territories? It becomes my duty to require your peaceable departure."

"As to the summons you send to retire," the commander replied, "I do not think myself obliged to obey."

And so began the fight to control the crucial area surrounding the Forks of the Ohio River, where Pittsburgh stands today—the French and Indian War. Although the sites bringing this conflict and Pontiac's Rebellion, which followed close after its conclusion, are a stretch and may be beyond the scope of a day trip for travelers in the Middle Atlantic region, the chance to explore yet another chapter in our country's past is worth the extra miles it takes to reach these destinations.

Some historians characterize the French and Indian War as a rehearsal for the Revolutionary War—as well as a contributing cause. During the first conflict, European colonial powers vied for control of the Forks of the Ohio, where the Allegheny and Monongahela Rivers converge. It was not inevitable that the fight for the forks would take place at this spot; that it did is largely due to the judgment of one man—George Washington.

Just twenty-one years old, Washington made his decision during the expedition he undertook on Dinwiddie's behalf. Governor Dinwiddie realized in early 1753 that the French had begun to build strategic forts along western waterways to secure control of the frontier and access to the country's central basin. From October 31, 1753, to January 16, 1754, Washington traveled hundreds of miles to deliver Dinwiddie's message to Fort LeBoeuf's commanding officer.

Washington's return to Virginia was so dramatic that Dinwiddie had the account Washington made of his adventures published and sent to Europe. On December 29, while Washington was crossing the ice-choked Allegheny River with Christopher Gist, an experienced trader, Washington tumbled into ten feet of bone-chilling water. He managed to grab onto the raft, but the pair was unable to reach either shore. Fortunately, they were passing near an island and were able to reach its safety. By the following morning, the ice had grown sufficiently thick for Washington and Gist to walk to the opposite bank and continue their journey. The pair also had to contend with blizzards as they crossed the mountains. While fording the Connoquenessing Creek during the mission, Washington was ambushed by a Native American, whose gun misfired, thus sparing his life.

Once Washington left Fort LeBoeuf, the French did not behave as casually as their commander's response might have implied. Winter had halted the French efforts to fortify the river, but Dinwiddie's message prompted them to ignore the inhospitable weather and begin the arduous task of stockpiling supplies. On April 16, 1754, the French troops and their Native American allies arrived at the Forks of the Ohio in 360 canoes and bateaux (light, flat-bottomed boats used especially in Canada). This combined force of fifteen hundred men encountered forty Virginia militiamen who had erected a fortified log storehouse they called Fort Prince George. The Virginians surrendered it "with great civility."

It was Washington's men who fired the shots that ignited the French and Indian War, which in Europe escalated into the Seven Years' War. Dinwiddie had promoted Washington to lieutenant colonel and dispatched him again to western Pennsylvania, with the ultimate objective of taking Fort Duquesne. Originally second-in-command, Washington became the ranking officer at the death of Col. Joshua Fry. Washington did not make it as far as Fort Duquesne on this mission; he encountered the French at Great Meadows, and the saga of that conflict is told in the Fort Necessity selection.

General Braddock tried to take Fort Duquesne in July 1755, after marching an army of nearly 1,500 men—weighted heavily with equipment and provisions—more than 125 miles and building the military road that Washington had started work on as they advanced. Braddock came within six miles of Fort Duquesne but lost everything to a force of two hundred French soldiers and four hundred Native Americans. Historians later called the British force a "red bulls eye" because retreating troops became entangled with advancing forces, and nearly a thousand men were killed or wounded in less than three hours. Braddock was wounded, and Washington was instrumental in helping him from the battlefield. He died approximately one mile west of Fort Necessity. Braddock was buried in the middle of the military road, so that the tread of marching soldiers would camouflage his grave, protecting it from plundering enemies. The Fort Pitt Museum exhibits artifacts recovered along Braddock's Road, including shoes, gun flints, nails, scissors, a canister shot, and pottery shards.

The British had failed miserably in thwarting French interests in western Pennsylvania, but in 1757, the newly empowered British secretary of state, William Pitt, took charge of the war effort. He devised a four-pronged attack against the major French fortifications, assigning fifty-one-year-old Gen. John Forbes the task of taking Fort Duquesne. Forbes planned the campaign but, plagued with declining health, depended on Col. Henry Bouquet, twelve years his junior, to execute his strategy. This story is recounted in the Fort Ligonier selection. As this British force reached a spot not far from the scene of Braddock's defeat, they heard a huge explosion—before abandoning Fort Duquesne, the French blew it up. The only artifact of this fort in the Fort Pitt Museum is a cannonball emblazoned with a fleur-de-lis.

Reversals for the French in the New World continued after their abrupt departure from the Forks of the Ohio. Fort Niagara and Quebec were lost in 1759, and Montreal the following year. By the Treaty of Paris of 1763, all of New France was ceded to Britain. Spain, which fought with France in the waning days of the Seven Years' War, received Louisiana.

Pontiac's Rebellion, a conflict that is little covered in most American history texts, was in many respects a continuation of the French and Indian War. Although the war had officially ended, nobody ordered the Native Americans to stop fighting. After they lost the war, the French encouraged their allies to continue fighting. Also, intertribal rivalries, which had influenced which side the Native Americans fought on, continued after the European combatants stopped warring.

Pontiac, an Ottawa war chief, united the Great Lakes tribes and attacked Fort Detroit on May 8, 1763. In just two months during the "Native American war for independence"—as some historians interpret it—the French and Indian allies had captured nine British forts, two were under siege and one had been abandoned. Fort Pitt, built by the British where Fort Duquesne had stood, was under siege by about a thousand Native Americans from late May to early August

1763. With six hundred settlers seeking protection of the fort, Capt. Simeon Ecuyer encountered difficulty feeding and supplying his garrison of 125 men and the extra settlers. In hopes of driving off the Indians, who continued their assault on his fort, Ecuyer sent them hospital blankets and handkerchiefs infected with smallpox—a grim, early episode of germ warfare.

When Gen. Jeffery Amherst, commander-in-chief of the British forces in North America, failed to receive word from Fort Pitt, he directed Colonel Bouquet to travel to the fortification from New York. His route passed Bushy Run, and the encounter there, fully explored in that selection, helped end the conflict. After the Native Americans fled the Bushy Run Battlefield, Bouquet's forces continued on to relieve Fort Pitt.

Despite the victory at Bushy Run, a third British campaign, in October 1764, was necessary before the end of Pontiac's Rebellion. Col. Henry Bouquet led an army of fifteen hundred from Carlisle, past Fort Pitt, and into Ohio. He met no resistance, and the Native Americans sued for peace. All captured Europeans and Africans were returned—206 persons in all (with another 100 returned the following May).

For Native Americans, Pontiac's Rebellion represented a turning point. It was one of the most important conflicts in their history, since it determined whether British colonization could be limited. This was also a war to see how far the Native Americans could be pushed west. Tribal leaders, realizing they must deal with the Europeans, who were predominant, had tried their best to negotiate settlements. But their hopes were disappointed. The concept of Native American hunting grounds west of the Alleghenies was now abandoned, and the door was open for the expansion of the frontier. Even more significant for Native Americans was the introduction of the containment concept, with decrees stipulating that Indian populations be kept west of the Alleghenies.

Pennsylvania

Bushy Run Battlefield

In October 1758, thirteen American Indian nations and the governors of Pennsylvania and New Jersey signed the Treaty of Easton, agreeing that the Ohio Indians would sever their alliance with France and would withdraw to west of the Alleghenies and that the lands in the west were to be Indian territory. But the British did not withdraw from this western region. Instead, they sent troops to occupy former French forts and, on the site of Fort Duquesne, erected Fort Pitt, their largest and most elaborate fortress in North America.

The Native Americans, sought as allies during the French and Indian War, were obstacles to settlement once that conflict was resolved. The British stopped selling the Native Americans gun powder, lead, and alcohol. Tribal members used their munitions not only in conflict, but also in hunting, from which they maintained their livelihood; so to be deprived of them was a severe blow. The westward expansion of European settlers threatened the hunting grounds and spread diseases, such as smallpox, throughout the tribes.

These provocations prompted Pontiac, an Ottawa war chief, to unite the Great Lakes tribes and attack Fort Detroit on May 8, 1763. Thus began a Native American war for independence, driving some settlers back east and prompting others to seek sanctuary in frontier forts such as Fort Pitt. Initially, the British command did not take this threat seriously. But within two months, nine forts were captured, another was abandoned, and Fort Detroit and Fort Pitt were under siege. In a not often-reported effort to undermine the Native American threat, Capt. Simeon Ecuyer, head of the 125-man garrison at Fort Pitt, employed germ warfare against the Delaware and Shawnee laying siege to the fort. He gave the warriors infected blankets and handkerchiefs from the fort's hospital.

Fearing conditions on the western frontier, General Amherst, in command of the British forces in North America, sent Henry Bouquet with troops from three regiments to resupply Fort Pitt. Bouquet left Carlisle, Pennsylvania, on July 18 and reached Fort Ligonier (see selection) on August 2. Trying to increase the speed of his march, as it had been over a month since any report had been heard from Fort Pitt, Bouquet abandoned the barrels and wagon train, repacking the flour into bags and loading them on 340 pack animals. Without the heavier equipment, he was able to take a less-traveled route in hopes of avoiding a surprise attack. But on August 5, near **Bushy Run**, the column was attacked by as few as ninety-five warriors (although Simon Ecoyer at Fort Pitt estimated the attacking force at four hundred). The warriors had terminated their siege of Fort Pitt to attack the fort's reinforcements. During the attack, Bouquet's men suffered fifty casualties and were forced to retreat. With nightfall, Bouquet used the flour bags to create a fortification to protect the wounded. Feigning a retreat the next morning, the British were able to catch the Native Americans in a deadly crossfire and force them to retreat. With more than a quarter of his troops killed or wounded, after regrouping Bouquet continued his march to reprovision the fort, covering the remaining twenty-six miles in four days.

Bouquet's ability to withstand and turn the tide of the Native American attack and his successful provision of Fort Pitt were significant contributions to British victory in **Pontiac's War**. In 1764, Bouquet continued westward into Ohio, and the Native Americans ceased their struggle and returned their hostages. Two hundred and six Pennsylvania and Virginia settlers were turned over; later, the Shawnees released another hundred captives. This victory opened the west for further colonial expansion.

When you visit this battlefield, use your imagination to populate the undulating hills with troops. Take a guided Edge Hill Battle Trail tour to retrace the course of the battle. You can also pick up a trail map for the Flour Sak [sic] Battle Discovery Trail and the Iroquois Nature Trail.

The visitor center features an exhibit, "The March to Bushy Run," that provides additional details about Pontiac's War. A fiber-optic map gives the positions and progression of the battle that occurred here, and mannequins are dressed in authentic garb of those on both sides of the conflict.

Bushy Run Battlefield is open Wednesday through Saturday from 9:00 A.M. to 5:00 P.M. On Sunday, the visitor center opens at noon. It is closed Monday, Tuesday, and holidays, except Memorial Day, July Fourth, and Labor Day. A nominal admission is charged. Flags, maps, munitions, and other artifacts fill the display cases.

Directions: From the east and south, take I-76, the Pennsylvania Turnpike, to Exit 8. Follow signs for Toll 66 north and take that to the Greensburg-Harrison City exit; go left off the exit onto Business 66 north, to Route 993 west. Turn onto Route 993 west for approximately three miles. From the west and north, take I-76 to Exit 6, follow Route 22 east for approximately ten miles to Greensburg exit. Follow signs for Business 66 south and take that to Route 993 west.

Fort Ligonier

There was a time when the Americans were not fighting against the British; they were fighting *with* them. The enemies in this early North American conflict were the French and Native Americans. George Washington, who later played a pivotal role in the war for independence, was a colonel in the Virginia provincial forces in service to King George II. The colonial powers were vying for control of the vast inland basin of this new empire.

In 1758, the British launched attacks against three of France's largest forts: Fortress Louisbourg in Novia Scotia, Fort Ticonderoga in New York, and Fort Duquesne at the Forks of the Ohio. Gen. John Forbes approached the task of taking Fort Duquesne by cutting a passage across the Alleghenies—the Forbes Road. Along this route a series of fortifications were built to provide provisions and a safe haven for troops traveling to and from Fort Duquesne.

Fort Ligonier was one of these outposts. Originally, it was named after the site of an old Delaware Indian village, Loyalhanna. In September 1758, fifteen hundred men under Col. James Burd built this square fort with bastions and a wooden outer retrenchment, an uncommon addition. On October 12th, Burd and his command withstood an attack by a combined force of French and Native Americans emanating from Fort Duquesne. (This event is commemorated annually during Fort Ligonier Days, on the weekend nearest the 12th.) Forbes's army moved west from Raystown (later Fort Bedford, see selection).George Washington and his men, who had suffered defeat at Fort Necessity (see selection), also joined the force gathering at Loyalhanna.

On November 18, 1758, General Forbes led twenty-five hundred men out of Loyalhanna to Fort Duquesne. The French had suffered reverses during the autumn, culminating in the Treaty of Easton. Although they were not a party to this treaty, it cost them most of their Native American allies (see Bushy Run Battlefield selection). With Forbes on the march, the French abandoned and burned Fort Duquesne.

Forbes, who was dying of a wasting disease, reported to Secretary of State William Pitt that he had renamed the French fort Pittsburgh, in his honor. He also renamed Loyalhanna, calling it Fort Ligonier for Sir John Ligonier, commander in chief of military forces and Raystown.

From 1758 to 1766, Fort Ligonier served as a vital link in the supply line to the West, and, though attacked, it was never taken. During Pontiac's War in 1763, the fort was attacked twice and under siege for two months before Col. Henry Bouquet's men broke through the Indian lines. It was between Fort Ligonier and Fort Pitt that Bouquet fought the decisive battle at Bushy Run (see selection). Fort Ligonier was retired from military service in 1766, although it was used by settlers in the area during Lord Dunmore's Indian War of 1774 and again by the Pennsylvania militia during the American Revolution. But by 1800, no aboveground trace of the fort was in evidence.

But it's back in evidence today. A full-scale reconstruction stands on the same commanding hilltop as the original fort. The sharpened wooden pickets of the retrenchment provide a photographic point of interest as you approach the fort. Before exploring the fort, stop at the visitor center to see the exhibits and film on Fort Ligonier and the French and Indian War. The film covers the military, political, and social ramifications of the war in the colonies and Europe.

One portion of the museum focuses on history and another on both military and civilian life during the colonial era, with emphasis on fine and decorative arts. There is a drawing room in the Georgian style that one would have seen in Field Marshall John Louis Ligonier's London residence. Hanging here is an original Joshua Reynolds portrait painted of Ligonier in 1760. When the fort was decommissioned in 1766, Arthur St. Clair was appointed civil commandant, and he built an estate several miles from the fort. The log parlor, exhibited in the museum, is the only portion of St. Clair's Hermitage that survived. It is furnished with eighteenth- and nineteenth-century English and American pieces, several belonging to the St. Clair family. There is a portrait of St. Clair over the mantle as well as silhouettes of Arthur and Phoebe St. Clair. Arthur St. Clair was a major general in the Continental army during the war for independence. He later served in Congress and was governor of the Northwest Territory from 1788 to 1802.

Fort Ligonier is a complete reconstruction of the original, with the surrounding retrenchment and gun batteries providing an outer circle of defense. The palisade, or stockade, provides an inner defensive picket wall around the interior buildings. Formed of tree trunks, these walls could stop musket balls but offered no protection against artillery.

The placement of the interior buildings was determined by an archeological dig. The dig yielded approximately 125,000 artifacts. Officers and the ranks ate, drank, and lived on vastly different levels, as you'll see in the officers' mess and sleeping quarters and in the soldiers' barracks. Soldiers originally slept in tents around the fort, but in 1763, barracks were added housing thirty to forty soldiers, two to a bunk.

Each of the fort's structures is filled with articles that may once have been stocked. The quartermaster's storehouse has a wide array: clothing, tents, packsaddles, blankets, kettles, cooking utensils, arms, gunflint, and assorted equipment. All supplies were dearly come by on the frontier, even the flags. Garrison flags were flown only on Sundays from 11:00 A.M. to 1:00 P.M. Today the Union flag, like the original, still flies. History buffs may observe that the cross of St. Patrick of Ireland is not part of this Union flag because Ireland did not become part of Great Britain until four decades after Fort Ligonier played its part in history.

Another vitally important part of the fort was the armory, which originally served as the powder magazine. When the underground magazine was added in 1759, weapons were stored in the heavy-timbered, old powder magazine. The underground structure was added because military engineer Harry Gordon felt the entire fort was endangered by the above-ground magazine: Enemy mortar fire could explode the magazine and lay waste to the fort.

The east side of the fort and half the north and south have an additional line of defense, a horizontal log wall that, unlike the palisade wall, could withstand an artillery bombardment. Its basketwork construction was filled with stones and earth, offering protection from cannon shot.

The fort's hospital was originally on Ligonier's Main Street, but it is interpreted in what was part of the storehouse. A surgeon's chest displays implements used in the eighteenth century, such as the bone saws, amputating knives, skull drills, and blistering irons. The only anesthesia was rum or whiskey; many died not from their wounds but from the surgeon's knife.

General supplies were stored at the quartermaster's, but food supplies were kept at the commissary. The daily ration for the soldiers was customarily a pound of flour, a pound of salt pork or beef, butter, and rice or dried peas. A diet this delinquent in fresh vegetables and fruit often led to malnutrition and scurvy.

Outside the fort's main gate is a reconstruction of the hut the ailing Gen. John Forbes requested. Like other high-ranking officers, Forbes traveled with his own supplies, servants, and aides. The hut contains tableware, linens, chests, and furnishings to suggest those he used while headquartered here. To get a sense of what it was like when the fort was fully garrisoned, visit during Fort Ligonier Days in October; call (412) 238-9701 for dates and details.

Fort Ligonier is open daily, April through October, from 9:00 A.M. to 5:00 P.M. Admission is charged.

Directions: From I-76, the Pennsylvania Turnpike, traveling west, take Exit 10, Somerset and follow Route 601 north to the intersection with Route 30. Take Route 30 west to Ligonier, and Fort Ligonier will be on your right. Traveling east on the Turnpike, take Exit 9, Donegal, and head north on Route 711 to the intersection with Route 30. Fort Ligonier is just beyond the intersection.

Fort Necessity National Battlefield

George Washington experienced a crucible at **Fort Necessity**. As a result of the action here, some accused Washington of assassination, while others proclaimed him a hero. This was Washington's first military engagement and the only one he ever fought in which he had to surrender. It was Washington's men who fired the shots that are thought to have been the first in the conflict that led to the Seven Years' War in Europe. The experience Washington gained during the French and Indian War, as it was called in the colonies, influenced the decision to appoint him commander in chief of the Revolutionary forces.

At the age of twenty-one, George Washington was sent by Virginia Governor Robert Dinwiddie to lead an expedition into the Ohio Valley to warn the French against intruding into what the English viewed as their territory. Young Washington was picked because he had done surveying in the disputed territory and because his older brother, Lawrence, was a major stockholder along with Dinwiddie in the Ohio Company of Virginia. This venture, begun in 1747, brought the English and French into direct competition for the rich fur trade and land in the Ohio Valley.

Washington first traveled to Fort LeBouef in November 1753 on a diplomatic mission to convince the French to withdraw. When this proved ineffective, a military force was assembled. Volunteers were promised land in the Ohio Valley. Troops were under the command of Col. Joshua Fry and Lieutenant Colonel Washington, who at Fry's death in Wills Creek (present-day Cumberland, Maryland), was put in charge and promoted to colonel.

As they proceeded from Wills Creek toward Fort Duquesne, Washington and his force of 150 men cleared a path through the forested region. After approximately four weeks, they had covered fifty miles and were in the Great Meadows area when they received word from American Indian scouts that a company of thirty-three French soldiers was five miles away.

Washington led a party of forty soldiers and surprised the French at dawn. In the first military skirmish of his career, Washington was victorious. The French leader, Ensign Jumonville, and nine others in his party were killed; within fifteen minutes the French surrendered. One member of the French party escaped and walked barefooted to Fort Duquesne. He reported Washington failed to order a cease fire when the French called out that they were on a diplomatic, rather than a military, mission.

Neither Washington, nor any of his men, had heard this appeal.

The yells of the American Indians, the cries of the wounded, and the noise of the battle may well have obscured the plea, if indeed it was made. This brief encounter was the start of the war that ended with the English acquiring full claim to all the French land in North America.

Washington returned to Great Meadows after the Jumonville incident and built a fort "of necessity" in case the French returned with a larger force. Washington continued to have his men build the road west. Little more than a month later, on July 3, 1754, a large French force did appear, led by Coulon de Villiers, Jumonville's brother. The French attacked Fort Necessity. Even though Washington had been reinforced by Captain McKay and his Independent Company from South Carolina, the British were still outnumbered. Washington's force was able to hold them off for eight hours, but then surrendered. In the terms, which Washington unknowingly signed, was a statement that he was responsible for the assassination of Jumonville. Washington and the British officers later stated that the French word assassin was incorrectly translated and that he believed the document read the killing or death of Jumonville in action. This signed statement by George Washington was used to discredit the English in Europe.

The visitor center has a slide presentation on the dramatic events in this opening chapter of the French and Indian War. The location of Jumonville Glen is marked, and Fort Necessity has been reconstructed. The fort is unbelievably small, making it difficult to believe that it is indeed the exact size of the fortification Washington fought so hard to defend on July 3, 1754. But extensive archeological excavation proved that this was indeed the size of the original fort.

A year later, Gen. Edward Braddock followed the road Washington had cut through the forest, although eventually he turned north toward modern-day Pittsburgh, while Washington's route veered west toward modern-day Brownsville. When Braddock was mortally wounded at the Battle of the Monongahela on July 9, 1755, General Washington, who was leading the retreat, was instrumental in removing the suffering Braddock from the battlefield. Four days later, Washington read the burial service at Braddock's grave, just a mile west of Fort Necessity. He was buried in the middle of the road, in hopes that the Native Americans would not find his grave. A monument stands near the site of his burial.

In 1770, George Washington returned to this area. He had purchased 234.5 acres around Great Meadows for $120.00 in 1770. This was only a portion of the thirty-two thousand acres of frontier land that Washington owned. As early as 1784, Washington recommended the land as an excellent spot for an inn, a claim he would repeat several times before he died in 1799. It was not until 1827 or 1828 that the **Mount Washington Tavern** was built along the National Road, which ran in front of the property. Today, the tavern is part of Fort Necessity National Battlefield. It has been restored to appear as it did when it was one of the most famous and lively inns on the National Road. A Conestoga wagon sits outside. The bar room, parlor, kitchen, and upstairs bedroom have been furnished to suggest the tavern's heyday. In the dining room, there is a display on the National Road and its many inns.

Fort Necessity National Battlefield is open daily during daylight hours, and the visitor center and tavern are open from 8:30 A.M. to 5:00 P.M. The park is closed on Thanksgiving, Christmas Day, and New Year's Day. A nominal admission is charged; children sixteen and under get in free.

Directions: From I-76, the Pennsylvania Turnpike, take Exit 8, New Stanton and follow Route 119 south to Uniontown. In Uniontown, Route 119 and Route 40 will become the same road for a short distance. Remain on Route 40 for approximately eleven miles past Uniontown. The park entrance will be on your right.

Fort Pitt Museum

The Forks of the Ohio meet at "the Point" in present-day Pittsburgh. This land was hotly contested during the French and Indian War, the mid-eighteenth century conflict between Britain and France for control of North America. The conflict's name is misleading, as Native Americans fought with both the French and the British.

In western Pennsylvania, control of the American frontier rested with whoever commanded the Forks of the Ohio. The first to fortify the Point were settlers from Virginia. It was this group that George Washington was planning to reinforce before he was stopped near Jumonville Glen and forced to build Fort Necessity in hopes of protecting his small military force from the French and their Native American allies (see selection). The French seized the British outpost at the Point, Fort Prince George, then attacked and defeated Washington and his men at Fort Necessity. Following these victories, the French erected Fort Duquesne and were able to control the Forks and the Ohio Valley until 1758.

In 1758, six thousand British and colonial soldiers under Gen. John Forbes marched against Fort Duquesne. Rather than surrender Fort Duquesne to a superior force, the French blew up the fort, burned the barracks, and retreated two days before the British arrived. (A bronze marker at Point State Park indicates the location of the Fort Duquesne.) The following spring, the British began constructing **Fort Pitt**, the most elaborate and largest British fortress in the American colonies. Virtually upon the heels of its completion, the French surrendered their territory in the New World to the British. Fort Pitt was used by the British as a base of operations and for trade with the Native Americans. It was attacked and under siege for six weeks in 1763, during the Native American uprising known as Pontiac's Rebellion (see Bushy Run Battlefield selection).

The British were stationed at Fort Pitt until 1772. With the American Revolution looming on the horizon, patriot forces occupied the fort while attempting to wrest control of British outposts in Illinois. Fort Pitt was abandoned in 1792, by which time the town of Pittsburgh had grown up around the former frontier outpost.

The **Fort Pitt Museum** has exhibits, dioramas, reconstructed rooms, and models that reveal the turbulent story of the frontier years leading to the founding of modern-day Pittsburgh. The main gallery hall of the museum extends into the fort's original Monongahela Bastion. In the center of this hall is a scale model of Fort Pitt, where visitors can listen to a taped explanation of the fort. Living-history presentations are offered by the Royal American Regiment, a modern volunteer group that re-creates the British 60th Regiment of Foote, which helped build and garrison Fort Pitt. On summer Sunday afternoons, the regiment brings to life the sights and sounds of the eighteenth-century British army. Call (412) 281-9284 for performance dates and times. Around the museum are excavations of the fort's earthworks and bastions. The fort's Blockhouse now serves as a welcome center and gift shop.

The Fort Pitt Museum is open Wednesday through Saturday, 10:00 A.M. to 4:30 P.M.; on Sunday, it opens at noon. The museum is closed Monday, Tuesday, and some major holidays. Admission is charged.

Point State Park is a popular congregating spot for visitors and residents. Throughout the year, festivals and celebrations are held at the park, including fireworks on the Fourth of July and on Holiday Light-Up Night in late November. During the summer, a two-hundred-foot fountain at the tip of the point provides a refreshing focal spot.

Directions: (This is about a four-and-a-half-hour drive from the Washington Beltway.) From the Pennsylvania Turnpike, I-76, take Exit 6, the Parkway, Route 376, to downtown Pittsburgh. Exit on Stanwick Street. Fort Pitt is located in Point State Park in the city's Golden Triangle.

Maryland

George Washington's Headquarters and Fort Cumberland Tunnels

In a one-room cabin at Fort Cumberland, George Washington studied military strategy and planned his first campaign. Having surveyed in the Cumberland Valley for Lord Fairfax in 1748, Washington, five years later at the age of twenty-one, was given a commission by Virginia Governor Dinwiddie to carry a warning to the French on the Ohio River not to remain in British-claimed territory. He carried out this fruitless mission, but on two occasions it nearly cost him his life. He was ambushed and fired upon by hostile Native Americans, and he fell into the icy Allegheny River.

A year later, in 1754, when the French still had not heeded the warning, Fort Mount Pleasant was built on the bank of Wills Creek. It was from here that Lieutenant Colonel Washington led a small force north to a spot just over the Pennsylvania state line (see Fort Necessity National Battlefield Park selection) and fought his first battle. Washington built a small temporary fort "of necessity," but had to surrender when he was attacked by a far superior force.

In 1755, a large fort was built on the Maryland hill overlooking Wills Creek. Fort Cumberland, as it was called, was the biggest fort in the colony at that time, measuring 400 feet long and 160 feet wide. The dimensions of the fort are marked on the streets of Cumberland, also the original location of Washington's headquarters.

General Braddock rode a chariot into Fort Cumberland in May 1755. George Washington, as his aide-de-camp, marched with him on the ill-fated attack on Fort Duquesne. The British lost the battle and their general; but the colonies gained their greatest hero (Washington's heroism would contribute to his appointment as commander of the American revolutionary forces). Though he had three horses shot from under him and his uniform was riddled with bullet holes, Washington helped two other officers carry the mortally wounded General Braddock from the battlefield. Then he returned to battle, riding all night to lead the men and wagons to safety.

As president, Washington came again to Fort Cumberland in 1794 to review the troops marching north to suppress the Whiskey Rebellion in Pennsylvania. Despite its historic significance, the fort fell into disrepair. When the land was sold to private developers, timbers from the one-room cabin that had been **George Washington's**

Headquarters were saved and eventually moved to the banks of Wills Creek near the site of the old fort (now Riverside Park), where it has been restored. When you peer through the windows of the cabin, you see a mannequin dressed in a Virginia militia uniform resembling a youthful Washington. A taped message provides background on Washington's involvement in the French and Indian War and on Fort Cumberland.

If you plan ahead, you can arrange through the pastoral offices of Emmanuel Episcopal Church (301-777-3364) to explore the **Tunnels of Fort Cumberland**. The church is built on the site of the fort, and some of the network of trenches that crisscrossed and surrounded Fort Cumberland are still visible amid the foundations of the church.

These stone-fined trenches are the only surviving earthworks from the French and Indian War. One section is identified as a possible powder magazine. Walking along these winding tunnels, you can get quite a thrill realizing that Washington may well have found his way along the very same route.

On your way to the tunnels, be sure to stop for a look at this Gothic church. Two of the windows were done by Tiffany himself, a third by his studio. The windows reveal such depth of color that they seem to glow with an internal fire. *The Adoration of the Shepherd*, by Bongereau, over the altar is not to be missed. The church is at 16 Washington Street in Cumberland's historic district (see History House selection).

Directions: From Baltimore, take I-70 west to Hancock (about 90 miles). From Hancock, continue west on I-68 to Cumberland. Take Exit 43A, right onto Lee Street. Continue to traffic light; turn right onto Greene Street. Proceed two blocks to where Greene Street turns left. Headquarters cabin is on the right. One block ahead on Greene Street, turn left onto Washington Street. The Emmanuel Church is on the left.

The Declaration of Independence

If the colonials couldn't obtain their rights as Englishmen, then they were determined to obtain them as Americans. The denial of their rights led them to sever ties with England and create their own laws. The concepts of equality and freedom expressed in the Declaration of Independence were the motivating force that inspired many of the early colonists. But few had previously envisioned freedom to the degree encompassed by this Declaration. Social and political reform, spurred in part by this document, would occur more slowly throughout Europe, Asia, and Africa. The Declaration of Independence is therefore one of the most important documents in American and world history.

The First Continental Congress met in Philadelphia in September 1774. This first attempt to get delegates from all thirteen colonies together was for the purpose of making a consolidated appeal to King George to listen to their grievances. They hoped their united plea would persuade the king to make policies more equitable to the colonial economy.

Rather than adopting a conciliatory stand, by the end of 1775, King George was considering sending a larger army to the colonies. Fights had already erupted between British redcoats and irate colonists; yet the laws became even more dictatorial.

In April 1775, the first shots of the Revolution were fired at Lexington and Concord. In May, Ethan Allen and his Green Mountain Boys captured Fort Ticonderoga on Lake Champlain, acquiring needed muskets for colonial forces. By the time the Second Continental Congress met in June, they were confronted with a situation already out of control. The delegates chose George Washington as commander in chief of the Continental troops. But the Congress still did not formally sever ties with England.

Early in 1776, Thomas Paine published a pamphlet called *Common Sense,* arguing the case for independence. It was highly influential, selling more than 120,000 copies in less than three months. Even the Prince of Wales was discovered reading it by the Queen Mother.

When the Second Continental Congress reconvened in Philadelphia on June 6, 1776, Richard Henry Lee proposed that the colonies declare their independence. John Adams seconded the motion, but it was not unanimously received. Many—especially those from the middle colonies—still felt that the differences with England could be reconciled. It was decided to postpone the vote until July, and a committee of five was chosen to draw up the document that would declare the colonists' intentions.

Committee members included Benjamin Franklin of Pennsylvania, John Adams of Massachusetts, Thomas Jefferson of Virginia, Roger Sherman of Connecticut, and Robert Livingston of New York. Jefferson was picked to draft the document, as he had already demonstrated a facility with words and a capacity to lead others. Livingston, who was not in favor of the proposed document, returned to New York and did not rejoin the Congress. Franklin already had too many other obligations, and Sherman was not adept at writing. Adams declined to write the document. As he explained to Jefferson, "Reason first—you are a Virginian, and a Virginian ought to appear at the head of this business. Reason second—I am obnoxious, suspected, and unpopular. You are very much otherwise. Reason third—you can write ten times better than I can."

Working each night after the regular session, Jefferson prepared the statement. He incorporated the ideas expressed by his fellow Virginian, George Mason, in his "Declaration of Rights." Both Adams and Franklin were delighted when shown the proposed declaration. It was presented to the Congress on July 1, 1776.

No vote was taken the first day, although the delegates met for nine hours. By the end of the second day, twelve colonies had voted, and all favored independence. Only New York abstained. The New York delegation was concerned about their fate with General Burgoyne's army about to occupy New York.

On the third day, the text of the declaration itself was read. The Preamble was accepted with much approval and only minor changes. The twenty-seven charges against George III were agreed upon after discussion and corrections. When the last charge was read, in which Jefferson accused King George of taking away the liberty of distant people and carrying them from their homeland to be slaves, the delegates from South Carolina and Georgia balked. Their economy was based on slavery, and they refused to vote in favor of a document that condemned slavery.

It was necessary for the thirteen colonies to act unanimously. With the tenuous nature of the new country, they could not afford to have any colony stand apart, which would be a base for English troops and a wedge to defeat all the Americans' hopes. Reluctantly, the other delegates agreed to drop the last charge condemning slavery.

In all, the delegates made eighty-six changes (changes Jefferson called mutilations) to the 1,817 word draft that Jefferson submitted. It was Thursday, July 4, 1776, when the delegates voted to adopt the Declaration of Independence. Contrary to popular thinking, it was not signed until August 2. The delay, necessary to permit the printer to strike a formal copy, gave the delegates time to ponder their action. As they signed, each knew that if the British succeeded in crushing the revolution, his signature on this document would be evidence of treason.

Their concern was well advised. Of the fifty-six patriots who signed the Declaration of Independence, nine died of wounds suffered during the war. Seventeen lost everything they owned. The houses of twelve signers were burnt to the ground. Five were captured and imprisoned. In many cases, wives and children of patriots were killed, jailed, or left destitute. Despite these considerable hardships and tragedies, not one signer defected to the British cause. Their honor, like their new country, remained intact.

Virginia

Berkeley

The story of Thanksgiving is inextricably linked to the Pilgrims at Plymouth Rock despite the fact that America's first Thanksgiving did not occur in Massachusetts. It took place in Virginia, a full two years before the Pilgrims arrived in the New World.

John Wooflief, captain of the forty-ton *Margaret*, landed his small party of thirty-eight settlers at Berkeley Hundred on December 4, 1619. They came ashore and gave thanks for their safe passage, reading the message prepared for their landfall by King James I, their English proprietor: "Wee ordained that the day of our ships arrival at the place assigned for plantacon in the land of Virginia shall be yearly and perpetually keept holy as a day of thanksgiving to Almighty God." Each year on the first Sunday of November, the landing of the *Margaret* and the First Thanksgiving are re-enacted at **Berkeley**. (The house is called Berkeley; the settlement, Berkeley Hundred.)

This would be quite enough to secure Berkeley's place in history, but it holds yet another distinction. It is one of only two houses in America to be the ancestral home of a signer of the Declaration of Independence (Benjamin Harrison) and two presidents of the United States (William Henry Harrison and William Henry's grandson, Benjamin Harrison). The other house with this historic significance is the Adams ancestral home in Braintree, Massachusetts.

Berkeley is also credited with the first distillation of bourbon. In the early days at Berkeley Hundred, the colonists worked hard to establish their settlement. George Thorpe, an Episcopal missionary, concocted a home-brew to encourage their efforts. His corn liquor proved more popular than their English ale.

The Harrison family acquired Berkeley in 1691, but it was not until 1726 that Benjamin Harrison IV built the Georgian-style main house, the oldest three-story brick house in Virginia. Benjamin Harrison's wife was Anne Carter, the daughter of Robert "King" Carter. It was their son, Benjamin Harrison V, who became a signer of the Declaration of Independence and three-term governor of Virginia. He held elective office for forty-two of his sixty-five years. His picture hangs over the mantle in Berkeley's northern drawing room.

Benjamin Harrison V's youngest son, William Henry, the future president, was born at Berkeley in 1773. He gained fame as an American Indian fighter at the Battle of Tippecanoe and became governor of the Northwest Territory. When William Henry Harrison ran for the presidency in 1840, he initiated campaign publicity. You see examples of his buttons and banners when you tour Berkeley. Although he was born to wealth and social position, Harrison was depicted on his commemorative handkerchiefs as a rude frontiersman standing in front of a log cabin home.

Harrison won the election and became the ninth president. He returned to Berkeley to write his inaugural address in the room where he was born. During the campaign, Harrison had been advised by party leader Nicholas Biddle to "say not one single word about his principles, or his creed—let him say nothing—promise nothing... " The opportunity to speak proved too tempting for Harrison; at slightly less than two hours, his was the longest inaugural speech ever delivered. He paid a high price for his vanity; he contracted pneumonia from his prolonged exposure to Washington's cold, wet weather and died thirty-one days later. His vice president was his

Berkeley Plantation was the ancestral home of the Harrisons, two of whom became president. The first settlers of the Virginia colony celebrated Thanksgiving after their 1617 landing, two years before the Pilgrims held a similar ceremony in Massachusetts.

Sherwood Forest neighbor, John Tyler, whose smooth succession to the presidency set a precedent for future mid-term transitions. In 1888, Harrison's grandson, Benjamin Harrison, became the twenty-third president.

Though Berkeley looks as if nothing has happened to it since colonial days, history tells us otherwise. In 1781, during the American Revolution, Benedict Arnold's troops plundered the plantation. Late in the Civil War, during July and August of 1862, General McClellan made Berkeley his headquarters. The Union army of 140,000 men camped on the grounds, and President Lincoln visited Berkeley twice to confer with McClellan. Linking the past with the present, Malcolm Jamieson, Berkeley's long-time owner, was the son of a drummer who served with McClellan's army at Berkeley.

Berkeley's preeminent role in history is highlighted in a slide program that precedes the guided tour of the house. After the tour be sure to explore Berkeley's grounds and gardens. The plantation is open daily from 8:00 A.M. to 5:00 P.M. Admission is charged.

Next door to Berkeley is **Westover Plantation**. Although the mansion is not open, the views you can get of the house from various parts of the sweeping grounds are worth your time. Westover is considered an outstanding example of Georgian architecture. If Westover looks familiar, it is because it is featured in the Williamsburg movie, *The Story of a Patriot.*

There are several dependencies on the grounds, including the kitchen, smokehouse, icehouse, and necessary. The formal gardens were re-established about 1900; within the garden you'll see the tomb of William Byrd II, founder of Richmond and Petersburg, buried here in 1744. Westover's grounds and gardens are open daily from 9:00 A.M. to 6:00 P.M. A nominal admission is charged.

Directions: From I-295 to the east of Richmond, take Route 5 along the James River toward Williamsburg. Berkeley and Westover, which are about twenty-two miles east of Richmond, are well marked.

George Wythe House

If Sir John Randolph (see Peyton Randolph House) was the most distinguished lawyer in Virginia in the first third of the eighteenth century, then another Williamsburg resident, George Wythe, may well lay claim to this distinction in the last third. While his neighbor, Peyton Randolph, was serving the colony in England, Wythe acted as attorney general. Wythe, a member of the House of Burgesses, was a good friend of Governors Fauquier and Botetourt. However, when the time came to choose sides, without hesitating, he joined the patriots and signed the Declaration of Independence for Virginia.

The document's author, Thomas Jefferson, was at one time a law student in Wythe's Williamsburg home. And in 1776, the Jefferson family stayed at the Wythe house for several weeks. A popular teacher, Wythe became America's first professor of law at William and Mary in 1779.

The **George Wythe House** was used by George Washington as his headquarters during the Yorktown siege. After the hostilities ended, Rochambeau moved here from the Randolph House. Centuries later, this Georgian mansion became the home of the Reverend W.A.R. Goodwin. Perhaps living here made him more attuned to the urgency of restoring Williamsburg to its former glory. In any event, he had the idea for Rockefeller's restoration. George Wythe established a miniplantation in the heart of Williamsburg, where you can see his outbuildings and gardens.

Admission to the Wythe House is included in the basic ticket sold at the visitor center. All attractions are generally open from 9:00 A.M. to 5:00 P.M. The days and times do change depending on the season.

Directions: From I-95 in the Richmond area, take Exit 238, I-64 east to Colonial Williamsburg and follow the signs to the visitor center.

Monticello

Monticello is one of the most interesting homes in America because Thomas Jefferson was one of the most original thinkers of his, or any, age. His home reveals the breadth and scope of his interests.

President Taft said that, in Charlottesville, "they still talked of Mr. Jefferson as though he were in the next room." When you visit Monticello and sense the individuality of its designer, it is easy to feel that Mr. Jefferson is in the next room.

Thomas Jefferson inherited the land on which he built Monticello at his father's death in 1757. He had played on the mountaintop as a child while growing up at neighboring Shadwell. Jefferson occasionally took time out from his law studies with George Wythe in Williamsburg and explored his Virginia hilltop, perhaps planning the home that he eventually built. The year after he finished reading law, 1768, he began to level the top of his 867-foot mountain so that he could begin building. He named his estate "Monticello," an Italian word for little mountain. The design is an example of Roman neoclassicism. Jefferson used architectural books to design his house. He borrowed heavily from the Palladian style popularized by Andrea Palladio.

Like so many of the skills Jefferson acquired, his architectural artistry was self-taught. He was an enthusiastic innovator in all that he attempted. One of the features that would become a Jeffersonian trademark was the dome he added to his house. His was the first private house in America to have a dome. His dome-room is only reached by a pair of narrow staircases, so visitors cannot enjoy an up-close look at this architectural feature. Jefferson loved domes but disliked grand staircases.

Another innovation was the seven-day clock Jefferson designed for the entrance hall. Cannonball-like weights indicate the day of the week. Because he ran out of wall space for the days of the week, Saturday's marker is below the hall on the basement level and can be seen in the archeological exhibit area below the main floor. Jefferson even designed a special ladder for the weekly winding of the clock. The hall also boasts elk antlers brought back by Lewis and Clark from their trip to the far west, as well as mastodon bones that Clark found in Kentucky.

When you tour Monticello, you quickly become aware of Jefferson's practical turn of mind. In the study there is a marvelous device that allowed him to write with one pen while a second, connected pen made a copy of the letter. Jefferson designed his bedroom so that he could have access to his bed from either the bedroom or the sitting room; the bed itself is a room divider. He also designed beds to fit in alcoves to conserve space. His practicality extended to other areas of the house. There is a lazy susan door in the dining room that allowed the kitchen staff to set the prepared dishes on the door shelves and then simply turn the door, fully stocked, for service in the dining room.

Much as Jefferson enjoyed designing, building, and embellishing his mountaintop home, his real passion was for horticulture. Indeed, this great leader, who served as president of the United States, vice-president, secretary of state, minister to France, and governor of Virginia, once said, "I have often thought that if heaven had given me a choice of my position and calling, it should have been on a rich spot of earth... and near a good market... No occupation is so delightful to me as the culture of the earth... "

The gardens of Monticello are not to be missed. Visitors should plan their day so that they can include an hour-long escorted tour of the garden, offered daily April through October. Jefferson's creativity certainly extended to his garden. As he proudly proclaimed, "I am become the most ardent farmer in the state." In his later years he would say, "Though an old man, I am but a young gardener."

He was twenty-three years old when he began the garden diary he would keep until two years before his death at age eighty-three. His precise records have enabled the Thomas Jefferson Memorial Foundation to accurately restore the landscape to its appearance following Jefferson's second term as president in 1809. A grid, drawn by Jefferson in 1778, gives the exact locations of three hundred trees. In all, his notes and planting plans indicate the positions of nine hundred trees. His enthusiasm for fruit trees unquestionably exceeded their usefulness. Even on his busy estate, there weren't enough people to consume the fruit from three hundred trees. Jefferson's orchard was one of the most extensive in America; he planted 122 varieties of 10 different types of fruit.

He also enjoyed experimenting with vegetables in his massive thousand-foot vegetable garden, located on a terraced area above the orchard. Peas were one of Jefferson's favorite vegetables, and he grew twenty kinds of English pea. In total, he cultivated 250 varieties of herbs and vegetables. Jefferson once said that the "greatest service which can be rendered any country is to add an useful plant to its culture."

Monticello is open daily, except Christmas, from 8:00 A.M. to 5:00 P.M., March through October, and from 9:00 A.M. to 4:30 P.M., November through February. Admission is charged. You can purchase a Presidents' Pass at the Charlottesville-Albemarle Visitors Bureau, a discounted combination ticket for Monticello, Historic Michie Tavern, and Ash Lawn. For more information, you can call (804) 984-9822 or check Monticello's Web site, www.monticello.org.

Directions: From I-95 in the Richmond area, take I-64 west to Charlottesville. Take Exit 121, Route 20 south, off I-64. From Route 20, turn left onto Route 53, the Thomas Jefferson Parkway, to Monticello. From the Washington, D.C., area, take I-66 west to Route 29 south, the Warrenton exit. Follow Route 29 south to Charlottesville. Take Route 250 West bypass to I-64 east toward Richmond. From I-64, take Exit 121A, the Monticello exit, which will put you on Route 20 south. Proceed as outlined above.

Nelson House

The **Nelson House** in Yorktown is filled not with furniture but with voices from the past. Exemplifying the best traditions of the National Park Service, the living-history programs performed here bring to life this important American family.

If you've ever wandered through a historic house and thought about the stories it could tell, you'll appreciate the Nelson House Drama. Two actors perform this minidrama as they re-create prominent Nelson family members and friends. The presentation brings alive the tumultuous days when America sought her independence. The program is given every half hour from noon to 4:00 P.M., except 2:30 P.M., throughout the summer.

The Nelson's family home was built around 1730 by "Scotch

Tom" Nelson, an Englishman born near the Scottish border. Young Thomas Nelson, Jr., just seven when his grandfather died, went on to play a pivotal role in Virginia history.

Following colonial tradition, he was educated in England at Cambridge University. When he returned to the colonies, he served as a member of the House of Burgesses. As the dispute grew between crown and colony, he sided with his fellow Virginians and became one of the signers of the Declaration of Independence.

The Nelson House still bears reminders of Thomas Nelson, Jr.'s, military career during the Revolution. As brigadier general of the Virginia militia, he directed his men to fire at his own home because he thought it was the headquarters of British Commander Lord Cornwallis. You'll see two cannonballs embedded in the east wall. They were placed in the wall in the twentieth century to fill scars left from the siege of 1781.

The Revolution not only threatened the very walls of Nelson's house, it also cost him a substantial fortune. He personally outfitted and provisioned his men during the Virginia campaign. Despite his financial reverses, the Nelson family house was the scene of a lavish gala honoring Lafayette on his return in 1824 to celebrate the victory at Yorktown.

Visitors are as welcome now as they were in the eighteenth century. Nelson House is open daily from mid-June to mid-August from 10:00 A.M. to 4:30 P.M. and in the spring and fall from 1:00 to 4:30 P.M. Hours may vary, depending on staffing. Before leaving, be sure to explore the twentieth-century formal English garden. For information on the living-history dramas, call (757) 898-3400, extension 58.

While in Yorktown, take the time to stroll along Main Street. Near the Nelson House are two interesting homes. The Dudley Diggs House was built in the early eighteenth century and, during the Revolutionary years, was the home of a council member for Virginia. You'll also see the Sessions House, built around 1693 and believed to be the oldest house in Yorktown.

To the left of the Nelson House on Main Street are five buildings of historical interest. Just across Read Street is the customhouse, reputedly built in 1721. Across Main street is another eighteenth-century residence, the Pate House. Next door is Somerwell House, which survived the siege of 1781 to become a hotel during the Civil War. Across Church Street is the medical shop, reconstructed to look as it did during the eighteenth century.

Facing the medical shop on Main Street is the reconstructed Swan Tavern and dependencies, now operated as an antique shop. Swan Tavern was built in 1722 by "Scotch Tom" Nelson in partnership with

Joseph Walker and destroyed during the Civil War. You can pick up a walking tour map at the National Park Service Visitor Center.

Directions: From I-95 in the Richmond area, take I-64 east to the Colonial Parkway. Follow Colonial Parkway to Yorktown.

Stratford Hall

The Washingtons were one of many families of prominence to have their roots in the Northern Neck. James Madison, James Monroe, John Marshall's father, and the Lee brothers were all born in the region. The Washingtons (see George Washington Birthplace National Monument selection) and the Lees were virtually neighbors. Richard Henry Lee, who became a signer of the Declaration of Independence, was born a year later than George Washington, on January 20, 1733. His brother and fellow signer, Francis Lightfoot Lee, was born two years later on October 14, 1734. It is provocative to imagine the mutual influence Washington and the Lees might have had on one another had they grown up together.

The Lees were the only brothers to sign the Declaration of Independence. Richard Henry Lee actually proposed the resolution for independence from England at the Second Continental Congress. It is likely that he would have been asked to draft the resolution had he not been called back to Virginia during the debate. That was perhaps for the best; Lee was considered an orator, while Jefferson was noted as a superior writer.

Richard Henry Lee was an activist. He established the first association in the colonies to boycott English goods, the Westmoreland Association. At the First Continental Congress, his efforts in this direction led to the Continental Association, the first step toward a union of the colonies.

The father of these distinguished patriots, Thomas Lee, had held the highest office in the Virginia colony as president of the King's Council. In the late 1730s, he built the family estate on the cliffs overlooking the Potomac River.

Stratford Hall, as it eventually came to be called, is far grander than the Washington home. It once encompassed 4,100 acres and even now includes 1, 670 acres. It is still a working farm with a herd of Black Angus. The house itself was an architectural anomaly in colonial America. It was not designed in traditional Georgian manner but in the Italian style, with the major living quarters on the second floor. The design features an H-shaped great house with two clusters of four chimneys each. The great hall forms the center of the H and is considered one of the hundred most beautiful rooms in America. Like the rest of the house, it is furnished with eighteenth-century pieces.

Thomas Lee's great-nephew, "Light Horse" Harry Lee, was a military hero of the Revolutionary War. He went on to serve three terms as governor of Virginia. His son Robert E. Lee was born at Stratford Hall. Visitors can see the bedroom where Robert E. Lee was born. The adjoining nursery contains a fireplace with two bas-relief winged cherubs said to be favorites of the young Lee.

Stratford Hall is open from 9:00 A.M. to 4:30 P.M., except Thanksgiving, Christmas, and New Year's Day. Admission is charged. If you decide not to picnic on the grounds, try the log cabin plantation dining room, which is open from 11:30 A.M. to 3:00 P.M.

Directions: From I-95 take Route 3 east at Fredericksburg. Take Route 3 to Lerty and turn left on Route 214 for Stratford Hall.

Thomas Jefferson's Poplar Forest

The visionary design can be discerned despite the ruinous inroads time has inflicted on **Poplar Forest**, Jefferson's country retreat, seventy miles south of Monticello just outside Lynchburg. Restoration work still continues on the masterpiece Jefferson created at the peak of his architectural maturity.

Jefferson acquired the land through his wife, Martha Wayles Skelton Jefferson, whose father owned the Lynchburg acreage. Jefferson designed the house as an escape from the crush of visitors that engulfed him at Monticello. Based on a Palladian plan, the house has four equal octagonal rooms grouped around a square dining room with an overhead skylight. It was the first octagonal residence in the New World.

Work on Poplar Forest began in 1806, and in 1812 Jefferson said, "When finished, it will be the best dwelling house in the state, except that of Monticello; perhaps preferable to that, as more proportioned to the faculties of a private citizen."

You can imagine Jefferson reading in the bright, airy rooms. Today, Jefferson's private sanctuary, where he said he enjoyed the "solitude of a hermit," is open to the public. Hours are 10:00 A.M. to 4:00 P.M. from April through November, Wednesday through Sunday. It is closed on Thanksgiving. Groups can tour by appointment year-round; call (804) 525-1806.

When Jefferson traveled to Poplar Forest, he often stopped for a visit at the **Miller-Claytor House.** You can add this stop to your outing. This modest house was the fourth house built in 1791 in the new town of Lynchburg. Legend has it that on one of Jefferson's visits, he took a bite of a "love apple" growing in the yard. It is believed to be the first time that a tomato, generally considered poisonous, was eaten in this part of the country.

The Miller-Claytor House at Miller-Claytor Lane and Treasure Island Road in Riverside Park is open May through September, Thursday through Monday, from 1:00 to 4:00 P.M. To arrange a tour, call (804) 847-1459. There are twelve sites of interest along Rivermont Avenue. They include richly embellished private residences, Randolph-Macon Women's College, and the Centenary United Methodist Church. Architecture runs the gamut from Beaux Arts to a Swiss Chalet style with Queen Anne influence.

Directions: From I-95 in the Richmond area take Route 360 southwest to Burkeville, then take Route 460 to Lynchburg. Or take I-64 west to Charlottesville, then Route 29 south to Lynchburg. The visitor center is at 12th and Church Streets.

Maryland

Chase-Lloyd House

Two lovely Georgian homes sit on opposite sides of Annapolis's Maryland Avenue. Both begun by men whose dreams were never fulfilled. The Hammond-Harwood House (see selection) was built by master builder William Buckland. Buckland also did some of the interior work on the Chase-Lloyd House.

In the 1770s, legal firebrand Samuel Chase, described by the mayor of Annapolis as "an inflaming son of discord," wanted to build a dream house. It turned into a nightmare for Chase when business reverses forced him to sell the uncompleted house to a wealthy Eastern Shore planter, Col. Edward Lloyd IV. Lloyd's opulent lifestyle earned him the nickname "Edward the Magnificent." When he acquired the unfinished Chase House, he employed William Buckland to oversee its completion. Buckland, too, had a sobriquet: He was called the "Taste Maker of the Colonies" for his influential style. The combination of Buckland's talent and Lloyd's wealth produced one of the finest eighteenth-century interiors in America.

The exterior of this three-story, Flemish bond brick mansion has a decorative cornice, projecting pedimented pavilion, and a Venetian doorway. But it is the lavishly decorated interior that marks this as one of Buckland's finest achievements. Beginning in the main hall, you can see graceful Ionic columns separating the entranceway from the grand staircase, a much-photographed architectural delight

The **Chase-Lloyd House** remained in the Lloyd family for seventy-three years and then ironically was purchased by Chase's descendants. The last surviving Chase niece arranged for the house to be preserved as a home for elderly ladies. It is, however, open to the public on afternoons from 2:00 to 4:00 P.M., except on Sundays. The small entrance fee, used to support the upkeep, includes the garden.

Chase's fortunes did not improve after he sold his Annapolis home. He went bankrupt in 1789. In 1805, his legal career ended in ignominy when he was impeached as an associate justice of the Supreme Court, though in the end he was not convicted.

Directions: From Baltimore, take Route 97 to Route 50 east. Take Route 50 to Rowe Boulevard exit. Follow to College Avenue (at "T" in road). From Rowe Boulevard, turn left onto College Avenue, then right at the first light, King George Street. Proceed on King George Street to the first light and turn right on Maryland Avenue. Chase-Lloyd House is on the right corner. Parking is very limited so it is a good idea to try to park on King George Street.

Thomas Stone National Historic Site

The United States has no aristocracy, having always favored a meritocracy. But if there was a roster of American nobility, it might well include the brave men who signed the Declaration of Independence at great risk to their personal safety and property. Had England won the Revolution, they would have been judged traitors. As it was, many lost their liberty and their belongings during the war.

Thomas Stone, a well-respected lawyer and prominent political figure, was a signer for Maryland. Stone not only served in the Second Continental Congress, he was also a State senator. He was selected as a representative to the Constitutional Convention in 1787, but his wife's ill health and his busy law practice forced him to refuse the honor. She died in June 1787, and he soon became ill and died on October 5 of the same year.

They are buried at **Haberdeventure,** the Charles County plantation Stone purchased in 1770. The following year, he began constructing his two-story, brick country home; it was finished in 1773. After the National Park Service acquired the estate in 1981, restoration work began on the fire-gutted central block of the house, which is being restored to its eighteenth-century appearance.

Originally, Stone's plantation consisted of 442 acres, but by the time of his death, the estate was 1,077 acres. Although he increased the plantation's size, Stone never seemed to regard Haberdeventure as a source of income. Only half of the original acreage was suitable for cultivation. The main crops were corn and wheat. He also concentrated on livestock production. Approximately twenty-five to thirty-five people are thought to have lived at Haberdeventure, including the extended Stone family and slaves.

The **Thomas Stone National Historic Site** visitor center has exhibits on the house and Stone's career. The site is open September through May, Thursday through Sunday, from 9:00 A.M. to 5:00 P.M. To check on expanded summer hours, you can call (301) 934-6027. The park is closed on Christmas and New Year's Day.

Mansion tours are offered hourly from 10:00 A.M. until 4:00 P.M. The park staff will also provide directions for self-guided tours and hikes. There are numerous points of interest within the park, including mid-nineteenth-century tobacco barns, corn crib, horse stable, and tenant house. Before exploring the grounds, check with the park rangers about restricted work areas.

Directions: From Baltimore, take the Baltimore-Washington Parkway, I-295, south to the Washington Beltway, I-495/95, south to Exit 3, Indian Head Highway, Route 210. Take Route 210 south to Potomac Heights and turn left on Route 225 east. Take this for approximately ten minutes, then make a right (south) on Rose Hill Road, which will take you to the Thomas Stone National Historic Site.

William Paca House and Garden

It is the colors you'll remember long after you visit the Annapolis home of William Paca (pronounced pay-ka). Five years of painstaking work peeled away twenty-two layers of paint and wallpaper to uncover the startling Prussian blue walls that have now been resplendently repainted. This sky-blue hue, so dramatically different from the muted Williamsburg shades that we think of as colonial, was the first commercially produced paint.

The restoration of the house was a remarkable achievement. The dramatic change can be seen in the before and after photographs displayed in the rear porch chamber. The additions made while the house was used as part of the Carvel Hall Hotel were all removed, and both the Georgian mansion and the eighteenth-century pleasure gardens were restored.

The house tour takes you to the blue parlor, which, like the rest of the house, has been furnished to reflect fashions ten years before the American Revolution. Because the house did not remain in the family, the furniture is not original, although one chair and several pieces of silver did belong to the Paca family. Each room shows a popular activity that the family might have enjoyed during that era. A card game is spread out on the parlor table. You'll see the hall, which, contrary to your expectation, is not a passageway but what we would call a family room, with the table set for tea. Again you will see the bright blue, used here for trim. In the dining room, the guide explains that colonial families frequently had their meals served in whatever room they were using and only resorted to the dining room when entertaining company.

The back porch, not traditionally a part of Georgian homes, was added to the house by William Paca, who, it can be conjectured, wanted a room where he could enjoy the garden on which he lavished so much time. You'll get your best overview of the garden from the upstairs window. Note how the terraces lead down to the wilderness garden, which is highlighted by a two-story, octagonal pavilion. This pavilion and the Chinese Chippendale trellis bridge were included in the background of the Charles Willson Peale portrait of Paca. The pleasure gardens look as though they haven't been touched since the days when the portrait was painted. They were all restored after detailed excavation work uncovered the old garden foundations.

Paca's interest in gardening is but one of many similarities between Paca and Thomas Jefferson, with whom he was often compared. Both were lawyers, both served in the Continental Congress, and both signed the Declaration of Independence. Paca went on to help draft the Maryland Constitution and served as governor of Maryland from 1782 until 1785 (Jefferson served as governor of Virginia). At Paca's death in 1799, he was serving as the first U. S. District judge from Maryland, the position to which he was appointed by President Washington.

William Paca House and Garden are open for tours. Many visitors return to enjoy his gardens as they change with the seasons. The house tours now also change every eight months, emphasizing different facets of eighteenth-century life. The William Paca House is open Monday through Saturday from 10: 00 A.M. to 4: 00 P.M. and on Sunday from noon to 4: 00 P.M. The William Paca Garden is open at the same times, except on Sundays, May through October, when it stays open an hour longer, until 5:00 P.M. Both house and gardens are closed Thanksgiving, Christmas Eve, and Christmas Day. During January and February, the house is only open Friday through Sunday. For additional information, you can call (410) 263-5553.

Directions: From Baltimore take I-97 to Route 50 east, then take Rowe Boulevard into Historic Annapolis. Turn left at the State House onto College Avenue; then make a right on King George Street; right again on East Street for one block to Prince George Street. Make a right on Prince George Street, and you'll see the William Paca House at 186 Prince George Street.

Pennsylvania

Declaration House

Thomas Jefferson is revered as the author of the Declaration of Independence and for his lifetime service in his country's behalf.

The **Declaration House,** part of Independence National Historical Park, is where Thomas Jefferson rented rooms during the Second Continental Congress. It was while staying here that Jefferson drafted the Declaration of Independence. These were his second accommodations in the city. The first rooms he rented were too noisy, so he moved to what was then the edge of town and rented two rooms on the second floor from bricklayer Jacob Graff, Jr., for thirty-five shillings a week. Jefferson worked in his rented parlor, writing on a portable writing-box that he had designed. He finished his draft in two weeks.

Jefferson attended the regular sessions of the congress in June 1776, then came back to his rooms and worked on a document to express the position of the American colonies regarding British tyranny. There is a short film on Jefferson's labors to bring forth a document that would have the support of the thirteen colonies meeting in Philadelphia.

The Graff, or Declaration, House has been completely reconstructed. The only original piece is the lintel in the western window. The bedroom and parlor are replicas of the rooms Jefferson used. An exhibit reveals the sources Jefferson found for some of his statements.

The Declaration House is located at 7th and Market Streets and is open at no charge.

Directions: From I-95 southbound (from points north), take Exit 17. Using the right-hand lanes of the exit, follow the signs for Callowhill Street/Independence Hall. At the bottom of the exit ramp, follow 2nd Street straight ahead to Chestnut Street. Continue a half block past Chestnut Street for the Historic Area Parking Garage on the left. It is best to park your car and walk to all the sites in the Historic District. Start at the Independence National Historical Park Visitors Center, one block away, at 3rd and Chestnut Streets, where you can pick up an easy-to-follow map of the district and a park schedule. If you are traveling northbound on I-95 (from points south), you will also take Exit 17. Stay in the left lane because you will exit on the left side of I-95. At the exit, stay in the right-hand lane and follow the signs for Independence Hall/Historic Area. Turn left at 6th Street to Chestnut and drive through the heart of the Historic District to 2nd Street. Turn right on 2nd Street.The entrance to the Historic Area Parking Garage is on the left.

Franklin Court

The spirit of Benjamin Franklin can be felt at **Franklin Court,** part of Independence National Historical Park in Philadelphia. The latest in museum technology was employed to create the imaginative and innovative exhibits.

The all-underground museum is literally explored from the bottom up. The Franklin Exchange has twenty-two noted Americans and twenty-six Europeans whom you can "telephone" for their opinions of this talented, complex figure. Original quotes from John Adams, Henry Steele Commanger, Jefferson Davis, Ralph Waldo Emerson, Thomas Jefferson, Harry Truman, Mark Twain, and George Washington offer interesting insights. Europeans heard from are Lord Byron, Charles Darwin, David Hume, Immanuel Kant, John Keats, Lafayette, D. H. Lawrence, and George Sand.

None of these personalities outshines Franklin himself when it comes to wit. His remarks on a wide range of topics appear on projected slides. Franklin's views on women, virtue, money, government, and ethics still seem timely. "Franklin on the World Stage" presents a series of miniature figures in a sound and light show depicting Franklin in such settings as before the House of Commons in 1766 and in 1778 before the Court of Versailles.

Next, the personal side of Franklin is showcased in the movie *Portrait of a Family,* about his early life and marriage. You'll see how his career affected his family. Franklin's wife died just before he returned to America after representing the fledgling country for a decade in England. He left again to spend eight years representing America's interests in France.

At street level, you discover that the foundation is all that remains of Franklin's home. Not enough documentation survive to support a historically accurate reconstruction. There is a colonial pleasure garden and five Market Street houses, three of which were owned by Franklin. Each house reveals a facet of his life.

Franklin, the builder, is the theme of the center house at 318 Market Street. Explanatory notes let visitors "read" the walls. Plaster, wallpaper, chair rails, chimney, and joists all date from the eighteenth century. Franklin was concerned about fires—in fact, he established the nation's first volunteer fire department. And in his designs, he made sure that the joists of one room did not meet those of another, which prevented fires from spreading rapidly from room to room.

Franklin the printer is the focus of another house, where you'll see a printing press he used to turn out handbills. Franklin's grandson, Benjamin Franklin Bache, had an office at 322 Market Street, which has been restored. The *Philadelphia Aurora* was published here.

Franklin was the first postmaster general of the United States, and the fourth house is a post office. Letters can be cancelled with the postmark Franklin made famous, "B Free Franklin." Postal museums are must-sees for stamp collectors. The fifth house is a park sales outlet. Franklin Court is open daily (except for some holiday closings).

Directions: Traveling north on I-95, take I-676 into Philadelphia, following the signs for Independence Hall. Turn left on 6th Street and continue down to Market Street; then turn left on Market Street. Franklin Court is between 3rd and 4th Streets.

George Taylor House

Even more profitable than marrying the boss's daughter is marrying his widow. When young George Taylor arrived in Philadelphia at age twenty from Northern Ireland, his first job as a "redemptioner" was in an iron foundry. He was working to pay back his passage. But shortly after the death of his employer, he married the widow and took over the management of the furnace.

Taylor was to be very successful in the iron business. The iron forge at which he spent most of his career was Durham Furnace, an 8,511-acre iron plantation. To get an idea of what such an operation was like, visit Hopewell Village (see Era Between the Wars: Industries.) It re-creates life on one of the eighteenth-century iron plantations.

During the American Revolution, George Taylor served as a colonel in the Army. He also was a delegate to the Continental Congress and signed the Declaration of Independence as a representative of Pennsylvania.

In 1767, he bought the land for this house in Catasauqua, Pennsylvania. It was part of a ten-thousand-acre tract that William Penn had deeded to his daughter in 1736. This lovely stone house was the first one that Taylor had ever planned and built for himself. His hopes for a leisurely life with his family in their new home were dealt a blow when his wife, Anne, died the same year the house was finished.

The George Taylor House is furnished to suggest its original appearance. Used as a summer residence, it was more elegantly designed than most houses in the Lehigh Valley. There is a formal walled garden in the park surrounding the house.

The house is open June through October from 1:00 to 4:00 P.M. on Saturday and Sunday. It is a good idea to call the Lehigh County Historical Society at (610) 435-1074 to check the current hours of operation

Directions: Take Washington Beltway Exit 27 (I-95) to Philadelphia. Then take Route 76 along the outskirts of the city; go right on Route 276 to the Route 476 exit. Follow Route 476 north to Allentown; then take a right on Route 22 to the Fullerton exit. Go north on 3rd Street to Bridge Street; then east on Bridge Street, crossing the river to Lehigh Street. Take a right on Lehigh Street to Poplar Street and a left on Poplar Street to Front Street and the George Taylor House.

OF NOTE: The only engrossed copy of the Declaration of Independence that was signed by all the delegates on August 2, 1776, is on display in the Exhibition Hall of the National Archives Building in Washington, D.C.

Revolutionary War Years

The "shot heard round the world" still echoes. The gallant fortitude of the men of the Continental Army—not only on the battlefields, but also through the cold winters at Morristown and Valley Forge—inspires each new generation of Americans.

It was on April 19, 1775, that Paul Revere hurried to the home where patriots Sam Adams and John Hancock were in hiding from the British. He brought word that there were six hundred redcoats marching on Lexington. The town's seventy-member Minuteman Brigade, so called because they could be called out at a moment's notice, formed ranks on the village green. Their ranking officer, Capt. John Parker, said, "If they mean to have a war let it begin here."

Seventeen minutemen were cut down in the first minutes of the skirmish, as the British easily overwhelmed the small force and proceeded to Concord to confiscate military supplies. But when they attempted to return to Boston, the redcoats fell under fire from a countryside swarming with militia. Lacking uniforms, training, and even experienced leadership, this farmers' army killed 73 British soldiers, wounded 174, and was responsible for the disappearance of 26 others. Only reinforcements from Boston saved the British from a total debacle. The British were confounded to find that the rebels would dare to fire on the king's troops. The Americans had shown that they would stand up to the British, as they would do again and again through the long struggle to defeat their former countrymen.

The British had not intended to start a war, but when they fired on this small band of colonials, it *was* war. It would be more than a year before independence was formally declared, but it was a year filled with skirmishes and confrontations. The first step had been taken.

It was only a matter of months after the skirmish in Massachusetts that the Second Continental Congress, meeting in Philadelphia, chose George Washington as commander in chief of the Continental Army. Washington is often depicted as reluctant to lead, anxious only to do his duty and return as quickly as possible to Mount Vernon. But it should be noted that he attended the Second Continental Congress, which was a political gathering, in the uniform of a colonel of the Virginia militia. He was the only delegate in uniform. His wearing of a uniform at that time in the turbulent state of colonial affairs was of marked significance. He may not have been as unwilling to command the army as history often implies.

The colonists were reluctant rebels; and while rebelling against the British crown, they remained loyal to many British principles—trial by jury, free assembly, free petition, and free speech. In a sense, the patriots were fighting to maintain the status quo, to defend their rights as Englishmen. George III, in denying them rights they considered their due, forced their hand. In their view, they could restore their rights only by creating a new country. At the same time, they broadened the scope of those rights and secured them from the whim of a king.

In attempting to wrest their independence from England, the Americans faced sizeable obstacles. They had to raise, equip, and train an army to meet one of the best and most often tested military forces in the world. England's population was three times that of the colonies; her finances enabled her to hire foreign troops to assist her own, and England had the largest navy of any colonial power.

The colonists also had to contend with a divided country, since not all citizens wanted to sever their ties with England. Their problems were compounded by inadequate financial support and woeful shortages of ammunition. The army itself was a constantly changing group. Men would be trained only to leave when their enlistment expired. It was not until halfway through the war that the standard term of enlistment became three years rather than one.

When Washington crossed the Delaware to attack the Hessians at Trenton on Christmas night 1776, it was a now or never proposition. At least fourteen hundred men of the Continental Army were scheduled to end their duty on December 31. Washington would be virtually without men, which could mean the end of hope for the Revolution.

Washington's action at Trenton and at the Battle of Princeton thwarted Britain's early objective in this conflict—that of dividing America in half geographically with its military force. General Cornwallis felt that, from a secure New York, the British would be able to subdue New England and the South bit by bit.

The last attempt to realize this goal was the Battle of Saratoga, one of the most crucial encounters of the war. The American ability to stand firm resulted in the surrender of General Burgoyne's entire army. It was a major defeat for the British and a significant turning point of the war.

There were two results of the Battle of Saratoga. The king sent peace commissioners to meet with Congress—but not to grant independence, and the Americans would settle for nothing less. Also, this victory convinced France to enter the war. The French had not wanted to squander money and men on a losing cause, but once the odds indicated the possibility of an American victory. France sent much needed men and ships. Other European powers also aided the new country as a means of weakening England.

The war would last six more years. But it was the government rather than the army that proved weak. Congress had so little power that it could not raise money to pay or supply the army. Soldiers risked their lives and served without regular pay and often without adequate food or clothes. Isolated mutinies occurred. It was a sad commentary that American troops marched on the newly formed American government before the war was even won.

In the last days of the war—after a long southern campaign in which the British under Cornwallis had lost a third of their army despite victories at Savannah in December 1778, Charleston in May 1780, and the capture of all major points in South Carolina—the British turned at last to the sea, which led to the final confrontation of the war. Washington was now able to cut off Cornwallis's escape by sea with the help of Admiral De Grasses and the French fleet.

The British army was trapped at Yorktown. On October 17, 1781, Lord Cornwallis and the eight thousand men of the British army surrendered. Two years later, the Treaty of Paris was signed, formally declaring the United States a free and independent country.

Pennsylvania

Brandywine Battlefield Park

When you visit **Brandywine Battlefield Park**, make the visitor center your first stop. The twenty-minute audio-visual show provides a concise perspective on the Revolutionary battle that occurred here in 1777. General Washington might well have wished for a similarly clear picture of what was happening as he led his men on September 11, 1777. Washington kept receiving conflicting reports on the position of the fifteen thousand British soldiers under General Howe. The fourteen-thousand-member American force, although lacking in equipment and experience, still managed to retreat rather than surrender—thus saving the Continental force to fight another day. From this encounter, the British moved to their comfortable winter quarters in Philadelphia, while the Americans endured the privations at Valley Forge.

Within the park, the houses used as headquarters by Washington and Lafayette have been restored. Both of these houses belonged to Quakers, whose sympathies were with the revolutionary cause. The **Benjamin Ring Farm**, General Washington's base, had to be completely rebuilt, as the original structure burned to the ground. The spacious farmhouse is again furnished to look as it did in 1777.

The Marquis de Lafayette stayed at the more modest farm of Gideon Gilpin, who later received permission to operate a tavern in compensation for the expenses he incurred during the Battle of Brandywine. A report filed by Gilpin listed as lost such items as 10 cows, 48 sheep, 28 swine, a yoke of oxen, 12 tons of hay, 230 bushels of wheat, 50 pounds of bacon, a history book, a clock, and a gun. There are dependencies at the Gilpin farm, including a root cellar, barn, and carriage house. A shed adjacent to the carriage house contains an original Conestoga wagon. Few people realize that this style of wagon was developed in the upper Brandywine Valley.

Brandywine Battlefield Park is open year-round, Tuesday through Saturday from 9:00 A.M. to 5:00 P.M.; on Sunday it opens at noon. Admission is charged.

Directions: From I-95 south of Philadelphia, take Route 322 west toward Concordville. Follow Route 322 to the intersection with Route 1; take Route 1 south for approximately five miles. The Brandywine River Museum is located on the left side of Route 1 in Chadds Ford; the Chadds Ford Barn Shops and the Battlefield Park are on the right.

Congress Hall and Old City Hall

On March 4, 1797, America's leaders assembled in the House of Representatives's chamber in **Congress Hall** to watch the inauguration of John Adams as the second president of the United States. George Washington was on hand to facilitate the nation's first transfer of executive power. There is a perhaps fictitious story about what happened after Adams took the oath of office. Washington, who was now a private citizen, motioned for Thomas Jefferson, the new vice president, to precede him from the room. Jefferson hesitated, then stepped in front of George Washington; thus did the nation achieve the transfer of power with dignity and smooth precision.

The young federal government met in Philadelphia, called by some the "capital of the New World," for ten years while the new federal city was built in Washington. The legislative branch used Congress Hall, then called Philadelphia Court House, for its sessions.

The lower house of Congress met on the lower, first-floor chambers. A large dais was added for the Speaker of the House, and rows of mahogany desks were built by a Philadelphia cabinetmaker. The county commissioners added a spectator's gallery for those interested in watching the federal government in session.

The upstairs was refitted for the Senate chambers. The senators had their own desks with comfortable leather armchairs. The vice president presided over the sessions. The upper floor also had committee and conference rooms and housed the office of the secretary of the senate. All are currently restored.

During the time Congress met here, three new states were added to the Union—Vermont in 1791, Kentucky in 1792, and Tennessee in 1796. On May 14, 1800, Congress adjourned to reconvene in the new capital. Philadelphia was no longer the center of the new country.

While the federal government operated from Philadelphia, the judicial branch met in **Old City Hall**. The chamber looks as it did in 1791, when the Supreme Court first met here. Called upon to define the law, but with no power to enforce it, the Supreme Court had initial problems in achieving the respect of the states.

In *Chishom v. Georgia*, the Court was asked to rule on whether a citizen of one state, in this case South Carolina, could bring a suit against another state, Georgia. The Court ruled that he could. Georgia did not even send a lawyer to argue its position. The Eleventh Amendment to the Constitution reversed this ruling.

Just outside Old City Hall is a colonial watch box. Such boxes contained buckets of water. As the city's watchmen made their rounds, keeping their eyes open for fires, each house had to have two buckets of water ready in case the watch sounded the alarm.

Congress Hall and Old City Hall are part of **Independence National Historical Park**. They have exhibits pertaining to the pivotal events that occurred in their chambers. Both are open at no charge from 9:00 A.M. to 5:00 P.M. daily.

Directions: From I-95 southbound (from points north), take Exit 17. Using the right-hand lanes of the exit, follow the signs for Callowhill Street/Independence Hall. At the bottom of the exit ramp, follow 2nd Street straight ahead to Chestnut Street. Continue a half block past Chestnut Street for the Historic Area Parking Garage on the left. It is best to park your car and walk to all the sites in the historic district. Start at the Independence National Historical Park Visitors Center, one block away, at 3rd and Chestnut Streets, where you can pick up an easy-to-follow map of the district and a park schedule. If you are traveling northbound on I-95 (from points south), you will also take Exit 17. Stay in the left lane; you will exit on the left side of I-95. At the exit, stay in the right-hand lane and follow the signs for Independence Hall/Historic Area. Turn left at 6th Street to Chestnut, which will take you through the heart of the historic district to 2nd Street. Turn right on 2nd Street. The entrance to the Historic Area Parking Garage is on the left.

Fort Mifflin

Four hundred and fifty men at Fort Mifflin withstood forty days of bombardment from ninety-four ships of the British fleet. General Howe's garrison in Philadelphia needed munitions and supplies before they could pursue General Washington's Continental army. **Fort Mifflin** and Fort Mercer, straddling the Delaware, blockaded the delivery of these supplies, thus delaying the British.

River traffic was halted by a cheval-de-frise, an obstacle consisting of tree trunks chained together and spiked protrusions. This type of obstruction was more frequently used to repel cavalry charges.

The British, stuck beneath the forts, began firing on October 11, 1777. After four days the guns were firing every half hour. Except for a brief time on October 22, when British guns turned to aid the Hessian land attack on New Jersey's **Fort Mercer**, the guns remained on the lower, more vulnerable Fort Mifflin. Howe began calling this obstacle "that cursed little mud fort."

The men manning the fort could be excused if they felt it was cursed; casualties had decimated their ranks. By November 7, only 115 of the fort's 320-man contingent could still man the guns. The men tried to rebuild the fort walls at night, but the constant bombardment was reducing the fort to rubble.

By November 13, three of the fort's four blockhouses were destroyed. Only eleven cannons could still be fired. By November 15, the British were firing a thousand shots every twenty minutes. The cheval-de-frise was released, either by accident or by treachery, and it fell to the bottom of the river, enabling the British to move into a better position and fire point-blank at the already crumbling fort.

By the afternoon of November 15, the men within the fort were out of ammunition. When night came, the forty defenders who were still able to walk left the fort. Estimates of American casualties ran as high as four hundred men; the British lost only seven lives.

But the British did lose valuable time. When the supply ships finally managed to destroy this small fort, the American army under Washington was beyond Howe's reach, and a major confrontation was avoided.

This ended Fort Mifflin's usefulness during the American Revolution. It was rebuilt in the 1800s during Adams's administration. Enlarged during the Civil War, it was used as a prison garrison for deserters, Confederate soldiers, bounty jumpers, and political prisoners. The fort conducted executions on what is now the Sunday drill grounds.

Fort Mifflin, which stands on Mud Island, still has its original moat. Some of the walls are from the Revolutionary period. The enlisted men's barracks, underground, bomb-proof vaults, and fortifications have been restored. On Sunday afternoons, in addition to fort tours, there are militia guard drills and living-history programs. A working blacksmith is often on hand to demonstrate how old weapons were made. A museum completes the historical picture of events at Fort Mifflin.

Fort Mifflin is open from April through November on Wednesday through Sunday from 10:00 A.M. to 4:00 P.M. The fort is open to pre-booked tours only during the off-season, from December through March. Admission is charged.

Directions: From I-95 if you are traveling south, take Exit 13 and follow the signs for Island Avenue. Make a left at the stop sign and follow the signs to Fort Mifflin. Traveling north on I-95, take Exit 10 for the Philadelphia International Airport. Drive past the airport to the large intersection of Island Avenue and I-291. Make a right at the light. Follow the signs to Fort Mifflin.

Thaddeus Kosciuszko National Memorial

Thaddeus Kosciuszko (pronounced Kos-Choos-Ko) was born February 4, 1746, into an impoverished eastern Polish family. After pursuing military studies in Warsaw and France, he lacked funds to purchase a military commission in Poland. He may also have left Poland because of a doomed love. In 1774, he was injured while attempting to elope with a Polish lord's daughter whom he was tutoring.

Kosciuszko came to America and offered his services to the American cause.

Kosciuszko arrived in Philadelphia a few weeks after the Continental Congress adopted the Declaration of Independence. The thirty-year-old had training but no experience. Additionally, he was the first foreign volunteer, so it took time before Congress responded to his offer. On October 18, 1776, a resolution was passed that "Thaddeus Kosciuszko, Esq. be appointed an engineer in the service of the United States, with the pay of sixty dollars a month, and the rank of colonel." This began a six-year tour of duty, during which he planned and built the fortifications at Saratoga and West Point. At war's end, Kosciuszko was promoted to the rank of brigadier general.

On July 15, 1784, Kosciuszko sailed back to a quiet country life in Poland. But by the 1790s, he was actively opposing Czarist Russia's domination of Poland. Kosciuszko drafted the Act of Insurrection, a document reflecting the ideas he had absorbed from America's Declaration of Independence. When Poland adopted a constitution on May 3, 1791, war with Russia ensued. Kosciuszko was made commander of the national armies but ultimately was seriously wounded in battle, defeated, and imprisoned at the Peter-and-Paul Fortress in St. Petersburg.

Only a promise never to return to Poland secured Kosciuszko's release in December 1796. His painful wounds left him partially paralyzed, but Kosciuszko traveled to London, via Finland and Sweden, arriving on May 30, 1797. Two weeks later, he left on a sixty-one-day journey to America. He arrived in Philadelphia to a hero's welcome. But because the then-capital city was fighting a lethal yellow fever epidemic, Kosciuszko visited Gen. Anthony White in New Jersey and Gen. Horatio Gates in New York.

With cold weather, the mosquitoes died, and the threat of yellow fever ended. In November Kosciuszko returned to Philadelphia and rented a small room on the second floor at Mrs. Ann Reif's boarding house at Third and Pine streets. The Polish hero spent the winter reading, also entertaining Thomas Jefferson and other distinguished guests.

Continued concern for Poland prompted him to return to Europe on May 5, 1798. After spending time in Paris, he retired to a friend's estate in Switzerland. He died in 1817 after falling from a horse. Before his death, he had emancipated all the peasants on his Polish estates. Kosciuszko was buried in the cathedral of Cracow, returning to his beloved Poland only after his death.

The **Thaddeus Kosciuszko National Memorial,** part of Independence National Historical Park, re-creates the room Kosciuszko rented for his last six months in America. Both the second-floor room and the exterior of the house are restored to reflect that time period. In addition to his rented room, exhibits detail Kosciuszko's contributions to the American Revolution, as does a four-minute video. The memorial is open 9:00 A.M. to 5:00 P.M. daily from June through October and Wednesday through Sunday from November through May.

Thaddeus Kosciuszko's valorous exploits also are celebrated at the **Polish American Cultural Center,** as are those of other noted Poles: Queen Jadwiga; Casimir Pulaski, the father of the American cavalry; Nicholas Copernicus, the father of modern astronomy; composers Frederic Chopin and Ignace Paderewski; scientist Marie Curie; novelist Henry Sienkiewicz; religious leader Pope John Paul II, and political leader Lech Walesa. There is also a copy of the portrait *Our Lady of Czestochowa.* Poland's May 3, 1791, constitution is pictured; it was after the drafting of this, the world's second oldest democratic constitution, that Kosciuszko took command of Poland's national army. The center has examples of Polish folk art, and the music of Chopin fills the air. A modest selection of handicrafts is for sale.

Directions: From I-95 southbound (from points north), take Exit 17. Using the right-hand lanes of the exit, follow the signs for Callowhill Street/Independence Hall. At the bottom of the exit ramp, follow 2nd Street straight ahead to Chestnut Street. Continue a half block past Chestnut Street for the Historic Area Parking Garage on the left. It is best to park your car and walk to all the sites in the historic district. Start at the Independence National Historical Park Visitors Center, one block away, at 3rd and Chestnut Streets, where you can pick up an easy-to-follow map of the district and a park schedule. If you are traveling northbound on I-95 (from points south), you also will take Exit 17. Stay in the left lane because you will exit on the left side of I-95. At the exit, stay in the right lane and follow the signs for Independence Hall/Historic Area. Turn left at 6th Street to Chestnut, which will take you through the heart of the historic district to 2nd Street. Turn right on 2nd Street. The entrance to the Historic Area Parking Garage is on the left.

Valley Forge National Historical Park

A family excursion to Valley Forge National Historical Park provides a splendid opportunity to instill a sense of pride in our country's past. The story of the bitter winter that the young Revolutionary army spent here in 1777 and 1778 is a stirring saga of courage, patriotism, honor, and dedication. Exploring this re-created encampment brings alive the victory at **Valley Forge.**

This victory was not won in battle. At Valley Forge, the enemies were starvation, disease, and the uncompromising elements. The road to Valley Forge began in August 1777, when the British under General Howe landed at the upper end of the Chesapeake Bay and headed north toward the patriot capital at Philadelphia. Washington failed to halt the British advance at Brandywine in September, and again at Germantown in October. With winter setting in, the British established themselves in Philadelphia, and the Continental army was forced to seek the cold comfort of Valley Forge, eighteen miles to the west.

To understand what happened during the army's six-month stay at Valley Forge, begin at the visitor center with the audiovisual program. There are four ways you can explore the park. First, from mid-May through Labor Day, you can join a bus tour that departs from the visitor center. The bus's taped narrative makes this a good way to get an in-depth look at the thirty-four-hundred-acre park. You can spend as much time as you like at the various stops because you can always catch the next bus. A fee is charged for these tours. Second, you can rent an audiotape and drive yourself. Third, if you just want an overview, use the park map and drive through on your own, stopping to read the roadside markers at the ten park stops.

Fourth, bring your bicycle and explore the park along the six-mile cycling trail, which starts at the visitor center and passes all the major points of interest. There are shorter footpaths for those who enjoy hiking and many miles of horseback trails. You can enjoy an al fresco meal at any of the park's picnic areas: Varnum's, Wayne's Woods, or Betzwood.

The area near General Varnum's Quarters is the **Grand Parade** grounds, where General von Steuben, formerly of the general staff of Frederick the Great of Prussia, transformed the ragtag Continental army into an effective fighting force. One of the major problems the army faced prior to Valley Forge was the lack of a standard training manual. Although soldiers did have minimal training, it was from a variety of field manuals. Thus, coordinated battle movements were all but impossible to achieve.

Benjamin Franklin sent Baron von Steuben from Paris with his personal recommendation to see if he could be of assistance to the Continental army. Franklin's idea proved to be invaluable; within six months of the Baron's arrival, he had produced a well-trained army. Von Steuben's work was all the more remarkable when seen against the formidable obstacles he overcame: He spoke little English; the men were weary from long marches and unsuccessful campaigns; and they were poorly fed and inadequately clothed and housed. At one point,

The first winter encampment for the entire Revolutionary army was at Valley Forge. Washington was determined to keep the men together despite privations and disease. NATIONAL PARK SERVICE PHOTO BY RICHARD FREAR

four thousand men were listed as unfit for duty. Baron von Steuben labored day and night to overcome these obstacles, and part of the victory at Valley Forge can be attributed to his perseverance and skill.

If you visit during the summer months, you will see authentically clad soldiers demonstrating various aspects of military life at the Muhlenberg Brigade. Visitors should plan to spend some time at the **Isaac Potts House**, used by General Washington as his headquarters. This fieldstone building has been restored to look as it did when Washington was in residence. At the visitor center there is a field tent used by Washington when he first arrived at Valley Forge. He chose to share the rough field conditions his soldiers were experiencing.

In addition to the redoubts, reconstructed fortifications, artillery park, and other officers' quarters, two privately operated sites are located within this park. The first is the **Washington Memorial Chapel**, which tells the story of the founding of our country in thirteen stained-glass windows. During the summer, tours are conducted of the chapel and bell tower. The chapel's carillon was purchased in 1926 with money collected from the original thirteen states. The second site, next to the chapel, is the **Valley Forge Historical Society Museum**, with a fine collection of Revolutionary memorabilia. A nominal admission fee is charged.

Valley Forge is a marvelous spot to visit at any time of year. You might want to plan your first visit for the summer months, when living-history re-enactments bring the camp dramatically to life. But a winter's visit captures the real spirit of Valley Forge. You will appreciate the army's accomplishments more fully on a bitter cold day when there is snow on the ground and a stiff wind blowing across the elevated plain. On President's Day weekend, hundreds of young Boy Scouts camp "under the same circumstances" as the Revolutionary soldiers. Spring is a delight because the park's one thousand pink and white dogwood trees are in bloom, and in the fall the bright foliage adds color. The park is open year-round from 9:00 A.M. to 5:00 P.M., except on Christmas Day.

Headquartered in Valley Forge in a park-like setting near the National Historical Park is **Freedoms Foundation**. The mood is set before you even arrive. A good distance from the entrance, you can see the American flag made especially for the foundation. Its bold red and white stripes extend for sixty feet. Also larger than life is the nine-foot bronze statue of a kneeling George Washington looking out over Valley Forge.

The foundation has an **Independence Garden**, which is designed around bricks and stones from the homes of all fifty-six signers of the Declaration of Independence. Although the homes of twelve signers were burned to the ground, five signers were captured and imprisoned, and nine gave their lives, not one signer defected to the British cause. It seems highly appropriate that the nondenominational chapel nearby is called Faith of Our Fathers Chapel. It has a stained-glass window duplicating the one in the chapel of the Capitol in Washington, D.C.

The exhibits in the Henry Knox Building honor the 3,414 recipients of the nation's highest military decoration, the Medal of Honor. A fifty-two-acre Medal of Honor grove provides a contemplative natural setting.

The Freedoms Foundation at Valley Forge is open by appointment only, and a nominal admission is charged. To make reservations to tour, call (215) 933-8825 or write Freedoms Foundation at Valley Forge, Valley Forge, PA 19481.

Directions: Take I-76, the Pennsylvania Turnpike, to Exit 24, the Valley Forge exit. Take Route 202 south to Route 422 west; then exit onto Route 23 west. The Valley Forge National Historical Park entrance is straight ahead through two traffic signals. The visitor center is the large glass building with flags at the entrance. From the Philadelphia area, take the Schuylkill Expressway, I-76, west to Exit 24, the Valley Forge exit. Take Route 202 south to Route 422 west; then exit on the Route 23 west exit. Follow Route 23 west through the park and through Valley Forge village. Freedoms Foundation is on your right at the top of the hill.

Washington Crossing Historic Park

Washington crossed the Delaware in defeat. His men were beaten in battle, their clothes were in tatters, and their stomachs were empty. Nobody—certainly not the celebrating Hessians—thought Washington's men would recross the ice-clogged river. The Hessian commander, Colonel Rall, was so confident and so disdainful of the ragtag Continental force that he didn't even read an intelligence report about Washington's imminent attack. Rall's arrogance cost him his life and his men the battle.

You can retrace the tumultuous events of December 25, 1776, when you visit **Washington Crossing Historic Park**. At the visitor center and Memorial Building, the best place to start your visit, you'll see a thirty-minute movie on the historic events that occurred here. The Memorial Building has a copy of a huge painting by Emanuel Letuze, *Washington Crossing the Delaware.*

As you discover when you visit the Durham Boat House and see the cargo boats used to transport the twenty-four hundred men who finally made it across the river, the famous painting erred in the depiction of the boat. Although all types of boats were used, it is doubtful that Washington crossed in a boat like the one shown in the painting. Additionally, Washington's standing pose, although typical of the artistic style of the 1840s, is unlikely to have been assumed during the hazardous crossing, complicated by a blinding snowstorm and virtually iced-over water. Finally, it is extremely doubtful that Washington even crossed the river during the evening hours.

Within the park you see the house from which Washington planned his unexpected about-face and the inn where he took Christmas dinner before his heroic attack. The **Thompson Neely House**, whose oldest stone section was constructed in 1702, was used by Washington's staff for conferences. They met in the kitchen, as it was the warmest room in the house. Guides dressed in eighteenth-century garb answer questions about the period furniture and the colonial artifacts on display in the building. Before leaving this section of the park, be sure to visit the gristmill. During the summer months, it is open for guided tours.

Authentically garbed guides escort visitors through McKonkey Ferry Inn, or Old Ferry Inn as it is also called, where Washington ate his Christmas dinner. A novel way to spend Christmas day, is to visit the park for the annual re-enactment of the crossing. On the weekend of George Washington's birthday, hot gingerbread is served at the Thompson Neely House. An annual birthday brunch is held each year with George Washington as a guest!

In the upper section of the park, commanding the hilltop from which sentries once kept watch, is the Bowman's Hill Tower. An extensive renovation program made it possible to reopen the tower, and an elevator now takes visitors to the top. Beneath this frequently photographed tower is the one-hundred-acre wildflower preserve dedicated to the brave Revolutionary soldiers serving under Washington who once camped here.

There are twenty-six trails and habitat areas in **Bowman's Hill Wildflower Preserve**. The best time to visit is April and May, but during the summer months, the field flowers are also colorful. Each season has its own appeal. A self-guiding trail map and a monthly blooming list are available at the Wildflower Preserve headquarters. The garden outside this building displays plants suitable for backyard gardens in this part of the state. Altogether, more than a thousand different kinds of native trees, shrubs, vines, and wildflowers are preserved in the park. There is a pond for flowering aquatic plants and a bog for those requiring a swampy terrain.

Washington Crossing Historic Park is open Monday through Saturday from 9:00 A.M. to 5:00 P.M. On Sunday it opens at noon. There is a nominal admission fee for some of the historic buildings.

Directions: From I-95 north of Philadelphia, take the Yardley Interchange. Signs will direct you north on Route 532 to Route 32. Washington Crossing Historic Park is located on both sides of Route 32.

New Jersey

Morristown National Historical Park

Winters were the real testing ground of the American Revolution, and George Washington's colonial troops spent two bitterly cold winters in Morristown, New Jersey. Visitors today fare much better; a cold weather outing gives the best appreciation of the problems that beset the colonial forces.

Most Americans finish their schooling with only a sketchy idea of the chronology of the American Revolution, and when they think of the winter encampments, they think only of Valley Forge. But in 1776 Washington crossed the Delaware on December 25 and defeated the Hessians. He then went on to beat the British at Princeton prior to leading his tired, cold army to their first winter camp at Morristown, New Jersey, in 1777. It was not until the winter of 1777–78 that they camped at Valley Forge. They spent the winter of 1778–79 at Middlebrook, New Jersey, and returned to Morristown for the winter of 1779–1780.

The best way to begin exploring **Morristown National Historical Park** is to stop at the visitor center, open from 9:00 A.M. to 5:00 P.M., except on Thanksgiving, Christmas, and New Year's Day. Maps of the park and explanatory brochures are available at the center. An eight-minute color film depicts the rigors endured by the Continental soldiers during their winters at Morristown. During their second winter camp (at Morristown), twenty-eight blizzards left the army stranded without supplies and reduced the men to a diet of tree bark, shoe leather, and—for the lucky ones—company dogs. There is a life-size diorama of a soldier's hut with a taped message telling about the men who served in the colonial army and the hardships they faced.

You'll find the **Wick House** near the visitor center. This building was used as headquarters for Gen. Arthur St. Clair and the staff of the Pennsylvania Line. Although certainly not so grand as the nearby Ford Mansion, this house was more substantial than most in the area. The simple, homemade furniture is complimented by the pewterware, called "poor man's silver." You'll see indications of the prosperity enjoyed by Henry Wick. His dining room table is a formal Queen Anne piece, although the chairs are in the "Country Queen Anne" style. In the kitchen herb garden adjacent to the house, vegetables and herbs are grown and carefully identified.

Your next stop should be **Jockey Hollow**, where costumed "soldiers" will answer questions about what it was like to camp at Morristown. There are also periodic musket firings and drills at Jockey Hollow. These events occur daily during July and August, and on weekends during the rest of the year as staffing permits. All officers below the rank of general lived with the men at Jockey Hollow. These officers often found it hard to imbue their men with confidence, and only George Washington's compelling leadership held the army together. He successfully quelled two attempted mutinies during their second winter encampment.

Washington's Headquarters is another pivotal section of the park. Here you can visit both the **Ford Mansion**, where the general stayed during the 1779–80 encampment, and the adjacent museum. The story behind Washington's use of this home for seven months is a testimonial to his concern and personal regard for his officers. When Col. Jacob Ford became sick and died during the 1776 New Jersey campaign, Washington ordered a military funeral with full honors for one of his "official" family. Ford's widow remembered Washington's consideration, and when he returned to Morristown, she invited him to use her home, the finest in all Morristown. Martha joined her husband here and spent most of her time trying to stay warm as she entertained guests and stitched in the upstairs bedroom. Also quartered here was Alexander Hamilton, one of Washington's aides. Perhaps Hamilton did not feel the cold as much as some of the other officers because, as the song goes, he had his "love to keep him warm." A romance grew between Hamilton and Elizabeth Schuyler, the niece of Dr. John Cochran, who was the chief physician and surgeon of the Continental army and a member of Washington's staff. The house where the young lovers met is not part of the park, but it has been restored. It also has an attractive colonial garden. The Schuyler-Hamilton House is at 5 Olyphant Place and serves as the headquarters of the Morristown Chapter of the Daughters of the American Revolution. It is open Tuesday through Sunday from 1:00 to 5:00 P.M. and is closed on major holidays.

But even Alexander Hamilton, along with Washington's other officers, had little time for romance. Washington kept them busy with scheduled staff meetings and conferences. He used the main meal of the day (which was served from 3:00 to 5:00 P.M.) for informal discussions of military matters. The Ford Mansion is open 9:00 A.M. to 5:00 P.M. daily. Costumed interpreters are available to answer questions as you take your self-guided tour of Washington's Headquarters.

At the museum a twenty-minute movie about life at the Ford Mansion during the Revolutionary War is shown on the half-hour. There is also a narrated slide show with more information on the solider's life at Morristown. Displays and dioramas give additional background.

Directions: Take I-95 north to US 1, then go north on I-287. Follow Route 287 to Exit 26B-Bernardsville. Make a right turn at Route 202N (the first stop sign), and then a left at the next stop sign onto Temple Wick Road, which will bring you to the visitor center, the Wick Farm, and the Jockey Hollow encampment. For Washington's Headquarters, you'll follow the park signs around Sugar Loaf Road and up Western Avenue. Then turn right on Route 24, drive around two sides of the green, and go straight to Morris Avenue.

Maryland

Chestertown

Every school child knows the story—the American colonists of Boston were incensed about the high tax England imposed on tea. A tumultuous meeting on December 16, 1773, led to decisive action. Under cover of darkness, 40 to 50 radicals, disguised as Indians, crept aboard three British ships and dumped 342 chests of tea into the Boston harbor.

Few school children, even in Maryland, realize there was a second tea party, more courageous and closer to home. Like their Boston counterparts, the people of **Chestertown** were angered by the tea tax. On May 23, 1774, in broad daylight, the irate townsfolk rowed out to the brigantine *Geddes* and dumped not just tea, but crew members as well, into the Chester River. The Maryland "tea party" is re-enacted each year on the Saturday before Memorial Day. It's part of a day-long festival that includes a parade, historical vignettes, music, crafts, and escorted walking tours.

The May celebration is an ideal time to get acquainted with Chestertown, but some visitors prefer it when the streets are empty and only the ghosts of the past share the old, brick sidewalks. A *Walking Tour of Old Chester Town* brochure, available at the visitor center on Cross Street or in most of the shops along Main Street, provides information on the historic district and the town's lovely Georgian and Federal houses. Many of these houses were built before the Revolution.

Chestertown, when it was one of Maryland's most prosperous ports, was a major stop between Philadelphia and Virginia. Cargo from around the world passed through the **1746 Customs House**, which is one of the largest surviving custom houses built in the thirteen original colonies. It's just one of twenty-eight locations marked on your tour map.

The **Geddes-Piper House**, headquarters of the Kent County Historical Society, at 101 Church Street is open regularly to the public (May to October, on weekends from 1:00 to 4:00 P.M.). The three-and-a-half-story, Philadelphia-style townhouse was the home of William Geddes, the collector of customs for the Port of Chester Town. It was his ship that his neighbors boarded and off-loaded so unceremoniously in 1774. Tea not only contributed to Geddes's livelihood, but also to the decor of his home. His lovely collection of teapots is proudly displayed.

If you find yourself wishing you could see the interior of the town's lovely old houses, plan to return on the third Saturday of September for the annual Candlelight Walking Tour, which is the only time some of these private residences can be toured. One other chance to see a selection of Chestertown's spectacular properties is during the December Historic House Tours. Call (410) 7780416 for additional information. You also can obtain information on the Internet at www.kentcounty.com, or write Kent County Tourism, 100 N. Cross Street, Chestertown, MD 21620.

Try to arrange your day so that you're in Chestertown at tea time (3:00 to 5:00 P.M. daily), and you can partake of a delightful colonial experience at the **White Swan Tavern**, an establishment that George Washington once patronized. It's now a bed and breakfast with five, eighteen-century rooms. For reservations call (410) 778-2300. One of the guest bedrooms was the one-room dwelling of the first owner of the property, John Lovegrove, the "Shoemaker of Chestertown." The property was enlarged by subsequent owners and served as a tavern between 1803 and 1853.

Reflecting turn-of-the-century style is the newly restored **Imperial Hotel**, which was built on High Street in 1903. Its twelve bedrooms and dining room are furnished in Victorian froufrou. For reservations call (410) 778-5000.

Chestertown has fewer shopping options than Annapolis or Ellicott City, but they are worth exploring as you roam along the town's red-brick sidewalks.

Twelve miles south of Chestertown in Rock Hall are two museums of interest. The **Rock Hall Waterman's Museum,** next to Haven Harbour Marina, is open daily without charge from 10:00 A.M. to 5:00 P.M. You'll see exhibits on oystering, crabbing, and fishing. There is a reproduction of a shanty house, like the "shanties" or "arks" the watermen built on a scrow or barge and towed behind their boats to the netting grounds on the Bay. The watermen frequently spent the night in these one-room shanty houses. The museum also has a collection of boats, decoys, and historical photographs.

In Oyster Court, you'll find **The Rock Hall Museum**, with a collection of arrowheads from the Ozini tribe, an indigenous tribe that once inhabited Kent County. The museum also has boat models and ship artifacts, including maps, clocks, lights, and compasses. There is a display of china and agateware, as well as paintings and prints. The museum is open daily.

Directions: From Baltimore, take Route 97 or Route 2 south to Route 50. Head east across the Bay Bridge. When Route 301 splits off Route 50, head north on Route 301. Take the Centreville/Chestertown exit and follow Route 213 north for twenty miles through Centreville and Church Hill to Chestertown. To reach Rock Hall from Chestertown, take Route 291 south and proceed 0.25 mile to Route 20. Turn right and travel twelve miles south on Route 20 to Rock Hall. Haven Harbour Marina is one mile south of the traffic light in Rock Hall, on the right.

Fort Frederick

Once there was a chain of forts protecting Maryland's western frontier; of these, only **Fort Frederick** remains. The frontier settlers wanted to stay out of the conflict between the English on the coast and the French, who were firmly entrenched in Canada. Neither nation was of much concern to the people struggling to carve homesteads out of the wilderness. But the French prompted their Indian allies to attack the homes along the Maryland frontier. In 1756, following General Braddock's defeat by the French at Fort Duquesne, the governor of Maryland insisted that the Maryland Assembly appropriate money to build a fort.

Governor Horatio Sharpe took a personal interest in the North (now Fairview) Mountain fort. After supervising much of the work, he named it Fort Frederick in honor of Maryland's Lord Proprietor, Frederick Calvert, Sixth Lord Baltimore. The flag you'll see flying over the fort shows the Grand Union Jack, indicating the colony's allegiance to England, plus the black and gold colors of the Calvert family.

Fort Frederick was a more formidable fort than was traditionally built along the frontier. Unlike other forts in the chain, it was larger and more durable and it had stockade walls of stone instead of wood or earth.

There is another reason why the fort still stands: It was never attacked. Perhaps the imposing walls deterred assault, even though the fort was important as a supply base for the English during the French and Indian War. In the American Revolution it was reactivated as a prison camp for British and Hessian prisoners and remained unmolested. A small skirmish was fought at Fort Frederick on Christmas Day, 1861, when Union troops held the fort against Confederate raiders.

To fill in the historical details about Fort Frederick, stop first at the visitor center and watch the seventeen-minute movie; it will make the self-guided walking tour more meaningful. The tour map (available at the visitor center) will direct you up the path to the fort. On your right you'll see the garrison garden. Eating salted meat (with occasional fresh game), dry beans, and bread could get monotonous, so the troops garrisoned planted vegetables outside the stone walls to supplement their diet. Food was so scarce during the American Revolution that fort commandant Colonel Rawlings permitted local farmers to hire his British and German prisoners, who were fed in return for their labor.

As you pass through the gateway, you'll see two barracks within the one-and-a-half-acre fort compound. Seasonally, interpreters dressed in uniforms of the French and Indian War period are on hand to answer questions about the fort and about military life from 1756 to 1763. The west barracks' rooms have been furnished to represent enlisted men and noncommissioned officers' quarters of the late 1750s. You're invited to step into the public room and get a feel of eighteenth-century barrack life. Don't try to bounce on the beds though; they're made of bare wooden planks.

Across the parade ground are the east barracks. These two barracks were planned to hold about four hundred enlisted men. The fort was rarely garrisoned up to strength, however, so the rooms were used for other purposes. In the west barracks you'll see a storage room, laundry, and dining area. The second floor has been converted into a museum depicting the history of the fort.

The location of the governor's house, which served as fort headquarters, is now indicated by stone foundations at one end of the parade ground. Also marked are the officers' quarters and a storehouse. Because of lack of sufficient documentation, these structures could not be rebuilt. Much of what restoration could be done was done by the Civilian Conservation Corps during the Depression in the 1930s.

The barracks and visitor center are open May through September. The hours are Monday through Friday from 8:00 A.M. to 4:00 P.M. and from 9:00 A.M. to 5:00 P.M. on Saturday and Sunday. There is a nominal charge. Each May the reactivated Maryland Forces present "The French and Indian Muster," depicting life during the French and Indian War, frontier skills, and ranger tactics. In late July, Military Field Day is held here, when roughly 450 uniformed men represent all three conflicts in which Fort Frederick played a role. In late September there are competitive matches during the Governor's Invitational Firelock Match. The schedule ends with an evening ghost walk on the Friday closest to Halloween.

You can picnic at Fort Frederick, and Captain Wort's Sutler Shop sells snacks, soft drinks, and crafts. Two nature trails provide more diversion if you have a day to spend at Fort Frederick. And there is a primitive family campground on the bank of the Potomac River. You can fish in the Potomac and in the ninety-two-acre Big Pool Lake. Rental boats are available.

Directions: From Baltimore, take I-70 west about eighty miles to Exit 12. Take Route 56 south toward Big Pool. Fort Frederick will be on your right.

Smallwood's Retreat

William Smallwood joined the Continental army as a colonel in January 1776. By October of that year, he was a brigadier general, and by 1780, he was a major general, the highest-ranking Marylander in George Washington's command.

We know little about the private life of this busy public man. He was a bachelor who lived on a five-thousand-acre plantation, part of his parents' holdings. He called his tidewater home Mattawoman Plantation; today it is known as **Smallwood's Retreat**.

Despite the peaceful sound of its name, the plantation served as an active meeting spot for political and military leaders. Smallwood and his neighbors across the river, George Mason of Gunston Hall and George Washington of Mount Vernon, would meet at their respective homes to talk of independence from England.

Smallwood was involved in the Revolutionary struggle from the earliest days. When Washington had to retreat after the Battle of Long Island, Smallwood's troops, the Maryland Line, protected his flanks and saved them all from annihilation. Smallwood was wounded at the Battle of White Plains but did not relinquish his command. It was this brave action that led to his promotion to brigadier general. After keeping the southern wing of the Continental army from disintegration following the bitterly fought Battle of Camden (South Carolina), Smallwood was formally commended for his bravery and promoted to major general.

Smallwood's friendship with Washington did not end when the war ended. Both were members of the Masonic Lodge of Alexandria. Smallwood also was active in the newly formed Protestant Episcopal Church. When Washington came to Southern Maryland, he and Smallwood often attended Old Durham Parish Church, built in 1732. Markers at this church indicate their attendance. The church is off Route 425 and open to visitors.

After the Revolution, Smallwood helped form the Society of the Cincinnati for former Continental army officers. Smallwood also resumed a political career interrupted by the war. He had represented Charles County in the Colonial Assembly during the 1760s and 1770s. In 1785, he was elected governor of Maryland and served three, one-year terms.

This distinguished Marylander is buried on the front lawn of his plantation. When he died, there was no will and the property was divided and sold. The house continued to be occupied for approximately one hundred years after Smallwood's death. It fell on hard times, though, and its last known use was as a storage barn for grain and hay. Only remnants of three walls and the foundation remained when the Smallwood Foundation was established to restore the general's retreat.

The fully rebuilt house is open for free tours, conducted by docents in colonial garb, on weekends and holidays from Memorial Day to Labor Day, noon to 5:00 P.M. Seven rooms have been finished with eighteen-century pieces similar to those Smallwood might have owned. Only three chairs in the dining room were owned by the family, they were made in Annapolis by John Shaw. In the great room a copy of a portrait of William Smallwood in his military uniform is displayed. It is surprising to see how much he resembles George Washington.

One curious feature of the house's design is the warming room, built off the dining room. The servants had to bring all the food through the dining room to the warming room before they started serving the meal. Then, because there was no exit door, they had to stay in the warming room until the meal was finished.

The layout of the downstairs rooms was determined by the debris patterns in the foundation. No such clues were available for the upstairs, so it was designed by conjecture. There is a guest bedroom, a gentleman's large bed chamber, and a dressing room. The tour ends in the restored out kitchen. After your tour be sure to see the herb and vegetable gardens. Throughout the year Smallwood's Retreat hosts special events such as garden parties, candlelight tours, military encampments, and craft demonstrations.

Located on Mattawoman Creek, a tributary of the Potomac River, **General Smallwood State Park** also has delightfully situated, waterside picnic tables. There are boats for rent and guided nature walks and canoe trips for which reservations are needed. For information on guided walks, special events, and canoe reservations call (301)743-7613.

Directions: From Baltimore take I-97 south to Route 301. Continue south on Route 301 to La Plata (eight miles south of Waldorf) and turn right on Route 225. Continue west to the "T" intersection with Route 224 and turn left. Proceed down Route 224 for about six miles to park entrance on the right at Sweden Point Road.

New Jersey

Rockingham

It is one of the ironies of colonial history that George Washington, a man whose greatest love was his Mount Vernon home, should have been forced to spend so many years so far away from his Potomac estate.

Rockingham, just outside Princeton, New Jersey, was the last in a series of military headquarters that Washington established up and down the East Coast. Congress abandoned Philadelphia because their sessions were so frequently interrupted by mutinous soldiers demanding back pay. The 1783 fall session of Congress met at Nassau Hall in Princeton. When General Washington was asked to attend the meetings, accommodations needed to be found for him and Mrs. Washington. Congress rented the Berrien house. The Berriens were fabulously wealthy people at the time. They came out of the Revolutionary War with a substantial amount of holdings still intact.

John Berrien, a New Jersey judge who built the house, came to an untimely end in 1772. After inviting a number of friends to witness the formal signing of his will, he drowned himself in the Millstone River in front of his guests. Surviving him was his wife and six children. The widow put the house up for sale.

Although the home no longer has the original furnishings, period pieces re-create Washington's bedroom and office. Martha Washington was suffering from a fever during her stay here and used the ground floor bedroom. Washington's upstairs office is called the Blue Room. Here he prepared his "Farewell Orders to the Armies of the United States," sending them to West Point to be distributed. The order can be found in the Orderly Book of the day at West Point. The house is open to visitors at no charge.

Directions: Take Washington Beltway Exit 27 (I-95) north past Philadelphia to the Trenton area; proceed north on Route 1. Make a right on Route 522 and head west to Rocky Hill, New Jersey. Once at the town center, proceed straight through Kingston, staying on what has turned into Laurel Avenue, Route 603. At the intersection of Route 603 and Route 518, proceed east on Route 518. Rockingham is up the hill on the left-hand side.

Wallace House

Yet another winter of the Revolutionary War is recaptured at the Wallace House, George Washington's winter headquarters from February until June 3, 1779. The army bivouacked at nearby Camp Middlebrook.

It was another cold winter, though not as cold as the preceding winter Washington had spent at Valley Forge. Martha Washington, who accompanied the general to this New Jersey home, later commented that her strongest impression was of the bitter cold nights spent huddled under quilts and comforters.

Wallace House was not quite complete when Washington rented it for a thousand dollars, but it was the finest house in the area. The other officers who were billeted in the area and even some of the enlisted men were invited to dine at Wallace House so that Washington could get better acquainted with the men serving under him. It was at the Wallace House that Monsieur Girard, the first ambassador from France to the self-proclaimed free colonies, presented himself to Washington.

Washington became good friends with the pastor of the Dutch Reform Church, Jacob Hardenberg, whose parsonage was adjacent to the Wallace House. This old church home, moved across the street from the Wallace House in 1914, was built in 1751 and is also open to the public. Its unique feature is a smokehouse on the third floor, rather than on the ground floor as was common. With hungry armies in town, the third-floor smokehouse proved to be a secure place to preserve meat and keep it from being pilfered.

Both the Wallace House and the **Old Dutch Parsonage** are open Wednesday, Thursday, and Friday from 9:00 A.M. to noon and from 1:00 to 6:00 P.M. On Saturdays they are open from 10:00 A.M. to noon and from 1:00 to 6:00 P.M., and on Sunday, from 1:00 to 6:00 P.M. They are closed Thanksgiving, Christmas, and New Year's Day.

Directions: Take Washington Beltway Exit 27 (I-95) to Route 206 north toward Princeton to Somerville. Both historic buildings are just south of Somerville, New Jersey, off Route 206 on Washington Place.

Virginia

Yorktown Colonial National Historical Park

The rights proclaimed in the Declaration of Independence—life, liberty, and the pursuit of happiness—were grounded in the rights the colonists felt were due them as Englishmen. These rights and privileges were asserted from the beginning; the first permanent settlement at Jamestown had a representative legislative assembly in 1619. At Williamsburg, colonists again heralded the cause of man's natural rights in their 1776 "Declaration of Rights." The final battle to insure these rights took place at Yorktown.

This Yorktown victory is given depth and substance at the National Park Service Visitor Center at the **Yorktown Battlefield**. A museum, with exhibits and a movie, provides an ideal introduction to your battlefield tour.

It was the end of September 1781, the seventh year of the American Revolution, and Cornwallis had moved his British troops into Yorktown following his campaign through Virginia and the southern colonies. Washington responded by moving his men from their New York camp down to Virginia, hoping to arrive before Cornwallis escaped by sea with his army.

Washington's men dug siege lines around the British, who were forced by a French naval blockade to hold their positions. With his army surrounded and his escape cut off, Cornwallis had run out of options. On October 14, two important British redoubts fell. (A painting in the Old Senate Chamber at the Virginia State Capitol captures this dramatic action.) On October 17, a drummer appeared on the British inner-defense line and beat a parley. The guns were silent at last. On October 18, surrender terms were drawn up at the home of Augustine Moore, and the next day, the British army surrendered. It would be another two years before the peace treaty was signed, but the war was, in fact, over.

A popular exhibit at the museum is the reconstruction of the gun deck and captain's cabin from a British frigate of the 1780s. It is similar to the *Charon*, a forty-four-gun frigate the British lost during the Battle of Yorktown. Also on display are German regimental colors surrendered to Washington on October 19, 1781.

Before starting your drive, take the time to view the battlefield from the visitor center observation deck. The seven-mile tour, marked by red arrows, includes six main points of interest: British inner-defense lines, Grand French battery, second Allied Siege Line, Redoubt 9 and 10, the Moore House, and Surrender Field.

An Allied encampment tour extends nine additional miles and is marked with yellow arrows. Its significant stops include: the American Artillery Park, Washington's Headquarters, the French Cemetery, the French Artillery Park, the French Encampment Loop, and an untouched British redoubt.

Yorktown Battlefield at Colonial National Historical Park is open daily, 9:30 A.M. to 5:00 P.M., with seasonally extended hours. An admission is charged.

Directions: From I-95 in the Richmond area, take I-64 east to the Colonial Parkway. Follow the Colonial Parkway to Yorktown.

The American Revolutionary War ended at Yorktown. At the York-
town Victory Center's re-created eighteenth-century farm site, visi-
tors can help with chores, like breaking flax so that it may be
processed into cloth.

Yorktown Victory Center

The Virginia peninsula, a fifteen-mile-wide strip, encompasses the historic triangle of Jamestown, Williamsburg, and Yorktown. On this land the first permanent English settlement was established, the colonial capital of Virginia thrived, and the War for American Independence ended. At the **Yorktown Victory Center** the story of the revolutionary struggle is told, from the beginning of colonial unrest to the formation of a new nation.

The victory at Yorktown was the culmination of a war that had begun more than six years earlier. Events that led to hostility between the colonies and Britain are chronicled along the "Road to Revolution," an open-air exhibit walkway. Sections of a time line, interspersed with quotes and illustrations, connect three themed pavilions that explore the impact of three issues: treaties, taxes, and tea.

At the end of the walkway, the museum exhibition building offers an introductory look at the Declaration of Independence before leading into a series of themed galleries. Attention is paid to three groups—African Americans, Native Americans, and women—to whom the early documents regarding freedom and equality did not apply.

History is not just a record of big events; it includes personal stories of ordinary individuals. Ten individuals provide a unique perspective in the "Witnesses to Revolution" gallery. Making up this group are two African American slaves who support opposing sides in the colonial conflict, a Mohawk chief who wants to keep his people neutral, a loyal British Virginia plantation owner, two Continental army soldiers, a woman captured and adopted by the Seneca Indians just before the outbreak of war, and three civilians who reflect on the homefront. The words you hear are their own, taken from diaries, letters, and other sources. The exhibit also includes graphics, artifacts, and life-size cast figures.

Pivotal events from the issuing of the Declaration of Independence to the significant victory at Yorktown are captured in photomurals along the ramp that connects the first theme gallery with the "Converging on Yorktown" gallery. Yorktown and Gloucestertown were on opposite banks of the York River. Multinational armies, clashing for one of the last times in this epoch struggle, converged on these small communities. One of the center's prized exhibits is a pair of pistols that belonged to Marquis de Lafayette, who was on hand in 1781 to witness the British defeat, which he helped to bring about. Again, "witnesses" from the various countries are represented here—American, British, French, and German. This personal look at the events that occurred in Yorktown is also presented in an eighteen-minute film, *A Time of Revolution*. Individuals in encampments around Yorktown reflect on the struggle.

Yet another gallery tells the story of ships sunk or scuttled in the York River, "Yorktown's Sunken Fleet." A re-creation of the bow portion of the British supply ship *Betsy* is the focal piece of the exhibit. Artifacts from the *Betsy*, the most extensively studied wreck in the area, add another dimension to the exhibit. There is a video on the excavation of the *Betsy* and a detailed scale model.

Outdoors, in re-creations of a Continental army camp and an eighteenth-century farmstead, costumed interpreters re-enact and discuss daily life during and just after the Revolution. The camp has two furnished officers' tents—one for the company commander and one for the regimental surgeon. There are several soldiers' tents and a massive earthen "kitchen," designed to serve a company of soldiers. Activities in the camp include demonstrations of musket and cannon loading and firing, eighteenth-century medical practices, military drills, music, and meal preparation. Visitors are "recruited" into military service or given the opportunity to prepare an herbal remedy.

Originals of many of the reproductions used in the encampment are exhibited in the Mathews Gallery, including uniforms, weapons, musical instruments, medical equipment, personal documents, and belongings.

The farmstead represents a typical small farm in post-Revolutionary Tidewater Virginia. Interpreters at the site engage in domestic activities, such as gardening, food preparation, and processing fibers for cloth, and during cool weather, making candles. During your visit, you may be invited to help out in the field or kitchen.

The Yorktown Victory Center is open daily except Christmas and New Year's Day from 9:00 A.M. to 5:00 P.M. A children's discovery room offers youngsters the opportunity to learn about the Revolutionary era through participatory activities. An adjacent adult resource room is equipped with computer monitors and printed materials. Admission is charged. A combination ticket is available that includes Jamestown Settlement (see selection); both are operated by the Jamestown-Yorktown Foundation. For additional information, you can call their toll-free number (888) 593-4682 or (757) 253-4838. You also can access the center's Web site at www.historyisfun.org.

Directions: From I-95, in the Richmond area, take I-64 east to Exit 247 and turn left onto Route 143. Take Route 143 to the traffic light and turn left onto Route 238. The Victory Center is four miles farther on the right, on Old Route 238.

War of 1812

Sea captains in the British Navy were "lords of all they surveyed," but it was an uneasy sovereignty. One of their responsibilities was to maintain a large enough crew to man their ships. The hard life of a British seaman did not encourage volunteers, so captains resorted to impressing men on streets, in taverns, and on British merchant ships. When even these methods failed to muster sufficient men, they turned to foreign ships—frequently American—and began seizing US seamen for duty in the British navy.

This unpopular practice mocked American sovereignty and was one of the factors that led to the "second war for independence" in 1812. Impressment was not new in 1812; in fact, in 1807, the British had fired on the USS *Chesapeake,* boarded her, and seized four seamen. Reaction ran high, but President Jefferson first tried economic rather than military action. An embargo forbade commerce with both England and France, which also was guilty of ignoring the neutral rights of the United States. The hope was that the loss of trade would force the European countries to respect American sovereignty. Unhappily, its principal effect was to ruin the economy of the New England port cities. There was even talk of secession by the impoverished New Englanders.

To make matters worse, impressment continued. When James Madison was inaugurated as the fourth president in 1809, there was growing popular support for war. The North, West, and South were suffering economic depression in 1811 and 1812 as a result of the curtailment of trade.

The West also was threatened by renewed incitement by the British of the frontier Indians. To the "war hawks" of the West, open conflict with England would provide a chance to rid Canada of the English and end this incessant provocation once and for all. Southerners also had their eyes on expansion—the rich Florida land beckoned.

Conservatives argued that the American navy could not hope to successfully challenge English superiority on the seas. It was ironic that the espoused cause, defense of the maritime rights of the North and East, was not supported in New England. It was the Southern and Western "war hawks" who forced Madison to declare war in June of 1812. There was a real question of whether the new government would be able to finance a war without bankrupting the country.

But it was finally a question of submission to continued humiliation, loss of national status, and taking a minor position in international dealings or fighting for the sovereign rights of the country. The vote in Congress did not achieve a two-thirds majority in either house—the count was seventy-nine to forty-nine in the House and nineteen to thirteen in the Senate in favor of declaring war on England.

Americans anticipated a four-pronged attack on the British in Canada. Though the war was envisioned as a land struggle, most of the significant encounters were to be on lakes or at sea. Military probes into Canada failed miserably, confounding those who felt, as Andrew Jackson did, that this would be a "mere military promenade."

Oliver Hazard Perry built a fleet on Lake Erie and won a stirring victory over the British fleet, forcing the English to abandon Detroit and giving the Americans their first real victory in this war. (Of note; Perry's battle flag from the Lake Erie campaign with the motto "Don't Give Up the Ship" can be seen in Memorial Hall at the US Naval Academy in Annapolis, Maryland.)

Another American victory at Plattsburg on Lake Champlain prevented the British army, now reinforced with troops no longer needed in Europe after the British victory over Napoleon, from advancing southward down the American coast. The British loss was most striking as their force was three times larger than the American contingent.

American victories at Plattsburg and at Fort McHenry, where the British were held at bay and failed to take Baltimore, convinced the British that it would be too costly to continue the struggle. Unfortunately, victory at Baltimore came after the American capital was ignominiously burned by the British following the Battle of Bladensburg.

News of peace did not come soon enough to prevent the war's greatest battle, that of New Orleans, which occurred two weeks after the war was over. It was almost as if this last battle fought between American and British troops replayed the first instances of their conflict with one important difference—the Americans won the battle. Just like the Battle of Bunker Hill in the early days of the American Revolution, the British, under Sir Edward Pakenham, marched in the open while the Americans, under Andrew Jackson, fired from behind a barricade, this time of cotton bales. The results were the same as at Bunker Hill; the British were cut down in rows, suffering terrible losses. After two, hours a third of the British force, some two thousand men, had been killed or wounded; their general was slain, and they were compelled to surrender. Only seven Americans died in the greatest American victory of the War of 1812.

The Treaty of Ghent was signed on Christmas Eve, 1814, and unanimously ratified by the Senate. But it did not even address the issues of the war. Impressment was not mentioned, no land changed hands, the protection of neutral rights at sea was not clarified; it simply restored the peace.

The War of 1812 can still be considered significant because it did establish the United States as a nation with the strength and the will to make her voice heard. Americans had gained confidence at home and respect abroad. American patriotism was enhanced by the stirring words of "The Star-Spangled Banner." Oliver Hazard Perry and Andrew Jackson joined the heroes of the American Revolution to instill pride in the strength of America's fighting force.

Maryland

The 1814 British Invasion Route

In August 1814, the British landed at Benedict, Maryland. They marched on the capital and burned the public buildings. While it is certainly not recommended that their example be followed, their route, at least, can be. It took the British a week on foot to reach Washington, but by car it can be done in less than a day.

The landing of four thousand British soldiers under Gen. Robert Ross on August 19, 1814, at the small seaport town of Benedict in Charles County, Maryland, was one of the easiest landings on a foreign shore in history.

News of this British invasion forty-five miles from Washington was rushed to the White House, then just a grey stucco mansion. The government was confused as to the British objective. Would it be Baltimore or Washington?

Secretary of State James Monroe, unbeknownst to the rest of the government, decided to scout the British position to determine their strength and, if possible, the direction of their attack. Some feel Monroe was meddling and adding to the confusion, hoping for further military glory. Others feel his efforts were of considerable assistance to General Winder. He did bring news indicating his strong opinion that the British were heading for Washington.

After resting at Benedict, the English land force, escorted along the Patuxent River by a small fleet under Admiral Sir George Cockburn, headed toward the port village of Nottingham. (For auto route, take Route 231 from Benedict; then north on Route 381; right on Route 382 and right again on Tanyard Road to the village of Nottingham.)

The strong British fleet bottled up a flotilla under Commodore Joshua Barney, whose ships had been forced to remain inactive in the Patuxent River during the summer of 1814. Barney had made his headquarters at Nottingham, but now with Admiral Cockburn sailing up the river, he had no choice—Barney had to salvage the guns and burn and scuttle his ships in the headwaters of the Patuxent River. Commodore Barney and his men set off for Washington to join forces with General Winder, contributing to the guns and ammunition.

By August 22, the British were in Upper Marlboro. (For auto tour, return to Route 382; join Route 301; and proceed north to Upper Marlboro.) General Ross, joined by Admiral Cockburn, made his headquarters at the home of the town's leading citizen, Dr. William Beane, who was taken hostage when the British retraced their route back to Benedict. His seizure by the British would prompt his good friend Francis Scott Key to try and negotiate with the British outside Baltimore, thus placing Key on a ship to witness the attack on Fort McHenry. This experience so moved Key that he wrote the words that have become our national anthem.

The Americans attempted to engage the British in battle while they were in Upper Marlboro, but inadequate intelligence foiled their efforts. The next day's march on August 23 took the British force to Melwood (located on Route 4 at Woodyard Road; the Americans were camped in what is now Forrestville, farther down Route 4). The Americans believed they might face a night attack and retreated back to the capital, burning the bridges leading across the Anacostia River to Washington.

The British headed for Bladensburg, which was considered the best place to ford the river. Marching up what is now Kenilworth Avenue in the intense August heat, they arrived in the Bladensburg area at noon on August 24, 1814. After an all-too-brief rest, the battle commenced.

The American force under General Winder was not a regular army, nor had it received military training as a group. The men had no uniforms and no standard equipment. General Winder did not even have a staff. The result was absolute confusion. In fact, while President Madison was inspecting the troops, trying to offer the men encouragement, he narrowly escaped walking into the main body of the British force. Madison left the battlefield and returned to Washington, where frantic residents were evacuating the city. Dolly Madison had collected many of the treasures of this fledgling country—the Declaration of Independence, Washington's portrait and other important documents. Then, the Madisons also left the capital.

The Battle of Bladensburg was quickly over; the British routing the American force. Only Commodore Barney stood firm with his men. The troops under Winder ran when the British fired their new Congreve rockets, which made a frightful noise and looked like flaming fireworks.

Having made quick work of the opposition, the British continued on to the capital. The British arrived so soon after the Americans had fled that the officers were able to enjoy the hot meal prepared by the White House staff for the Madisons and forty invited guests. Not ideal guests themselves, the British not only ate and ran, but burned the house as they left. Most of the government buildings were destroyed as well as some private homes. It should be pointed out that the Americans had burned the British city of York in Canada earlier in the war.

The next day, after a violent tornado struck the city, the British began their return trip to Benedict and their ships. (They returned on what is now Route 202, the most direct route.)

In all, the British force was on American soil for twelve days; they were victorious, and the Americans were humiliated by their poor showing and the burning of their capital. But the forces of war would turn soon at Fort McHenry, when the British tried to take Baltimore.

Fort McHenry National Monument and Historic Shrine

The play of history is often sensed best in the places where our forebears lived and fought. At **Fort McHenry** the cannons and walls stand in silence, but once they spoke out in defense of liberty. The sight of the thirty foot- by forty-two-foot American flag triumphantly waving over the fort inspired Francis Scott Key to write "The Star-Spangled Banner," our national anthem. The September 13, 1814, battle was a turning point in the War of 1812 and led to the cessation of hostilities with Great Britain five months later.

Lieutenant Clagett and the thousand other soldiers and sailors manning Fort McHenry that September night had the job of defending the fort and saving Baltimore from the fiery fate suffered by Washington, when the British captured that city. Rain made it difficult for the British to keep their powder dry, but the Americans had a greater problem—their guns could not reach the British ships. The British were in range to bombard the fort with their guns and the new Congreve rocket; they fired between fifteen hundred and eighteen bombs, rockets, and shells. It is amazing that the heavy barrage resulted in only four deaths and twenty-four men wounded. Despite the strength of their firing position, the British could not subdue the fort, and thus the attack on Baltimore failed.

The gallant defense of the fort is captured in a sixteen-minute film that is shown at the Fort McHenry Visitor Center. The film packs an emotional wallop—don't miss it!

You'll get more out of your walk around the fort if you see the film. The present fort is not the first to stand on this pivotal ground guarding the approach to Baltimore. Fort Whetstone protected the city during the American Revolution. The star-shaped fort you'll explore was built between 1798 and 1803. The design was chosen to make surprise attacks impossible, each point of the star being visible from the points on either side.

As you explore the star fort, you'll notice along the base of the walls the remains of the dry moat that once encircled it. The fort is entered through an arched doorway, or sally port, which is flanked by bombproof underground rooms built immediately following the bombardment. Across from the sally port is a ravelin, consisting of angled embankments used to protect the sally port from enemy attack. Guardhouses, barracks, and junior commanding officers' quarters have been re-created. This fort was used not only during the War of 1812, but also during the Civil War, World War I, and World War II.

On the weekends during the summer months, members of the Fort McHenry Guard, in replica US uniforms of 1812, perform drills and military demonstrations in the fort. Make sure you check out the electric map, which illustrates the troop movements during the Battle of Baltimore. Fort McHenry is open daily at a nominal charge from 8:00 A.M. to 5:00 P.M. In the summer it is open until 8:00 P.M. It is closed Christmas and New Year's Day. From mid-June through Labor Day, ranger-guided activities are offered daily. Check the directory board behind the information desk in the visitor center for the schedule. On some Sundays in June, July, and August at 6:30 P.M., military tattoos (programs of music and drill) are performed. Each September, a Defenders' Day program celebrates the anniversary of the Battle of Baltimore with a mock bombardment, military drills, music, and fireworks. For details of this and other special events, you can call (410) 962-4290 or check the Web site at www.nps.gov/fomc.

Those who want a different perspective of Fort McHenry should take one of the several excursion boats that provide narrated tours to

US Marine Corps units perform at the Fort McHenry Tattoo Ceremony. The fort flies a replica of the flag that inspired the "Star-Spangled Banner." NATIONAL PARK SERVICE PHOTO BY RICHARD FREAR

the fort from the Inner Harbor. These boat tours give you the chance to see the fort from the vantage point of the British ships anchored off Baltimore. Boat tours and water taxis are offered in the spring, summer, and fall.

Directions: From Baltimore's Inner Harbor area, go south on Light Street. Proceed past the Light Street Pavilion and the Maryland Science Center, and turn left on Key Highway. Take Key Highway for one mile then turn right on Lawrence Street. Take Lawrence Street to Fort Avenue and turn left and proceed to Fort McHenry National Monument. From I-95, take Exit 55, Key Highway, and follow Fort McHenry blue/green directional signs on Key Highway to Lawrence Street. Turn left on Lawrence Street and then left on Fort Avenue. Proceed one mile to the fort.

Fort Washington

In 1794, George Washington selected this bluff overlooking the Potomac River as the site of the first fort to be built to protect the country's new capital. Fort Warburton, as it was originally called, was destroyed only five years after its completion, during the War of 1812. Ten years later, its replacement, the present Fort Washington, began a much longer life as capital defender and military post.

Fort Washington (its name was changed by 1810) was destroyed without firing any shots at the British. So how did it meet its fate? Some reports suggest that this question is what the army asked fort commander Capt. Samuel Dyson before he was stripped of his commission. Dyson's verbal orders were to destroy the fort if it came under land attack from British troops during the War of 1812. The United States government did not want Fort Washington to fall into enemy hands. But it was from the Potomac River that the threat was posed on August 27, 1814. A British fleet of seven ships under Captain Gordon had with great difficulty—the ships ran aground twenty-two times—made its way up the Potomac. Positioned off the fort, the ships opened fire. Dyson and his men were under fire for two hours before he destroyed all of the equipment and spiked the cannons. As he and his men were leaving the fort, they laid a powder trail and blew up almost three thousand pounds of black powder to prevent the British from seizing it.

The British threat prompted quick action, and barely twelve days after the fort was destroyed, Secretary of War James Monroe commissioned Maj. Pierre L'Enfant, architect of the nation's capital, to rebuild it. The French engineer ordered two hundred thousand bricks and a large quantity of stone and lumber. But work proceeded slowly; so slowly that after the Treaty of Ghent, which ended the war, was signed on February 13, 1815, the need for defense was tempered by the desire for economy.

L'Enfant was insulted when requested to submit reports on the work in progress and his plans for the fort's construction. He simply ignored the request. Work was then halted, and he was dismissed. On September 6, 1815, Lt. Col. Walker K. Armistead took over. When the new Fort Washington was finally completed on October 2, 1824, the total cost was more than $426,000.

Little has changed since 1824, as you will see when you cross the drawbridge over the dry moat and enter the walled fort. From the sally port entrance, there is a panoramic view of the construction design, which incorporates three levels of defensive positions. The lowest level is the V-shaped water battery, positioned sixty feet below the main fortifications. This battery was started under L'Enfant's direction. Next are the casemate positions, bombproof gun sites from which defending soldiers could fire upon ships on the Potomac. From the high ramparts two half bastions commanded the river above and below the fort.

Uniformed guides will explain the advantages and disadvantages of these three-gun positions. On Sunday afternoons costumed volunteers re-create military life of the mid-1800s. On selected occasions a cannon is fired on the parade ground. To obtain more background on the fort, stop at the visitor center, located in the historic Commanding Officer's House.

A different perspective is gained by touring Fort Washington during the Torchlight Tattoo ceremonies, which are presented several times each summer on Saturday evenings (call 301-7634600 for schedule and information). You'll be briefed before the ceremony begins; then the clock is turned back to the tense Civil War days. You will be treated as visiting Washingtonians, anxious about southern attacks on the capital. Fort Washington, manned by only forty marines in January 1861, was the sole fort protecting the city. By February units of the regular army and militia took over. When Fort Foote was built on the Maryland side of the Potomac in 1864, the military significance of Fort Washington was eliminated. The masonry fort was closed in 1872, but the reservation remained an active artillery post until 1945.

Fort Washington is open daily, year-round, from 9:00 A.M. to 5:00 P.M. Picnicking is encouraged. Tours are given on weekends at 2:00 and 3:00 P.M. and on weekdays by request. There is a nominal entrance free—either per vehicle or for walk-ins.

Directions: From Baltimore, take I-95 south to the Washington Beltway and proceed south (still on I-95) to Exit 3A (Route 210, Indian Head Highway). Take Indian Head Highway south for four miles to Fort Washington Road. Turn right and go three miles to the fort.

Star-Spangled Banner Flag House

Oh, say can you see by the dawn's early light,
What so proudly we hailed at the twilight's last gleaming?
Whose broad stripes and bright stars, thro' the perilous fight
O'er the ramparts we watched were so gallantly streaming?
And the rockets' red glare, the bombs bursting in air,
Gave proof thro' the night that our flag was still there.
Oh, say does that star-spangled banner yet wave
O'er the land of the free and the home of the brave?

The flag that inspired Francis Scott Key to write the national anthem was made in this Baltimore row house by Mary Pickersgill, at the request of Major Armistead, Commandant of Fort McHenry.

On September 14, 1814, Francis Scott Key wrote these stirring words that became the first stanza of our national anthem. Key was trying to negotiate the release of his friend, Dr. William Beanes, who was taken hostage after the British burned Washington during the War of 1812. From his position aboard an American truce ship anchored outside Baltimore's harbor, Key witnessed the British attack on Fort McHenry, and he anxiously awaited the coming of dawn to see if the flag still flew and the fort still held.

The flag he searched for had been designed with visibility very much in mind. Major Armistead, commandant of Fort McHenry, had wanted a giant flag so big "that the British will have no difficulty in seeing it from a distance." He commissioned Mary Pickersgill to fashion the oversize flag. Mary, with some help from her teenage daughter and niece, worked for ten hours a day for six weeks to make the thirty foot-by forty-two-foot flag. It was the largest battle flag ever designed and weighed eighty pounds. Eleven men were needed to raise it.

Mary Pickersgill, a young widow, had moved from Philadelphia in 1807 to this row house at 844 East Pratt Street with her seven-year-old daughter, Caroline, and her mother, Rebecca Young, also widowed. Mrs. Young had worked as a flag and banner maker in Philadelphia and had made the first flag of the Revolution at the request of George Washington. That flag, the Grand Union or Continental Colors, was raised by General Washington on January 1, 1776, at Cambridge, Massachusetts.

The furnishings in Mary Pickersgill's home are from the Federal period, popular when she lived here. In the parlor there is a Charles Willson Peale portrait of Mary's uncle, Colonel Flower, who was George Washington's commissary general. Mary Pickersgill made the flag on the first floor of her house. The material for the flag was four hundred yards of English wool bunting. It was Mary's military connections and her mother's reputation as a flag maker that prompted Major Armistead to choose her to make the Fort McHenry flag.

Visitors enter the **Star-Spangled Banner Flag House** by way of a small building, which is both a gift shop and a small 1812 War Military Museum. A short audiovisual program serves as a background for understanding the War of 1812 and the part played by Mrs. Pickersgill's flag—a symbol of defiance to the British and a source of inspiration for Francis Scott Key. Guided tours of the house are given after the program.

Mary Pickersgill's tattered flag is displayed at the Smithsonian Institution's National Museum of American History in Washington. A replica, made by hand in 1964, is on display at the Flag House.

Another replica may be seen at Fort McHenry (see selection). Mrs. Pickersgill's receipt for the flag is owned by the Flag House; a photostatic copy is on display. She received $405.90.

The Star-Spangled Banner Flag House and 1812 War Military Museum are open Tuesday through Saturday from 10:00 A.M. to 4:00 P.M. A nominal admission is charged.

Directions: Take Pratt Street east past the Inner Harbor to the 800 block. The Star-Spangled Banner Flag House is on the left at the corner of Pratt and Albemarle streets. Free parking is available on Albemarle Street.

US Frigate *Constellation*

Britannia indeed ruled the waves during the War of 1812. When the newly established United States Navy challenged her sea, it was akin to David attacking Goliath. England had some 400 large warships, 350 of which were outfitted with 50 or more cannons. She also had smaller brigs, sloops, schooners, and cutters. Against this, the United States had three forty-four-gun frigates, the *Constitution,* the *President,* and the *United States,* and four frigates with between thirty-two and thirty-eight guns.

The *Constellation* was a seasoned veteran by the time the young country became involved in the War of 1812. She had the distinction of being the first US Navy ship to engage and defeat a man-of-war from Europe. In 1799, the *Constellation,* reacting to attacks on American ships by French privateers and men-of-war, triumphed over the French frigate *L'Insurgente* off Nevis in the Caribbean. She also had engaged the Barbary pirates (and would continue to do so after the war). Unfortunately, she was unable to contribute during the War of 1812 because the "Yankee Race Horse," as she was called, was penned up in Hampton Roads, Virginia, for the duration of the conflict by a seven-ship British fleet under Admiral George Cockburn.

The *Constellation* was to achieve other distinctions. It was aboard this ship that the US Navy signal book was written by the ship's first captain, Thomas Truxtun. The signals and regulations he wrote still serve as basic operating guides. Later in the *Constellation's* service, while circumnavigating the globe in 1842, she became the first US man-of-war to enter China's inland waters.

The *Constellation* is one of the only surviving American warships that saw action in the Civil War. Recognizing the *Constellation's* historic significance, President Franklin Roosevelt ordered her back to active duty during World War II as the flagship of the US Atlantic Fleet. She was the only sailing ship to hold this honor. Fleet Admiral Chester Nimitz called the *Constellation* "perhaps the most important link that the United States Navy and the American people have with our early historic efforts to preserve our liberty."

The *Constellation's* long career means that she has the longest record of service of any U.S. warship. She is also the oldest ship in the world that has been continuously afloat. Purists may argue that the extensive rebuilding undermines this distinction, but most Americans are grateful that this historic link with our past has been saved.

The *Constellation* has been undergoing significant restoration efforts. Admission is charged.

Directions: The USF *Constellation* is docked at the Baltimore Inner Harbor.

District of Columbia

Octagon House

It was George Washington who persuaded fellow Virginia planter, Col. John Tayloe III, to build a town house in the new capital city. When city planner Pierre L'Enfant was laying out lots, Tayloe picked a challenging, triangular-shaped lot within two blocks of the White House. To build on this lot, he commissioned Dr. William Thornton, first architect of the US Capitol, who designed a unique, six-sided house containing round and triangular rooms and curved doors. How did a six-sided house come to be called the **Octagon House?** In the eighteenth century, round rooms such as the entrance hall and upstairs parlor were often constructed with eight angled walls plastered smooth and were called "octagon salons."

The Octagon became the nation's temporary White House when President James Madison and his wife, Dolly, returned to Washington after the British burned the executive mansion during the War of 1812. The Madisons lived at the Octagon House from September 1814 until March 1815, while Benjamin Henry Latrobe oversaw the repairs of the White House.

In his circular office on the second floor, Madison signed the Treaty of Ghent on February 17, 1815, ending the War of 1812. The Treaty Room still holds the table where Madison signed this historic document.

A wide, oval staircase leads to the second and third floors. The staircase is the architectural centerpiece of the house, which figures prominently in a ghostly tale told about the Octagon's first owners. According to the story, Colonel Tayloe had an argument with one of his daughters over a suitor. During their heated exchange, she fell over the stair railing to her death (a few versions hint she was pushed). Since then, some claim to hear her crying on the stairs.

The Octagon House is now the headquarters for the American Architectural Foundation. The house contains handsome Federal furnishings that belonged to the Tayloe family. It is also worth visiting for its architectural interest and the decorative interior design work, including the original Italian marble floor and ceiling molding in the entrance hall. The house is open Tuesday through Sunday 10:00 A.M. to 4:00 P.M. For more information, you can call (202) 638-3105.

Directions: The Octagon House is located in Washington, D.C., at 1799 New York Avenue, N.W., at 18th Street.

Delaware

Zwaanendael Museum

It sounds like a mythical kingdom—the land of the whale, the swan, and the unicorn—but this symbolic trinity figured prominently in the tales of the founding of Lewes (pronounced Loo-is), Delaware.

Henry Hudson discovered the Delaware Bay in 1609, but the first Dutch settlers didn't arrive until 1631. They sailed on their ship *De Walvis* (the whale) into the quiet inlet where the Delaware Bay meets the Atlantic Ocean. Because the marshy region was abundantly populated by wild swans, the thirty-three newcomers called their settlement Zwaanendael, the valley of the swans.

The figurehead on their ship was not, as you might expect, a whale, but a unicorn, part of the heraldic coat of arms of Hoorn, their hometown in Holland. The curious Delaware Indians were fascinated by this single-horned beast and wanted the Dutch to give them the large wooden talisman. When the Native Americans were denied it, they burned the stockade and massacred the settlers.

To see a model of the early settlement, visit the **Zwaanendael Museum**. Despite their inauspicious beginning, this was not the end of Dutch efforts to establish an outpost in the area. Their second settlement suffered the same fate as the first, but from a new foe. On Christmas Eve 1673 the second enclave was burned by Calvert supporters from the neighboring Maryland colony who did not want the

Dutch infringing on their territory. By 1682, the English had wrested control of the area and renamed the settlement Lewes.

Later, on two occasions, pirates attacked the town, and ultimately on April 6 and 7, 1813, during the War of 1812, the townspeople had to defend themselves against the British. This tumultuous history is covered in the museum.

The museum's collection includes a wide variety of domestic articles, handmade coverlets, quilts, and samplers, which speak for the skills of yesteryear. China and silverware indicate changing tastes. There are also a few pieces of seventeenth-century pewter.

Another display is devoted to antique toys. An 1860s stagecoach is driven by a team of miniature horses. A later form of transportation is the 1922 Toonerville Trolley, complete with driver. There are also dolls, dishes, puzzles, cradles, and carriages.

The medicinal display has a number of interesting features. Do you know the derivation of sugarcoating? You'll find out when you read about the pill roller, which was recovered from a drug store in Milton, Delaware. The paste, or main component of the pill, was placed on an iron cutter and sliced to size. Then the segments were put in a round box with sugar and shaken until they were properly shaped and coated.

The museum, built in 1931 to commemorate the 1631 settlement, replicates the Town Hall in Hoorn, Holland. The brick building, with its colorful blue trim and red and white shutters, has a statue of founder David Pietersen de Vries atop its peaked facade.

The Zwaanendael Museum, at Savannah Road and King's Highway, is one of twenty-three points of interest on the town's walking tour. A Lewes guide can be picked up at the Lewes Chamber of Commerce office in the Fisher-Martin House at 102 Kings Highway. Pick up penny candy at the old store, then check out the gift shop in a former blacksmith shop. You'll be able to tour a one-room plank house, furnished as it would have been by settlers in the 1700s. The straw-filled mattresses in the sleeping loft and crude wooden kitchen furniture bespeak a Spartan existence.

In contrast, the eighteenth-century Burton-Ingram House represents a much more elegant lifestyle. Lovely Chippendale and Empire furnishings from old Lewes families fill the rooms. The lower level of the house was constructed using ballast from the cargo holds of one of the first ships to dock at Lewes.

Also in the complex are the Hiram Burton House, which was furnished by a local antique dealer, and the Rabbit's Ferry House, now used as an artist studio This ferry house was built using a technique called brick-nogging. Bricks were laid between wooden beams and then whitewashed. Lastly, an 1850s doctor's office is outfitted with old medical equipment.

The walking tour includes many more historic structures, including the Maull House, where in 1803 Jerome Bonaparte, the brother of Napoleon, reputedly brought his wife when stormy seas forced them ashore. Legend has it that Betsy Bonaparte would not take her seat at an elaborate dinner until the silver candlesticks from the ship were brought to the table.

A house that survived a barrage during the War of 1812 is known today as the Cannonball House and Marine Museum. The exterior still has a cannonball embedded in the wall, and inside you'll see nautical exhibits. Opposite the town post office is the 1812 Memorial Park, where a defense battery stood. You'll see four large guns and a smaller one, which were supposedly seized from a pirate ship. On the lower terrace of the park is a World War I naval gun.

The Zwaanendael Museum is open on a limited basis; call (302) 645-1148 for current hours. For information on the Lewes Historic Society Complex, call (302) 645-7670, or you can call the Lewes Chamber of Commerce to inquire about both sites, (302) 645-8073.

Directions: Take the Beltway I-495/95 to Route 50 exit and proceed east on Route 50 across the Bay Bridge. At Route 404 turn right and continue east past Bridgeville to the merge with Route 18 to Georgetown. At Georgetown continue east on Route 9 into Lewes.

Era between the Wars

Presidential Homes

America has no royal family, no castles that have stood since the Middle Ages. The great diversity in the homes of the men we have chosen to hold the highest office in the country testifies to the opportunity for even the poorest to reach great heights.

In fact, it was sometimes incumbent on would-be office seekers to rusticize their origins. When William Henry Harrison campaigned for the presidency, he depicted his birthplace as a log cabin—a far cry from the gracious splendor of his ancestral plantation, Berkeley.

But the homes of the American Presidents do reflect the diverse backgrounds of our nation's leaders. Our presidents have been farmers, lawyers, tavern keepers, scholars, businessmen, and soldiers. Their homes provide an insight into the private side of these public figures.

Patterns do emerge; of the first ten presidents, six were of the Virginia landed aristocracy. Their homes were elegant plantations, reflecting taste, intelligence, and a mastery of vast domains. Some of these homes are represented in earlier sections—Mount Vernon, Monticello, and Berkeley.

No section on presidential homes would be complete without including the one home they all, with the exception of George Washington, shared in common—the White House.

The White House

The most famous home in America is the focal point of government; the president not only lives there, he works there. The history and traditions of our democracy are reflected in the home of our presidents. The White House also is a mark of the special nature of the American government: It is the only residence of a chief of state in the world that is open regularly to the public without charge.

In 1790 George Washington signed a measure to create a "Federal City" on the Potomac. However, he would not live to see John and Abigail Adams move into the President's home on November 1, 1800. Mrs. Adams felt the house needed a good deal of work just to make it livable. Even though she was a veteran of New England winters, she was accustomed to a snugger environment; the Adams's called this house their "chilly castle." They lived there for only four months before Thomas Jefferson replaced Adams.

Jefferson was certainly the right man at the right time. He was never happier than when remodeling. His own plantation, Monticello, was always being altered as he conceived new innovations. The job of running the country did not allow Jefferson to give full rein to his enthusiasm, so he hired a professional architect, Benjamin Henry Latrobe. An architect was certainly needed as the White House roof had been so poorly constructed that the Washington rains caused the East Room ceiling to collapse. But gradually, the house took shape.

Though Jefferson devoted time to the building's interior, being a widower, he did not provide a woman's touch. When Dolly Madison moved in after the inauguration of 1809, she immediately began redecorating. Barely a year after she had the house decorated to her taste, the British inconsiderately burned it to the ground during the War of 1812.

James Monroe was president when the house was again livable in 1817. The Monroe furnishings were purchased by the US government in 1817. They were in the French Empire style.

Each successive administration has added something to and made changes in the White House as a result not only of taste and personal preference, but also of the incredible wear and tear caused by the endless procession of guests and visitors that seem to perpetually populate the house.

It wasn't until Theodore Roosevelt's administration in 1902 that funds were appropriated to build executive offices and provide some separation between the president's living and working quarters. Work to expand the office space of the executive mansion continued on and off through 1934.

But problems with the house continued. Chandeliers trembled, upper floors sagged and swayed, and plaster peeled and flaked away. In 1948, an architectural study indicated evidence of instability—the White House gave signs of collapsing. The Trumans moved across the street to Blair House and work began again on the house. Some people even suggested total demolition, beginning again with granite or marble. But the desecration of what many considered a national monument was forestalled. Extensive rebuilding was necessary, requiring twenty-seven months to reinforce and rebuild the White House. The Trumans moved back in on March 27, 1952.

No perspective on presidential homes would be complete without visiting the country's "first house." The White House is open Tuesday through Saturday from 10:00 A.M. to noon. During the summer, it stays open until 12:30 P.M. Though there is no charge, due to larger summer crowds advance tickets are required and must be picked up on the Mall in person the day of the tour.

One spring and fall weekend each year, the White House gardens are open for free tours; call the White House Visitor Center for information at (202) 208-1631. Just as Jefferson concerned himself with the architectural details of the house, he also contributed to the landscaping of the White House grounds, adding sloping mounds south of the mansion for greater privacy. From John Quincy Adams on, the presidents and their families have planted one or more trees in the eighteen-acre **President's Park**. The tradition began when Adams planted an American elm on the south grounds. He also employed a full-time gardener and took a great interest in the White House landscape, setting out many of the plants himself.

And so the presidents and their families each began to contribute something to the grounds. Now when you walk through President's Park, you can see these tangible links with our country's past.

Some presidents made other contributions to landscaping. In 1867, Andrew Johnson, the seventeenth president, added a fountain to the south side of the White House grounds, and his successor, Ulysses S. Grant, added one to the north side in 1873.

As twentieth-century development encroached on the White House, additional plantings were added to preserve the natural setting of the mansion and shield it from the city. A grove of trees, primarily elm, extends from Pennsylvania Avenue along the north side of the house.

Of the three specific garden areas that comprise President's Park, the Rose Garden is the best known. The design that you see today was done in 1962 by Mrs. Paul Mellon at President Kennedy's request. But some of the roses date back to 1913, when the first Mrs.

Wilson planted them. The Rose Garden was redesigned to provide space for entertaining large groups. The new design was anything but contemporary, being laid out like an eighteenth-century American garden.

The Rose Garden is used by the president for ceremonial occasions. French doors lead from the Oval Office into the garden. Foreign dignitaries are often greeted in the garden before entering the office for a working session. In 1976, an elegant state dinner for Queen Elizabeth II was held there alfresco. The 1971 wedding of Tricia Nixon to Edward Cox was celebrated in this garden.

On the east side of the mansion, a second garden, the Jacqueline Kennedy Garden, is used by the first lady to receive guests. This intimate, more miniature, garden is shaded and delineated by a row of lindens. Finally, there is the Children's Garden, added to the grounds by the Lyndon B. Johnson family. Children can enjoy historic President's Park every Easter Monday at the children's Easter Egg Roll, the only occasion other than the spring and fall weekend tours that the White House grounds are open to the public. You can call the White House Visitor Center for information on tours at (202) 208-1631.

Directions: The White House is located at 1600 Pennsylvania Avenue, N.W., Washington, D.C.

Virginia

Ash Lawn–Highland

Improbable but true, three of America's first five presidents died on July 4: Thomas Jefferson and John Adams on the very same day in 1826 and James Monroe in 1831. After fifty years of public service, Monroe had hoped to retire to Highland (now called **Ash Lawn–Highland**), his rural Virginia home. His long years of government work, however, had so impoverished him that he was forced to sell Highland in 1826. The loss was undoubtedly easier to bear than Jefferson's death that same year.

Monroe built Highland at Jefferson's urging. The sage of Monticello wanted to create "a society to our taste." He envisioned surrounding himself with a coterie of interesting and stimulating friends. The young James Monroe, who had studied law with Jefferson after the American Revolution, was happy to oblige his mentor.

In 1793, Monroe spent a thousand dollars for a thousand acres adjoining Monticello. Before he could begin building, President

Washington, another Virginian with whom Monroe had close ties, having served under him at Valley Forge, appointed Monroe minister to France. In the entrance hall of Ash Lawn–Highland is a copy of the Leutze painting, *Washington Crossing the Delaware*, which portrays Monroe holding the flag behind his commander.

Not wanting the house project to languish while Monroe was out of the country, Jefferson enlisted the help of James Madison, and the two of them, with Monroe's uncle, Joseph Jones, began the planning of Monroe's house. Jefferson also sent his gardener over to begin landscaping the grounds. Monroe dubbed his home a "cabin-castle" because, though the exterior was simple, the interior was furnished with Neoclassical French Empire pieces that the Monroes acquired abroad. On your tour of the house, you'll see a portrait of their daughter Eliza's life-long friend, Hortense de Beauharnais, daughter of the Empress Josephine, who became Queen of Holland and the mother of Napoleon III. There is also a portrait of the headmistress of the French school attended by Eliza and Hortense. In the drawing room you'll see a marble bust of Napoleon Bonaparte, a gift to Monroe. The study has a copy of the Louis XVI desk used by Monroe when he was president.

Monroe, like his friend George Washington, was taller than average. The highpost bed was big enough to accommodate his six-foot frame. Although it is the only Monroe piece in the master bed chamber, the rest of the furnishings are from Monroe's time. You'll learn that the wooden working parts of the case clock were greased with fat, which attracted mice and may have provided the inspiration for the popular nursery rhyme, "Hickory Dickory Dock."

Ash Lawn–Highland is operated today by James Monroe's alma mater, the College of William and Mary. Thomas Jefferson and John Tyler were also alumni. The college maintains the 535-acre estate as a nineteenth-century working plantation. A dozen peacocks strut in the boxwood garden, and an abundance of nature can be enjoyed year-round. Spring and summer bring flowers and herbs, as well as the Ash Lawn–Highland Summer Festival, two months of opera, musical theater, and family entertainment. Vegetables are harvested in the fall, and in winter, Christmas trees can be cut at Ash Lawn–Highland. Traditional farm crafts are demonstrated throughout the year.

Ash Lawn–Highland is open March through October from 9:00 A.M. to 6:00 P.M. From November through February, hours are 10:00 A.M. to 5:00 P.M. It is closed on Thanksgiving, Christmas, and New Year's Day. Admission is charged.

Directions: From I-95 in the Richmond area, take I-64 west to Charlottesville; then use Exit 121. Follow signs to the Charlottesville/Albemarle County visitor center and continue past that, then turn left on Route 53. Pass Monticello, and make a right turn on Route 795, the James Monroe Parkway, for Ash Lawn–Highland.

The Monroe Presidential Center

In the famous painting *Washington Crossing the Delaware*, James Monroe is depicted as the young man behind George Washington holding the flag. Monroe did not stay in the background for long. (He wasn't actually in the background on that icy crossing. Still a very young lieutenant, Monroe wasn't with Washington when the general crossed the river. Monroe and Washington's nephew, Capt. William Washington, crossed the river the day before to scout for British troops. The two young men spent the night depicted in the painting spying on Hessian troops in the town of Trenton.) Monroe had an illustrious career: He went on to become US senator; American ambassador to France, England, and Spain; four-term governor of Virginia; secretary of state, secretary of war, and two-term president of the United States.

It is the young James Monroe who is remembered in Fredericksburg, where he began his legal practice after reading law with Thomas Jefferson in Williamsburg. **The Monroe Presidential Center** is in a brick building on the site where Monroe practiced law from 1786 to 1789. For many years it was thought that Monroe actually practiced law in this building, but studies have shown it was not here prior to 1815. Monroe probably worked in a wooden structure on this town lot, which he sold for a nice profit between 1792 and 1793.

Inside the center you'll see reminders of Monroe's long career of public service. Perhaps the most significant is his Louis XVI desk. It was at this desk in 1823 that Monroe signed the message to Congress containing the section that has become known as the Monroe Doctrine. The desk has three secret compartments that were not discovered until 1906. They held two hundred letters that Monroe had received from Alexander Hamilton, Benjamin Franklin, and other statesmen of his day.

James Monroe, fifth president, was the first to occupy the White House after it was burned by the British in 1814. Since all the furniture had been destroyed, the Monroes had to fill the house with their own pieces. While in France representing the United States, they had acquired a great many Louis XVI pieces of mahogany and brass. Today, you can see the originals in this Fredericksburg museum. (The

White House has copies, made at Mrs. Hoover's direction in 1932.)

Among the museum's most popular exhibits are selections of Mrs. Monroe's gowns. There are citrine jewels and a stunning Empire-styled velvet gown that she wore to the Court of Napoleon and a green velvet suit worn by Mr. Monroe.

For scholars, the museum has an extensive library about James Monroe and his pivotal foreign policy doctrine. A reconstruction of a nineteenth-century Virginia gentleman's library is also housed here. You'll leave the museum through an old-fashioned walled garden with a bronze bust of James Monroe. The bust is by Margaret French Cresson, daughter of Daniel Chester French, who created the *Sitting Lincoln* in marble at the Lincoln Memorial in Washington, D.C.

The Monroe Presidential Center is open 9:00 A.M. to 5:00 P.M. from March through November. From December through February, it is open 10:00 A.M. to 4:00 P.M. It is closed on Thanksgiving, Christmas Eve and Day, and New Year's Eve and Day. Admission is charged.

Directions: From I-95, take the Fredericksburg exit and follow Route 3 east to the heart of town. Turn right on Charles Street, and you will see the Monroe Presidential Center at 908 Charles Street.

Montpelier

President James Madison's **Montpelier**, acquired by the National Trust for Historic Preservation in 1984, was the last home of one of America's Founding Fathers to pass into public hands. This twenty-seven hundred-acre estate in Virginia's Piedmont affords a tantalizing glimpse of the Madison family plantation. But you need to realize that this plantation is presented in a distinctly different manner than most familiar sites, like Washington's Mount Vernon and Jefferson's Monticello.

Montpelier is a work in progress—ongoing archeological work is revealing new facets of the plantation grounds, while architectural historians are still uncovering new dimensions to the mansion. Many of the rooms are unfinished and unfurnished. Several of the lavishly appointed rooms represent the duPont years, the final private owners of the estate.

James Madison's family arrived in Virginia in 1653, and his grandfather acquired and settled the Montpelier estate in 1723. James (who was actually James, Jr.) was born on March 15, 1751, the eldest of twelve children. He was educated and pursued a career in law and politics. Some historians claim that America's greatest contribution to Western civilization is the thinking of James Madison, whose work in formulating and winning approval for the US Constitution and Bill of Rights shaped the framework for modern democracy, not only in the United States, but around the world as well.

Madison's public service career spanned fifty-three years. He served as a delegate to the Continental Congress. He was a member of the Virginia House of Delegates, a United States congressman, Thomas Jefferson's secretary of state and United States president from 1809 to 1817. After his second presidential term, Madison retired to Montpelier with his wife, Dolley, whom he had married in 1794. He died breakfasting in the dining room on June 28, 1836.

The Montpelier mansion has changed a great deal over the years, but docents help you see the stages of the main house beginning with the central and earliest portion of the house that was built in 1760 for James Madison, Sr. After James and Dolley were wed, they moved into one wing of the house, with her son John Payne Todd by her first marriage. For the first five years, Montpelier was open to the public; it was thought that the newlyweds occupied what was essentially a duplex in the northern section of the mansion. But archeological research uncovered an interior doorway indicating the two suites were connected.

During the last years of his father's life, James began work on a thirty-foot addition to the northeast end of the house. The dining room was added, and the front portico work was completed by 1800. Nine years later, additional projects were launched, including interior renovation and the addition of one-story wings at each end of the house. The mansion's first inside kitchens were in the basements of these wings. After consulting with his good friend, Thomas Jefferson, Madison had the entire mansion stuccoed.

After the death of her husband, Dolley Madison moved to Washington. She sold Montpelier in 1844; most of the furniture had already been sold at auction. For over five decades, the estate changed hands frequently, until in 1901 it was purchased by William duPont, Sr. The duPont family made significant alterations and additions to the house and grounds. The last owner, Marion duPont Scott, added a steeplechase course. The Montpelier Hunt Races, which she inaugurated, are still held the first weekend each November.

When you visit, you will view a brief audiovisual program on Madison's career before touring the first floor of the fifty-five-room mansion. Some of the rooms reflect the senior Madisons and the 1760s, during the president's youth. The post-White House years are captured in other rooms, with furnishings from the 1820s. The lifestyle of the senior duPonts during the Gilded Age is depicted in the Morning Room and Adam Room, which are noted for ornate plasterwork, elaborate chandeliers, embossed silk wallpaper, and other elegant decorative touches. The distinctive Art Deco period is captured in Marion duPont Scott's Red Room with photomurals of her beloved horses. After touring the house, wander through the two-acre garden, with its photogenic temple, added by Madison in 1811. Madison took the extravagant step of hiring a French gardener, who was paid a generous seven hundred dollars a year. Madison's terraced garden covered four acres, including the two-acre formal area that has been restored by the Garden Club of Virginia. You also can take a tree walk, using a self-guided brochure that pinpoints over forty species of trees. Madison introduced trees and exotic plants from around the world, like the large cedar of Lebanon at the entrance to the formal garden.

With all the changes the main house experienced over the years, one constant was the unobstructed view from the portico of the Blue Ridge Mountains. The grounds fluctuated from the early days as a colonial-era working plantation to the later, country equestrian years. You will see elements from each as you drive around the twenty-seven hundred-acre estate, past more than a hundred buildings. They include smaller houses, barns, a bowling alley, stables, and a family cemetery, where both James and Dolley Madison are buried. Much of the acreage is open pasture, and the stables are still filled with horses.

Montpelier is open daily, March through December from 10:00 A.M. to 4:00 P.M. and weekends only in January and February. It is closed on Thanksgiving, Christmas, and New Year's Day. There is a well-stocked Country Store Museum Shop with a nearby picnic area. Admission is charged.

Directions: From I-95, take the Fredericksburg exit and proceed west on Route 3 to the intersection with Route 20. Make a left on Route 20 to Orange. Montpelier is four miles southwest of Orange on Route 20.

Sherwood Forest

It doesn't seem possible, but **Sherwood Forest** is today owned by President John Tyler's grandson, Harrison Tyler. John Tyler was sixty-three when he fathered his youngest son, Lyon, who in turn, at the age of seventy-five fathered his youngest son, the current owner, Harrison. Hence, the home has been remarkably unchanged by time. Few, if any, historic homes have retained as complete a collection of family furnishings, and nowhere else are you as likely to hear as many colorful anecdotes about them as you do here.

You learn that when John Tyler and his wife, Julia Gardiner, moved into the White House, Congress would not allocate any funds for redecoration. The Tylers brought their own furniture to the White House and took it back to Sherwood Forest at the end of John Tyler's term in 1845. Tyler, the tenth president (1841–1845), was the first to gain office by the death of his predecessor, William Henry Harrison. This was also the first and only time neighbors followed each other into this high office, as Tyler's home was next to Harrison's birthplace, Berkeley Plantation (see selection).

Sherwood Forest was under construction from 1660 to 1845. By the time it was finished, its 301-foot length made it the longest frame house in America, the same length as a football field. One of the last extensions to be built was a narrow ballroom, added specifically for dancing the Virginia Reel. Sherwood Forest is the only James River plantation to have a ballroom. The long hall on the other side, which connects the kitchen with the main house, was called the colonnade and used as a "whistling walk" and storage area. Legend has it that slaves carrying dishes to the dining room had to whistle as they walked to prove they weren't sampling the fare.

According to family legend, one room at Sherwood Forest is haunted by the "Gray Lady." The family sitting room, known since 1840 as the Gray Room, is connected by a narrow staircase with the nursery above. The children's nurse customarily brought the youngest child downstairs to rock in front of the fireplace. When the youngster died, the devoted nurse was inconsolable. Since that time, a phantom rocker has been heard at night in this room.

Behind the house is a ginkgo, one of thirty-seven tree varieties at Sherwood Forest that are not indigenous to the area. The ginkgo was brought to America by Admiral Perry when President Tyler reopened the trade routes to the Far East.

The house and grounds at Sherwood Forest opened to the public on March 29, 1993, President Tyler's 203rd birthday. Tours are given daily, 9:00 A.M. to 5:00 P.M., except Thanksgiving, Christmas, and New Year's Day. Admission is charged.

Directions: From the Richmond area, take I-295 east to Exit 22A, Route 5. (Sherwood Forest is approximately thirty-five to forty-five minutes from the city limits.) Take Route 5 east toward Williamsburg. Sherwood Forest is on the right. From the Williamsburg and Virginia Beach area, take I-64 east to Route 199, Exit 242, toward Jamestown. At Route 5, turn left and travel west approximately twenty miles, and you will see Sherwood Forest on the left.

Pennsylvania

Wheatland

The scene had all the elements of a Hollywood historical drama: the elderly politician in shirt-sleeves; the shady porch in the June heat; then the unexpected news: At long last, the party nomination to run for the presidency! It all happened just that way in June of 1856 when, after three unsuccessful bids, James Buchanan finally got the Democratic nomination. He was Pennsylvania's first, and thus far, only president. His Federal-style mansion is much the same as it was back on that eventful day when he delivered his acceptance speech from his front porch.

Buchanan once said that he "never intended to enter politics... but as a distraction from a great grief which happened at Lancaster when I was a young man... I accepted a nomination." He was talking about his broken engagement to Anne C. Coleman, who died shortly after they became estranged. This unhappy experience resulted in Buchanan's remaining a bachelor, the only one to ever become president. His niece, Harriet Lane, served as his official hostess both at **Wheatland** and while he was in the White House.

Although Buchanan may have entered politics reluctantly, he went on to devote forty-two years to public service in various capacities. His list of titles is formidable: He served in Congress as representative and senator from Pennsylvania; he was Jackson's minister to Russia, Polk's secretary of state, and Pierce's minister to Great Britain.

The lavish Victorian ambience of Wheatland reflects Buchanan's years of travel and diplomacy. Some of the decorative pieces were gifts from heads of state. The two-hundred-pound fishbowl was a gift from the Japanese Mikado when trade was inaugurated between the United States and Japan. A message from Queen Victoria commemorates the completion of the Trans-Atlantic Cable. Signed portraits of the Queen and Prince Albert recall Buchanan's years as minister to Great Britain.

Many of the furnishings represent the White House years. In the corner cupboard of the family dining room is the French porcelain used by Buchanan in the White House.

After exploring the house, step out on the famous porch and imagine Buchanan's emotions on that long-ago day. The estate has a garden and several outbuildings. Don't miss the carriage house where Buchanan's old Germantown wagon is exhibited.

Wheatland is open daily, April through November from 10:00 A.M. to 4:00 P.M. Admission is charged. For more information, you can call (717) 392-8721.

Directions: From I-76, the Pennsylvania Turnpike, traveling west, take Exit 22, Route 222 south; then take Route 30 west to the Harrisburg Pike exit. Head south on Harrisburg Pike to President Avenue; turn right and head south to Route 23, Marietta Avenue, and turn right. Wheatland is twenty yards on the left at 1120 Marietta Avenue. If you are traveling east on I-76, take Exit 19, Route 283 south, to Route 30 west and take that to the Harrisburg Pike exit.

Private Homes

The popular interest in antiques has long encompassed the old homes in which old furnishings are so often found. History buffs and avid collectors appreciate the careful restorations that provide a complete picture of life in an earlier era.

This revival of the past is even more significant when, as often happens, it re-creates the home of some important figure from the pages of our history books.

Great men, great houses, and great objects all combine to provide fascinating footnotes to events on the larger stage of history. Sometimes what makes a house worthy of consideration is not its style, but that it survived. The fact that it still exists and that William Penn, Benjamin Franklin, or George Taylor once lived and worked in it make it significant. Even when the house hasn't itself survived, but enough records, inventories, diagrams, or pictures remain to allow it to be authentically rebuilt, it becomes significant historically.

In the forty-seven years between the War of 1812 and the Civil War, America developed, expanded, and grew. These houses represent that period of growth.

District of Columbia

Decatur House

The **Decatur House** owes its prominence to its distinguished architecture as well as its association with one of American's most important nineteenth-century leaders. Naval hero Stephen Decatur built his home on one of the lots he purchased with prize money won fighting the Barbary pirates and the British. Stephen Decatur's father was also a prominent naval officer, who achieved early fame by capturing the French ship *Le Croyable* during the undeclared naval war with France in 1798.

Young Stephen soon followed in his father's footsteps, dropping out of college in 1800 to enlist. In 1804 during the war with the Barbary pirates, he was credited by the famous British Lord Nelson with "the most daring act of the age." Decatur's fame stemmed from the raid he led with roughly seventy volunteers into the harbor of Tripoli to burn the captured US frigate *Philadelphia*, thus preventing it from being used in battle against other American ships. Later during the War of 1812, he captured the British frigate *Macedonian*.

Stephen Decatur moved to Washington early in 1816 to serve on the Board of Naval Commissioners. Approximately a year later, he hired the noted architect Benjamin Latrobe to design his house, which is one of only three private residences designed by Latrobe that has survived the vicissitudes of time. Over the years the house has been occupied by George M. Dallas, vice president under Polk and three secretaries of state—Henry Clay, Martin van Buren, and Edward Livingston. France, Britain, and Russia used it as a legation.

Stephen Decatur and his wife, Susan, lived in their Washington town house for only fourteen months. In 1800, at the age of forty-one, Decatur was killed in a duel by Commodore James Barron, who blamed Decatur for ruining his naval career. Congress and all of official Washington attended his funeral, and he was mourned throughout the country.

The first floor rooms at the house reflect the Federal style popular during the Decaturs' brief residency. The upstairs is furnished in the opulent Victorian style of the Beales, the last residents. It was Beale who spread the news of the discovery of gold in California across America.

The Decatur House is open Tuesday through Friday, 10:00 A.M. to 3:00 P.M., and weekends from noon to 4:00 P.M. Admission is charged. For additional information you can call (202) 892-0920 or check its Web site at www.decaturhouse.org.

Directions: The Decatur House is at 748 Jackson Place, N.W., on Lafayette Square across from the White House.

Virginia

Centre Hill Mansion

Two totally different homes in Old Towne Petersburg evoke the nineteenth century. **Centre Hill**, overlooking the town, is the third hilltop home of the wealthy Bolling family. In 1823, Robert Bolling built Centre Hill for his fourth wife, Sarah Melville Minge Bolling. The architectural eclecticism of Petersburg is nowhere more evident than at Centre Hill, built in the Federal style but remodeled twice. Robert Buckner Bolling, who inherited the house from his father in the late 1840s, added a Greek revival look to Centre Hill. At the turn of the century, Mr. and Mrs. Charles Hall Davis purchased the house and remodeled it along the then-popular colonial revival style.

It is the affluent era before the siege of Petersburg that is re-created today at Centre Hill. Your entrance to the house is less dramatic than it was in the 1850s. Entrance is through the basement, where one can view a service tunnel, which was used as an entryway to the house by the slaves who used the basement as a work area.

Centre Hill has some unique furnishings. On the marble mantelpiece in the library is a clock commemorating Lord Nelson's victory at the Battle of the Nile. In the dining room is the forerunner of the wet bar, a copper-lined compartment in a sideboard, ideal for storing wine and beverages. But it is the twenty-four-karat, gold-trimmed dinner service that has an interesting story. If you think you have troubles with delivery service today, consider that it took five years for dishes to get here from the Minton factory in England. The ship on which they were sent had to bypass the Union naval blockade around Petersburg. Then the shipment had to be smuggled past Grant's forces surrounding the city. The dishes finally were delivered during the Christmas season of 1864, and by that time, there was no food to serve on them. During that Christmas season, Petersburg citizens celebrated by hosting "starvation parties."

Two presidents visited Centre Hill. After the fall of Petersburg, Centre Hill served as Union headquarters. Once Union forces captured Petersburg, President Lincoln visited Centre Hill to confer with Gen. George L. Hartsnuff. In 1901, President William Howard Taft visited Petersburg to dedicate the Pennsylvania Monument to the soldiers from Pennsylvania who had lost their lives during the Battle of the Crater. There was an al fresco luncheon held at Centre Hill for President Taft.

You can visit Centre Hill from 10:00 A.M. to 5:00 P.M. daily, except on major holidays. Tours begin every hour on the half hour. There is a charge. Parking for Centre Hill is located at Tabb and Adams Streets.

The **Trapezium House**, just a few blocks away, is named for its odd shape. Its owner, Charles O'Hara, an Irish bachelor, built the house in 1817. There are absolutely no right angles in his house—walls, stairs, floors, windows, and even the mantles were all set at an angle. Legend has it that O'Hara built it this way to ward off evil spirits. Other local tales claim that O'Hara kept unusual pets, including a monkey, parrot, and white rats. The stories say that he found the animals more compatible than his boarders. His mistrust of people is obvious from the way he numbered the logs beside the fire so that no one would steal from his stockpile. This house at Market and High streets can be toured for a charge, 10:00 A.M. to 5:00 P.M. daily, except major holidays from April through October.

Directions: Take I-95 to Petersburg; then use Exit 52 onto West Washington Street into Old Towne. Turn right on S. Sycamore and proceed to the end of the street. Then turn right for the visitor center parking lot.

John Marshall House

In an era when their contemporaries were marrying for wealth and position, John Marshall and Mary "Polly" Willis Amber married for love. It was a love that was to last a lifetime and influence the career decisions of a major figure in American history.

John Marshall, who was to become chief justice of the US Supreme Court, met Polly Ambler when she was a girl of fourteen. When Marshall first proposed, Polly burst into tears; he was taken aback and left in despair. A cousin of Polly's caught up with Marshall as he was leaving and gave him a lock of Polly's hair. Marshall kept the talisman and proposed again several years later. She accepted, and they were married in 1783, when he was twenty-eight and she was seventeen.

Along with his good fortune in obtaining the hand of the girl he loved, Marshall also inherited the law practice of Edmund Randolph, who relinquished it to run for governor of Virginia. With this practice and his own clients, Marshall had a thriving practice. He also had a growing family, and in 1788, John Marshall purchased a one-block lot in the center of Richmond. While their house was being built, the Marshalls lived in a small two-story cottage on the grounds. They moved into the two-story brick house in 1790. The main house still stands, though the large kitchen dependency, laundry, smokehouse, carriage house, and Marshall's law office are gone.

The **John Marshall House** itself has been open to the public since 1913, and it contains the largest collection of Marshall memorabilia in existence. The Marshall silver, returned to the house for his 225th birthday celebration, is here as is the French porcelain purchased by Marshall when he was ambassador to France in 1797. His wife's invalidism and nervous disorders meant that Marshall did far more of the housework and child care than men typically did in the eighteenth century. Although Polly did not enjoy entertaining, he frequently invited thirty fellow attorneys for his "lawyer dinners."

His tenure as ambassador was one of the rare times Marshall accepted an appointment away from Richmond. As chief justice, he was able to do much of the casework at home. When you look at the portrait of Polly Marshall at age thirty-three, you can see why he was reluctant to leave her. She was a gorgeous woman despite her ill health, which came in part from bearing ten children and suffering several miscarriages. Marshall also had health problems; he had over a thousand gallstones removed with only alcohol for an anesthetic. Despite their problems, both lived long lives; Polly Marshall to age sixty-six and John to just prior to his eightieth birthday.

John Marshall may well have attributed some of his long life to his wine cellar. He spent a tenth of his income on wine. His Richmond home boasted a superb wine cellar that has been restored. A reproduction of a sundial John Marshall set in place in the eighteenth century can be seen on the lawn.

The John Marshall House is open Tuesday through Saturday from 10:00 A.M. to 5:00 P.M. Admission is charged, either for this house alone or as a Court End block ticket, which provides reduced admission to three houses and St. John's Church on a self-guided walking tour, which includes ten additional points of interest. The block ticket provides admission to the Marshall House, the Wickham-Valentine House, and the John Brockenbrough House, which served as the White House of the Confederacy (see selections).

Directions: From I-95 south, take Exit 74C to Broad Street west. Travel to 9th Street and make a right. The John Marshall House is at 818 East Marshall Street on the corner of 9th and Marshall streets.

Lee-Fendall House

Nothing succeeds like excess—Philip Richard Fendall was not content with one Lee wife, he had three! Philip, himself the grandson of

Philip Lee of Blenheim, first married a cousin, Sarah Lettice Lee. He next wed Elizabeth Steptoe Lee, widow of Philip Ludwell Lee and the mother of Matilda, who grew up to marry Henry "Lighthorse Harry" Lee. To further complicate the matter, Philip's third wife was "Lighthorse Harry's" sister, Mary.

Visitors will be thoroughly confused if they try to keep track of the thirty-seven Lees who lived at the **Lee-Fendall House** from 1785 to 1903. (As a historical footnote, the last resident-owner of the house, from 1937 to 1969, was labor leader John L. Lewis.)

Philip Fendall built this rambling frame house in 1785. Both George Washington and Harry Lee were frequent visitors. In March 1789, the mayor of Alexandria interrupted dinner at the Fendall House and asked Harry Lee to write a farewell address from the citizens of Alexandria to their favorite son. George Washington was to ride through town on his way to his inauguration in New York. Lee moved from the table to a nearby desk and wrote the requested farewell message. He would write another, and final, farewell to his old friend ten years later, expressing the esteem in which he was held throughout the nation: "First in war, first in peace, and first in the hearts of his countrymen."

Though the Lee-Fendall House is furnished with family heirlooms spanning the 118 years of Lee occupancy, it is the way the house appeared in the 1850s, as a grand mansion, that you see on your tour. Lees were born in this home up until 1892. Favorite toys through the years can be seen upstairs. There is Minerva, a doll with a tin head, ordered from the first Sears and Roebuck catalog. An antique doll house collection is also displayed.

Tours are given at the Lee-Fendall House, 614 Oronoco Street, on the hour from 10:00 A.M. until 3:00 P.M., Tuesday through Saturday, and from 1:00 to 3:00 P.M. on Sunday. Admission is charged.

Directions: From I-495/95, the Washington Beltway, take Exit 1, US 1 north into Alexandria. Turn right on Oronoco Street, which is ten blocks past Franklin Street.

Morven Park

From the outside, **Morven Park** suggests Scarlet O'Hara's Tara, but the opulent interior is more reminiscent of William Randolph Hearst's San Simeon. The mixture of architectural styles—the Renaissance grand hall, French drawing room, and Jacobean dining room—is matched by furnishings collected from around the world by the twentieth-century owners, Governor Westmoreland Davis and his wife.

The house the Davises purchased in 1903 has changed dramatically over the years. Originally, the land was farmed by Pennsylvanians who settled in the area in the late 1700s. An unpretentious stone house was built here around 1781. In 1800, Thomas Swann acquired the land and built a Federal-style home, which he enlarged after he retired. It was Swann who added the Greek Revival, four-columned entrance portico. Swann named his estate after the Princeton, New Jersey, home of Commodore Robert F. Stockton, who was flattered by his gesture but suggested that he add "Park" to the name because of the vast acreage (roughly 2,562 acres at that time).

After inheriting his father's estate, Thomas Swann, Jr., was too involved in business and politics to spend much time at this Leesburg estate. His position as president of the Baltimore & Ohio Railroad made it necessary for him to spend time in Baltimore. He maintained Morven Park as a summer residence while living in Annapolis as governor of Maryland and in the Washington area as a five-term congressman. Despite the claims on his schedule, he still exerted a great deal of influence on Morven Park. It was Thomas Swann, Jr., who embarked on the last major building program, integrating the three separate buildings into the one imposing mansion you see today.

If the exterior reflects Governor Swann, the interior reflects the taste of Governor and Mrs. Davis. They filled the house with treasures from Europe, including the 1550 Brabant tapestries that line the great hall. Their grandeur is matched by the red velvet thrones from the Pitti Palace that sit beneath them. The ornately carved dining room furniture is reflected in huge rococo mirrors.

The house tour at Morven Park is just the beginning. There is a great deal more to see. The **Museum of Hounds and Hunting** traces fox hunting in America from George Washington's day to the present. The Winmill Carriage Collection was bequeathed to the estate. It provides a mini-history of transportation in the eighteenth century. Names you may only have encountered in books take on fascinating form, as you examine landaus, sulkies, breaks, and phaetons, as well as the more easily recognized carriages, sleighs, carts, coaches, and buggies, in the seventy-vehicle collection, which rotates exhibits.

Nature lovers will find an extensive garden. The Marguerite G. Davis Boxwood Garden has the largest living stand of boxwood in the United States. Spring bushes and bulbs add color, and in the summer months, roses, dahlias, and crepe myrtle bloom.

Morven Park is open April through October from noon to 4:30 P.M. weekdays and 10:00 A.M. to 4:30 P.M. on weekends. In November, it is open weekends. There are special December hours; call

The exterior of Morven Park is quintessentially Southern, but inside the decor is decidedly European. Museums on the grounds provide a mini-history of fox hunting and eighteenth-century transportation.

(703) 777-2414 for details. Admission is charged.

Directions: From I-95 in the Fredericksburg area, take Route 17 northwest until it merges with Route 29/15. Turn right on Route 29/15 and continue north. Once you are beyond Warrenton, Route 29/15 divides. Take Route 15 north toward Leesburg; Morven Park is off Route 15 on the right just past Leesburg. From the Washington Beltway, I-495/95, take Route 7 west to Leesburg, then Route 15 south toward Warrenton.

Oatlands

Oatlands traces its lineage back to Virginia's early days. The land was purchased by the Carter family from Lord Fairfax as part of the 11,357-acre Goose Creek Tract. George Carter drew close to five thousand acres in a lottery held by his father for his ten surviving children. In 1804, Carter built a post-colonial country house on his estate. George Carter married a thirty-nine-year-old widow, Elizabeth Grayson Lewis, when he was sixty. He died after only nine short years of wedded life.

Elizabeth and their two sons briefly abandoned Oatlands at the start of the Civil War. The boys served in the Confederate army, and the house served as a billet for Confederate troops. After the war the Carter family had difficulty maintaining the house. They took in boarders for a time but eventually were forced to sell the family home and sixty acres.

The Greek Classical Revival house has a three-story pavilion flanked by two-story wings. In a break with tradition, it has a staircase on each end of the house rather than one in the center. Oatlands, like its neighbor Morven Park, did undergo some remodeling over the first twenty years, 1804–1829. When the vogue for octagonal rooms caught on, a square-shaped room was converted to an eight-sided drawing room. One of the most distinctive features of the interior design is the elaborate plasterwork done in the 1820s.

The house and garden you see today were reclaimed by Mr. and Mrs. William Corcoran Eustis after years of neglect. He was the grandson of the founder of the Corcoran Gallery in Washington, D.C. They furnished the house with American, English, and French pieces. The dessert plates you'll see on the dining table once belonged to George Washington.

The Eustises restored the boxwood garden laid out by George Carter, reclaiming and expanding to create what is now considered one of Virginia's finest gardens. Mrs. Eustis, in describing the garden, said it was noted for "mystery, variety, and the unexpected." It is the only garden in the country to use boxwood for the preached, or tunnel, walk. The wisteria walk is a springtime delight. Specialty areas include a rosarium and an herb garden.

Oatlands is open April through late December, Tuesday through Saturday and federal holiday Mondays from 10:00 A.M. to 4:30 P.M. and Sunday from 1:00 to 4:30 P.M. Admission is charged.

Directions: From I-95 in the Fredericksburg area, take Route 17 northwest until it merges with Route 29/15 and continue north. Once you are beyond Warrenton, Route 29/15 divides. Take Route 15 north toward Leesburg, Oatlands is off Route 15 on the right just before Leesburg. From the Washington Beltway I-495/95, take Route 7 west of Leesburg; then Route 15 south toward Warrenton. Oatlands is on Route 15, six miles south of Leesburg.

Sully Historic Site

Sully Historic Site, Richard Bland Lee's Virginia country house, was built in 1794. Lee combined two architectural styles he had grown to love: the Georgian colonial of his native state and the more delicate Federal style he had admired while serving in Philadelphia as northern Virginia's first congressman.

The Philadelphia influence helped make his wife feel at home. Elizabeth Collins was the daughter of a prominent Quaker merchant in Philadelphia. They married in 1794 and had a family. The Lees and their four surviving children made Sully home until 1811. During this time, the plantation was operated by slave labor, which included field hands, domestics, and skilled artisans.

The Haights, later owners of Sully, were Quakers from the North. Their pacifist beliefs did not protect them during the Civil War. The men were forced to leave their southern farm and retreat behind the Union lines. The women of the Haight family stayed at Sully and protected their home from the foraging armies of both North and South.

Today, Sully is restored and decorated with Federal furnishings. After a guided tour of the main house, you can see the dependencies: the kitchen-laundry, smokehouse, and stone dairy. Visitors can enjoy the kitchen and flower gardens, a walking trail, and the museum gift shop.

Sully hosts a variety of living-history programs on the weekends. Programs highlight aspects of the work of slaves as well as gentry daily life. Perennial special-event favorites are the Antique Car Show in June and the Annual Quilt Show. Sully Historic Site is open daily from 11:00 A.M. to 4:00 P.M. It is closed on Tuesdays, Thanksgiving, Christmas, and New Year's Day. Admission is charged. For additional information, you can call (703) 437-1794.

Directions: From the Washington Beltway, I-95/495 in Virginia, take Exit 9, Route 66 west. Continue on Route 66 to Route 50 west and proceed for 5.5 miles to Route 28 north. Turn right on Route 28 and go 0.75 mile to Sully. An alternative route for Sully from I-495/95 is the Dulles Toll Road west to exit 9A, Route 28 south and proceed 4.5 miles to Sully on the left.

Maryland

Beall-Dawson House

Upton Beall, son of Maryland tobacco merchant Brooke Beall, built his Rockville "mansion house" around 1815. The exact date is not known, but a Beall family legend says that the lumber Upton Beall acquired for construction of his house was used instead by American troops retreating through Rockville in 1814, during the War of 1812. Tax records for 1820 valued the house Beall built at fifteen hundred dollars. When Beall was a forty-year-old widower, he married seventeen-year-old Jane Neil Robb, daughter of a prominent Rockville tavern keeper. Upton and Jane Beall had five children. Three of the girls lived, but none married, so this Rockville house remained their home.

After the Civil War, when death claimed two of the sisters, Margaret Beall invited her cousin, Amelia Holliday Somerville, to live with her. When Amelia married John Dawson, the newlyweds made their home with Miss Margaret, a condition she demanded before giving her permission for their union. Margaret Beall died in 1901 at the age of eighty-four. The house was inherited by the Dawsons and did not pass from the family until 1946.

This Federal-style, brick house is now the headquarters of the Montgomery County Historical Society. It has been restored to its nineteenth-century appearance. The downstairs rooms are furnished to represent the years Upton and Jane Beall lived here, 1815 to 1847. About six pieces actually belonged to the Bealls; other pieces duplicate items listed on the inventory of Upon Beall (1827) and Jane Beall (1847). Over the parlor mantel hangs a portrait of Upton Beall. The parlor also has a pianoforte bought for Margaret Dawson in 1834. One of Amelia and John Dawson's nine children, Margaret, used it when she gave dancing lessons to Rockville youngsters. Several of the upstairs rooms are used for changing exhibitions on different aspects of county history.

Many of the society's books are in the adjacent frame library, built in the late 1940s. The library can be used by genealogical and local history researchers. Hours are the same as for the Beall-Dawson House, from Tuesday through Saturday, noon to 4:00 P.M., and on the first Sunday of the month from 2:00 to 5:00 P.M. Admission is charged for the house tour. For more information, you can call (301) 762-1492 or (301) 340-9853.

The **Stonestreet Museum of 19th Century Medicine** is on the grounds of the Beall-Dawson House (and is included in the admission fee) in what was once the medical office of Dr. Edward E. Stonestreet. He practiced medicine in the Rockville area from 1852 to 1903. During the Civil War, Dr. Stonestreet was an examining surgeon for local Maryland draftees. A photograph of the doctor, his wife, and their six daughters hangs in the museum. His saddlebags and boots still hang behind the door. He kept them in the office to be used on his frequent house calls.

When you see the nineteenth-century medical instruments, you'll be glad the doctor isn't in; this is one collection that certainly doesn't evoke nostalgia for the good old days. Some of the medical tools on display here were put to gruesome use, and look it. There are sharp blades for amputation and devices for bloodletting. The drugs certainly must have helped patients forget their problems, even if they did not cure. Many of the old nostrums included a considerable amount of opiates. The human skeleton on display is a favorite with the younger set.

Directions: From Baltimore, take I-95 south to the Washington Beltway, I-495, and head west to Exit 34N (Rockville Pike, Route 355). Take Rockville Pike to Middle Lane, across from the Rockville Metro Stop. Turn left on Middle Lane and go two blocks; then turn left on Adams Street and right on West Montgomery Avenue. The Beall-Dawson House is at 103 West Montgomery Avenue.

Hampton National Historic Site

The Ridgely family always seemed to be at the right place at the right time. The first to emigrate to America from England was Robert, who held several governmental positions including deputy secretary of the Colony. Two more Ridgely generations were planters in the rich farmland of Anne Arundel County. After the family was in Maryland for about one hundred years, they moved to the frontier of Baltimore County, where they developed an iron furnace that supplied cannons and shot to the Continental army and navy.

Capt. Charles Ridgely took the vast fortune he acquired during the Revolutionary War and built what was the largest mansion in the United States. **Hampton Mansion's** opulence survives today, almost unchanged. The eye-catching design pulls your eye up the white columns at the front door, past the second floor balcony, to the octagonal, white, dome cupola, eighty-six feet above the ground. The mansion's distinctive pink color comes from iron oxide in the sand used to mix the stucco.

There were those who questioned Captain Ridgely's judgment when he began the seven-year project of building his house. Built deep in the woods, eleven miles from Baltimore, the neighbors, believing it an impossible task, called it "Ridgely's folly." Captain Charles, the builder, died approximately six months after the mansion was finished, leaving behind a childless widow. His nephew inherited the property on the condition that he change his name from

Charles Ridgely Carnan to Charles Carnan Ridgely. Young Charles had a distinguished career as a representative in the Maryland General Assembly, senator in the Assembly, and governor of Maryland. He and his wife, Priscilla, had thirteen children.

It was Charles Carnan Ridgely who undertook the landscaping that is as spectacular as the mansion itself. The famous landscape architect Henry Winthrop Sargent said: "It has been truly said of Hampton that it expresses more grandeur than anyplace in America." The gardens are laid out in huge parterres, or falls, planted in a formal geometric style. Bulbs, boxwoods, and flowers adorn some of the parterres, while others feature heirloom rose varieties. The estate reached its peak under the second owner, who amassed some twenty-four thousand acres. More than three hundred enslaved African Americans, as well as indentured servants and craftsmen, lived on the estate and contributed to its wealth.

The first owner built it, the second owner landscaped it, and the third owner and his wife spent a fortune and a lifetime furnishing Hampton. Eliza Ridgely, whose famous portrait hangs in the Great Hall, traveled Europe acquiring art treasures and furniture for her grand Maryland home. The park today has about forty thousand original items, many of which were purchased by Eliza. Present plans are for each room to reflect a decorative period popular during the lifetimes of the seven generations that lived at Hampton. One of the most striking rooms is the dining room, painted a brilliant Prussian blue. The blue is picked up in the curtains, where it is combined with gold and trimmed with gold and orange tassels—quite a striking window treatment!

After your house tour, take a walking tour of the grounds and gardens. Five trees on the site are Maryland state champions. Slave quarters, stables, and other buildings remain from the heyday of the estate.

The grounds are open daily from 9:00 A.M. to 5:00 P.M. Tours of the mansion are offered on the hour from 9:00 A.M. until 4:00 P.M. Admission is charged. A tearoom serves lunch every day except Monday. Hampton is a part of the National Park Service.

Directions: From the Baltimore Beltway (I-695), take Exit 27B, Dulaney Valley Road. From Dulaney Valley Road, make an immediate right onto Hampton Lane; proceed 0.5 mile. Hampton is on the right.

Riversdale

Riversdale felicitously blends the New World with the Old. The five-part, stucco-covered brick mansion was built between 1801 and 1807 by Henri Joseph Stier, a Flemish financier, who fled Flanders with his family during the French Revolution just before French troops invaded his country. Stier was a descendant of Peter Paul Rubens and brought with him an outstanding art collection, including a number of paintings by his famous relative.

After a little more than a year in Philadelphia, at the end of 1797, the Stier family moved to the William Paca House (see selection) in Annapolis. While staying in the Maryland capital, the family made the acquaintance of George Calvert, a descendant of the family who founded the colony and served as the first governor. On June 11, 1799, Stier's youngest daughter, Rosalie Eugenia married Calvert.

Although the Stiers had hoped to return to Flanders, by April 1801, they had purchased 729 acres just north of Bladensburg. The house plan was in the five-part style favored in the mid-Atlantic, but the three ground-floor parlors were reminiscent of the Chateau du Mick, built in 1790 and the newest of the Stier family homes in and around Antwerp. When you tour the house, you will see the fine decorative work in the central salon, with triple-arch motif on each wall and heavy mahogany doors.

When the Stier family returned to Belgium in the spring of 1803, Rosalie and George Calvert, with their first two children, made Riversdale their home. Although Rosalie corresponded with her family until her death in 1821 and received architectural and horticultural advice as well as numerous art objects to embellish the house, they were never reunited. Rosalie's letters to her father were discovered in the family archives and provide a rich source for interpretation of the house. (The letters have been compiled in *Mistress of Riversdale*, available in the gift shop.) Steir's art collection was sent back to Belgium in 1816, but before it was packed for transport, there was a two-week exhibit at Riversdale for artists and politicians. Auctions in 1817 and at Mr. Steir's death in 1821 have dispersed the collection.

Rosalie Calvert is buried near Riversdale with four of her nine children. Her tombstone was carved by an Italian sculptor who was embellishing the US Capitol under Latrobe's direction. George Calvert died in 1838, and one of his two sons, Charles Benedict, made his home at Riversdale with his wife, Charlotte A. Norris, and their six children.

Charles B. Calvert represented his county in the state legislature and was the principal founder of the Maryland Agricultural College, which became the University of Maryland. The school was situated on Calvert's 428-acre "Rossburg Farm." The cannon on the lawn at Riversdale was a gift to Charles Calvert from St. Mary's City. It was said to have come from either the *Ark* or *Dove* (see Historic St. Mary's City selection). Calvert was a close friend of Henry Clay, the noted political figure and presidential candidate, who often stayed at Riversdale. Local legend claims that he drafted the Compromise of 1850 at the mansion. Calvert died in May 1864. In 1887, the mansion and 475 acres were sold to a New York real estate syndicate that created the community of Riverdale Park, which became the nucleus of the town of Riverdale Park.

In 1912, the mansion, which had fallen into disrepair, was renovated by Thomas H. Pickford. The east hyphen and wing was converted to a two-story banquet hall, and the west wing became a garage. Pickford also filled several rooms with period furnishings. The house was then leased from 1916 to 1929 to Senator Hiram Johnson, one of the founders of the Progressive, or Bull-Moose, party. He was Teddy Roosevelt's running mate on the national ticket in 1912.

Pickford sold the house to Arkansas Senator Thaddeus Caraway. When Caraway died in 1931, his wife, Hattie, was chosen to finish his term, and she was elected in her own right in 1932, the first woman elected to the United States Senate. She served until early 1945. A mortgage default enabled Pickford to regain the house, and he sold it in 1933 to former Oregon congressman Abraham Lafferty. It was Lafferty who sold the mansion and grounds in 1949 to the Maryland-National Capital Park and Planning Commission.

Tours of Riversdale are given year-round on Sundays from noon to 4:00 P.M. A nominal admission is charged, and there is a gift shop in the mansion. The mansion also can be rented for special events. Call (301) 864-0420 or, on Sundays, (301) 864-3521.

Directions: From Baltimore, take the Baltimore Washington Parkway south to the Washington Beltway, I-495/95. Head northwest on the Beltway to Exit 23, Route 201, Kenilworth Avenue south. Continue for approximately three miles and turn right on East West Highway, Route 410. Proceed 0.5 mile and follow Maryland History signs to the mansion, which is off East West Highway at 4811 Riverdale Road.

Union Mills Homestead and Gristmill

The Shrivers, founders of **Union Mills**, are savers. This becomes apparent as you tour the family homestead. In addition to the furnishings and memorabilia accumulated by the six generations of Shrivers who have lived here, there are also diaries, accounts, and records. Only the Adamses of Massachusetts have more detailed family records; but then their family had two presidents, John and John

Quincy Adams.

The Shriver brothers, Andrew and David, came to Maryland in 1797. Each built a two-room log house separated by a "dog walk." The cost for building both houses was eighty-six dollars; the exact figure is listed in the accounts kept from the very beginning. On their hundred acres, the brothers next built a sawmill, followed by the gristmill you'll see on your visit. Records show that a hundred thousand bricks were fired for the gristmill, but only seventy thousand were used. A tannery and shops for a blacksmith, cooper, and carpenter were added later.

Once the family businesses were functioning smoothly, David Shriver moved to the Shellman House in Westminster, and then to Cumberland, on the National Road that he surveyed. Andrew stayed at Union Mills, where both his family and his home expanded over the years. Andrew fathered eleven children, and the house was eventually enlarged to twenty-three rooms. The various additions are easily seen from outside.

Andrew Shriver campaigned for Thomas Jefferson. The grateful president rewarded Andrew with the postmastership of the Union Mills community. Andrew's original eight-slot postmaster's desk still sits in his office, one of the house's four original rooms.

The Civil War divided the country—it also divided the Shriver family. Andrew Shriver's son Andrew Kaiser inherited the homestead and tannery. His brother William had a nearby house, called The Mills, and the gristmill. Andrew Kaiser was a Protestant, a Republican, and though he owned slaves, a Northern supporter. Two of his sons served in the Union army. William, a convert to Catholicism and a Democrat, did not own slaves but he supported the South. Four of his sons fought for the Confederacy.

The tensions within the family reached their peak just before the Battle of Gettysburg, when troops from both armies were fed at the homestead. On June 29, 1863, J. E. B. Stuart's twenty-four hundred rebels camped in the farm's apple orchard, which has been replanted. At about 2:00 A.M. they were all fed pancakes prepared in the kitchen's huge fireplace by "Black" Ruth Dohr. Not long after the Confederates had departed, Union general Barnes arrived. He was given a bedroom at the homestead, and he and his officers were entertained in the parlor by the Shriver daughters, who sang and danced. Accounts of the evening mention that one song heard that night was "When the Cruel War Is Over."

When the war was over, the Shrivers returned to the business of business. The family tannery won an award at the 1876 Centennial in Philadelphia. The certificate, which still hangs at the homestead, commends their "oak sole leather from Texas hides." The house itself served as an inn for travelers along the coach road from Baltimore to Pittsburgh. Washington Irving stayed here, talking late into the night in front of the fire. James Audubon also enjoyed the hospitality of Union Mills Homestead while he was researching and writing about Baltimore orioles. Audubon watched an oriole build a nest in the willow tree outside his window.

Unlike other historic homes, Union Mills Homestead has no period rooms. Here, you'll find an amiable, lived-in mix of furnishings. As one of Andrew Shriver's descendants remarked, "No one seems ever to have thrown anything away!"

Across from the house is the restored water-powered gristmill. The mill operated from 1798 to 1942 and was one of the first mills to use the revolutionary designs of Oliver Evans. Evans's *The Young Millwright and Miller's Guide,* published in 1795, included the greatest innovations in milling since before the time of Christ. The first mill to incorporate these ideas was at Ellicott Mills (see selection). Both George Washington and Thomas Jefferson employed the new design. The Union Mills gristmill is one of the most accurate restorations of an Evans design in the country.

You can buy flour milled at Union Mills, as well as other items, at the gift shop in the restored Miller's House. Also restored is the Old Bark Shed, where, on selected weekends, blacksmithing, carpentry, and woodworking are demonstrated.

Union Mills Homestead and Gristmill are open June until September, Tuesday through Friday from 10:00 A.M. to 4:00 P.M. and Saturday and Sunday from noon to 4:00 P.M. In May and September, they are open on weekends only. Admission is charged.

Directions: From Baltimore Beltway, I-695, take Exit 19 to I-795 to Route 140 west to Westminster. Then head north on Route 97. Union Mills is on the right on Route 97, seven miles north of Westminster.

Pennsylvania

Ebenezer Maxwell Mansion

The idea of commuting to and from work can be traced to the advent of rapid transportation. By the 1850s one of America's earliest commuter railroad lines linked downtown Philadelphia with rural Germantown. What had been primarily a summer retreat became a year-round green suburb.

One of Philadelphia's up-and-coming businessmen who built in Germantown was **Ebenezer Maxwell**. His Gothic villa is one of the town's most striking residences. The stone house was built of local Wissahickon schist with red sandstone used as a decorative element. Following a popular building practice of that day, coal dust was added to darken the mortar; and sand was added to the paint to give texture to the wooden window frames. A massive tower soars over elaborate Flemish cornices. There's a patterned mansard roof, and seven different shapes of windows, two of which are set with stained glass, contribute to the visual effect.

When the Maxwell house was finished in 1859, it incorporated all the latest conveniences—running water, gaslights, central hot-air heating, and even vents to allow the vitiated (used or polluted) air to escape. These newfangled ideas were viewed with caution. Several of the rooms were still heated by a fireplace to avoid any possible ill effects from the new heating system.

New decorating techniques allowed the middle-class Maxwells to imitate the homes of the wealthy. Thus, you'll see that the fireplace has marbleized slate and the wallpaper is made to look like marble. The linoleum entranceway was designed to resemble tile, and the wood-graining created a moneyed appearance. The Maxwells lived here fewer than three years before moving to a house they built next door.

It is hard to imagine how anyone could consider demolishing this wonderful period piece, but it came close to the wrecker's ball. It is fortunate that it was saved because the Maxwell mansion is the only Victorian house museum in the Philadelphia area.

Two time periods are reflected in the interior. The first floor furnishings are of the 1850s and 60s, the second floor, the 1870s and 80s. The rooms appear to be wrapped in brocades and velvets, while feathers fill a pair of parlor vases. Ceilings, walls, and doors, painted in intricate patterns in the 1880s, have been carefully restored. From the entrance hall, you can see three different floor patterns. The decor assaults the senses.

Though it must have been difficult to live in such a busy decorative environment, it's fascinating to visit. Even the garden continues the dual ambience achieved by the interior. The front yard captures the landscaping of the early 1850s, while the ribbon garden and hemlock arch at the back represents the 1880s.The yard is still enclosed by the original iron fence.

The Ebenezer Maxwell Mansion is open April through December, Friday through Sunday, from 1:00 to 4:00 P.M. Admission is charged. While you are in the neighborhood, you might want to stroll along West Tulpehocken Street and West Walnut Lane, where there are numerous architecturally interesting houses.

Directions: From the center of Philadelphia, take the Benjamin Franklin Parkway toward the art museum and continue along Kelly Drive on the east side of the Schuylkill River until it merges with Lincoln Drive. Then take the Harvey Street exit; turn right on Harvey Street and follow to Greene Street and turn left. The Maxwell Mansion is on the corner at 200 West Tulpehocken Street. You also can take the Schuylkill Expressway, Route 76, west to the Lincoln Drive exit. Follow Lincoln Drive to Harvey Street. Turn right and follow the directions above.

Todd House and Bishop White House

At the time of the American Revolution, Philadelphia was one of the largest English-speaking cities in the world. On forty-eight acres in downtown Philadelphia, the Independence National Historical Park has forty historic buildings and numerous eighteenth-century park areas that bring back those bygone days. The park encompasses government buildings where the nation was organized and initially run, as well as homes, such as the Todd and Bishop White houses, that reflect the private side of this tumultuous era.

In a perhaps legendary American version of *The Student Prince,* the niece of a Haddonfield, New Jersey, tavern keeper succeeded where the original heroine failed. Young Dolley Paine, after attracting the admiring attention of the eager soldiers and legislators who frequented her uncle's Indian King Tavern, did succeed in becoming America's first lady—albeit by a circuitous route. Dolley Paine married John Todd, Jr., a promising young Philadelphia attorney. A year later, the Todds moved to the Philadelphia house, now part of Independence National Historical Park.

They lived in the gracious town house from 1791 to 1793. During this period Dolley had two children. The Philadelphia yellow fever epidemic was a tragic time for the Todd family. Even though Dolley left the city, one of her children, already ill from other causes, died, as did her husband, who had remained in the city. Perhaps a third of the population fled the city; many who stayed perished.

When cold weather killed the mosquitoes, the epidemic ended. Dolley returned to the city a widow with a two-year-old son. She had three choices: take in boarders as her own widowed mother had done, open a small shop, or marry again. Being young and attractive, she took the last alternative. Aaron Burr introduced her to James

Madison, and after only a few months, they married. Madison had an illustrious career, culminating in the presidency.

The **Todd House** is an example of an "end of row" house, a style found predominantly in Pennsylvania, New Jersey, and Delaware. It is furnished from exact inventories, representing a middle-class Quaker house in the eighteenth century. One indication of the era's frugality is the forerunner of the Xerox, a press-like device that created a copy of correspondence. Unfortunately, the copy came out backwards, so a mirror was placed on the desk to enable the copy to be read. The mirror served a secondary function of doubling the candle power by reflecting the flame.

Bishop William White's House has none of the Quaker sparseness of the Todd House. White's house was built for him in 1786 while he was in London being consecrated as the first Protestant Episcopal bishop of Pennsylvania. The house has a number of floors. At the very top is a loft and below that is the boys' floor, where initials are carved into the wood. The third floor is the girls' room, with White's bedroom and library just below. The formal rooms are on the first floor; beneath that is the kitchen area, the scullery, the wine cellar, root cellar, and the ice well.

White and his wife, their five children, a cook, and a coachman filled this large house. The Whites entertained frequently, as Bishop White served as chaplain of the Continental Congress and of the United States Senate. He lived here for fifty years after his wife died.

This upper-class home is quite elegant. The details have been so faithfully re-created that two half-smoked cigars have been added to duplicate those shown in an artistic rendering of the room. Archeological research led to the discovery of silver and crockery in the drain under the house, permitting exact copies of the original pieces.

The Todd House and the Bishop White House are open daily. As the number of visitors that can be accommodated is limited, tickets are required; but they can be obtained at the INHP Visitor Center.

Adjacent to the Todd House is a re-created formal colonial garden, which is just one of the gardens that capture the "greene Country Towne" that William Penn foresaw in 1682. Philadelphia was one of America's first cities to be developed according to a plan that included plants. The Pennsylvania Horticultural Society has planted a colonial garden at 325 Walnut Street. Like many gardens in the 1700s, this garden is in three sections: a formal garden, an orchard, and the herb and vegetable area. In the formal parterres, or sections, you can see seasonal flowers. There are also gardens on the grounds of the Norris House and the Pemberton House.

Directions: From I-95 southbound (from points north), take Exit

17. Using the right-hand lanes of the exit, follow the signs for Callowhill Street/Independence Hall. At the bottom of the exit ramp, follow 2nd Street straight ahead to Chestnut Street. Continue a half block past Chestnut Street for the Historic Area Parking Garage on the left. It is best to park your car and walk to all the sites in the Historic District. Start at the Independence National Historical Park Visitors Center, one block away, at 3rd and Chestnut Streets, where you can pick up an easy-to-follow map of the district and a park schedule. If you are traveling northbound on I-95 (from points south), you will also take Exit 17. Stay in the left lane because you will exit on the left side of I-95. At the exit, stay in the right-hand lane and follow the signs for Independence Hall/Historic Area. Turn left at 6th Street to Chestnut, which will take you through the heart of the Historic District to 2nd Street. Turn right on 2nd Street. The entrance to the Historic Area Parking Garage is on the left.

Delaware

Rockwood

Rockwood has great style. The highlight of this Rural Gothic manor house is the newly restored conservatory, one of the oldest of its type in the United States. This Victorian fancy has been carefully returned to its turn-of-the-century splendor, down to the original gingerbread plant stands that support the palms and ferns. Its unusual color scheme mixes five shades of beige with yellow; it sounds dreadful but it works.

Rockwood was built between 1851 and 1857 by Joseph Shipley, whose family founded Wilmington, Delaware. His great-grandfather was the first chief burgess for the city. Shipley planned his Delaware estate to resemble his country home in Liverpool, where he lived and worked for many years.

The tour includes fifteen rooms filled with family treasures that combine furniture of the William and Mary period with decorative pieces from Europe and the Orient. One of the most stylistically interesting touches is the fanlight you see as you enter. Such cut-glass fans were costly and almost always found over front doors, where they could be admired by all who came to call. In the entrance hall you also will see the lovely wooden banister and raised ceiling, which gives an illusion of great spaciousness. Within this hall hangs a collection of portraits of the four generations who lived in this house over a 120-year period.

The drawing room has gold fabric walls, ornate gold cornices over the windows, and huge gold scrolled mirrors. Even richer is the family's collection of overlay glass, which was popular during the Victorian era. It is one of the best collections on the East Coast.

Upstairs, the rooms are smaller and more intimate. In earlier periods, it was not unusual for a lady to entertain in her bedroom while she continued her needlework; but by this time, bedrooms were viewed as private sanctuaries.

Rockwood is the only estate in Delaware to employ a gardenesque landscape design for the grounds. Essential to the gardenesque concept was the unity of buildings and grounds. The gray Brandywine granite of the house blends with the boulders that were left on the 211 acres of grounds. The success of this goal is still evident today.

One-hour tours are given Tuesday through Saturday from 11:00 A.M. until 3:00 P.M., and the house closes at 4:00 P.M. Admission is charged. To take a one-hour grounds tour, you must make reservations by calling (302) 761-4340. The grounds are open at no charge daily from dawn to dusk.

Rockwood hosts a number of annual events: a summer concert series in June, an Old-Fashioned Ice Cream Festival in July, and a Victorian Christmas celebration in December. Victorian reproductions and other gift items are available at Rockwood's shop.

Directions: Take I-95 to the Wilmington area. Use Exit 9, Marsh Road. Follow brown signs to the museum, which is located at 610 Shipley Road at the junction of Shipley Road and Washington Street Extension.

Transportation

After the American Revolution and the subsequent "second war for independence" in 1812, the American people finally had a chance to contemplate the magnitude of their achievement and to consolidate the strengths of the new nation.

Since the most abundant resource the United States had was land, one of the principal occupations in the era between the wars was to build routes to the western territories. Roads, canals, and railroads pushed resolutely forward through the mountains to the vast lands waiting to be tapped in the Northwest Territory.

The roads came first. The major highway to the West at the beginning of the eighteenth century was the Pennsylvania Road, now US 30. Another important thoroughfare was the National Pike, or Cumberland Road, started in 1808. Conestoga wagons, loaded with all the worldly possessions of the pioneers, made the dangerous trip. It was a rugged life. The pioneers needed constant vigilance to protect themselves from the Native Americans, to keep the animals on the road, and to provide water, firewood, and food for the family.

Water travel was smoother and offered the advantage of company. But since goods could flow down stream and not up, canals were dug for easy movement both up and down by water. The first major canal was the Erie Canal, finished in 1825. This started a wave of canal building that peaked in 1828, when the Chesapeake & Ohio Canal was started on the same day that the first stone of the Baltimore & Ohio Railroad was formally laid.

The trains were faster and reached a greater number of destinations. They quickly superseded the canal system, and many canals reverted to great grassy ditches.

Maryland

B&O Railroad Museum

The story of the American railroad begins at Mount Clare in Baltimore, when Maryland's Charles Carroll laid the first stone for the Baltimore & Ohio Railroad on July 4, 1828 (coincidentally on the same day President John Quincy Adams turned over the first shovel of soil for the building of the Chesapeake & Ohio Canal just outside Washington, D.C.). Carroll said about his involvement in the B&O Railroad inauguration, "I consider this among the most important acts of my life, second only to the signing of the Declaration of Independence, if second even to that."

At the **B&O Railroad Museum** you can explore this pivotal transportation revolution. Fifty locomotives and full-size models are housed in the museum's Mount Clare station roundhouse. The station is considered the birthplace of the American railroad and the oldest station in the United States. The first American trains ran from this spot to Ellicott City (see selection), and it was here that Peter Cooper built the engine he called his Teakettle, nicknamed by others "Tom Thumb."

Cooper's Tom Thumb is known as the early locomotive that lost a legendary race with a horse. As sometimes happens with such stories, fiction has clouded fact in this tale. Although a race evidently did take place, just when and where have never been firmly established. It might have been on August 28, 1830, during the engine's inaugural thirteen-mile run between the Mount Clare station and Ellicott City. No horse, however, could have matched the engine's time of 26:22 minutes, and the many news accounts of the run do not mention a race. It is far more likely that the race took place in 1831, during the celebration of Charles Carroll's ninety-fourth birthday. The fan belt broke during this run, slowing the train enough for a horse to beat it.

The B&O Railroad Museum is known worldwide for the size and scope of its collection. Many of the prize railroad cars rest on the roundhouse's twenty-two turntable tracks. There are vintage Pangborn engines, Imlay coaches, and trains from the Civil War (when the military first used railroads) and later wars. From World War I, there are "40 and 8" trains, so called because they carried forty men and eight horses.

Trains overflow to the front and back of the museum and are popular with young visitors, who play conductor and engineer on the vintage engines. The museum is open daily from 10:00 A.M. to 5:00 P.M. It is closed on Thanksgiving, Christmas, and Easter. Admission is charged.

Directions: The B&O Railroad Museum is located at 901 W. Pratt Street, a few blocks west of Martin Luther King Jr. Boulevard in downtown Baltimore and ten blocks west of Baltimore's Inner Harbor.

C&D Canal Museum

The **C&D Canal Museum** in Chesapeake City is well worth a stop. A six-minute audio-visual program introduces visitors to the C&D Canal. The canal opened on October 17, 1829. Crossing the Delmarva Peninsula to connect the Chesapeake Bay with the Delaware River, it cuts three hundred miles of passage between these two bodies of water by eliminating the voyage around Cape Charles. Today the C&D Canal is one of the world's busiest canals, with thousands of vessels a year taking this shortcut. Most museum visitors have the chance to watch huge ships slip beneath the bridge that connects the north and south sides of Chesapeake City.

A working model at the museum demonstrates how the canal's lift lock works. There are also models of vessels that have plied the canal. The most colorful ship represented is James Adams's floating theater, which once brought entertainment to Chesapeake City and other towns along the canal. There is also a model of a canal barge, a pipeline dredge, and various Chesapeake Bay sailing craft. Those interested in the mechanical operation of the canal locks will be fascinated by the two steam engines and the cypress-wood lift wheel in the Old Lock Pump House.

The C&D Canal Museum is open at no charge Monday through Saturday, 8:00 A.M. to 4:00 P.M. Chesapeake City has a number of specialty shops and restaurants. The Bayard House, at Bohemia Avenue and the C&D Canal, is a restored Federal-style tavern and inn with great views of the canal (410-885-3314). The Inn at the Canal is a bed and breakfast with six guest rooms in an old Victorian house (410-885-5995). Italian food is featured at The Tap Room, on the corner of Second and Bohemia (410-885-9873). The Canal Creamery, 9 Bohemia Avenue, is an ice cream parlor with freshly baked pies and other tempting desserts, including their special hot fudge brownie sundaes.

Directions: From Baltimore take I-95 north. Just before you reach Delaware, exit on Route 279 south. When you intersect Route 213, continue south on Route 213 to Chesapeake City. The C&D Canal Museum is at the intersection of Second Street and Bethel Road. The address is 815 Bethel Road.

C&O Canal National Historical Park (Lower)

The outlook for transportation in America changed on July 4, 1828. In Baltimore, Charles Carroll was laying the first stone for the Baltimore & Ohio Railroad, while outside Washington, President John Quincy Adams turned over the ground to begin construction of the Chesapeake & Ohio Canal.

The C&O Canal was first envisioned by George Washington as a waterway connecting the Potomac and Ohio Rivers. He anticipated Georgetown becoming a major hub of commerce, linking Pittsburgh with the capital. This plan was never realized as construction ended in Cumberland, just 185 miles from Washington. The simultaneous construction of the B&O Railroad made the canal obsolete.

However, the portion of the canal that was completed represents an engineering masterpiece, as it presented numerous construction complications. The major difficulty was the necessity of raising the water level 605 feet from the canal's origin in Georgetown to its final stop in Cumberland. A series of seventy-four locks enabled the barges to negotiate this gradual upgrade. This incline was not the only problem facing the builders. The canal spans eleven tributaries of the Potomac River, so Roman-style aqueducts were used to float the barges above the river level. As the canal moved into the mountain area of western Maryland, a third difficulty complicated its progress. Great stone cliffs extended all the way down to the water. The only option was to tunnel. So the 3,118-foot Paw Paw Tunnel (see C&O Canal National Historical Park [Upper] selection) was dug through the mountains, enabling the barges to continue on their way.

The best way to experience canal life is to take a boat ride on the *Canal Clipper*, a canal boat that plies the narrow waterway from mid-April through October. Right after you board the boat, the captain blows the giant lock horn and begins the "locking through" maneuver designed to bring the boat up to a higher water level. The boat enters a lock and then a valve is opened, raising the water level eight feet in five minutes. In 1870, there were seventy-four of these lift locks on the 185.5 miles of canal stretching from Georgetown to Cumberland.

Once the boat is locked through, mules are hitched to the boat, and the one-hour canal voyage begins. The boats usually covered only four miles an hour, the speed limit imposed by the Canal Company so that the wake of the boats would not erode the sides of the canal. It took about ten minutes for each locking through maneuver; a minimum of twelve hours was needed to pass through all seventy-four of the canal's locks. If a boat traveled at the maximum allowable speed of four miles per hour for ten hours a day, it could travel the distance from Cumberland to Georgetown in about six days.

On quiet evenings the boat captain, who often traveled with his entire family, would pull out his harmonica or jew's harp, and passengers and crew alike would join a sing-along. Some of the park interpreters use music in their programs and invite visitors to help recreate these songfests on the boat ride. Other interpreters tell about the history of the C&O Canal.

In the spring and fall, the boat trips run Wednesday through Friday at 3:00 P.M. and on weekends at 11:30 A.M., 1:30 and 3:00 P.M. From mid-June through Labor Day, boat rides leave Wednesday through Sunday at 11:30 A.M., 1:30 and 3:00 P.M. Boat tickets go on sale the day of departure during visitor center hours. They sell out quickly on weekends. For more information and specific times, call (301) 299-3613. There is a per vehicle entrance fee for Great Falls park (a splendid natural setting with overlooks providing an awesome look at the tumbling falls of the Potomac River). Boat rides also are given at the C&O Canal in Georgetown; tickets are sold at the Georgetown Visitor Center on Thomas Jefferson Street. Call (202) 653-5190 for information.

Directions: From Baltimore, take I-95 south to the Washington Beltway (I-495) and head west to Exit 4l. Take the Clara Barton Parkway heading toward Carderock and Great Falls. At the end of the Clara Barton Parkway, turn left onto MacArthur Boulevard, which leads directly into the park at Great Falls. From I-270, take Exit 5, Falls Road, heading toward Potomac. Follow Falls Road through Potomac until you come to the end of Falls Road, where it intersects with MacArthur Boulevard. At this intersection turn right and you will enter the park.

C&O Canal National Historical Park (Upper)

The B&O Railroad and the C&O Canal once vied for travelers and trade. Now they are merely reminders of the early years of westward expansion. It is a rueful footnote to this rivalry that the **C&O Canal National Historical Park** Visitor Center is located in Cumberland's Western Maryland Station Center on Canal Street.

This impressive and commanding station reflected the railroad's success. It was built in 1913, at the height of the railroad era. Inside the station is an exhibit center for the C&O Canal National Historical Park. The C&O Canal National Historical Park Visitor Center is open Tuesday through Saturday from 9:00 A.M. to 5:00 P.M. during the winter. During the summer, it is also open on Sunday from 9:00 A.M. to 5:00 P.M. Hours do vary, so it is advisable to call ahead at (301) 722-8226 to

The Canal Clipper, *the National Park Service's nineteenth-century mule-drawn barge, glides through history on the C&O Canal. Boarding for the picturesque tour begins at the Great Falls Maryland Tavern.*

confirm the times. The Western Maryland Station, which reopened after a major restoration effort was completed in 1999, is part of the major Canal Place Project, which includes the Footer Dye Works Complex and the reopening of the Railroad Gift Shop and the ticket office of the again operational Western Maryland Scenic Railroad.

A path leads from the station to the C&O Canal terminus. From this point, it was 184.5 miles along the canal to Georgetown in the District of Columbia. On July 4, 1828, President John Quincy Adams turned the first shovel of earth to begin construction of the canal. On that same day, Declaration of Independence signer Charles Carroll laid the first stone in Baltimore for the B&O Railroad. It was to be a race to the West!

The canal did not reach Cumberland until 1850, eight years after the B&O Railroad got there. By the time the canal was fully operational, it was practically obsolete. The last three locks of the canal, numbers 73, 74, and 75, were finished in the 1840s. Stop at North Branch and see these locks, as well as a canal boat replica. The boat has a re-created captain's cabin, hay house, and onboard mule stable. The canal boats almost always had two teams, so that one team could rest while the other worked. Canal traffic was seasonal from the very beginning, because the boats couldn't maneuver once there was heavy freezing. Tours are given of the canal boat on weekends from 1:00 to 5:00 P.M., June through August.

One last canal site you might enjoy is the **Paw Paw Tunnel**, thirty miles below Cumberland. This was one of the most astonishing engineering achievements of the entire canal project. It was also completed late, twelve years behind schedule. The tunnel, through 3,118 feet of solid rock, was built to eliminate a six-mile set of bends in the Potomac River.

Today, you can walk through the tunnel. Wear comfortable shoes and be sure to bring a flashlight. Imagine the tunnel in operation, 1850 to 1924. Talk about a traffic jam! Only one boat could negotiate the tunnel at a time, so there was often a one-mile backup at each end of the tunnel.

It takes approximately twenty minutes to walk through the tunnel; as you get near the middle, the light dwindles, and the sense of being beneath an enormous rocky mountain grows. It's easy to empathize with the workers who hacked and blasted their way through this rock. Violence between the immigrant work crews, cholera epidemics, and frequent accidents added to the ordeal.

If time permits after you explore the tunnel, you may want to hike along the Tunnel Hill Trail that leads up and over the ridge above. This is a strenuous walk that takes about an hour.

Directions: From Baltimore, take I-70 west ninety miles to Hancock; then go south on Route 522 to Berkeley Springs, West Virginia. Turn right on Route 9 and continue for twenty-eight miles to Paw Paw. Head over the Potomac River bridge back into Maryland and follow signs for the Paw Paw Tunnel on your right. For Cumberland and the C&O Canal National Historical Park Visitor Center, take I-68 west from Hancock to Cumberland, Exit 43C. Turn left off the ramp onto Harrison Street; follow Harrison Street through the first stoplight into the Western Maryland Station Center parking lot. For North Branch locks, take Exit 43B, Route 51 south from Cumberland. Turn right five miles south at the sign that reads "C&O Canal Lockhouse 75 Area." This is the PPG Road; follow it to Lock 75 parking area about 0.5 mile.

The Cumberland Road

No discussion of transportation in the early days of the Republic would be complete that did not include the Cumberland Road, or National Pike. This American Appian Way linked Cumberland, Maryland, with Wheeling, West Virginia. It eventually extended as far as Illinois and was the main land route connecting the eastern seaboard with the West.

The Cumberland Road was built by the federal government between 1808 and 1829. Like the Chesapeake & Ohio Canal, this was a project that George Washington, a former surveyor, first proposed. Jefferson also was interested in this effort to expand the country's boundaries and make the interior more accessible. Once built, it was heavily used by Conestoga wagons and stagecoaches traveling over it until 1850. After that, the railroad, having made the canal route obsolete, also diverted much of the traffic from the Cumberland Road.

Built as it was, through the Allegheny Mountains, there was no problem obtaining stone for its construction, and in places the road was as wide as eighty feet. Large boulders were covered by smaller stones, which much later were macadamized and still later re-done in concrete. A keen-eyed passenger traveling along the National Pike will see many old buildings constructed of stone that was quarried when the road was dug out of the mountain.

The Cumberland Road is now part of US Route 40. One of the interesting features still remaining from the old road are the great stone bridges spanning the mountain streams. The largest one still standing, erected in 1813, crosses the Castleman River in western Maryland.

Just west of Washington, Pennsylvania, there is another interesting bridge, which was built in 1818 in the noteworthy "S" shape. Engineers found it more economical and easier to build their bridges at an angle to the flow of the stream, so they snaked across in an "S" pattern.

Bridges are not the only interesting reminders of the early days along the Cumberland Road. Even more closely associated with the first years of the National Pike are the tollhouses. Only three remain, of which the most striking architecturally is the one just over the Maryland state line in Addison, Pennsylvania. Built of stone, this hexagonal building looks more like a teahouse than a tollhouse.

Ellicott City B&O Railroad Station Museum

It was August 28, 1830, when the first cars were attached to the steam engine known as "Tom Thumb" for the run from Baltimore to Ellicott City, thirteen miles away. On a later run, when the Tom Thumb passed the relay house on the return trip to Baltimore, a race began between the train and a horse-drawn coach. Guess who won? As the engine passed the horse, it looked as though Tom Thumb would be the victor, but mechanical difficulties changed the outcome of the race. The engine slowed and the horse surged ahead—and won!

A replica of the Tom Thumb is in the Baltimore & Ohio Transportation Museum in Baltimore, but it's also worth a trip to visit the terminus at the other end of this historic line. At the Ellicott City B&O Railroad Station Museum a model of the thirteen-mile trip has been built, with an authentic HO-gauge, model-train layout. A "sight and sound" show that depicts the creation of the railroad and its first terminus, Ellicott Mills, is one of the award-winning video programs shown in the restored Freight House (circa 1885) at the B&O complex in Ellicott City.

The old stone station, built in 1831, houses a visitor center, restored stationmaster's quarters, Superintendent's Office, Ticket Office, Waiting Room, and Engine House. A partially excavated turntable is located between the two buildings, and a restored caboose is also open for inspection.

The museum hours change with each exhibit; for a current schedule, call (410) 461-1944. Admission is charged.

Directions: From the Washington Beltway, I-495/95, take Exit 30, Route 29/Columbia Pike to Old Frederick Road. Follow that to Ellicott City and the Ellicott City B&O Railroad Station Museum. From I-695, take Exit 13, Frederick Road, toward Catonsville. Head west on Frederick Road until you reach Ellicott City. The museum is located on the corner of Maryland Avenue and Frederick Road.

La Vale Toll Gate House

Have you ever become hopelessly confused trying to navigate a road with multiple names? Such confusion is as old as one of the country's earliest links between the Eastern Seaboard and the West: the National Road or Cumberland Road.

This link, now US 40, was called the **National Road** because it was the first and only road built and maintained by the federal government. George Washington had wanted to build a road, as well as a canal, linking East and West ever since he had surveyed as a young man in western Maryland.

When Congress began debate on the road's construction, the legislators called it the **Cumberland Road** in honor of the city. The contract for the first stretch from Cumberland to Eckhart was granted on May 8, 1811, but work was not completed until 1818. At a cost of $21.25 per 24fl cubic feet of road, the construction proceeded slowly and expensively. By 1830 it was decided that the states could assume the costs of any additional building as well as maintenance.

Ohio and then Maryland took over their portions of the National Road and built tollhouses to collect money to pay for them. The **La Vale Toll Gate** was the first toll house built along the Maryland section of the National Road and is now the only surviving toll gate house in the state.

The tollhouse has a two-story, seven-sided main section flanked by two one-story sections. The main part looks like a stunted lighthouse. From the windows in the upstairs bedroom the gatekeeper could see clearly in both directions. He was paid in the first year of operation two hundred dollars, or 12% of the gross receipts. The report of the superintendent of the National Road for the following year, 1837, noted that twenty thousand travelers had used this section of the National Road and recommended raising the gatekeeper's salary to three hundred dollars.

The toll rates posted on the gate house windows reveal that a horseback rider was charged four cents, and a four-wheel carriage with two horses, twelve cents. It also cost twelve cents if you were driving a score of cattle, but only six cents for a score of sheep or hogs. There was no toll for vehicles with wheels eight or more inches wide, nor for mail carriers, soldiers, or anyone going to church or a funeral.

When the railroad reached Cumberland in 1842, traffic along the National Road diminished. In 1878 the toll gate house became the property of Allegany County, which collected tolls until around 1900. Later it was sold to a private owner for use as a residence. The Maryland Historical Trust assumed ownership in 1969 and began its restoration. For many years the M.F.W.C. (Maryland Federation of Women's Club) La Vale Century Club maintained the restored and furnished toll gate house. Allegany County assumed ownership of the house in 1989, adding a picnic pavilion and benches on the landscaped grounds, as well as public restrooms. From mid-May through late October, it can be toured on Saturday and Sunday from 1:30 to 4:30 P.M. A nominal donation is requested.

Just five minutes from the Toll Gate House is one of Maryland's best dining bargains—**Fred Warner's German Restaurant.** Don't miss the chance to taste Fred's Wiener Schnitzel (the most tender, delicate veal) served with wafer-thin potato pancakes. Housed in an old stone building that is decorated with needlework, coats of arms, beer mugs, painted plates, and hanging grapes, the restaurant offers inexpensive lunch platters, including homemade breads and your pick of a well-stocked salad bar. Fred Warner's puts on special festivals four times a year during the first part of May, August, October, and December.

The restaurant is open year-round, Tuesday through Sunday, for lunch and dinner, except during July when it is closed on Sundays and Mondays. Call (301) 729-2361.

Directions: From Baltimore go west ninety miles on I-70 to Hancock. Continue west on I-68 to Cumberland. Stay on I-68 to LaVale Exit 39, which is Route 40 Alternate. The Toll Gate House is on the left 0.25 mile after you exit. To get to Fred's German Restaurant, go east on Route 40 Alternate for a short distance. Just before the first traffic light, bear right on Route 53. Turn left on Route 220, which takes you to Cresaptown and Fred Warner's (on your right).

Virginia

James River and Kanawha Canal

There are two things you should know about the **James River and Kanawha Canal**: It was the first canal system built in America, and it is one of the coolest spots in Richmond on a hot summer afternoon. Beneath the 13th Street arched overpass, built in 1860, a picnic pavilion is shaded from the sun and cooled by the canal. Display cases in the pavilion provide the history on this significant canal.

It was George Washington's dream to have a "great central American waterway" linking the Atlantic Ocean to the Ohio River. In order to realize that dream, the James River had to be made navigable for carrying tobacco and other goods. From the earliest days, settlers had encountered the obstacle of seven miles of rapids at the falls. On May 24, 1607, ten days after landing at Jamestown, a party of twenty-one explorers, including Capt. John Smith, sailed up the James River only to be halted by these falls. The falls broke the connection between the Atlantic Ocean, some 125 miles down the river, and the 200 miles of navigable river extending into the Alleghenies.

Land along the falls was sold in a lottery by Col. William Byrd II in 1737 and again in 1768, by his son William Byrd III. This settlement formed the nucleus of the city of Richmond. Although early lot purchasers hoped the James River would be cleared for navigation, it was not until George Washington became president that the work was actually started. In January 1785, the Virginia Assembly established the James River Company with the object of "clearing and improving the navigation of the James River." Washington served as its first president.

By the end of 1789, large boulders were removed from the James River and two short canals were built around the falls. In 1800, an eastern terminus called the "Great Basin" was built in Richmond between the area that is now 8th, 12th, Canal, and Cary streets. The next step needed to complete the canal system was to connect the Great Basin in the town of Richmond with the docks located in the tidewater below Shockoe Creek—the Tidewater Connection. Between 1810 and 1812, thirteen wooden locks were built by Ariel Cooley.

In 1826, Charles Crozet, chief engineer for the canal, proposed that Cooley's decaying wooden locks be replaced with stone locks. He estimated the cost at $350,000. By 1854, when the five stone locks and two basins Crozet recommended were finally open to commerce, the price tag was $850,000.

The canal has not been used since the end of 1870, but you can still visit restored locks number four and five of the Tidewater Connection at the canal locks park. Each of these large granite-blocked locks is a hundred feet long and fifteen feet wide. This National Historic Landmark is open at no charge from 9:00 A.M. to 5:00 P.M. daily. The Tidewater Connection and the surrounding park was preserved by the Reynolds Metals Company incorporating the canal path and lock system into the design of the Reynolds Wrap Distribution Center.

Directions: The James River and Kanawha Canal Locks can be seen in downtown Richmond at 12th and Byrd Streets. Parking is available alongside the canal.

Pennsylvania

Hugh Moore Historical Park and National Canal Museum

Riding a mule-drawn canal boat is the best way to understand what life was like along the canals from the 1820s to the 1930s. Historical interpreters in period dress bring canal days to life during the forty-five- to sixty-minute ride along a two-and-a-half-mile stretch of the **Lehigh Canal**. The longer two-and-a-half-hour trip includes a fascinating locking through maneuver in one of the three restored canal locks. During this procedure, the canal boat enters the lock, and a valve is opened, lowering the water level eight feet in about five minutes, thus allowing the boat to move ahead at the new elevation.

Lehigh Coal and Navigation Company founders Josiah White and Erskine Hazard tamed the turbulent Lehigh River in 1820 by creating a descending navigation system using their own unique "bear trap," or hydrostatic locks. Converted to a two-way navigation system by 1829, it gave the Lehigh Canal the largest carrying capacity of any canal in the country. The Lehigh linked up with the Morris and Delaware Canals to connect this part of Pennsylvania with New York and Philadelphia. These large metropolitan markets encouraged the development of early industrial parks at power sites along the canal.

One such industrial park was the Abbott Street area, which had a dozen manufacturing establishments employing more than a thousand workers by 1840. This area, near Lock 47, is now part of the **Hugh Moore Historical Park**. Also part of the park are the ruins of the Glendon Industrial Area and the piers and cables of Change Bridge. Built in 1857, Change Bridge is the oldest existing bridge using machine-made wire rope. Efforts are now underway to restore the bridge.

When the park was established in the early 1960s, restoration work was done on the locktender's house. Now a museum, this house provides an opportunity to step back in time to the days when the locktender and his family lived there. A costumed interpreter is on hand to answer questions.

A second museum, the **National Canal Museum,** is located in historic downtown Easton. In the Two Rivers Landing Building (also the location of The Crayola Factory and a Visitors Center for the Delaware and Lehigh National Heritage Corridor), the museum has exhibits on canal life, industries along the canal, and the coal-mining industry that used the canal to transport coal-laden canal boats to America's population centers.

Hugh Moore Historical Park stretches for six miles beside the Lehigh River. The scenic parkland has a three-mile paved bike trail. There is a towpath and river hiking trail plus a picnic and playground area.

The National Canal Museum is open year-round, Tuesday through Saturday from 9:30 A.M. to 5:00 P.M. and Sunday noon to 5:00 P.M. During the summer, the museum opens at 9:00 A.M. and closes at 6:00 P.M. except on Sunday, when it opens at 11:00 A.M. The museum is closed on major holidays, but open on most Monday holidays. A nominal admission is charged. On some busy weekends, the building's capacity limits visitors.

The canal boat ride at Hugh Moore Park is open Tuesday through Sunday from the first Saturday in May through Memorial Day. The ride operates daily from Memorial Day through Labor Day, after which they are given on weekends only until the end of September. The Locktender's House Museum is included with the canal boat admission, but it is open for limited hours. You also can rent canoes and pedal boats during the operating season.

Directions: From I-78 take the Easton exit. The National Canal Museum is 1.4 miles north of the Easton exit. The museum is two blocks south of Route 22, in historic downtown Easton in the southwest quadrant of Center Square, off S. Third Street. For the Hugh Moore Park, take the Easton exit and follow signs for Route 611 north (1.3 miles); then turn left at the end of the bridge onto Larry Homes Drive. Turn left onto Lehigh Drive, go two miles, and then turn left onto the bridge into Hugh Moore Park. From the National Canal Museum, take Route 22 to 25th Street south. Continue on 25th Street for 1.6 miles to Lehigh Drive and turn right. Proceed for 0.5 miles to the stop sign and turn right at the entrance bridge to Hugh Moore Park.

New Hope Mule Barge Company and New Hope & Ivyland Railroad

Travel back in time on a mule-drawn barge on the historic Delaware Canal or the New Hope and Ivyland Railroad to experience a community that dates back to the colonial era. In the early 1900s a group of internationally known artists moved to New Hope and opened a series of popular galleries and shops.

The charms of **New Hope** include picturesque eighteenth-century stone houses, narrow streets and alleys lined with quaint row houses, intriguing courtyards, wooded trails, and towpath walks. You can also sample the competing transportation alternatives that vied for supremacy in the late 1800s and early 1900s.

The **New Hope Mule Barge Company** lets you travel back more than 150 years and experience life along the canal. The Delaware Canal runs parallel to the Delaware River from Easton to Bristol. Construction started in 1827 and was completed in 1832, but engineering and construction problems kept it from opening for another two years. It wasn't fully operational until 1840. By 1862, between twenty-five hundred and three thousand boats traveled on the Delaware Canal, passing through twenty-five lift locks. The canal is now a national heritage corridor, as well as a Pennsylvania State Park.

Trips run on Wednesdays, Saturdays, and Sundays in April and November at 11:30 A.M., 1:00, 2:00, 3:00, and 4:30 P.M. From May through October trips are daily, and a 6:00 P.M. tour is added to the schedule. For current prices call (215) 862-2842.

Even if you don't have time to take a barge ride, be sure to walk along the canal towpath to see the old locks and perhaps photograph one of the barges as it travels the still water. If you book one of the two-hour rides on one of the few preserved canals in the country, you will pass Revolutionary cottages, artists workshops, and colorful gardens. On many of the trips, barge musicians and historians entertain passengers.

Another alternative is a half-hour cruise aboard the *General George Washington* on the Delaware River. The big blue pontoon boat departs from Coryell's Ferry, 22 South Main Street, beginning at noon daily from April through October. For additional information call (215) 862-2050. Coryell's Ferry is located on the river directly behind Gerenser's Exotic Ice Cream store, which makes roughly forty-five flavors, including such offbeat options as Ukrainian rose petal, Jewish malaga, Magyar apricot brandy, and Oriental green tea.

The noisier iron horse provides a different experience from the slow, tranquil barge rides. Tickets for the **New Hope & Ivyland Railroad** are purchased at the New Hope Station, on W. Bridge Street, where a small exhibit area evokes the early days of locomotive travel. The New Hope line was built between 1889 and 1890 and gradually supplanted the canal as the major carrier to the region.

On the nine-mile journey, fans of old movies may recognize the curved trestle bridge the train crosses as the one used on the matinee serial *Perils of Pauline*. The train ride through the countryside gives you an idea why so many artists make their home here. The train travels to Lahaska and back to New Hope. You won't have time to appreciate all this little community offers, so plan to return and enjoy the noteworthy collection of shops at Peddler's Village and Carousel World (see selection).

Trains run daily from April through November and on weekends January through March. During December there are Santa rides. Call (215) 862-2332 for updated hours and fares.

Be sure to save some time to browse through the unusual craft and antique shops in New Hope. It's easy to spend hours exploring the hundreds of shops along the tree-lined streets and tucked-away alleys. If you find yourself wishing you could tour the inside of one of the lovely old homes, head over to the 1784 **Parry Mansion** on Cannon Square. Tours of this museum of decorative arts (1775–1900) are given by the New Hope Historical Society, May through October on Friday, Saturday, and Sunday from 1:00 to 5:00 P.M. Admission is charged.

Directions: From I-95 north of Philadelphia take Exit 31, Route 32, the New Hope/Yardley exit. Route 32 becomes Main Street in New Hope.

Robert Fulton Birthplace

Visiting homes associated with figures from the pages of history fills in the blanks. Take Robert Fulton, for example. He's well known as the inventor of the steamboat, although there was an extensive litigation disputing his claim to originality and his monopoly of the steamboat service. His patents were improvements on basic ideas of both American and European steamship designs. It was, however, unquestionably Fulton who developed the steamboat into a commercially successful venture.

At Fulton's Lancaster County birthplace you'll get to know the man behind the legend. Fulton was a Renaissance man who combined a lifelong love of art with a talent for scientific endeavors. At an early age, Fulton showed artistic promise. He visited local gun shops and designed firearms and drew designs for the etchings engraved on them. Fulton also drew political and military caricatures and painted tavern signs. His family moved from this stone house in Lancaster when he was only a few years old.

When he was seventeen, the handsome and charming Robert Fulton moved to Philadelphia and studied art. He began painting the miniatures for which he became noted; his tiny portraits were among the finest in the country. His talent brought him in contact with the leading families in the state. With political and social contacts to assist him, Fulton headed to London for more training at the London Academy of Art, under the direction of American-born painter Benjamin West. Fulton's personal appeal and artistic ability made him popular with the leading figures in London. He was befriended by two men: the Duke of Bridgewater, who was deeply involved with canal research, and Lord Stanhope, an inventor and engineer. These associations brought out Fulton's own scientific bent. He patented devices for marble sawing, flax-spinning, rope twisting, and a double inclined canal boat plane. A move to Paris brought Fulton to the attention of fellow countrymen Joel Barlow and Robert Livingston, who became his main financial supporters. Fulton's interest expanded to torpedoes, submarines and steam navigation.

After a twenty-year sojourn in Europe, Fulton returned to the United States in the fall of 1806 and built the *Clermont,* his famous steamboat, which was dubbed Fulton's Folly until its inaugural trip on the Hudson on August 17, 1807. People lined the riverbanks expecting to see the newfangled boat sink. After its success, Fulton supervised the building of seventeen steamboats, a torpedo boat, and several ferryboats. His financial partner in these endeavors was Robert Livingston, the American minister to France. The day after the *Clermont's* successful voyage, Fulton became engaged to Livingston's niece, Harriet. Fulton only lived eight more years, dying of pneumonia at the age of forty-nine on February 24, 1815.

The **Robert Fulton Birthplace** was once part of a commercial hamlet that grew up around the Swift stop on the Peach Bottom Railroad, later called the Lancaster, Oxford and Southern Railroad and known locally as the Little, Old, and Slow. Although only a few buildings remain, there was once a creamery, butcher shop, country store, post office, doctor's office, and other businesses. Tobacco and grain warehouses still stand, and the granary is being transformed into a heritage center. The Fulton's three-story fieldstone house is within a hundred feet of the railroad tracks.

Visitors can tour the first floor of the Fulton birthplace, which is modestly furnished with period pieces. An exhibit room provides a chance to see several miniatures done by Robert Fulton as well as a model of the *Clermont.* An herb garden is behind the house. The Robert Fulton Birthplace is open by appointment and from Memorial Day to Labor Day on Saturdays, 11:00 A.M. to 4:00 P.M., and Sundays, 1:00 to 5:00 P.M. A nominal admission is charged.

Directions: From I-76, the Pennsylvania Turnpike, take Exit 22, Route 222 south of Lancaster. The Robert Fulton Birthplace is on Route 222 just south of the Swift Middle and Clermont Elementary Schools.

Strasburg Rail Road

How can you resist a trip to Paradise? Steam trains departing daily from **Strasburg Rail Road**, the nation's oldest short-line railroad, travel to a quiet picnic spot in Paradise, Pennsylvania. This is an ideal getaway for the extended family; grandparents can regale the younger generation with tales of traveling on the network of rails that crisscrossed America. It is also a chance to experience an authentic, operational railroad in contrast with the cars that carry crowds around larger theme parks.

You can't stay in Paradise, alas. The forty-five-minute round trip takes you through the picturesque Lancaster farmland. From the train's windows, you will glimpse straw-hatted Amish farmers working the fields with plows drawn by horses and mules. Somber clothes hang neatly on wash lines outside immaculate white farmhouses, and in front of barns you'll see black buggies. The entire experience provides a sense of slipping into a time warp.

At Strasburg Rail Road, there are reminders of the past wherever you look. Trains depart from an 1892 Victorian railroad station that is enhanced by an old water tower and several pieces from the line's rolling stock. The entire panorama seems designed for a period movie; indeed, several of the railroad cars have been used in films. An open observation car and several others made a colorful backdrop in the movie *Hello Dolly*. The world's oldest standard-gauge coach, called the Willow Brook, shared billing with Elizabeth Taylor in *Raintree County*.

You can climb aboard several of these interesting old cars, including the private coach of the president of Reading Railroad, which once epitomized traveling elegance. With its separate sitting, dining, and sleeping areas, the car cost a hundred thousand dollars to build in 1916. Designer touches include cut-glass ceiling lamps, lace-curtained windows, and mahogany paneling inlaid with rosewood. Some claim that Harry Truman used this car in his famous 1948 whistle-stop campaign across the country.

Preservationists restored the cars in the Strasburg collection to the way they looked in the late 1800s. They have puffer-belly engines, plush seats, inlaid wood paneling, kerosene lamps, and pot-bellied stoves. When you ride aboard one of these coaches, the conductor moves down the aisle punching tickets. He'll also answer your questions and tell stories about the early days of rail travel. If you want, you may disembark for a picnic, but you have to bring your own supplies.

It's easier and more in keeping with the train theme to eat at the nearby Red Caboose, a local restaurant located in an actual dining car. There are rooms available in coach cars for overnight guests. Each converted caboose has either regular or bunk beds, plus a fully equipped, though tiny, bathroom. Television sets are even hidden in the potbellied stoves. Call (717) 687-6646 for details.

This area is a mecca for train enthusiasts. Directly across from the Strasburg Rail Road is the **Railroad Museum of Pennsylvania**, which offers a treasure trove of railroad memorabilia, plus a substantial collection of rolling stock. The best vantage point from which to get an overview of the museum's collection is the second-floor observation bridge. From there you can see all the cars on the museum's four tracks. More than thirty-one classic locomotives and railroad cars date from 1835 to the present. Platforms give you a glimpse into the windows of these old Pullmans, passenger cars, mail and baggage cars. There are still more cars behind the museum, although many of these will go indoors once the museum completes its expansion project. You can easily spend hours wandering around this fascinating place.

If the life-size cars remind you of the train sets from your childhood, head over to the nearby **Toy Train Museum**, opposite the Red Caboose. Here, you get a miniaturized view of railroading as you study cases filled with train models. Three layouts show standard-gauge, American Flyer, S-gauge, and O-gauge trains. About two hundred toy trains chug around the tracks. This museum also serves as the headquarters of the Train Collectors Association.

Another spot you shouldn't miss is the **Choo Choo Barn** and its elaborate, seventeen-hundred-square-foot model train layout. Thirteen trains travel through some 130 animated scenes. Every twenty minutes the scene switches to a nighttime view. The shop that sells tickets also sells just about everything a model train enthusiast could possibly want. This is a great spot to visit at Christmas time.

If time remains, be sure to explore Strasburg's Main Street, part of the town's National Historic District. This street was once part of the Conestoga Highway, the first westward route from Philadelphia. The district has at least a dozen log houses; the Christopher Spech House dates to 1764. Other historic buildings date from the eighteenth and nineteenth centuries. On a hot day there's no better place to stop for a treat than the Strasburg Country Store and Creamery, where old-fashioned ice cream is served at an 1890 soda fountain.

The Strasburg Rail Road is open daily from mid-March through November. It is closed on Thanksgiving. There are special Santa Claus runs the first two weekends in December. Call (717) 687-7522 for a current steam train schedule. The Railroad Museum of Pennsylvania is open from 9:00 A.M. to 5:00 P.M., Monday through Saturday, and noon to 5:00 P.M. on Sundays. From November through April the museum is closed on Mondays. The Toy Train Museum is open Monday through Sunday, 10:00 A.M. to 5:00 P.M., from May through October, and on weekends only between those hours in April, November, and the first two weekends in December. The Choo Choo Barn is open daily, 10:00 A.M. to 5:00 P.M., from late March until mid-Novem-

All aboard… The Strasburg Rail Road is ready to transport visitors back to the time of steam railroading as it travels through the scenic countryside of Lancaster County, Pennsylvania. PENNSYLVANIA DUTCH VISITORS BUREAU

ber. During the summer months it stays open until 6:00 P.M., and it is open weekends only in November and December.

Directions: From the Washington Beltway, I-495/95, take I-95 north to the Baltimore Beltway and head northwest towards Towson. Take Exit 24, I-83 north to York, Pennsylvania. At York take Route 30 east through Lancaster; then turn right on Route 896 to Strasburg.

Industries

Within a year of the settlement of Jamestown in 1607, two profitable enterprises had begun: Tobacco was being planted, and a small glass factory was in operation. These early beginnings of American business were only two of the endeavors attempted by the settlers.

The Middle Atlantic area later prospered both in peacetime and wartime because of the iron industry and the manufacturing of machinery. The factory system began slowly prior to the War of 1812, but that conflict accelerated the process. With the English blockade and the federal government restrictions on trade, domestic manufacturing was essential. The iron industry also was vital to the production of weapons to fight the war and later to capitalize on the new status of the United States.

Advances in transportation—roads, canals, and railroads—provided new markets for goods. Concurrent advances in industrial productivity demanded even more expansion so that new materials and manufactured goods could move back and forth smoothly from the western markets to the eastern manufacturing regions.

Larger businesses brought another change. Formerly, the master craftsman had worked beside his apprentices. Now, with industrialization, the owner no longer stood side by side with the factory worker. A great chasm developed between the life of one and the other.

In the south, industrialization locked the planters into the slave system. Eli Whitney's cotton gin made slavery profitable because the new machine could clean fifty pounds a day if operated by hand or a thousand pounds using water power; before, a laborer could only clean about one pound a day. Thus, cotton plantations expanded, and the economy of the south rested on "King Cotton."

By 1820, it was clear that the three sections of the country were developing differently. Agriculture was big business in the south, independent farming was prevalent in the northwest, and manufacturing prospered in the north. The regional interests were so vastly different that by 1830 citizens were loyal to the section in which they had a vested economic interest. This division of interest, this sectionalism, would sorely test the new nation.

Virginia

Colvin Run Mill

"Down by the Old Mill Stream" is more than a pleasant folk song in this area: It's a great destination. Virginia's Tysons Corner is a bustling commercial hub, just as, in earlier times, **Colvin Run Mill** was a community center for a variety of neighborhood services. The mill was built circa 1811 along Difficult Run, which flowed near the Leesburg/Alexandria Turnpike, a major transportation artery connecting the farms of the Shenandoah Valley with the bustling port in Alexandria.

Colvin Run Mill was built according to the design of Oliver Evans, whose 1794 book *The Young Millwright and Miller's Guide* introduced the automated machinery that revolutionized eighteenth- and nineteenth-century milling technology.

Water from Difficult Run was diverted into a pond and millrace; then it flowed over the waterwheel to power the milling process. On each floor of the mill, a different process was performed. Grain moved by elevators and chutes from floor to floor and process to process. This smooth, efficient operation was necessary for large merchant mills, like Colvin Run, that produced flour and meal for foreign markets, including Europe, Canada, and the West Indies.

Colvin Run Mill Historic Site includes several additional restorations. The circa 1810 Miller's House now serves as a museum with a permanent exhibit, "The History of Milling and the Restoration of Colvin Run Mill," and a changing exhibit about the Millard family, which owned and operated the mill from 1883 to 1934. The barn, representing a nineteenth-century dairy barn, is used for interpretative exhibits and demonstrations and includes an adjacent working blacksmith shop. The general store, an original structure dating from 1900, served the local community during the early twentieth century. Visitors can purchase whole wheat flour and cornmeal ground at the mill as well as candy, books, works by local artists, and other unique items.

Throughout the year, Colvin Run Mill hosts special events including Civil War encampments, concerts, woodworking and blacksmithing demonstrations, seasonal celebrations, and a traditional Christmas program, which features Santa in the Mill.

Colvin Run is open daily except Tuesdays, 11:00 A.M. to 5:00 P.M., March through December. During January and February, it closes at 4:00 P.M. It is closed Thanksgiving and Christmas. Admission to the site is free except during some special events. Guided tours of the mill and miller's house are offered on the hour. A fee is charged for the tours.

Directions: From the Washington Beltway, I-95/495 in Virginia, take Exit 10B, Route 7, Leesburg Pike, west for seven miles. Colvin Run is on the right.

McCormick Farm and Historic Museum

A historic mill on the farm where Cyrus McCormick was born and a working farm with an operational gristmill make a dandy country duo.

Walnut Grove Farm, while not widely known, is picturesque, educational, and historical. The oak log gristmill, built in 1778, stands beside the blacksmith shop, where in 1831 Cyrus McCormick designed and built the first successful horse-drawn mechanical reaper. Twenty-two-year-old Cyrus worked with his father, Robert, who was also an inventor and tinkerer. They tested the reaper in John Steele's neighboring grain field. It was a two-man operation. Jim Hite drove the horse and Jon Anderson raked the grain. In half a day, they had reaped six acres of oats, or as much as five men with scythes could harvest in a day. Despite such a demonstration, there were no buyers when Cyrus offered his marvel for sale at fifty dollars.

The following season, the McCormicks harvested their own fifty acres with the new reaper. Gradually, buyers were found. Between 1831 and 1846, when Cyrus left Walnut Grove at age thirty-six, he built and sold a hundred reapers, and the price doubled to a hundred dollars. The American Agricultural Revolution started slowly, but, unquestionably, this out-of-the-way Virginia **McCormick Farm** (now named for its famous native son) was its birthplace.

In the blacksmith workshop, which was the only "factory" McCormick had during the 1830s, you'll see an anvil he used to build the first reaper. A working reproduction of the reaper has the place of honor among the numerous McCormick Farm inventions displayed in the museum above the shop.

As part of the nation's bicentennial, this old reaper was operated for a BBC program. Getting it out of the museum was like trying to take a ship from a bottle. It had to be disassembled to get it through the door and then rebuilt. This was not the end of the problems—a young horse

Large merchant mills like Colvin Run Mill were significant community gathering spots in the eighteenth and nineteenth centuries. Colvin Run produced flour that was sold to foreign markets. DON SWEENEY, FCPA

harnessed to the noisy reaper bolted and ran it into a fence. Finally, an old workhorse pulled it into the field for the film. The TV crew might better have used the models, whose details are so exact that they look full-size when photographed outdoors. You'll see models of the reaper and binder, as well as the combined reaper and mower.

The McCormick homestead, built in 1821, now serves as head-quarters for the Virginia Polytechnic Institute's Shenandoah Valley Research Station. Visitors are welcome to explore the sheep barns and other livestock areas. There is also a picnic area, and restrooms are in the old slave quarters. The farm is open daily, 8:00 A.M. to 5:00 P.M., at no charge. Located just a half-mile off I-81, it's a great place for an interstate break.

Down the road four and a half miles is **Wade's Mill**, listed on the National Register of Historic Places. Capt. Joseph Kennedy, who built two of the earliest mills in Rockbridge County, built this mill in 1750. In 1882, James F. Wade purchased the mill, and it was operated by his family for four generations. A major historic renovation has returned the interior and mill workings to their appearance in the late 1880s. Power for the mill is supplied by a twenty-one-foot water-wheel fed by a nearby stream. The old-fashioned method of water-powered stone grinding uses stone burrs to slowly crush and grind the entire wheat kernel into flour, producing what many purists believe is a better tasting, more nutritious flour.

Wade's Mill produces a wide variety of flours with no bleaches, additives, preservatives, or chemicals. The flours include whole wheat, buckwheat, cornmeal, cracked wheat, natural white, and a buckwheat pancake mix. Wade's Mill offers gift boxes with a variety of their products. These can be purchased in shops in Virginia, in D.C. Safeways, or by mail. Write Wade's Mill, Inc., Route 1, P.O. Box 475, Raphine, VA 24472. You can stop by the mill Thursday through Saturday from 9:00 A.M. to 5:00 P.M., April though mid-December.

Directions: From I-95 in the Richmond area, take I-64 west to Charlottesville. From Charlottesville take the scenic Blue Ridge Parkway south. Exit the parkway at milepost 27.2 on Virginia Route 56 to Steele's Tavern. At Steele's Tavern go south on Route 11 for about a hundred yards and turn right on Route 606 to McCormick Farm. For Wade's Mill, take Route 606 four miles past I-81. The mill will be on the right as indicated by the sign on Route 606. Or, from I-81 take exit 205 (Raphine/Steele's Tavern) and go west on Route 606 for Wade's Mill or east for McCormick Farm.

Maryland

Carroll County Farm Museum

Over the years Hollywood has turned its spotlight on rural America with movies such as *Places in the Heart, Country,* and *The River.* But this kind of attention is not as personal and hands-on as the **Carroll County Farm Museum** in Westminster, which, since 1966, has been depicting the lives of nineteenth-century independent farmers.

Although a few display cases are filled with carefully labeled articles, Carroll County Farm Museum is not a museum in the traditional sense. It is primarily a re-creation of the way of life of a landowning farm family in the nineteenth century. On such farms the farmer planted enough to feed his family and his livestock. He acquired mechanized equipment very gradually, relying primarily on horsepower. His wife preserved and canned the excess crop, and the seeds were saved for the next year. Market days were major events for the entire family.

The house at the Carroll County Farm Museum was built in 1852 to serve as the County Almshouse. In the nineteenth century it was customary to house the poor in such a community dwelling. The house, which opened in May 1853, was called the "County Home." It was run by a "steward of Almshouse," who was paid four hundred dollars annually. For a time, as many as fifty people lived here, with the women on the third floor, the stewards on the second, and a separate men's dormitory. At times hobos and tramps stayed at the Almshouse, and it wasn't uncommon to have criminals or mentally impaired individuals housed here. Able residents worked on the farm to raise food.

The farm was worked from the late 1850s until 1965, when it became this museum. Six rooms of the house are now furnished (many would say over-furnished) in the Victorian style of the late nineteenth century. Ornate picture frames are draped with swags to draw the eye from one picture to the next.

As you tour the house, the only building where a guided tour is offered, it becomes evident that although the days were long and the life hard, farming did enable a family to acquire a few of the finer things. While you're exploring, see how many objects you can name. The kitchen offers a treasure trove to be identified. Few can pin a name on the whipped cream churner, though most can identify the apple corer.

The guides, dressed in period costumes, will direct you to the outbuildings, where blacksmiths, weavers, spinners, quilters, and tinsmiths, when available, demonstrate their skills and wares. After watching these artisans, you can check out the farm support buildings, which include a bank barn, blacksmith shop, broom shop, 1890 veterinary surgeon's office, springhouse, smokehouse, and one-room schoolhouse. There are farm animals and a fish pond. The farm is part of a 140-acre parcel. Two pavilions and a gazebo in the garden are popular for reunions, wedding receptions, and other private functions. There are nature trails, including a bluebird trail, to hike if you have the time and a place to picnic on the grounds under the trees.

The Carroll County Farm Museum is open weekends, noon to 5:00 P.M., May through October, and daily, except Monday, from 10:00 A.M. to 4:00 P.M. during July and August. Throughout the year the farm sponsors a series of special events (see Calendar of Events). The General Store, which suggests the 1800s, sells items crafted by museum artisans and well as nickel candy and souvenirs.

Directions: From Baltimore take Route 140 northwest to the Westminster area. From Route 140 west in Westminster, turn left onto Center Street. Go one mile and the Carroll County Farm Museum is on the right at 500 South Center Street.

Furnace Town

The south had plantations worked by slave labor, while the north had industrial villages worked by laborers who were virtual serfs on feudal-like estates. Just a few miles from Snow Hill, you can visit a re-created nineteenth-century industrial town that was run in this manner. The Nassawango Iron Furnace operated from 1832 to 1847. Step back in time at this remarkable historic site.

Bog ore was discovered along the Nassawango Creek as early as 1789. But forty years passed before the Maryland General Assembly, in 1829, granted a charter to the Maryland Iron Company, after which the company acquired five thousand acres of forest and swampland around the creek. Originally it built a cold blast furnace, but it switched between 1834 and 1837 to the hot blast technique developed in Scotland. It is this hot blast furnace you'll see today and that calls up mental pictures of the miners, sawyers, colliers, molders, firemen, carters, draymen, and bargemen who lived and worked in **Furnace Town** in its heyday.

Originally the ore was thought to be a higher grade than it actually was; thus the furnace was never as profitable as had been anticipated. The bog ore was obtained beneath the creek waters by min-

Restored stone buildings and reconstructed wooden ones at Hopewell Village National Historic Site provide a glimpse of industrial life in an iron-making community. Living-history demonstrations bring colliers, moulders, and blacksmiths to life. NATIONAL PARK SERVICE PHOTO BY RICHARD FREAR

ers using picks, shovels, and rakes. Ore was then carried to the shore in flat-bottom boats. It was smelted day and night in the thirty-five-foot-high furnace.

The furnace is recognized by historical experts as one of the finest examples of its kind in the country. It offers insights into how the smelting process worked. Because the trough, in which the molten ore was cooled after it had passed through the casting hearth, looked to some people like a sow with piglets, this cast iron came to be called "pig" iron. The entire iron-making process is explained at the Furnace Town museum. Be sure to stop there before you see the furnace; it will give you an appreciation and understanding of what you'll be seeing. Other buildings at Furnace Town include a company store selling wares made by Furnace Town's artisans, a blacksmiths shop, smokehouse, broom house, nineteenth-century print shop, and the Old Nazareth Church, circa 1874.

A fictional account of the decline of the Nassawango Iron Furnace is included in George Alfred Townsend's novel, *The Entailed Hat*. The book, published in 1884, is out of print but can be obtained through the Maryland public library system.

The **Nassawango Creek and Swamp** come under the jurisdiction of the Nature Conservancy. If you have the time, take the one-mile nature trail that begins at the furnace site. The trail is particularly enjoyable in the spring, when the wildflowers bloom. It is always a mecca for bird lovers.

Furnace Town hosts many festivals throughout the spring, summer, and fall. Living history is an integral part of these special events. Furnace Town is open daily from 11:00 A.M. to 5:00 P.M. Admission is charged. For additional information, you can call (410) 632-2032.

Directions: From Baltimore take Route 2 south to Route 50. Take Route 50 east about ninety miles to Salisbury; then take Route 12 south about sixteen miles to Old Furnace Road. Turn right at the highway sign for Furnace Town.

Pennsylvania

Cornwall Iron Furnace

Think about any contemporary commercial corridor, and you'll picture ubiquitous fast-food chains. Fast forward a century and imagine that only one survives. That is the analogy you should make when you visit **Cornwall Iron Furnace**. Cornwall was the first iron furnace in this part of Pennsylvania, but with passing years it became one of many. Now it is, again, one of the few. Nowhere else in the United States, and in few other places in the world, has an iron furnace been as well preserved as Cornwall.

What you have at Hopewell is a reconstructed iron furnace; the village at Hopewell is preserved, not reconstructed. Robert Vogel, of the Smithsonian Institution, says of the restoration of iron-working sites, "There are two sites of transcendent significance, noteworthy as a consequence of their being true survivals from important periods in American ironworking. These are the Cornwall and Sloss Furnace sites." (The latter is a nineteenth-century Alabama furnace.) Vogel continues, ". . . I doubt that elsewhere in the world is there a 19th century iron furnace complex with the degree of historical integrity to be found at Cornwall, where it has been estimated that fully 95% of the fabric is original."

Remarkably, the entire iron-making complex at Cornwall survived intact, providing the visitor an authentic look at nineteenth-century iron-making. Cornwall produced bars of "pig" iron as well as cast-iron products. Pig iron was sent to nearby forges for further refining.

Cornwall was built in 1742 by Peter Grubb to use the deposits in the Cornwall Ore Banks, once the greatest known deposit of iron in the country. Cornwall was the seventh furnace in the colony but the first in the area. From 1856 to 1857, the furnace was extensively renovated by the Coleman family, which then owned the complex. The Colemans also owned Hopewell Forge (see Hopewell Furnace selection) and Colebrook and Elizabeth Furnaces. By 1883 the Cornwall Iron Furnace was obsolete and went out of blast.

As you walk through the complex, a guide will explain the complex process by which iron was separated from the ore taken from the nearby pit mines. First the iron was heated to the melting point by charcoal in the core of the furnace. It took an acre of wood *per day* to make the charcoal used in the furnace. One acre of forest equaled twenty-one cords of wood. The bulk of the workforce was involved in making charcoal for the furnace. Each year, Cornwall schedules a charcoal making demonstration. The visitor center is situated in one of the charcoal storage rooms. There were four other equally large storage areas.

Every hour, charcoal, iron ore, and limestone were added to the furnace. The thirty-two-foot-tall furnace was built beside a hill to make it easier for the workers to load the materials into the furnace. Every twelve hours, molten iron was removed from the bottom of the furnace, while slag and waste material were removed at thirty- to sixty-minute intervals. At its peak, the furnace employed sixty men and boys and used forty-six horses and mules. Visitors may be surprised to learn that, for the first couple of generations, roughly a third of the workers were black slaves who were the property of the furnace owner.

After you peer thirty-two feet down to its base, metaphorically looking into the mouth of the furnace, you will discover its lungs. Oxygen needed to keep the fire burning was blown in at the base of the furnace. When Cornwall was first built, air was pumped in using large bellows powered by a waterwheel. Later, blowing tubs were added; these were were powered at first by the waterwheel and eventually by steam engine. (Note the difference if you visit Hopewell, which is water powered.) Furnace heat was then recycled to create more steam.

This process was hot and noisy and filled the air with charcoal dust and sulphur fumes. The roar of the furnace could be heard throughout the village, and its glare created an unholy glow. Both owner and workers lived near the furnace. When you visit Cornwall, you can see (but not tour) the owner's house, the mines where the ore was extracted, and the miners' and workers' sturdy stone houses.

During the Revolutionary War, some ironmasters became gun founders, which was the case at Cornwall, where forty-two cannons were cast. During the Civil War, gunblocks were cast at Cornwall, but these did not prove successful. A defective cannon still sits in the casting area, where you'll discover why they call it pig iron. The molten ore was channeled into sand troughs that reminded workers of a row of hungry pigs lined up beside their mother for lunch.

Cornwall Iron Furnace is open Tuesday through Saturday from 9:00 A.M. to 5:00 P.M. On Sundays, it opens at noon. It is open Memorial, Independence, and Labor Days. Admission is charged.

Directions: From I-76, the Pennsylvania Turnpike, take the Lebanon/Lancaster Interchange and proceed north on Route 72. At the traffic signal at Quentin, turn right onto Route 419 north. Follow signs 1.7 miles to the Cornwall Iron Furnace on Rexmont Road at Boyd Street.

Hopewell Furnace

Hopewell Furnace does for the travel buff what John Jakes's novel North and South did for the historical novel buff—it presents a rarely captured look at a paternalistic iron plantation. Like the Hollywood movie sets of the plantations of the Old South, Hopewell looks a lot cleaner now than it did in the 1770s. From the late eighteenth century until 1883, the furnace ran day and night, filling the air with smoke and coating the village with ash and cinders.

Now the dust is long settled. You can see an idealized, picture-perfect iron-making community, operating as it did between 1820 and 1840. It's interesting to compare the small houses of the ironworkers (still planted with their kitchen gardens) with the luxury of the iron-master's home, the Big House. Like their counterparts in the South, the ironmasters were community leaders. In fact, James Wilson and George Ross, both ironmasters and brothers-in-law of Hopewell's founder, Mark Bird, were members of the Continental Congress and signers of the Declaration of Independence. Another Pennsylvania signer, George Taylor, was the ironmaster at Durham Furnace.

When you arrive at this National Historic Site, managed by the National Park Service, you will begin your exploration at the visitor center, where an easy-to-follow, ten-minute orientation slide program provides an idea of how an iron furnace operated. This will, in turn, give you a greater appreciation of what you will see on your self-guided walking tour.

Many of the seventeen stops on your tour route are concerned with the iron-making process. Hundreds of acres of timber had to be cut annually to make charcoal for the furnace. The massive iron furnace was the linchpin of the village. You'll see the cast house, where the molten iron was formed into armaments for the Continental Army and such utilitarian products as stoves, sash weights, and cookware. Taped messages will help you understand the process as you follow the step-by-step procedure on your tour route.

The voices of those bygone days, heard on taped recordings, reveal intriguing details about daily life and concerns. Some villagers have serious problems: One worries about child labor, while a widow laments the hardship of her life.

Although interesting year-round, it is in the summer that Hopewell is most alive. During July and August the living-history program presents authentically clad blacksmiths, cooks, and moulders as well as other craftspeople, who talk about their lives and demonstrate their skills. Hopewell Furnace is open daily from 9:00 A.M. to 5:00 P.M. except for major holidays. Hopewell is accessible to the handicapped.

Adjacent to this historical site is a natural one—**French Creek State Park**—where you can enjoy a picnic lunch. This 7,339-acre park, with its three lakes, offers a variety of activities. Hiking, fishing, swimming, and camping are popular in pleasant weather. During the winter months, you can ski, sled, toboggan, skate, or ice fish.

"If you can't see it here, it isn't worth looking for." That's an accurate summation of the sixty thousand items that Henry Mercer collected to tell the story of work, play, and other aspects of daily life in America before the age of steam. MILTON RUTHERFORD, BUCKS COUNTY HISTORICAL SOCIETY

Another nearby attraction is **St. Peters Village**, a picturesque Victorian village where you can enjoy lunch, hike along French Creek, and browse through well-stocked boutiques. While having lunch on the outdoor patio of the Inn at St. Peters, you can watch the French Creek Falls, which drop 155 feet in less than half a mile.

Directions: From I-76, the Pennsylvania Turnpike, take Exit 22 at Morgantown and pick up Route 10, south. Take Route 10 south for 0.75 mile into Morgantown. In Morgantown turn left, east on Route 23, and go five miles to the intersection with Route 345. Take a left, north, on Route 345. This leads into Hopewell Furnace, which is ten miles from the turnpike. Follow the above directions for St. Peters Village and continue on Route 23; make a left on Route 8 and go north to the village.

Mercer Museum

"See Henry Mercer's Three Concrete Extravaganzas" may sound like a huckster's come-on, but Henry Mercer was no sideshow performer. Mercer was a daringly innovative archeologist, anthropologist, historian, and ceramist.

Mercer's explorations of the detritus of other civilizations enabled him to spot the "archeology of recent times." This is what he called the spinning wheels, rope machine, and salt boxes he spotted at a junk dealer's yard in the spring of 1897, a find which led to the amassing of fifty thousand objects that tell the story of work, play, and other aspects of daily life in this country before the age of steam.

Mercer not only felt a mission to salvage these fragments of Americana, he also had the daring to house them in an incredible concrete castle far more likely to be seen on some English moor than in Doylestown. Mercer designed and built his castle from 1913 to 1916 without using an architectural blueprint. Like castles of old, Mercer's monument is cold and damp. Hollywood could easily film a scary movie among the castle's labyrinth of dark passages, twisting staircases, high-vaulted ceilings, and absorbing, all-pervasive clutter. Mercer considered himself a writer in the tradition of Edgar Allan Poe and Ambrose Bierce. You might even get a sense of the macabre as you wander through the assortment of caskets, hearses, and gallows.

The mood at the **Mercer Museum** shifts with the changes in the motif of the exhibits. Tools used for more than fifty crafts can be found in four galleries that extend around a central court, where other items hang from the high ceiling or are lashed to the railings. A

Conestoga wagon and a whaleboat are just two of the pieces from the transportation field. As one visitor remarked, "If you can't see it here, it isn't worth looking for."

Henry Mercer was also fascinated with early American redware pottery. Colonial settlers originally made dishes, or trenchers as they were called, out of wood. Later they were made from gray and red clay. After studying the technique, Mercer himself began making decorative red clay tiles.

Never one to do anything on a minor scale, he began a factory in 1912 within the cavernous concrete edifice or "extravaganza" that became the **Moravian Pottery and Tile Works.** The decorated tiles Mercer produced were sold around the world. The tiles grace such haunts of the rich as a Rockefeller home and the casino at Monte Carlo. Mercer's varied designs number approximately two thousand and include scenes copied from old-fashioned cast-iron stove plates, as well as Indian and medieval motifs. Prices start modestly and extend to four hundred dollars. A slide show and lecture introduce visitors to the tile works. After that, you can take a self-guided tour through the still-operational factory.

There is yet one more Mercer "extravaganza" to be visited. **Fonthill** was Mercer's home and the first of the three concrete structures to be built. It's fun to imagine the comments of the Doylestown citizenry who watched the turreted, balconied, and pinnacled Fonthill go up. Working with only his own ideas and no architect's drawings, Mercer hired local unskilled laborers to build his house room by room, improvising as he went along. "Ceilings, floors, roofs, everything concrete," he wrote to a friend in 1909. Continuing, "You stand up a lot of posts-throw rails across them-then grass-then heaps of sand-shaped with groined vaults then lay on a lot of tiles upside down & throw on concrete. When that hardens pull away the props & you think you're in the Borgia room at the Vatican."

One might believe that the museum castle would be sufficient to display Mercer's collection, but it wasn't. Mercer's five-storied home has endless nooks and galleries filled with memorabilia, as well as walls of tiles. This collection ranges farther afield than that displayed in the museum. It includes artifacts Mercer gathered on his travels around the world. He seems to have kept everything he ever picked up!

It takes at least a day to cover the three Mercer "extravaganzas," and you'll want to wear comfortable walking shoes. All three sites are open daily, 10:00 A.M. to 5:00 P.M.; on Sunday they open at noon. Admission is charged. Reservations are suggested for Fonthill, where guided tours are given. Call (215) 348-9461. The Mercer sites are closed on Thanksgiving, Christmas, and New Year's Day.

Directions: From I-95 in Philadelphia, take Route 611 north to Doylestown. For the Mercer Museum, turn right off Route 611 on Ashland Street and continue to the intersection with Green Street. For Fonthill, continue up Ashland and turn left on Pine Street. Take Pine to East Court Street and turn right. Fonthill is on East Court Street on your left. To reach the Moravian Pottery and Tile Works, continue up East Court Street to Route 313; turn left and proceed about 0.1 mile to the parking lot on the left.

New Jersey

Wheaton Village

Wheaton Village was constructed to represent a glassmaking town that evokes the Victorian era, a time when the flames never died in the furnaces of South Jersey. The gingerbread architecture, village green, quaint one-room 1876 Central Grove Schoolhouse, and the General Store replicate the turn of the century. You'll see thousands of examples of glassmakers' skills in the **Museum of American Glass**, which boasts the finest and largest American glass collection in the country. Visitors can watch skilled workers create objects of great beauty in the fully functional glass factory.

The Museum of American Glass reveals the scope, complexity, and artistry of glassmaking. Exhibits trace the development of glassmaking and give examples and a brief history for each pivotal era. The foyer itself re-creates a Victorian Cape May, New Jersey, hotel lobby. The chandelier once hung in Atlantic City's Traymore Hotel; the brass wall sconces decorated the walls of the Waldorf Astoria in New York. A series of period rooms include numerous decorative and utilitarian glass items. Particularly interesting are the elegant dining room and well-stocked kitchen.

In all, the museum has more than sixty-five hundred pieces of American glass dating from 1609, when glassmaking began in the New World at Jamestown, Virginia. The first glass factory in the country was established in New Jersey as early as 1739.

The earliest pieces were functional and were used to store medicine and preserve food. The museum dispels the myth that the term "booze" is derived from the E.G. Booz Bottle in which Old Cabin Whiskey was sold. The expression derives from the sixteenth-century English slang word "boozy," meaning drunk.

By the middle of the nineteenth century, craftsmen were creating decorative glass. One outlet for creativity was the crafting of paperweights, and the museum has many imaginative examples. To start your own collection, stop at the village's Arthur Gorman Paperweight Shop. The selection here spans a wide price range from reasonable to extravagant (such as Tiffany glass and art nouveau pieces).

After the museum you'll be ready to see glass made at the **T.C. Wheaton Glass Factory**. Carl Sandburg described the original 1888 Millville factory as follows: "Down in southern New Jersey, they make glass. By day and by night, the fires burn on in Millville and bid the sand let in the light." They did indeed burn the factory fires seven days a week, twenty-four hours a day.

The fires still burn, but not as intensely. Three times a day, 11:00 A.M., 1:30 and 3:30 P.M., glassmaking demonstrations are given in the factory. A skilled craftsman explains the process and shows how blown ware and paperweights are made. If you want a hands-on experience, call ahead at (800) 998-4552 and make reservations to make your own paperweight. Only visitors twenty-one and older may register, and there is a fee. Both spectators and participants find it fascinating to watch as the glass takes shape and the flowers, leaves, and bubbles are added.

Glassmaking is only one of the crafts demonstrated at Wheaton Village. In Crafts and Trades Row you get to watch potters, woodcarvers, and flameworkers plying their craft. Picturesque Victorian shops along Main Street include the Paperweight Shop, Stained Glass Studio, Down Jersey Folklife Center, Gallery of American Crafts, Brownstone Emporium, and General Store.

Children appreciate the playground and half-scale steam train, the C.P. Huntington, which leaves from the 1880 Palermo Train Station. The open-sided cars wind around the perimeter of the village; the ride is particularly scenic in the spring when the azaleas bloom and in the fall when the leaves are colored.

Wheaton Village is open daily, 10:00 A.M. to 5:00 P.M., April through December. During January, February, and March, the village is only open Wednesday through Sunday. The village is closed on major holidays. Admission is charged, but children under five are free.

Directions: From the Washington Beltway I-495/95, take I-95 north to Wilmington, Delaware, where you will cross into New Jersey and take Route 40 east to Route 55. Continue on Route 55 south to Exit 26. Bear right at the exit and take the first left turn. The entrance will be a half-mile on the right.

Delaware

Hagley Museum

If you want to take a family excursion to a "theme" park that is more interesting than entertaining and more authentic than ersatz, then head down to the Brandywine Valley in Delaware.

Upper Delaware became a virtual du Pont family fiefdom from the time the du Pont powder mills along the Brandywine River began to prosper. There was a vigorous market for gunpowder and iron in the newly emerging country. As the Brandywine operation expanded into chemicals and textiles, the wealth of the du Ponts increased.

At the Hagley Museum just outside Wilmington, Delaware, you can see the re-created life of an industrial worker in the nineteenth century. There is so much to see, and it is such a picturesque spot, that you should plan a picnic lunch and make a day of it. It takes about three or four hours to do justice to the museum.

A jitney takes you around the two-hundred-acre grounds, stopping at more than twenty-four areas of interest included on the walking tour map. Demonstrators show how the waterwheel, water turbine engine, and steam engine were used in the powder mills.

Not only has the gun powder equipment been restored, but also the workers' homes. Community life in the mid-nineteenth century is further revealed by the Brandywine Manufacturer's Sunday School, where you can sit at the low desks as a worker in period dress explains the lessons of the day.

Overlooking the powder mills is the wisteria-covered, Georgian-style du Pont residence, Eleutherian Mills, built in 1803. Following the French tradition of sharing the dangers with his workers, Eleuthere du Pont built his home on the site of the highly volatile powder work mill. The confidence he hoped to instill was undermined several times when the house was severely damaged by explosions, the last and most serious in 1890.

Twelve rooms of the house have been restored and are furnished with antiques to reflect the lives of five generations of du Ponts who lived there. As you leave the house, you see the two-acre garden, now restored to its 1803–34 appearance. In addition to the seasonally changing flowers in the parterres, there are dwarf fruit trees trained en quenouille, a practice popular in France during the nineteenth century. E. I. du Pont planned his garden to be a mixture of French and American plants.

Also close to the house is a reconstructed summerhouse, an

arbor, and a barn containing a collection of nineteenth-century farm tools, weathervanes, wagons, a rare Conestoga wagon, and a cooper shop. Just down from the mansion is the first office of the du Pont company. It is interesting to see the precautions taken to protect the candlelight office from the highly explosive powder.

This indoor-outdoor historic complex is well worth exploring. The main museum building tells the story of America's early industrial development through a series of audio-visual presentations, automated displays, and a "talking" map. The Hagley Museum is a thoroughly professional and eminently enjoyable look at a part of our history all too often overlooked.

From March 15 through December, the Hagley Museum is open daily from 9:30 A.M. to 4:30 P.M. January through mid-March, the hours are the same on weekends, but on weekdays the museum is open only for a 1:30 P.M. tour. Hagley is closed on Thanksgiving, Christmas, and New Year's Eve Day. Admission is charged. Picnic tables are available.

Directions: Take I-95 south to Exit 7, Route 52 north. Follow Route 52 to the intersection with Route 100. Turn right on Route 100 and continue to Route 141. Make a right; continue on Route 141 until you reach the Hagley Museum on your left.

Civil War Period

Private Homes

The houses of the Civil War period are important because of what happened either in the house or on the grounds. Houses of earlier eras gained prominence and were restored because of the famous personalities associated with them; they served as the backdrop to personalities rather than events.

Homes that have been restored from the Civil War period are of historic interest because of the battles that occurred in their front yards, like Belle Grove, or because they served as a field hospital, like Chatham. Others are noted as the backdrops of conspiracy, as is the case with the Mary Surratt House and the Petersen House.

These homes became part of the events that took place in and around them. For instance, the Clara Barton House served not only as a home, but also as headquarters and office for the American Red Cross.

This utilitarian emphasis is reflected in the architecture and furnishings of the homes of the Civil War period.

Virginia

Belle Grove

Yost Hite emigrated from Strasbourg, Germany, to England in 1709. A year later he joined a group of three thousand commissioned by the English government to make tar for the Royal Navy in New York in exchange for the cost of their transportation. The project collapsed, and Hite with friends and his family went to live in Ulster County, New York. By 1716, they moved to Germantown, Pennsylvania. Still searching for the perfect spot to settle, Yost became the first recorded settler in the Shenandoah Valley.

Yost's grandson, Maj. Isaac Hite, who fought in the American Revolution, built **Belle Grove** between 1794 and 1797. Isaac married James Madison's sister, Nelly Conway Madison. In 1794, his brother-in-law, the future president, married Dolley Paine Todd, and the couple honeymooned at Belle Grove. James Madison's friend and neighbor, Thomas Jefferson, provided architectural advice during the building of Belle Grove. Jefferson's touch can be discerned in the graceful symmetry of the house, in the T-shaped halls and the top and bottom opening windows. The house is built of native limestone and has two large porticoed porches.

Looking out over the blue haze on the nearby mountains, you don't question how the range got its name; but you do wonder why the house isn't called Belle View. The house is furnished with many pieces made in the Valley, and many that belonged to the Hite family. In the parlor the Charles Peale Polk portraits, commissioned by Major Hite in 1799, can be viewed today in their original home.

During the Civil War's Valley Campaign, military action occurred in and around Belle Grove. In the fall of 1864, Gen. Philip Sheridan made his headquarters at Belle Grove. At 5:00 A.M. on October 19, Confederate soldiers made a surprise attack on the Union soldiers camped at Belle Grove. Sheridan was in Washington, D.C., conferring with Secretary of War Stanton. Sheridan heard the gunfire from Winchester as he returned. Confederate forces were already counting this a victory when Sheridan's timely arrival turned the tide of battle. More than six thousand men died at the Battle of Cedar Creek, the last major battle for control of the Shenandoah Valley.

Confederate general Stephen Dodson Ranseur, a classmate of George Custer's at West Point, was mortally wounded and died at Belle Grove. General Custer visited him before his death. There was a ladder to a rooftop platform where Sheridan's men sent messages to a lookout on Signal Mountain. Candle smoke graffiti in the attic says, "U.S.A. Signal Corps 1864."

In the cellar you can see the winter kitchen and learn the derivation of the expression "too many irons in the fire." If cooks during the Federal period tried to use more than one cookie press, the irons got too hot and burnt the cookie wafers; thus there were too many irons in the fire. Near the kitchen is an extensive demonstration garden to explore. Before you leave be sure to visit the large museum shop, which specializes in needlecraft supplies. For additional details on Belle Grove, call (540) 869-2028.

Belle Grove is open April through October, Monday through Saturday, with tours from 10:00 A.M. to 4:00 P.M.; Sunday, 1:00 to 5:00 P.M.; and by special appointment. Admission is charged.

Directions: From I-95 in the Richmond area take I-64 west to Route I-81. Travel north on I-81 to Exit 302; proceed west to Route 11. Then take Route 11 south through Middletown to Belle Grove, on your right two miles past Middletown.

Booker T. Washington National Monument

The video presentation at the **Booker T. Washington National Monument** is inspirational, but that is not surprising. The subject is the phenomenal journey of a young boy, born here in slavery, who grew up to found Tuskegee Institute and become an unofficial advisor to three United States presidents. The images of this fifteen-minute program are poignant, and the evocation of the life of young Booker T. Washington striking. It sets the stage for your walking tour of this Civil War era plantation.

The Plantation Trail takes you through a partial reconstruction of James and Elizabeth Burroughs's two-hundred-acre tobacco farm, which was typical of the area's working-class farms, on which slaves were used to grow a cash crop of tobacco. A reconstructed kitchen cabin stands near the location of the original cabin where a slave child, simply called Booker, was born in the spring of 1856. Like many slave cabins of the period, it has no windows, just crude openings and a bare earth floor. Booker, his mother, Jane, his brother John, and his sister Amanda slept on rags piled in the corner of a similar cabin. The video quotes young Booker on the discomfort of a new flax shirt. It felt like chestnut burrs pressed against his skin. He also complained about the slaves' crude wooden shoes.

As a child, Booker carried water, fed the livestock, took corn to the mill, and fanned flies away while the Burroughs family ate. Though his ambition as a boy was to "secure and eat ginger-cakes" like his owner's daughters, he developed more ambitious goals. After emancipation in 1865, he moved with his family to West Virginia. Life was still hard, but he was finally permitted to learn reading and writing. His workday at a salt furnace began at 4:00 A.M., and he studied the alphabet at night. When he heard about the Hampton

Normal and Agricultural Institute for African Americans, he became determined to attend although he had no idea where it was located or how he could get there.

Booker walked and begged rides across Virginia to reach Hampton. His experiences at this school changed his life. Because of his outstanding scholastic performance, the principal at Hampton recommended Washington for a position as principal at a school in Tuskegee, Alabama. When Washington arrived in Tuskegee, there were no teachers, classrooms, supplies, or campus. Washington, however, established the school and made it successful.

Booker T. Washington's roots were in the rural Piedmont farm where he lived as a slave, and he referred to his early days on the plantation throughout his life. In fact, his most autobiographical book was called *Up from Slavery*. It is amazing to reflect, as you walk the paths of this out-of-the-way farm, that a slave boy born here ended up having tea with Queen Victoria and informally advising Presidents McKinley, Roosevelt, and Taft.

The National Park Service maintains the farm today. On this living historical farm are reconstructed nineteenth-century buildings, farm animals, a kitchen garden, and fields of tobacco and other crops. Scheduled tours are offered daily. The visitor center at Booker T. Washington National Monument is open year-round. Park hours are from 9:00 A.M. to 5:00 P.M. daily, except Thanksgiving, Christmas, and New Year's Day.

Directions: From I-81 in the Roanoke Valley, take I-581 south to Route 220 to Rocky Mount. At Rocky Mount follow directional signs north on Route 122 to the park.

Boyhood Home of Robert E. Lee

There is a link between the Lee and Washington families. Martha Washington's grandson, George Washington Parke Custis, married Mary Fitzhugh on July 7, 1804, at this Oronoco Street house. Twenty-seven years later, their daughter, Mary Anne Randolph Custis, married Robert E. Lee. He had spent part of his boyhood growing up in the house where his bride's parents had married.

William Fitzhugh, formerly the owner of Chatham (see selection), purchased this Alexandria house two years after it was built in 1795 by businessman, John Potts. In 1811, another hero of the war, "Lighthorse Harry" Lee rented the house and moved here with his wife and five children. It was just prior to the War of 1812, and at that time Alexandria was part of the District of Columbia. When the British burned the Capitol in 1814, they sacked the warehouses of Alexandria. It was a tense time for all the citizens including seven-year-old Robert E. Lee, who perhaps felt it more keenly because his father had left his family and traveled to the West Indies in a fruitless attempt to improve his health. In the upstairs bedroom, you can imagine young Robert anxiously watching the Potomac both in hopes of his father's return and in fear of the British. Robert lived here until 1825.

When Robert E. Lee was preparing for West Point, his father's famous friend, the Marquis de Lafayette, paid a courtesy visit to Ann Hill Carter Lee, the widow of his comrade-in-arms, Gen. "Lighthorse Harry" Lee. The downstairs parlor, or sitting room, is called the "Lafayette Room" in honor of his October 1824 visit. This short call was followed by a dinner visit in December of the same year.

The Boyhood Home of Robert E. Lee at 607 Oronoco Street is open Monday through Saturday, 10:00 A.M. to 4:00 P.M., and Sunday, 1:00 to 4:00 P.M. Admission is charged.

Directions: From I-495/95, the Washington Beltway, take Exit 1, US 1 north into Alexandria. Turn right on Oronoco Street, which is ten blocks past Franklin Street.

Chatham

Within Fredericksburg National Military Park is **Chatham**, a gracious eighteenth-century Georgian mansion. The house, overlooking the Rappahannock River, was a front-line headquarters for Union general Edwin V. Sumner and others. Chatham was also a field hospital, served by Clara Barton, known as the "Angel of the Battlefield." Walt Whitman, one of America's most revered poets, also worked in the hospital.

Chatham is also noteworthy because it is the only home still standing where both George Washington and Abraham Lincoln are known to have been entertained. Local enthusiasts claim that George Washington wrote in a letter to William Fitzhugh, "I have put my legs oftener under your mahogany at Chatham than anywhere else in the world, and have enjoyed your good dinners, good wine and good company more than any other." The builder of Chatham, William Fitzhugh, achieved such a reputation for hospitality that he was exhausted by a steady stream of guests. He finally sold Chatham and moved to a smaller house in Alexandria, now known as the Boyhood

315

Home of Robert E. Lee (see selection), where he could more readily restrict his social calendar.

You can tour Chatham and see several rooms of museum exhibits. The gardens have been restored, and from the front yard there is a panoramic view of Fredericksburg. Chatham and the Fredericksburg Battlefield Visitor Center are open at no charge daily from 9:00 A.M. to 5:00 P.M., with extended hours in the spring, summer, and fall.

Directions: From I-95 take Exit 130A. Take Route 3 east into town. Turn right on Littepage Street and right again on Lafayette Boulevard to reach the Fredericksburg Battlefield Visitor Center. Chatham is two miles from the visitor center, off Route 218, east of the Rappahannock River.

Stonewall Jackson House

Jackson was nicknamed Square Box and Tom Fool by his young charges at Virginia Military Institute, who thought "his classes too dull, his methods too rigid and his discipline too severe." It is said that when he was asked for clarification by a student, he would simply repeat his statement using the same words and intonation. His lectures were not lightened by explanations or discussions. Yet those who survived the carnage of the War between the States grew old bragging that they were taught natural philosophy or artillery tactics by Old Jack.

The teacher who memorized his lessons standing at his desk in his Lexington home went on to glory by standing firm at Bull Run. He became known as Stonewall after that opening Civil War battle when General Bee spotted Jackson's brigade and cried, "There stands Jackson like a stone wall. Rally behind the Virginians."

But it is the days Jackson spent in Lexington before the war that are remembered at the **Stonewall Jackson House**. A short slide program introduces you to the young, handsome Virginia instructor. He was a deeply religious and disciplined military man who began each day with a cold bath and a brisk walk around town before his morning devotions. During the week, he taught his classes at VMI. On Sundays he taught at a Sunday school that he had founded for African American youngsters. When he left for the war, he earmarked part of his pay so that these religious classes could continue. Jackson regularly contributed a tenth of his income to the Presbyterian Church.

Two years after he arrived in Lexington, he married Elinor Junkin, whose father was president of Washington College. The newlyweds lived on campus with Elinor's parents in what is now called the Lee-Jackson House. Their life together was brief; she died the following year in childbirth. In 1857, after three years as a widower, Jackson married Mary Anna Morrison, and in 1858 they purchased this house on Washington Street.

The furnishings you can see today are personal possessions and period pieces that match the inventory made following Jackson's tragic death after the Battle of Chancellorsville in 1863. The first room on the tour is the kitchen, which is furnished with a six-burner wood cookstove. The Jacksons owned one like it that was valued at fifty dollars on the estate inventory. On a twenty-acre farm at the edge of town, Jackson, with the help of three slaves, grew much of the food for his table. He would often supervise the preserving of his crops, keeping an eye on the kitchen slaves and lending a hand to seal jars of tomatoes.

In Jackson's study there is a desk like the one he stood before while memorizing his lessons. In the parlor are a loveseat and two chairs that belonged to the Jacksons. Representing Jackson's one extravagance is a piano like the one he purchased for Mary Anna for five hundred dollars. Even though he was a devout churchgoer, he was known to occasionally waltz his wife around the parlor. (He learned to waltz and polka while serving in the Mexican War.) Jackson's rocking chair is in the bedroom. An early picture of Jackson reveals just how handsome he was without his beard. Legend has it that he vowed not to shave until the South was victorious, a story that is suspect as he did carry his shaving kit with him to war. At least one British journalist described him during the war as having "thin colorless cheeks, with only a very small allowance of whiskers; [and] a cleanly-shaven upper lip and chin."

The dining room was used every morning and evening for Bible reading and prayers. On Sunday evenings slaves in the neighborhood would join the Jacksons for devotions. Before ending your visit, be sure to view the exhibits that focus on General Jackson, the Civil War era, and life in Lexington during its "golden age."

The Stonewall Jackson House, at 8 East Washington Street, is open for guided tours 9:00 A.M. to 4:30 P.M., Monday through Saturday, and 1:00 to 4:30 P.M. on Sunday. During the summer it stays open until 5:30 P.M. Admission is charged.

To discover other city sites associated with Jackson, stop at the Historic Lexington Visitor Center just down Washington Street at number 106. You'll realize that this is a town with character when you read the historic plaque on the house next to Jackson's. It says:

"N.O.N. Historic Marker
On this Spot February 29, 1776 Absolutely Nothing Happened."

While you are exploring the nineteenth-century houses, inns, and quaint shops, join Lexington natives at the Sweet Things Ice Cream Shoppe at 106 W. Washington Street. Here you can get homemade ice cream in homemade waffle cones—a double delight. For an extra taste treat, try a waffle cone sundae.

Directions: From I-95 in the Richmond area, take I-64 west. At Staunton head south on either I-81 or Route 11. From I-81 take Exit 188B, then follow the signs to Lexington's visitor center. If you are on Route 11, it will divide and you should take Main Street, not Route 11 Bypass. From Main Street, turn left on Washington Street for the Stonewall Jackson House.

Maryland

Barbara Fritchie House and the Home of Roger Brooke Taney

Some students of history may dispute the facts, but if the details are questionable, the sentiment and character are true—Barbara Fritchie was a stalwart Union supporter during the Civil War who proudly flew the Stars and Stripes from her upstairs window in Frederick. The story passed down by Frederick townsfolk is that a youngster was sent to warn ninety-six-year-old "Auntie" Barbara that Confederates were going to be marching through town. Fritchie, who also kept a small silk US flag in her Bible, misunderstood the message. Believing it was Federal troops coming, she went out with her small flag and waved it to the passing soldiers. The resulting confrontation was immortalized by the abolitionist poet John Greenleaf Whittier:

> Up rose old Barbara Fritchie then,
> Bowed with her four score years and ten,
> Bravest of all in Frederick-town,
> She took up the flag the men hauled down;
> In her attic-window the staff she set,
> To show that one heart was loyal yet.
> Up the street came the rebel tread,
> Stonewall Jackson riding ahead.
> Under his slouched hat left and right
> He glanced, the old flag met his sight.
> "Halt" — the dust-brown ranks stood fast,
> "Fire'—out blazed the rifle-blast.

It shivered the window, pane and sash;
It rent the banner with seam and gash.
Quick, as it fell from the broken staff
Dame Barbara snatched the silken scarf,
She leaned far out on the windowsill,
And shook it forth with a royal will.
"Shoot, if you must, this old gray head,
But spare your country's flag, " she said.
A shade of sadness, a blush of shame,
Over the face of the leader came;
The nobler nature within him stirred
To life at that woman's deeds and word,
"Who touches a hair on yon gray head
Dies like a dog! March on!" he said.

Thus, Barbara Fritchie's name became enshrined among the heroines of American history. Doubt may exist about the details of this Civil War confrontation, but this feisty lady did indeed make her mark on Frederick. She was forty when she married twenty-six-year-old John Fritchie, son of suspected Tory spy Caspar Fritchie, and the match kept local tongues busy with gossip. The story of her life is reviewed in the orientation video program you'll see before you begin your tour of the **Barbara Fritchie House.**

Rooms both upstairs and down have furnishings that belonged to Barbara and John Fritchie. Many historic heirlooms have been lost due to the repeated flooding of Carroll Creek. In the room where Barbara once entertained local townspeople and family, you'll see the desk where Federal general Jesse Reno penned a letter to his wife on his way through Frederick. He died two days later at the Battle of South Mountain. Upstairs, there is the poet's corner dedicated to Whittier's tribute and the bedroom where Barbara died thirteen years after her younger husband. Outside, there is a triangular garden with eighteenth-century herbs and flowers.

The Barbara Fritchie House at 154 West Patrick Street is open April through November, Monday and Thursday through Saturday from 10:00 A.M. to 4:00 P.M. and Sunday 1:00 to 4:00 P.M. The house is closed on Tuesdays and Wednesdays. For additional information, you can call (301) 698-0630.

Just up the road, at 121 South Bentz Street, is the house of Chief Justice Roger Brooke Taney, who delivered the Supreme Court opinion in the famous 1857 Dred Scott case. Among other things, the decision concluded that under the US Constitution, slaves were not citizens and that freed blacks could not be citizens either—an ember that helped ignite the Civil War. Even though he had freed his own slaves years earlier, Taney felt that the compromise of the Constitutional Convention was the only safe ground for the Court.

In his earlier years, Taney had set up a law practice in Frederick with Francis Scott Key. Key eventually moved to Baltimore, but Taney, who had married his partner's sister Anne, remained. The house on South Bentz Street was his country home, which he visited on weekends.

Today it is furnished with Taney heirlooms. You'll see the drawing room, dining room, and bedroom. Upstairs, there is a small collection of memorabilia associated with both Taney and Key. The kitchen and slave quarters are outside. **The Home of Roger Brook Taney** does not have regular hours, so you must arrange your visit in advance by calling The Tourism Council of Frederick County, (301) 663-8687.

Directions: From Baltimore, take I-70 west to Frederick; use the South Market Street exit. Go left at the truck stop on Market Street to West Patrick Street. Turn left on West Patrick Street; the Barbara Fritchie House is at 154 West Patrick Street. You can park at metered spots along West Patrick and South Bentz Streets. You can then take a short walk up to the Taney House on South Bentz.

Clara Barton National Historic Site

Clara Barton gave this account of one of her experiences at Antietam: "A man lying upon the ground asked for drink. I stooped to give it and, having raised him with my right hand, was holding the cup to his lips with my left, when I felt a sudden twitch of the loose sleeve of my dress. He poor fellow sprang from my hands and fell back quivering in the agonies of death. A ball had passed between my body and the fight arm which supported him, cutting through the sleeve, and passing through his chest from shoulder to shoulder." (See Antietam selection.)

Barton was working as a clerk in the patent office in D.C. immediately before the Civil War. With the outbreak of hostilities, she devoted her time to aiding injured soldiers. Filling wagons with needed supplies—bandages, linens, anesthetics, and oil lanterns—she worked with the field surgeons at the Battles of Second Manassas, Antietam, Fredericksburg, the Wilderness, and Spotsylvania (1861–65).

After the war the Angel of the Battlefield made it her mission to locate and identify soldiers the US Army had listed as missing. Total

Clara Barton, noted for nursing the wounded during the Civil War, went on to establish the American Red Cross. Her home, built in 1891, overlooks the C&O Canal and the Potomac River.

Civil War casualties numbered 359,528, with only 172,400 identified. In four years of grueling work, Barton located and identified twenty-two thousand missing soldiers. She was instrumental in having the burial grounds of the infamous Andersonville prison in Georgia declared a national cemetery in 1865. It contained the graves of nearly thirteen thousand Union soldiers.

Such work took its toll, and Barton suffered an emotional breakdown. She went to Europe to recover; but rather than rest, she became involved in the great cause of her life, the International Red Cross. Barton's supposed convalescence included duty with the Red Cross in the Franco-Prussian War. She returned to the United States and devoted herself to establishing the American Red Cross, of which she served as president from 1881 to 1904. Barton significantly expanded the scope of Red Cross relief work by involving the organization in peacetime aid, such as the Johnstown Flood of 1889 and the Galveston Hurricane in 1900.

On a hilltop overlooking the C&O Canal and Potomac River, Edward and Edwin Baltzley built Miss Barton a house in 1891 as part of their Glen Echo development. Now a National Historic Site, this Victorian house is architecturally intriguing. From the main hallway you look up to railed galleries on the second and third floors; the latter gallery is seemingly suspended over the floors below. A top floor bedroom seems to hang from the sides of the house with no visible means of support, a delightful structural oddity.

One thing this house doesn't lack is closets—the main hallway is lined with them. These storage areas were used for disaster supplies. Two rooms are re-creations of the home offices Barton used from 1897 to 1904, and the house still has some of her furniture. She spent the last fifteen years of her life in this house and died at Glen Echo on April 12, 1912, at age ninety. After your tour, you are apt to agree with one of Miss Barton's guests who wrote, "I often think of your nice warm house, so full of your individuality. The crime of being commonplace can never be laid to your door—and your home is just as it should be, unlike anybody's else."

Barton was not without her flaws. She was ousted from her position with the Red Cross not only because members felt she was too old, but also because they found her disorganized and un-businesslike. There was even talk of a congressional investigation of her financial records before her resignation in 1904.

The heroism and the flaws of this remarkable woman are presented during a guided tour of the house. The **Clara Barton National Historic Site** is open daily at no charge. The house is shown only by guided tours, which are given on the hour from 10:00 A.M. to 4:00 P.M. The house is closed Thanksgiving, Christmas, and New Year's Day. Call (301) 492-6245 for details or log onto their Web site at www.nps.gov/clba.

Barton accepted Glen Echo for her home because she was interested in the Chautauqua self-improvement movement, which used facilities at Glen Echo. She was considerably less enthusiastic about the amusement park built here after 1899. The only reminder of the artistic Chautauqua years is Glen Echo's old stone tower, now an art gallery, which was used for Chautauqua gatherings in 1891. However, the spirit of the Chautauqua does remain; **Glen Echo Park** now offers workshops and classes in the arts. Artists create, teach, demonstrate, and sell their work on the grounds.

Directions: From the Baltimore Beltway, take I-95 south to the Washington Beltway (I-495). Head west on I-495 to Exit 40, for the Clara Barton Parkway to Glen Echo. Exit from the parkway at MacArthur Boulevard and turn left. Proceed on MacArthur Boulevard to Oxford Road and turn left; signs will indicate the parking lot for the Clara Barton National Historic Site.

Dr. Samuel A. Mudd House Museum

Dr. Samuel A. Mudd's grandson, Dr. Richard D. Mudd, and his family have worked for a number of years trying to obtain a complete exoneration for the doctor. Doctor Mudd's youngest grandchild, Louise Mudd Arehart, is president of the Dr. Samuel A. Mudd Society. Through her efforts, Dr. Mudd's plantation farmhouse has been successfully restored. The building looks today as it did on April 15, 1865, when history rode to the door and forever changed the lives of Dr. Mudd and his family. The home, St. Catherine on the Sekiah, has been on the National Register of Historic Places since 1974 and has been open to the public since 1983.

The drama began at Ford's Theatre the preceding night when John Wilkes Booth shot President Lincoln. Booth fractured his leg when he leapt on stage to make his escape. The injured Booth and his accomplice, David Herold, rode out of the capital and made their way into Southern Maryland. The two men stopped at Mary Surratt's Tavern (see selection). Booth's leg was causing problems; they decided to get medical help and set out for Dr. Mudd's farm farther south. Booth had traveled through this part of Maryland before, ostensibly to buy land and horses. Indeed, one of the horses the two were riding as they made their escape was purchased by Booth from Dr. Mudd's neighbor. However, his agenda had also included efforts to enlist support from the region's Southern sympathizers for various plots and plans that were constantly being made. On one of Booth's visits, he had met and dined with Dr. Mudd; their paths had crossed again in Washington. Booth and Herold arrived at Mudd's door at 4:00 A.M. Easter Saturday and left at 2:00 P.M. that day.

Herold dismounted and roused the Mudd household. Dr. Mudd had been out late with a patient, but Mrs. Mudd awakened him rather than answer the knock. She was afraid it might be floaters, or free blacks, who were often found in this state that bordered the Confederacy. Herold gave Dr. Mudd false names (Tyler and Tyson) as the doctor helped the wounded Booth into the house. According to some reports, Booth, an actor, had disguised himself with a false beard. Herold and Dr. Mudd helped Booth to the red velvet couch in the parlor (this historic piece of furniture has been returned to the house by a Mudd descendant) so that the doctor could examine his leg. Dr.

Mudd then moved Booth to an upstairs bedroom, cut off the boot and set the leg. The boot was tossed under the bed and forgotten. It would later be used as evidence.

Later that Saturday morning, Dr. Mudd and Herold set out to find a carriage for the two travelers to use on the rest of their journey. When none could be found, Herold and Booth set off on horseback at 2:00 P.M. As they left, Mrs. Mudd got a look at Booth's face, which, heretofore, he had kept hidden. She remarked to the doctor that he appeared to be wearing a disguise. This is how the Mudds later explained to authorities why they did not recognize a man who had been a guest in their home.

Dr. Mudd, who claimed not to have known of President Lincoln's assassination when he ministered to Booth, was nonetheless convicted by a military court of aiding and harboring an escaping fugitive. He was found innocent of charges that he was involved in the conspiracy to assassinate Lincoln. Mudd was sent to Fort Jefferson Prison in the Dry Tortugas off Key West, Florida.

Dr. Mudd served part of his sentence in chains after an escape attempt. But when a yellow fever epidemic decimated the prison population and the prison doctor died, Mudd was unshackled and began treating his fellow prisoners. Shortly after the end of the epidemic, he was pardoned by President Andrew Johnson for his humanitarian work. Dr. Mudd returned to his Maryland farm, and then toured the country lecturing on yellow fever. (He had contracted and survived the disease while at Fort Jefferson Prison.) Dr. Mudd died of pneumonia thirteen years after his release from prison.

The **Dr. Samuel A. Mudd House Museum** is filled with furniture and mementos, each piece prompting the costumed docents to tell another story about Dr. Mudd's experiences and the family's travail when Federal troops camped around the house. History comes to life at this out-of-the-way farmhouse, where the clock seems to have stopped in 1865.

The Dr. Samuel A. Mudd House Museum is open Wednesday from 11:00 A.M. to 3:00 P.M. and weekend afternoons from noon to 4:00 P.M. from April to late November. Admission is charged.

Directions: From Washington Beltway, I-495/95, Exit 7, take Route 5 south to Waldorf. Make a left on Route 205. Continue to Poplar Hill Road and make a right. Drive for approximately four miles. Turn right on Dr. Samuel Mudd Road and go 0.4 mile to the house. There is a sign at the entrance.

John Wilkes Booth Escape Route

Benedict Arnold, Aaron Burr, Edward Teach, and John Wilkes Booth—there is continuing fascination with these historical villains and their treacherous activities. This accounts for the popularity of The Surratt Society's biannual **John Wilkes Booth Escape** tours. Each spring and fall, a bus full of history buffs is escorted on the route Booth took after he assassinated President Lincoln at Ford's Theatre.

While it is undoubtedly enjoyable to travel in a group, the tour also can be done on one's own, keeping in mind, of course, that many of these stops are private property. There is a sense of drama to be felt in literally tracing the footsteps of history. The day's adventure begins in downtown Washington at Ford's Theatre at 511 10th Street (see Ford's Theatre National Historic Site). Booth shot Lincoln at 10:15 P.M. on April 14, 1865. After grappling with Major Rathbone, he leapt to the stage, tangling himself briefly in the "Treasury Guard" flag. This slight miscalculation resulted in a fracture of his left leg as he landed.

The injury slowed his escape and provided clues that helped those tracking him. Mounting a horse he had arranged to have standing at the back of the theater, Booth galloped down "F" Street and crossed Judiciary Square to Pennsylvania Avenue. He was spotted as he rode just south of the Capitol. Following Booth on his ride from the now hostile city was another conspirator, David Edgar Herold, who had been involved in a plan to kill Secretary of State Seward while Booth shot Lincoln.

Both men crossed the Potomac at the Navy Yard Bridge at the bottom of 11th Street. The Federal guard, Sergeant Silas Cobb, stopped each of them, but after asking their destination, permitted them to cross. The purpose of the guard was to prevent unauthorized entry into the city, not out of it, so it wasn't surprising that they were permitted to leave.

They continued up what is now Good Hope Road through Anacostia (formerly Uniontown) and then between the Civil War fortifications Fort Baker and Fort Wagner near Branch Avenue. After riding eight miles outside Washington, Herold caught up with Booth at Soper's Hill, which according to historians' best guess is the high ground just outside the Beltway at Exit 7.

The two fugitives stopped two miles before Surratt's Tavern around midnight. A young boy, George Thompson, and Henry Butler, a black man who worked for Dr. Joseph Blanford, the brother-in-law of Dr. Samuel Mudd, were stuck in a broken wagon where Branch Avenue now intersects with "Jenkins Corner." Booth asked them if there was a doctor in the area as his leg was giving him trouble after riding almost two hours.

They next stopped at Surratt's Tavern (see Mary Surratt House). Booth did not dismount. He had dropped off a pair of field glasses earlier in the day at Mary Surratt's boarding house in Washington. She took them down to the tavern and left word that they were to be given to the travelers who would stop by that night along with the guns that had been hidden in the tavern. Only one of these guns was taken that night by Herold. Booth was having too difficult a time with his leg to carry a carbine. The remaining gun was hidden in the dining room ceiling at the tavern.

After just a few minutes at the Surratt Tavern, they continued on to the town of T.B. Though their next stop is known, the route is uncertain. From T.B., they next showed up at the farm of Dr. Mudd, a Southern sympathizer and local doctor. Their probable route leads past St. Peter's Church.

St. Peter's also played a role in the larger drama. At Sunday service on April 16, Dr. Mudd asked his cousin to inform the authorities that two strangers had been at his farm the preceding day. Dr. Mudd's use of the term strangers was significant, as he had met Booth in November of 1864 at St. Mary's Catholic Church just down the road off Route 231 outside Bryantown. (The route passes St. Mary's, the site where Dr. Mudd would much later be buried.) Booth and Mudd met again in December at the Bryantown Tavern on Routes 5 and 232 and later in the month in Washington on business relating to various Confederate agents. Though he may not have known that Booth assassinated Lincoln, it is possible that Dr. Mudd was aware of the Lincoln kidnap plot.

While at St. Peter's Church, it is worth noting that this is also the burial spot of Edman Spangler, another of the convicted conspirators in the Lincoln plot. Spangler served time but was pardoned by President Johnson in 1869. He moved into the Mudd household and lived there until his death in February 1875.

It was 4:00 A.M. when Herold and Booth arrived at the Mudd farm, located where Route 382 and 232 meet. Dr. Mudd set Booth's injured leg. They left the farm Saturday afternoon, but Mudd didn't suggest the authorities be contacted until after service on Sunday morning.

Making their way through the Zekiah Swamp, now part of Cedarville State Park, the fugitives were seen in the vicinity of "Oak Hill," the home of Dr. Mudd's father, on Route 232. Actually only Herold was spotted when he asked directions from one of Mudd's employees.

Still needing directions, they stopped at the farm of Oswell Swann, which was at that time situated one mile south-southwest of what is now Hughesville. They hired this black tobacco farmer to lead them to "Rich Hill," the farm of Samuel Cox at Route 6 and Bel-Alton Newtown Road. There was conflicting testimony as to whether Cox let them come into the house. He denied it, but their guide said they were inside three or four hours.

The tired assassins did spend the night in the pine thicket several miles from "Rich Hill" off what is now Route 301. Booth and Herold stayed hidden in the woods for several days. Cox had his son contact Thomas A. Jones of "Huckleberry," a Confederate agent who was to get the two men across the Potomac River as soon as it was safe to do so.

It wasn't until Thursday, April 20, that they attempted to cross the Potomac into Virginia. Their first attempt failed. They tried again the next day and landed up Gambo Creek just south of the Route 301 toll bridge at a house along the water. They got food and were put in contact with a guide to take them to "Cleydael," the summer home of Dr. Richard Stuart. Word had been circulated of the assassination of the president, and Dr. Stuart was wary of the two strangers. Though he gave them food, he would not let them come in nor would he treat Booth's leg. He sent them for refuge to a free black, William Lucas. The racially bigoted Booth was highly insulted. He sent a bitter note to Stuart with a meager sum to pay for the food. His surly temper forced the Lucas family out of their own cabin for the night. Booth and Herold did hire Lucas's son to take them by wagon to the Port Conway ferry for twenty dollars.

While waiting on arrangements to get across the Rappahannock River, they met three Confederate soldiers. Herold's boasting talk soon revealed that they were the men who killed Lincoln. The three Southerners agreed to help them make good their escape. The addition of three more members to the group, men who were known in the area, eventually made the capture of Booth and Herold easier.

The five of them crossed the river and found a hiding place for Booth at a local farm owned by the Garretts. Booth stayed there while the other four went on into Bowling Green. The next day they returned and left Herold at the farm with Booth. As the soldiers started north, they saw the Federal cavalry heading in their direction. Federal agents had learned at Port Conway that the fugitives were in the area. The cavalry had crossed the Rappahannock and were on their way to the Garrett farm.

At 2:00 A.M. Colonel Baker posted his men around the barn while Booth and Herold slept inside. When they woke up they were trapped. Despite an hour of threats, Booth refused to come out. When Baker threatened to burn the barn, Herold surrendered but not Booth. At 4:00 A.M. they set fire to the barn. Booth, limping and with a pistol in one hand and a carbine in the other, started for the door. Before he came out, one shot was fired, hitting Booth in the neck.

The shot paralyzed Booth, and Federal soldiers dragged him out of the burning building. He died before dawn. A soldier named Corbett admitted firing through the barn siding, and evidence indicated this to be the shot that killed Booth. Rumors continued, however, that Booth had shot himself or was shot to prevent him from revealing a government conspiracy to kill Lincoln.

Neither the Garrett house nor barn is standing today. A marker on the Fort A. P. Hill military base marks their former location.

With Booth dead, the main villain could not be punished. But the lesser band stood trial. Herold, Mary Surratt, and two other plotters were hung. Dr. Mudd was given a prison sentence for his role in the tragic events, as were three additional bit players.

For those interested in joining the Surratt Society tours, advance reservations are required. For additional information call (301) 868-1121 or write the Surratt Society at P.O. Box 427, Clinton, MD 20735. You also can get information on-line at http://www. clark.net/pub/surratt/surratt.html.

The Surratt House

The Victorian era greatly influenced modern times. At the **Surratt House** in Clinton, visitors can find out how by viewing ever-changing exhibits and taking part in special events. You may see lacy Valentines of the Golden Age (1840–1900) or somber mourning memorabilia. Other exhibits have included "Washington of Yesteryear," a photographic history, and a festive look at Christmas traditions of the Civil War era.

Mary Surratt's mid-Victorian home, the Surratt House, has a tragic history. Although the extent to which Mrs. Surratt was involved in the criminal conspiracy to assassinate Lincoln is still debated, it was sufficient for the government to execute her, the first of her sex to suffer that fate at the hands of the federal government.

Mary Surratt was widowed in 1862, ten years after her husband, John Surratt, built a house and tavern in Surrattsville (now known as Clinton). From the beginning the tavern served as a gathering spot for the community. As the country grew ever more bitterly divided, Southern dissidents gathered here to repudiate Maryland's Northern alignment. When John Jr. left college to help his widowed mother run the family business, he quickly fell in with Confederate sympathizers and became a party to a scheme to kidnap President Abraham Lincoln.

The tavern also became a safe house for Southern agents. John Wilkes Booth was one such agent who knew he could find help here. As Booth made his way south after shooting the president, he stopped at the Surratt House to pick up his field glasses, left for him earlier in the day by Mary Surratt, and the "shooting irons" that had been hidden in the ceiling as part of the earlier kidnapping plot. His accomplice took one of the guns, but Booth decided against carrying any because his injured leg made it difficult for him to ride. Testimony that Mary Surratt had indeed helped Booth led to her conviction by a military court and her death by hanging on July 7, 1865. Two years later when her son, John, Jr., was tried on similar charges in a civil court, the jury could not reach a verdict.

In the spring and fall, the Surratt Society sponsors a full day's excursion along the route John Wilkes Booth took from Ford's Theatre to present-day Fort A. P. Hill, where he was finally cornered and shot. To reserve a spot on the next **John Wilkes Booth Escape Route** (see selection) tour, write the Surratt Society at 9118 Brandywine Road, P.O. Box 427, Clinton, MD 20735, or call (301) 868-1121.

The Surratt House can be toured from March through mid-December on Thursday and Friday from 11:00 A.M. to 3:00 P.M. and Saturday and Sunday from noon to 4:00 P.M.

Directions: From the Washington Beltway, I-495/95, take Exit 7A (Route 5, Branch Avenue) south to Woodyard Road (Route 223) in Clinton. Turn right on Woodyard Road and continue to the second traffic light, where you turn left onto Brandywine Road. The Surratt House is on the left at 9110 Brandywine Road.

District of Columbia

Ford's Theatre National Historic Site and Petersen House

The audience expected light comedy, but they saw high tragedy. It was the night of April 14, 1865. There was a full house for **Ford's Theatre's** production of *Our American Cousin*. President and Mrs. Lincoln watched from the State Box. In the balcony, a young actor followed the play line by line, waiting for his entrance. The actor was John Wilkes Booth, and he had written his own part into the production. Booth waited until late in the play, when there was only one actor on stage and the audience was laughing; that was the moment he chose to enter the president's box from the dress circle and put a pistol to Lincoln's head. Major Rathbone, attending the play with the Lincolns, tried to hold Booth, but the agile actor jumped to the stage. Although Booth injured his leg in his leap, he was able to escape.

The audience was paralyzed, but quick thinking doctors in the audience rushed to the president's box and carried the wounded Lincoln across the street to Petersen House, where he died the next morning. Booth escaped as far as Port Royal, Virginia, where he was shot eleven days after the assassination.

The tragedy forced Ford's Theatre to close. The federal government purchased the building and used it to house the files of Union soldiers and the Army Medical Museum. This ill-fated building suffered yet another tragic incident on June 9, 1893. The third floor collapsed, killing and injuring a number of federal employees.

Exhibits connected with Lincoln's assassination have been exhibited at Ford's Theatre since the 1930s. Many years were to pass, however, before the theater was restored to its appearance on that fateful night. In 1968, Ford's Theatre reopened. The State Box had reproductions of Lincoln's rocker and his wife's straight-back chair. The red sofa is original; so also is the framed engraving of George Washington on the front of the box. Although plays are again performed at Ford's Theatre, this box bears silent witness to its last patrons.

You don't have to attend a performance at Ford's Theatre to explore the **Lincoln Museum** in its basement, where you can see the Oldroyd Collection, which has been on display since the 1930s. The most significant item is the single-shot derringer Booth used to slay Lincoln. The display includes the clothes Lincoln and Booth were wearing.

Ford's Theatre is open 9:00 A.M. to 5:00 P.M. daily. There is no admission. If Thursday and Sunday matinees are being performed, the theater is not open, but the Lincoln Museum can still be toured. Due to frequent rehearsals, set work, and matinees, you should call ahead to be sure the theater is open; call (202) 426-6924. You also can log onto the theater's Web site, http://www.nps.gov/foth.

After touring Ford's, cross the street to **Petersen House**. When the wounded president was carried out of the theater, a boarder staying at the Petersen House suggested they bring Lincoln into the empty back bedroom. The president, because of his height, was placed diagonally on the small cottage bed. His wounded head rested on the pillow over the edge of the bed.

Mrs. Lincoln spent the long night in the parlor of the boarding house. She was joined by her eldest son and close friends. Dr. Charles Leale, who had been at the theater, monitored the dying president. During the night, Secretary of War Edwin Stanton also established himself at the Petersen House, using another bedroom as a command post as he began an investigation of the assassination. Government officials stopped at the house all through the night to pay their respects to the dying president.

At 7:22 A.M. on April 15, Lincoln died. His body was taken immediately to the White House. A boarder took a photograph of the bed on which Lincoln died. This picture, which was not circulated until a hundred years after Lincoln's death, was used in the restoration of Petersen House in the 1930s.

The Petersens did not profit from their brush with history, despite the public's interest in Lincoln's assassination. William Petersen died of a drug overdose in 1871. His wife died later that same year from a heart attack. Their boarding house was sold to the government in 1896. The Petersen House is open at no charge, 9:00 A.M. to 5:00 P.M. daily, except Christmas Day.

Directions: Ford's Theatre and the Petersen House are located inside the Washington Beltway in downtown Washington. Ford's Theatre is at 511 10th Street, N.W. The Petersen House is directly across the street at #516.

Civil War Forts

The Confederate firing on Fort Sumter in Charleston, South Carolina, actually began the Civil War, but the stage had been set when Lincoln won the presidency in 1860.

Not even waiting to see what action Lincoln would take to heal the profound differences separating the North and South, seven states seceded before his inauguration. The states justified their decision to secede by the fact that Lincoln's Republican party had not received a single popular vote in ten of the southern states. South Carolina was first to leave in December 1860, followed by Mississippi, Florida, Alabama, Georgia, Louisiana, and Texas in February.

Virginia, Arkansas, Tennessee, and North Carolina held off. They awaited Lincoln's inauguration to see what action the government would take regarding the seceded southern states.

On March 4, 1861, Abraham Lincoln provided some answers. In his inaugural address, he declared that there would be no invasion of the South, but also that the Federal union must be preserved. He told the South, "You have no conflict without being yourselves the aggressor."

Events would not wait long to test that judgment. The day after his inauguration, Lincoln received an urgent communication from Maj. Robert Anderson telling him that Fort Sumter was woefully low on supplies and ammunition. Only Fort Sumter and Fort Pickens in Pensacola maintained a Federal presence in the South. All other Federal forts had fallen into Confederate hands without resistance.

Lincoln faced a problem. If he sent supplies, Confederate President Jefferson Davis would undoubtedly take it as an invasion of Confederate sovereignty and attack the fort. But failing to provision the fort would be a sign of weakness and lead to its loss. Lincoln reluctantly decided to send supplies by naval expedition on unarmed ships. He then informed the governor of South Carolina of his peaceful purpose; food and supplies would be sent without any additional men or munitions.

This attempt to smooth over a difficult impasse failed. When Major Anderson refused to surrender the fort, a rocket was fired in the early morning hours of September 12, 1861. The Civil War had begun!

Virginia

Fort Marcy

While Richmond was a psychological prize coveted by the North and defended by the South, the city of Washington was viewed even more covetously. If the South could capture the capital of the United States, it would give their cause greater legitimacy, perhaps even persuade European countries, still anxious for Southern cotton, to support them in this internal struggle.

Recognizing the strategic importance of Washington, the Federal government made sure that it was heavily fortified. One of the forty-eight forts that protected the city was Fort Marcy, located on the old Leesburg Pike on the Virginia side of the Potomac River. Fort Marcy secured Chain Bridge, along with Fort Ethan Allen, on the other side. Confederate access across Chain Bridge would also have jeopardized the C&O Canal, the principal supply link for Washington.

Though Forts Marcy and Ethan Allen were on Confederate soil, the land was seized during the opening stages of the war. Federal troops under Gen. W. F. Smith crossed the Potomac on September 24, 1861, and began construction of both earthwork forts.

Visitors today can still clearly see this ground defense. It is worth keeping in mind that this form of defense was considered in many ways stronger than bricks. Forts constructed of bricks were rigid and collapsed when struck by cannonballs. Earthworks would merely be loosened but would still provide protection.

General Smith's command was staffed by West Point graduates, considered the best engineers in the world, who were well trained in the technique of defensive fort construction. A fellow graduate, Robert E. Lee, realized the efficacy of these fortifications and, for the most part, did not choose to risk his men against them.

Though the fort was first named Fort Baldy Smith, in honor of the commanding officer, in the late fall of 1861 the name was changed to Fort Marcy. Gen. Randolph Barnes Marcy was not only a chief on General McClellan's staff, he was also McClellan's father-in-law. Marcy's daughter, Nellie, had been courted by West Point roommates George McClellan and Ambrose Powell Hill. Her rejected suitor served the Confederate cause so well that one of McClellan's men is supposed to have remarked once in exasperation, "Nelly, why didn't you marry that man?"

Fort Marcy sits 275.4 feet above the Potomac at low tide. Eighteen guns—a ten-inch mortar, two twenty-four-pound mortars, and fifteen smaller cannons—were in place during the Civil War. The perimeter of the fort was 338 feet. Though no structure exists, the remaining earthworks of this fort can be visited during daylight hours and make an interesting outing that is close to Washington. For additional information, check out the homepage at http://www.nps.gov/gwmp/vapa/FtMarcy.htm.

Directions: Fort Marcy is located four miles north of Key Bridge. Access is from the northbound lane of the George Washington Memorial Parkway. The fort is situated on top of Prospect Hill, just one mile west of Chain Bridge.

Fort Monroe and the Casemate Museum

Edgar Allan Poe, tired of army life after spending the dark winter of 1828–29 at **Fort Monroe**, sold his enlistment for seventy-five dollars, ending his career as an army artilleryman. After wandering through the gloomy chambers of the **Casemate Museum**, you may wonder if he hadn't just decided that he had had enough inspiration for his tales of horror. Casemates—the damp, dungeon-like artillery vaults within the fort's mammoth stone walls—make a perfect setting for a Poe story, as well as for exhibits on the people and events in the history of Fort Monroe.

If Poe found the casemates inspirational, Robert E. Lee more than likely found them educational. Lee, an army engineer, worked from 1831 to 1834 on the construction of Fort Monroe. During the Civil War, Confederate forces never attacked the "Gibralter of Chesapeake Bay." The name was well deserved. Fort Monroe was the largest stone fort built in North America. At the time it was completed, it was also the largest enclosed fortification in the United States. The designer, Gen. Simon Bernard, had been trained to think big as aide-de-camp to Napoleon Bonaparte.

The fort's impenetrable stone walls imprisoned Jefferson Davis at the conclusion of the Civil War. He was charged with plotting to assassinate Lincoln, mistreating Union prisoners, and treason. After his capture on May 22, 1865, the former president of the Confederacy spent five months in casemate cell two. For the first five days, he was kept manacled in leg irons; but even after these were removed, his dank, spartan cell was a bitter home for a man who had just led the Confederacy, albeit to defeat. After five months Davis was transferred to better accommodations in Carroll Hall; its location is marked on the Fort Monroe Walking Tour. On May 13, 1867, Davis was released on $100,000 bail. Two years later, all charges were dropped.

Though Davis was a most reluctant resident, some Federal officers made comfortable homes in the casemates. Photographs from the 1900s show four such living quarters. You wonder as you look at the piano in the re-created casemate parlor if the fort kept a tuner on the payroll.

Another exhibit focuses on the four-hour Civil War battle that occurred just off Fort Monroe in Hampton Roads between the ironclads *Monitor* and *Merrimack* (the traditional spelling is without a *k*, but naval historians prefer Merrimack, after the New England river for which it was named).

Scale models of weapons from the army's coast artillery branch are also exhibited here. The Coast Artillery School was located at Fort Monroe, which served as the headquarters for the defenses of the Chesapeake Bay during World War II. Fort Monroe has an extensive collection of artillery pieces. On the walking tour, you can see a fifteen-inch Rodman gun, called the Lincoln gun in the president's honor and used to bombard Confederate batteries on Sewell's Point. You also can drive along Fenwick Road on the Chesapeake Bay and see Fort Monroe's seacoast batteries.

The Casemate Museum is open at no charge, 10:30 A.M. to 4:30 P.M. daily, and closed Thanksgiving, Christmas, and New Year's Day. For additional information, you can call (757) 727-3391.

Directions: From I-95 in the Richmond area, take I-64 east to Exit 268 for Hampton. The entrance to Fort Monroe is immediately before the Hampton Roads Bridge Tunnel.

Fort Ward Museum and Historic Site

On May 23, 1861, Virginia seceded from the United States, creating panic in the capital. Washington, D.C., found itself on the front lines of a divided country and without any defenses. The realization of the city's peril brought quick action. On the very day that Virginia's secession became effective, Union troops crossed the Potomac River and seized Alexandria and Arlington Heights with the intention of building defensive forts on these sites. Troops also began working on forts at three sites south of the river.

When the South won the first major battle of the war on July 21, 1861, at Bull Run (Manassas), the work to defend Washington intensified. Forts were begun that would encircle Alexandria, Washington, and Georgetown. These fortifications were modeled on seventeenth-century fieldworks designed by the French military genius Sebastien

Le Prestre Vauban. By the end of 1862, more than forty forts had been built.

With this degree of protection, Federal confidence was restored until August 1862, when the South won the Battle of Second Manassas (also called the Second Battle of Bull Run). After this setback, some of the forts were enlarged, more guns were added, and new forts were built. By the end of 1863, Washington was the most heavily defended location in the Western Hemisphere. There were sixty-eight forts and ninety-three batteries bristling with more than nine hundred guns, linked by over thirty miles of trenches and roads.

Fort Ward was the fifth largest of the forts surrounding Washington. It was begun in September 1861 and named for Commander James Harmon Ward, the first Union naval officer killed in the Civil War. Maj. Gen. John G. Barnard, chief engineer of the defenses of Washington, considered Fort Ward to be "one of the major forts in the defense system." After the Battle of Second Manassas in August 1862, the fort's firepower was strengthened. A one-hundred-pound Parrott rifled siege gun was positioned in the fort's southwest bastion on a center pintle carriage that permitted it to fire in any direction. A south and northwest bastion were added. When completed, Fort Ward had thirty-six guns mounted in five bastions. Work continued on the star-shaped fort throughout the war, and finishing touches were added after General Lee surrendered the Army of Northern Virginia at Appomattox on May 9, 1865. Work on the ceremonial entrance gate, crowned by the turreted castle and symbolizing the Army Corp of Engineers, was completed in May 1865. By the end of 1865, however, Fort Ward had been dismantled.

Today, visitors can see much of Fort Ward as it was more than a hundred years ago, during the Civil War. There is a replica of the fort's 1865 ceremonial gate. The northwest bastion has been carefully restored, complete with reproductions of the cannons that once stood there. Using original Corps of Engineers drawings, an officer's hut and Civil War headquarters building (the latter serves as a museum) also have been reconstructed.

Fort Ward Museum contains a large collection of Civil War items. The museum hosts frequent special exhibits relating to the Civil War period. Before exploring the fort, take the time to watch the twelve-minute video *Fort Ward, Silent Guardian of the Capital City.*

Fort Ward Museum and Historic Site is open daily at no charge (although donations are gratefully accepted) from 9:00 A.M. to sunset. The museum is open 9:00 A.M. to 5:00 P.M. Tuesday through Saturday and noon to 5:00 P.M. on Sunday. The museum is closed on Mondays, Thanksgiving, Christmas, and New Year's Day. The museum and historic site are surrounded by the forty-five-acre Fort Ward Park.

Directions: From I-95/495, the Washington Beltway, take Exit 2N, Telegraph Road. Follow the signs, and take Route 236 west. Turn right on Quaker Lane and proceed to the second traffic light. Turn left on West Braddock Road and travel approximately 0.5 mile to Fort Ward entrance. From I-395, take Seminary Road exit east and proceed to the fourth traffic light. Turn left on North Howard Street; then right onto West Braddock Road. The museum is immediately on the left.

Fort Wool

Fort Wool is strategically located on an uninhabited island at the mouth of Hampton Roads Harbor, directly across from Fort Monroe, which is the only moat-enclosed active duty military installation in the country (see selection). Getting to Fort Wool is definitely part of the fun; it's accessible only by boat.

The sixty-five-foot *Miss Hampton II* is moored at the picturesque Hampton Harbor right beside the visitor center, where tickets are purchased. The two-and-a-half- to three-hour cruise sails out on the Hampton River, past Blackbeard's Point, where legend claims the pirate's head was displayed on a post after his violent death in November 1718 off Ocracoke Island, North Carolina. Ocracoke legend claims that after the decapitation, Blackbeard's body swam around his adversary's boat seven times looking for its head.

The cruise takes passengers along the coast of Old Point Comfort, named by Capt. John Smith because of the "great comfort" it brought his crew to discover a safe navigable channel for the passage of their ships. The point was the site of one of the earliest forts in America, built in 1609.

It was decided that companion forts would be built to guard the entrance to Hampton Roads. The War of 1812 and the British burning of the White House in Washington reinforced the idea that fortifications were needed to protect the East Coast and Gulf Coast. A panel in 1818 suggested building twenty-six forts from Maine to Florida and along the Gulf. Among them was a fort across from Point Comfort, to create crossfire to guard this significant harbor.

In 1819, construction was begun on Fort Monroe and Fort Wool. Lt. Robert E. Lee, an Army engineer, was involved in supervising construction of both forts. Fort Monroe, completed in 1834, was the largest stone fort ever built in the United States. Before beginning work on Fort Wool, an island had to be created on which to build. Workers needed to haul forty thousand to fifty thousand perch (a cubic measure for stone) of stone to the mouth of the harbor before they could begin building Fort Wool. Stones were brought in from riverbeds and quarries. Cranes and rails were used to dump the stone into the water to create an island. Between 1819 and 1823, the workers managed to raise the island six feet above high water, and construction began. The plan for Fort Wool consisted of three tiers of casemates and a barbette tier (4 tiers designed to mount 232 guns). About half of the second casemate as well as one tier and a part of the second tier was completed before work stopped in 1830. The island was sinking at a rate of eight inches a year. Originally the fort was named Fort Calhoun (although informally it was called Castle Calhoun) after the secretary of war, John C. Calhoun.

Although incomplete, President Andrew Jackson was so taken with the island's seclusion, he brought family and friends to the fort for a summer getaway in 1829, 1831, 1833, and 1835. Guests were housed in the officers' quarters. Jackson entertained dignitaries here, including the Prussian ambassador. In 1842, President John Tyler sought the seclusion of the island to mourn the death of his wife.

Thousands of pounds of additional stones were added to the island and work resumed on the casemates in 1858. The onset of the Civil War halted construction. The fortification remained in Union hands throughout the conflict. The fort finally got 10 cannons in 1861, a small part of the 232 planned for the completed facility. The Union troops at Fort Wool fired on the Georgia battery occupying Sewell's Point across the harbor in June 1861. The shots landed past the Southerners' position, but it was clear that the cannon would reach across the water. The following March, two newfangled ships, the ironclad *Monitor* and *Merrimack*, met in Hampton Roads Harbor.

The *Monitor* was launched from a New York City shipyard on January 30, 1862. Six weeks later, on March 9, it encountered the CSS *Virginia,* formerly the USS *Merrimack.* The Union had scuttled their wooden steam frigate to prevent it from falling into Confederate hands, but the South was able to salvage the vessel and convert her into an ironclad. For four hours the ironclads lobbed cannon balls at each other's hulls at point-blank range. When a Confederate shell exploded in the sight-hole of the *Monitor,* it temporarily blinded Capt. John Worden. The *Monitor* withdrew, and so the South claimed victory. Neither side was a clear victor; the only decisive winner was the metal ship.

Lincoln visited Fort Wool in 1862. From this vantage point he supervised the unsuccessful invasion of Norfolk. (Later, General Wool successfully captured Norfolk and Portsmouth, but Lincoln was not on hand.) Secretary of War Stanton ordered Fort Calhoun's name changed in order to honor Wool, rather than a Southern secessionist.

In the early 1900s, the fort entered a new phase of construction. The walls were torn down and replaced with concrete fortifications to defend against new weapons. Eight of the casemates remained, and the outside stone wall was incorporated into the new concrete structure. Six three-foot rapid-fire guns and six 611 disappearing guns were added. A third stage of construction took place in World War II, when battery No. 229 was added. On December 7, 1941, troops reoccupied the island, but the fort never came under fire and the men never saw combat. Today, you can tour Fort Wool beginning with the pre-Civil War section of the fort, then moving through the World War II portion.

Cruises are given aboard the *Miss Hampton II* from April through October, and crew members conduct the Fort Wool tours. While aboard the *Miss Hampton,* you'll be able to see the behemoths of modern warfare when you cruise past the two-mile waterfront of Norfolk Naval Base, which is the world's largest naval installation (see selection). Onboard narrators will provide information on the aircraft carriers, guided missile cruisers, destroyers, and nuclear-powered submarines that you will see moored at the base.

Times and fees vary. Reservations are recommended, so be sure and call ahead at (800) 800-2202 or (757) 727-1102. Tickets are sold at the Hampton Visitor Center.

Directions: From I-64, take Exit 267, Hampton University and follow Routes 60/143 west-bound to old downtown Hampton. The excursion boat to Fort Wool departs from Hampton's main dock near the visitor center. There is a parking garage at the dock.

Maryland

Point Lookout State Park

From a summer resort, to a Civil War prison camp, and then back to a recreational retreat—that is the story of **Point Lookout.**

In the early 1860s, on the southernmost tip of Maryland's western shore, there was a beach hotel, roughly a hundred cottages, a large wharf, and a lighthouse. The onset of the Civil War signaled the end of an era for the Point Lookout resort. The US government leased it for use as an army hospital, and the first Union army patients arrived on August 17, 1862. During the winter of 1863, some Confederate prisoners were sent here, primarily Southern Marylanders accused of helping the rebel cause.

After the Battle of Gettysburg, in July 1863, a prison camp was built at Point Lookout to hold ten thousand Confederate prisoners of war. By the following summer, double that many were crowded into this camp. A year later, in June 1865, the last prisoners left. With a total of 52,264 Confederates imprisoned here, Point Lookout was the largest prison camp of the Civil War. For a time, Point Lookout had more rebel soldiers than General Lee had in his army.

The overcrowded conditions took their toll. Filth bred disease, and the men alternately froze and baked. More than thirty-five hundred prisoners died. One survivor wrote, "If it were not for hope how could we live in a place like this?"

One of the ironies for these Confederate prisoners was that many of their guards were former slaves. Some masters found their own slaves now in a position of authority over them. As one prisoner remarked, "The bottom rail's on top now."

The Union soldiers and guards who worked at the prison were stationed at Fort Lincoln, built on the banks of the Potomac River between 1864 and 1865. The fort's earthworks were reinforced by a wooden wall, and there was a guardhouse, enlisted men's barracks, and two officers' quarters.

Today, if you walk up from the park's beach along the historic trail, you can see the remains of Fort Lincoln. The earthworks are original, and part of the wooden walk and the walled entrance walk have been rebuilt. The guardhouse has been rebuilt and furnished and is open daily. The officers' quarters and the enlisted men's barracks have been rebuilt and are open daily. From the fort's southeast corner, you can see a section of the prison stockade fence just 150 yards away. It too has been rebuilt, although not from chestnut trees, which were used for the original, but are no longer abundant in this area.

To get a better idea of how Fort Lincoln looked during the Civil War, stop at the Visitor Center Museum, where a complete model is displayed and audio-visual exhibits highlight prison camp life. An additional presentation points out the recreational options available at Point Lookout State Park.

The visitor center also has live specimens of animal life at the park: Eastern box turtles, black rat snakes, and fiddler crabs. Check with the park naturalist or park historians about guided hikes, canoe trips, seafood cooking demonstrations, Civil War weapons demonstrations, nature crafts, junior ranger programs, and special events (call 301-872-5688).

From the visitor center, you can take **Periwinkle Point Nature Trail,** which winds through marshy terrain. This wet ground means that there are mosquitoes, so bring bug repellent.

Many visitors come to Point Lookout not for history but for the excellent fishing along the park's three miles of sandy beaches, where the Potomac River empties into the Chesapeake Bay. Anglers also fish from the causeway, sitting beside their cars with their rods in the bay waters. This part of St. Mary's County is considered one of the ten best fishing areas in the United States. Croakers, blues, flounder, and Norfolk spot are all found here, as are crabs, oysters, and soft shell clams. Boats can be rented at the park marina, or you can try your luck from the shore. Many fishermen enjoy camping at the park.

Point Lookout State Park is open 8:00 A.M. to sunset, and the visitor center is open daily from 10:00 A.M. to 6:00 P.M. from Memorial Day to Labor Day and on weekends in April, May, September, and October. It is closed the rest of the year.

Directions: From I-495/95, take Route 5 south. Point Lookout is located sixty miles south of Waldorf at the southern end of Route 5.

Delaware

Fort Delaware State Park

During the War of 1812, a primitive earthwork fortification designed to protect Philadelphia and its harbor was built on Pea Patch Island, in what is now Fort Delaware State Park, just one mile from the present Delaware City. This fortification was dismantled, and in 1819 a masonry fort was built. It was destroyed by fire in 1832. In 1848 work began on a fort that surpassed even Fort Sumter in size. Fort Delaware was not completed until 1859, just two years before the Civil War.

The fort covers six acres and is surrounded by a thirty-foot moat. Considered by knowledgeable architects as an example of the finest brick masonry work in the country, the fort has solid granite walls that are thirty feet thick and thirty-two feet high in certain spots. There are three tiers for guns and circular granite staircases. Entrance to the fort is by a drawbridge. It is an impressive structure.

Fort Delaware was first occupied in February 1861. After the battle of Kernstown in 1862, some 250 prisoners from Gen. Stonewall Jackson's Virginia force became the first Civil War prisoners and were housed on Pea Patch Island. Space was limited, so wooden barracks were built in 1862 for two thousand men. The prisoners of war kept pouring in; by June 1863, eight thousand men were imprisoned on Pea Patch Island, which was equipped for ten thousand but still insufficient. After the Battle of Gettysburg, Confederate prisoners, including Gen. James J. Archer as well as foot soldiers, brought the total population to 12,500. Of these, roughly twenty-seven hundred died at Fort Delaware. All were buried at Finn's Point National Cemetery in New Jersey.

Though the fort was modernized in 1896 in preparation for the Spanish-American War and garrisoned during World War I, it never fired a shot during it's entire military history. The fort was closed entirely in 1944 and later turned over to the state of Delaware.

Visiting Fort Delaware is fun as well as educational. Getting to Pea Patch Island is an experience in itself, as the only way is by boat. The boat to the fort leaves Delaware City, Clinton Dock on Saturday, Sunday, and holidays at frequent intervals for the fifteen-minute trip. A nominal round trip fare is charged, but the fort itself is open at no charge from the last weekend in April through the last weekend in September from 11:00 A.M. to 6:00 P.M. From mid-June through Labor Day, the fort is also open Wednesday through Friday from 11:00 A.M. to 4:00 P.M. For information, call (302) 834-7941.

Once on the island, a jitney transports visitors the short distance to the fort's entrance, or "Sally Port" as it's called. A good way to get acquainted is to view the thirty-minute film *The Story of Pea Patch Island* before exploring the fort. Various groups maintain museums within the Fort Delaware complex. Another point of interest is the difference in quarters for various soldiers. Those of high-ranking Confederate officers were spacious; the more crowded area with its three-tiered bunks was for those over the rank of captain; and the "dungeons" were used for solitary confinement of difficult prisoners. The rank and file were quartered in temporary barracks, which no longer remain.

A walk along the ramparts provides an overview of the island as well as the emplacements for artillery. If time permits, visitors also should take the nature trail on the island, which leads to an observation platform overlooking one of the largest nesting areas for egrets, herons, and ibis in this part of the country.

Directions: Take Washington Beltway Exit 27 (I-95) north. Exit on Route 77 east to Route 13. Exit on Route 72 east to Route 9 into Delaware City.

Civil War Battlefield Sites

There are a great many similarities between the Confederacy during the Civil War and the self-proclaimed independent colonies during the American Revolution. Like the colonies, it seemed the South could win the conflict by holding out, by fighting defensively on their home ground. But no single battle could break the South because there was not a vital center that would paralyze the Confederate States of America. This also proved to be the case during the American Revolution, to the frustration of the British.

French aid had helped make the difference during the Revolution, but during the Civil War, the South ended up fighting alone. They had been confident that England, at least, would come to their aid. Seventy percent of the cotton used in British textile mills came from the South, and there was every hope that "King Cotton" would save the South, but it did not.

The position of the North during the Civil War had many parallels with that of England in 1776. Both enjoyed superior resources—more men, money, transportation facilities, manufactured goods, and food. Also, both had established systems of government and trade, while the Confederacy, like the colonies, was just in the process of organization. But if the war had been as short as most predicted, these Northern advantages would not have proved significant. At the beginning of the war, the armies were essentially equal in size. It would not be until after 1863 that Southern losses would deplete manpower and there would be no reinforcements.

The American colonies had more able military and civil leadership than the British sent to wage the war. The Southern military leadership consisted of West Point's finest graduates—Lee, Jackson, and Stuart. They provided inspired leadership in the field. The North had trouble finding generals to stand up to this triumvirate. On the other hand, the Northerners fared better on the political scene; Lincoln proved more effective than Jefferson Davis at running a country fighting for its life.

The Civil War was a transitional type of conflict, having elements of older styles of warfare as well as being in many respects a "modern" war. It was the last of the old wars in which chivalry played a role. Officers of both armies had studied together at West Point; in some battles roommates who once worked on homework assignments together planned battle strategy for life and death struggles.

These men treated each other with respect even though they showed no mercy. This attitude of respect extended to the men in the field. It was quite common for pickets to exchange tobacco and coffee with those they were supposed to be on guard against.

New inventions were changing the methods of warfare. Railroad lines were vital to both sides during the Civil War. It was the first time that armies arrived at the battlefield by train, and enormous field armies were supplied by rail. Telegraph lines, ironclad ships, observation balloons, and long-ranged rifles with telescope sights all marked this as a new style of fighting. Trench warfare, which would later be so significant in World War I, was really inaugurated in the long sieges of the Civil War.

The Civil War was also the first instance in America of "total war." The civilian population of the South was not exempt from their own kind of combat. For ten months the people of Petersburg fought their own battle against starvation. The women of the South took over the job of providing food and running the farms and businesses, while almost all the able-bodied men aged seventeen to fifty served in the army. As the war dragged on, the North adopted a scorched earth policy to compel the South to surrender. The extent of the losses both in terms of manpower and economics was overwhelming. Much of the war was fought in the South, and the landscape was devastated by the conflict. Recovery would prove to be long and slow.

Harpers Ferry National Historical Park

The Civil War is rife with ironies, but events associated with **Harpers Ferry** rank high on any list of these contrary, or unexpected, episodes. Eighteen months before the war began, John Brown raided the town's Federal arsenal, and all hope of reconciliation between the abolitionists in the North and slave owners in the South was shattered.

Each summer that turbulent era comes alive at Harpers Ferry. The streets of the West Virginia town at the confluence of the Potomac and Shenandoah Rivers fill with costumed shopkeepers and soldiers who bring back the Civil War years. Escorted walking tours include fascinating tales about historical events.

One of the most popular tours covers the raid that made Harpers Ferry famous around the world. On October 16, 1859, John Brown, a Northern abolitionist, led eighteen followers (three more supporters waited with the group's supplies across the river in Maryland) in a raid. Their objective: the guns in the Federal arsenal.

Brown was gambling that if he obtained weapons, blacks in the

South would rally to his banner, which he believed would force the South to renounce slavery. One of his inspirations was Nat Turner's 1831 slave revolt that forced a vote on slavery in the Virginia Legislature; the measure to abolish slavery lost by only one vote. Be sure to stop at the **John Brown Museum** (listed as Stop #15 on the park's self-guided walking tour map) to explore the story of John Brown and the struggle over slavery.

Brown and his band entered the town quietly, but the townsfolk became alarmed at the sight of blacks carrying guns. When the alarm sounded, the raiders barricaded themselves in the firehouse, ever after called John Brown's Fort. (Promoters took the fort to the 1923–33 World's Fair in Chicago, but it attracted only eleven tourists.)

It is ironic that the Federal force against Brown was led by Lt. Col. Robert E. Lee and Lt. J. E. B. Stuart. Both resigned their commissions when war became certain and later became famous Southern generals.

There never was any question of the outcome of Brown's raid. Federal troops stormed the firehouse. They killed ten of Brown's men and captured Brown and four others; five managed to escape. In less than two months, the captives were tried, convicted, and sentenced. On December 2, 1859, John Brown was hanged. In the crowd that watched were John Wilkes Booth and Stonewall Jackson, two men who would play pivotal roles in the years to come.

As John Brown prepared for the gallows, he wrote a message that predicted the Civil War. You can take a walking tour that focuses on the military confrontations fought in and around Harpers Ferry during the war. The arsenal was a magnet for the North and South. Both armies wanted to acquire additional munitions, but neither wanted their enemy to re-arm.

Among the walking tours offered at the park is one that focuses on the guns of Harpers Ferry, and on selected (call ahead at 304-535-6748 for schedule) weekend afternoons, volunteers demonstrate how the early flintlock rifles and muskets worked. Visitors appreciate why these guns had to be replaced when they watch volunteers try many times before successfully firing one. While this may be embarrassing for the volunteers, for the army it was often lethal. You'll discover that the expression "going off half-cocked" originated from the unhealthy habit the guns had of doing just that. You'll also discover that many of the early guns were each made by several craftsmen. One artisan would do the stock, another the lock, and perhaps yet a third the barrel. When they combined the process into the hands of one craftsman, he made the gun "lock, stock, and barrel."

The Civil War totally disrupted the operation of the Harpers Ferry gun factory, which had been established by George Washington in 1796. When Federal soldiers were unable to hold their position in the town, they burned the arsenal and armory as they retreated. Throughout the war, the town seesawed between Union and Confederate forces. In September of 1862 Harpers Ferry was in Federal hands when it was attacked by Stonewall Jackson, who defeated the small Union garrison. Fighting here was over in two days, enabling Jackson to rejoin Lee just in time to adequately defend the Confederate position at Sharpsburg and salvage the Southern line at the Battle of Antietam.

The National Park Service tours at Harpers Ferry provide details about the Civil War era, so try to take at least one. A well-annotated map also makes it easy to explore on your own. A short background slide program is given on the hour at the John Brown Museum. Every half hour, a twenty-six-minute film on John Brown is shown.

It's fun to wander in and out of the restored shops along the historic town's main street. In the Dry Goods Shop an authentic looking ad encourages patrons to purchase pieces of the rope used to hang John Brown. Another sign suggests that the men of the town should buy a Colt pistol to protect their loved ones.

If you want to take a short hike, explore the trails on Virginius Island, the site of the old John Hall Rifle Works. Another option is the path behind St. Peter's Catholic Church to Jefferson Rock, a scenic overlook. When Thomas Jefferson saw the view, he claimed that it was "worth a voyage across the Atlantic." This endorsement may be true, but it is worth mentioning that at the time Jefferson supposedly made the remark, he had yet to make the crossing.

Harpers Ferry National Historical Park is open daily, 8:00 A.M. to 5:00 P.M. During the summer, the park remains open until 6:00 P.M. The admission fee is per vehicle.

Directions: From the Washington Beltway, I-495/95, take Exit 35, I-270 west to the Frederick area. Pick up Route 340, which will take you to Harpers Ferry.

Maryland Heights and Kennedy Farm

The historic town of Harpers Ferry is in West Virginia. But a sizable portion of Harpers Ferry National Historical Park (see selection) is in Maryland, as is the **Kennedy Farm**, which served as the staging area for the historic 1859 raid by John Brown and his band of abolitionists.

Behind St. Peter's Catholic Church in the town of Harpers Ferry, you'll find the stone steps that lead up to Jefferson Rock and the famous view, which Thomas Jefferson described as "worth a voyage across the Atlantic." (At that time Jefferson had not yet crossed the Atlantic.) Across the Potomac River on **Maryland Heights**, another overlook provides a vantage point for viewing the town, which is nestled on the mountainside. Two trails traverse Maryland Heights: Overlook Trail and Stone Fort Trail. The latter leads to the remains of a Civil War fortification. On the West Virginia side of the river, the Loudoun Heights Trail connects with the Appalachian Trail.

To trace the events that put Harpers Ferry on the map, start at the Kennedy Farm, known locally as the John Brown Farm. Here, Brown and his followers hid while planning their raid on the Harpers Ferry arsenal. The community was curious about the newcomers, particularly because it was known that they included blacks. John Brown kept all his band inside, however, and refused to admit any visitors into the widow Kennedy's farm house. A month after the raid, Frank Leslie's *Illustrated Newspapers* printed a sketch of the farm. Newly restored, it looks much today as it did in that sketch.

In the steps of Brown and his committed band, you will make your way from the farm to the Harpers Ferry arsenal. As you travel, think back to October 16, 1859, when the raiders attacked the Federal arsenal hoping to obtain arms for the slaves they anticipated would flock to their banner. They gained neither recruits nor arms.

At the Harpers Ferry Visitors Center, you can learn more about this dramatic incident, and more details are provided at the John Brown Museum just down the street. Throughout the day the National Park Service offers special tours that are well worth catching. Authentically clad mid-nineteenth century "residents" introduce you to the community and the gun factory that employed many of the townsfolk. The armory was defended by the North and seized by the South. You'll miss a lot of local color if you explore on your own, but there is a helpful guide for those who just want to amble around.

Most Harpers Ferry sites can be enjoyed without charge. If you bring a picnic to enjoy along the river, you can have a very inexpensive, but pleasant, family outing. For those who feel no outing is complete without shopping, the town does offer a number of quaint shops and boutiques.

The Kennedy Farm is open weekends, May through October, from 9:00 A.M. to 1:00 P.M. For additional information, call (301) 791-3130. The Harpers Ferry National Historical Park Visitors Center and exhibits are open daily, 8:00 A.M. to 5:00 P.M. During the summer, the special tours are given from 10:00 A.M. to 4:00 P.M. The entrance fee is five dollars per vehicle or three dollars per person for cyclists and walk-ins. For more information, call (304) 535-6029.

Directions: From Baltimore, take I-70 west to Frederick. At Frederick, take Route 340 west toward Harpers Ferry. Before crossing the Potomac River into Virginia, take the Harpers Ferry Road north to Samples Manor and then go north on Chestnut Grove Road to Kennedy Farm. For Harpers Ferry, continue west on Route 340 and follow signs.

Manassas National Battlefield Park

The story goes that on July 21, 1861, *the* thing to do was pack a picnic lunch and journey by carriage or horseback to rural Virginia to see the Union soldiers put an "end" to the rebellious Confederacy. Everybody wanted to see the fun. By four o'clock the outing was a rout, with picnickers as well as soldiers in a panic. Warfare was not what anybody expected.

Neither side was ready to fight in July. Both were still training their recruits. But the Northern army under Gen. Irvin McDowell was made up, for the most part, of three-month volunteers who had signed up in April after Fort Sumter was captured. Their time was almost up, and they were getting ready to head home. McDowell had to fight while he still had an army. There was also considerable pressure from Washington to get started—the battle cry "On to Richmond" echoed throughout the capital. So McDowell headed south with thirty-five thousand untrained men.

They encountered the Confederate force at Manassas, defending the vital railroad junction leading to the important regions of the South. The Southerners, numbering about twenty thousand, were led by Gen. P. G. T. Beauregard. Though the war had hardly begun, he was seeing action for the second time. He had led the Southern troops that captured Fort Sumter in April. As would be the case in so many battles in the next four years, the men leading the opposing armies were friends and classmates. Both McDowell and Beauregard graduated from West Point in 1838.

Another Southern army, a group of about twelve thousand men under Gen. Joseph E. Johnston, which was supposed to be pinned down in the Shenandoah Valley near Winchester, was moved to Manassas. When Johnston was informed of the Northern activity at Manassas, he transferred his brigades by train to this Virginia railroad center in order to bolster Beauregard's force. This was the first time an army was ever moved to battle by railroad—and the trains were on time. Some of the soldiers went directly from the train to the battlefield.

The opening shots of the first major battle of the Civil War were fired soon after dawn on July 21, 1861. The Union army, in a diversionary tactic, attacked the Confederates, who were positioned at a stone bridge over Bull Run (this is Stop 1 at **Manassas National Battlefield Park**). There is a hiking trail from the bridge to Ford Farm, where Gen. William T. Sherman's troops crossed Bull Run during the morning's fighting.

Col. Nathan Evans, who was guarding the stone bridge, saw the dust from the Union force as it tried to move around the Confederate position. Evans, leaving a small force at the bridge, rushed with the bulk of his troops to Matthews Hill (Stop 2) to halt the forward advance of McDowell's men. He was reinforced by two brigades under Gen. Bernard Bee and Col. Francis Bartow, but the Confederates were still pushed back, and the men broke ranks. The retreat became a rout, with soldiers turning and running from the fighting.

As the troops were pushed back to Henry Hill, General Bee spotted Gen. Thomas J. Jackson's brigade drawn up in orderly ranks behind the crest of the hill. He shouted to his men, "There stands Jackson like a stone wall! Rally behind the Virginians!"

The brigade held firm against the Union onslaught and was afterward called the "Stonewall Brigade"; its general, "Stonewall" Jackson. The brigade held the line for more than three hours until even the Stonewall Brigade began to weaken. But at that crucial junction, the last train carrying Johnston's men arrived at Manassas. The addition of fresh troops was too much for the tired Union soldiers. They panicked and ran, the picnickers were in full retreat as well, and the army became a mob. Lincoln himself watched the wild flight into Washington from the White House windows.

One additional point of interest, which figured not only in this battle but would also play a role in the Second Battle of Manassas, was the stone house (Stop 2) that served as a field hospital. Originally a turnpike inn for teamsters, it provided some protection for the wounded. Though the thick stone walls could protect the injured from the battle raging outside, it couldn't protect them from the inadequacy of the surgeons responsible for helping them. Many regiments had only one surgeon and one assistant, which was not nearly enough to handle the volume of wounded. Seriously injured men were left to die, and those with arm or leg wounds had the limb removed in a five-minute operation that lacked antiseptic or sterile refinements. Surviving this brutal surgery was difficult; death usually occurred within three days of "surgical fever." The casualties after Second Manassas were even greater. Nearly twenty thousand men were wounded and many languished on the battlefield for days without attention. Today, there are guided tours of the Stone House Field

Hospital during the summer months.

One year later, the Union and Confederate armies were back once more on the battlefield at Manassas. But this time they were no longer untrained recruits, they were battle-trained troops.

In the summer of 1862, Lee had driven McClellan's Army of the Potomac from the Richmond battle lines into a fortified camp on the James River. The Confederacy was at its zenith, both in terms of morale and military strength—all things still seemed possible. Though Lee had but half of McClellan's strength in numbers, he never hesitated to take a gamble, and he split his force in half, sending Jackson north to deal with the new Army of Virginia.

The War Department in Washington was not pleased with McClellan's showing and so created a new Army of Virginia under the command of Maj. Gen. John Pope. This army would fight only one battle, that of Second Manassas. Their dismal showing caused them to be disbanded subsequent to that encounter. Pope, a collateral descendant of George Washington and a relative of Mary Todd Lincoln by marriage, was not a popular or effective leader. He was a self-proclaimed fighter who declared his headquarters to be his saddle. A military joke of the day had it that Pope didn't know his headquarters from his hindquarters. His stubborn refusal to accept military intelligence and his complete mishandling of Northern troops at Manassas caused him to be sent to Minnesota to fight the Indians.

But he was riding high before Manassas, determined to defeat Jackson and bring new laurels to the North. When McClellan was ordered to proceed north to join with Pope, Lee decided to attack before the two forces could be combined.

In order to achieve this objective, Lee ordered one of the boldest military movements in history. On August 24, he sent Jackson with twenty-four thousand men on a fifty-four-mile flanking march around Pope's right flank. Their two-day march took them between Blue Ridge and Bull Run Mountain and east through Thoroughfare Gap to seize Manassas Junction. Jackson and his men reached their objective by August 26 and destroyed Pope's supply base. Pope felt that Jackson, with only twenty thousand men, could easily be taken by his own fifty-five-thousand-man army. Jackson had meanwhile found a secure defensive position in the same area where the First Battle of Manassas had been fought. In an unfinished railroad bed, Jackson deployed his men to await the arrival of Lee and Longstreet.

To prevent Pope from moving east of Bull Run and merging with the rest of McClellan's troops, on August 28 Jackson revealed his position by firing on Pope's troops (Battery Heights, the scene of the opening attack of the Second Battle of Manassas, is Stop 1 on the twelve-mile auto route that covers the three-day battle). It was 5:15 P.M. when Jackson ordered the three Confederate artillery batteries to open fire. With fewer than a hundred yards between the two sides, casualties were heavy. When darkness fell, the losses were tallied, and it became apparent that the Stonewall Brigade had suffered heavily; they had started the battle with 635 men and had only 100 left standing. Of the twenty-eight hundred Federal soldiers who saw action that afternoon, more than eleven hundred were hit. Word was sent to Pope that Jackson and his twenty thousand men had been pinned down. Pope assumed Jackson was trying to escape to the mountains and made plans to wipe out this Confederate nuisance once and for all.

The next morning, Jackson strung out his three Confederate divisions for two and a half miles along the unfinished railroad bed (Stop 3). Here Jackson's men held the line against numerous Union assaults as they waited to be reinforced. All day, the Confederates held their position, until darkness ended the Northern attacks.

On August 30, Pope still felt he had a weakening Confederate force trapped, despite various dispatches that told of large Confederate forces on the march toward Manassas. The orders Pope gave his generals on the 30th were to pursue the supposedly fleeing Jackson and "capture the whole lot of them." It was to be the shortest pursuit on record, as Pope would be heading into the cleverly planned trap that Lee had set (Stop 4, the Deep Cut Trail, is a one-mile hiking trail that covers much of the action on the afternoon of August 30). The Confederates were spread out like two huge jaws ready to swallow the unsuspecting Union line. The fighting was so intense that Jackson's beleaguered force ran out of ammunition and resorted to throwing rocks at the Yankees, who were only twenty yards away. With Lee and Longstreet now on the field, the jaws closed and the Union lines crumbled. It was the second debacle at Bull Run, with Pope losing 14,462 men, plus his command. The Army of Virginia was disbanded.

The victory at Manassas, though it cost Lee 17% of his men (9,474 men had fallen), still provided the impetus for the South to carry the war into the North—the next battle would be on the banks of another creek, this time in Maryland, at the village of Sharpsburg.

Tour Stops 4 and 5, the Sudley Church and the Stone House, both served as Union field hospitals. Other stops mark isolated incidents in the three-day fighting. At Stop 8, Henry Hill, there is a visitor center where two audio-visual programs provide orientation to the major battles that took place at Manassas.

The Manassas National Battlefield Park is open daily in the summer from 9:00 A.M. to 6:00 P.M. and in the winter from 8:30 A.M. to 5:00 P.M. It is closed on Christmas Day. There is a nominal entrance fee. Living-history programs are scheduled for the summer months.

Directions: Take Washington Beltway Exit 9 (I-66) west seventeen miles to the intersection of Route 23 north, where the battlefield is located.

Stonewall Jackson's Headquarters

Gen. Thomas Jonathan Jackson's career as Lee's ablest general was short-lived. Jackson served only two years before being tragically shot by his own troops in a moment of triumphant victory at Chancellorsville.

In the fall of 1861, Gen. Stonewall Jackson came to Winchester to command the Valley District. Lewis Tilghman Moore (great-grandfather of actress Mary Tyler Moore), a lieutenant colonel in the Fourth Virginia Infantry Stonewall Brigade, offered his Hudson River Gothic house to Jackson as his headquarters. The general wrote to his wife, "The situation is beautiful. The building is of cottage style and contains six rooms. I have two rooms, one above the other. My lower room, or office, has matting on the floor, a large fine table, six chairs and a piano. The walls are papered with elegant gilt paper. I don't remember to have ever seen more beautiful papering..."

His wife, Mary Anna Morrison Jackson, joined him in Winchester at Christmas time and stayed until March 1862 (see Stonewall Jackson House selection). These three months were their longest time together since Jackson had left his teaching duties at Virginia Military Institute. You'll see the table where they enjoyed Christmas dinner, Jackson's office (just as he described it), and his bedroom.

The military strategy that Jackson planned is so highly regarded that it is still studied in military academies both in America and in Europe. The able strategy, rapid movement, and brilliant execution are high points of the Confederate army campaign.

As commander of the Army of the Shenandoah in late May and early June, Jackson marched with his men nearly four hundred miles in thirty-two days, fighting almost daily, including five major battles. They defeated three Union armies, capturing twenty much-needed artillery pieces and taking four thousand Federal prisoners. In his "Valley Campaign," fewer than one thousand of Jackson's men were killed or wounded. His troops were between fifteen and twenty thousand strong, while more than sixty thousand opposed him.

This highly effective tactical campaign can be traced by car along US 11 and Route 340 between Lexington and Winchester. There are eleven road markers that provide information on Jackson's "Valley Campaign." The Virginia Civil War Trails brochure is an excellent resource.

Stonewall Jackson's Headquarters has photographs and a large collection of personal memorabilia from Jackson and his staff on display. The gift shop sells rare first edition books, old hard-to-find books on the Civil War, and Confederate money. The house, at 415 Braddock Street, is open 10:00 A.M. to 4:00 P.M. daily, April through October, and on weekends only during the winter months. Guided tours are conducted through the house. Admission is charged.

Directions: From I-95 at Fredericksburg take Route 17 north to Marshall. Pick up I-66 west, which will connect with I-81. Proceed north on I-81 to Winchester, Exit 80, Millwood Avenue. Head into Winchester on Millwood Avenue and turn right on Pleasant Valley Road past Abram's Delight (see selection). Turn left on Cork Street and right on Cameron Street. Continue to North Avenue and turn left. Go two blocks to Braddock Street and turn left. Stonewall Jackson's Headquarters is half way down the first block of Braddock Street, on the right.

Richmond National Battlefield Park

From the first days of the Civil War in 1861, Richmond was a prize sought by the North and defended by the South. Seven major Federal drives were launched against this symbol of the Confederacy. Both sides considered the city a prime psychological objective. Losing Richmond, the capital of the Confederacy, would be a devastating blow to the spirit of the South; it would also be a military disaster, because Richmond was the principal supply depot for Southern troops.

The first of the two Federal drives that came close to success was Gen. George B. McClellan's Peninsula Campaign of 1862. At **Richmond National Battlefield Park's** Chimborazo Visitor Center, an audio-visual presentation covers this campaign plus the climactic 1864 drive of Gen. Ulysses S. Grant, which helped bring the Civil War to an end. Displays, information on the park's frequent living-history programs, and maps of the sixty-mile battlefield trail are all available. You also can rent or buy audiotape tours. There are two distinct battlefield areas. Red dot markers indicate McClellan's campaign, while blue dots represent the 1864 Grant offensive.

There are five stops along McClellan's 1862 route. To his credit, Gen. George McClellan had taken the ragtag, defeated Union troops after the First Battle of Manassas and forged them into the one-hundred thousand-man Army of the Potomac. His goal was to mount a combined land and water attack on Richmond.

On May 15, 1862, the Federal naval attack on Fort Darling (battlefield tour stop at Drewry's Bluff) was repulsed. Union ships numbered five gunboats and included the famous ironclad *Monitor*. By repulsing this early effort, the Confederates saved Richmond from being shelled and also protected the city from forays up the James River. A self-guided trail with explanatory markers outlines the Civil War action around this fortification.

It wasn't until May 24, 1862, that McClellan reached the outskirts of Richmond, deploying his men on both sides of the Chickahominy River six miles from the city. From this position he waited for additional troops. The Confederates, seeing the Union army divided with half their force on each side of the river, decided to seize the initiative. On May 31, Gen. Joseph E. Johnston attacked the Federal force at Fair Oaks and at Seven Pines. (Battle site markers indicate these locations on the Richmond tour map.) Though the fighting itself was inconclusive, there were two strategic results from this first confrontation. First, the Confederate initiative and showing made an already cautious McClellan even more careful, a disposition that would impede the Federal battle plan and eventually cause him to forego the chance to take the city. Second, Johnston was wounded in this encounter and was replaced by Gen. Robert E. Lee, who gave the troops new leadership and a new name, the Army of Northern Virginia.

General Lee summoned his Southern hero, Gen. Stonewall Jackson, who had just wrapped up the Valley Campaign. These additional troops brought Lee's strength to more than eighty thousand, very near that of the Union force.

From this position of strength, Lee decided to attack on June 26 and began what is called the Seven Days Battle for Richmond. Watching from earthworks on Chickahominy Bluff (now a battlefield tour stop with an audio interpretative marker), Lee oversaw the opening attack at Mechanicsville, where the Confederates were successful. Later that same day, attacks north of the Chickahominy River on Beaver Dam Creek did not succeed, and the Confederates suffered heavy losses. (Beaver Dam Creek is also a battlefield tour stop.) To reach the Union position, it was necessary to first cross the creek and then a waist-deep millrace in the face of artillery fire. It was an impossible situation, and the Confederate attack at Beaver Dam Creek failed.

During the night of June 26, the Union troops abandoned their position behind Beaver Dam Creek and moved to Gaines' Mill, the location of the next day's fighting. There is now a self-guided trail around the battlefield at Gaines' Mill. The Watt Farm House, that Union Gen. Fitz John Porter used as his headquarters for the June 27 battle, has been partially restored, though it is not open to be toured. The self-guided trail leads to Breakthrough Point where Texas and Georgia troops penetrated the Union line. From the trail the shallow trenches used by Union troops are still discernible. Union reinforcements enabled Porter to hold the line, but McClellan, reflecting the cautious streak that would undermine his efforts, decided to abandon the Chickahominy positions and ordered a retreat. If McClellan's will had been stronger, he might have ordered an attack on Richmond, as the Confederate force standing between him and his goal was only a thin line. But though not beaten in battle, he was beaten in spirit.

General Lee now needed to anticipate McClellan's next move. When he learned that the Army of the Potomac was indeed leaving the battle, he started in pursuit. Fighting erupted at Savage Station, White Oak Swamp, and Glendale (all marked, though not part of the Battlefield Park). The Union army made a stand on July 1 at Malvern Hill. They were waiting for the supply train to reach Harrison's Landing at Berkeley Plantation on the James River. (See Declaration of Independence: Berkeley.) The Union position on Malvern Hill was almost impossible to attack; in fact, so impregnable was it, surrounded by swamp and water and protected by the Union navy, that they needed no trenches. The Federal troops stood in lines of battle with their massed artillery and mowed down the Confederates attempting to advance up the open slope. One Confederate officer said later, "It was not war—it was murder." Lee lost more than five thousand men to no avail.

Though they could not defeat the Union army at Malvern Hill, the Confederates felt victorious. They had stopped McClellan's drive to capture Richmond. The campaign cost thirty-five thousand men, North and South. It would be repeated again in 1864.

For the next two years of the Civil War, though there was activity in Virginia, Richmond's entrenched position was not seriously challenged. After the savage Battle of the Wilderness and Spotsylvania, Grant moved south to find a new battlefield. On May 30, 1864, he was stopped in the vicinity of Mechanicsville by Lee's troops.

Grant felt that the Southern line was weak in the center near Cold Harbor and attacked there on June 3. But he underestimated the strength of the Confederate fortifications and the will of Lee's veterans to resist. After only thirty minutes of fighting, Grant had lost several thousand men and gained no ground. For ten days Lee's men held the line, sweltering in the heat, humidity, and stench of battle. At the end of the Battle of Cold Harbor, Grant had more than thirteen thousand casualties, while Lee sustained a loss of at least three thousand men. Grant conceded the position as hopeless and withdrew his men, moving next to Petersburg, the railroad connection for the South. After Cold Harbor the war around Richmond shifted from active encounters to a state of siege.

At Cold Harbor, a visitor center provides an orientation for this stage of the conflict. The 1.25-mile battlefield tour road passes well-preserved field fortifications. The restored Garthright House served as a field hospital for wounded Union soldiers and after the Union retreat, for Southern casualties. The house is not open; only the exterior has been restored. Cold Harbor National Cemetery and Hanover County Battlefield Park are nearby.

While the major portion of Grant's Army of the Potomac was involved in the siege of Petersburg, sporadic raids on Richmond still occurred. On September 29, 1864, a surprise attack by Union soldiers succeeded in capturing Fort Harrison, part of the Southern fort defense of Richmond. Federal troops occupied and enlarged the fort. They then built a second fort opposite Fort Darling on Drewry's Bluff. A self-guiding trail covers the Fort Harrison Battlefield area and leads to the second Federal bastion, Fort Brady. Fort Harrison has a visitor center that is open during the summer months.

When Lee retreated from Petersburg on April 2, 1865, Richmond's mayor informed the Union army that the Confederate army had abandoned the city. They burned warehouses and supplies as they left. Before the ruined buildings cooled, Lee had surrendered to Grant at Appomattox Court House.

Richmond National Battlefield Park's Chimborazo and Cold Harbor visitor centers are open 9:00 A.M. to 5:00 P.M. daily, except Thanksgiving, Christmas, and New Year's Day. There is no admission charge.

Directions: From I-95 in the Richmond area, take Exit 74C if you are northbound; take Exit 74B if you are traveling south. Take East Broad Street to the Chimborazo Visitor Center at 3215 East Broad Street.

Antietam National Battlefield Park

The Union army seemed fated time and time again to snatch defeat from the jaws of victory. History abounds with "what ifs," but you cannot help feeling that if Lee had served the North rather than the South, the war would have been far shorter. The generals he faced were not his equals. McClellan failed at Antietam, though he had everything going for him—advance information, which gave him a decided edge, more men, and fresh troops, while Lee's army stood on the ragged edge of exhaustion. Yet McClellan let all these advantages slip through his fingers, and the only Northern gain was in preventing Lee from successfully invading the North.

The South needed to capitalize on their victory at the Second Battle of Bull Run. Lee hoped that he could carry the war to the North. Doing so, he felt, would achieve two important objectives: First, it might convince the North to work toward a negotiated settlement with the Confederacy; second, it might persuade England and France to recognize the Confederate States of America. The Union blockade of the South was causing economic hardship not only in the southern cotton area, but also in the English textile mills.

It was September 1862 when Lee crossed the Potomac into Maryland. Lee, the master of the bold stroke, decided to risk dividing his army, sending half his force under Jackson to capture Harper's Ferry and the remaining twenty thousand under Gen. James Longstreet to continue north. Longstreet, with Lee, headed for the eventual goal of Harrisburg, the capital of Pennsylvania. This risk was compromised when McClellan fortuitously obtained a copy of Lee's orders to Jackson and Longstreet on September 13 and learned the details of the Southern battle plan. The North now knew how thinly the Confederate forces would be spread over the Maryland countryside.

Once again, the North had a chance to quickly end the war. They knew Lee's game plan! But rather than acting quickly on this information, McClellan moved slowly, overcoming the small Confederate outposts in the South Mountain passes on September 14. Interpretive markers now indicate the skirmishes at Turner's, Fox's, and Crampton's Gap on South Mountain.

Then McClellan, with fifty thousand men, moved on September 15 into the Sharpsburg area, where he *knew* Lee waited with only half the Confederate force. Still McClellan waited, and victory faded with the passing time. By September 16, the Union army numbered seventy thousand, with the Confederates fielding only twenty thousand. The other part of Lee's plan progressed smoothly. Jackson captured Harper's Ferry on September 15 and quick-marched his men all night to rejoin Lee at Sharpsburg the next day. As the much needed reinforcements arrived to bolster the Confederate position, McClellan decided the time was right—not realizing he was at least one if not two days late for his appointment with destiny. At dawn on September 17, the bloodiest day of the Civil War began.

The opening attack was particularly brutal. From the Joseph Poffenberger Farm (Site 2 at Antietam Park), General Hooker's artillery attacked Jackson's force, which was positioned in the Miller cornfield (Site 4). The line of battle crossed this field fifteen times. Hooker, commenting on the encounter, reported, "every stalk of corn... was cut as closely as could have been done with a knife, and the slain lay in rows precisely as they had stood in their ranks a few moments before." Jackson's men were subjected to almost an hour of constant shelling, but yielded only about one-half mile until bolstered by additional troops around 7:00 A.M.

At 9:00 A.M. the Union army under General Mansfield counterattacked. Mansfield was wounded at the East Woods as he led his men into battle (Site 3). His men were cut off around the Dunker Church (Site 1; the original church was destroyed in a 1921 storm, but it was reconstructed in the early sixties), and Gen. John Sedgwick's division lost twenty-two hundred men in fewer than thirty minutes as they charged into the West Woods (Site 5) to extricate Mansfield's men. The morning fighting had taken a terrible toll. Neither side had made a substantial gain, and the day had just begun.

Fighting diminished until Union troops under Sumner attacked the Confederates along the Sunken Road, afterwards called the "Bloody Lane" (Site 6). Almost four hours of continuous fighting resulted in four thousand casualties. Sheer exhaustion stopped the battle at this point, around 1:00 P.M. Neither side had profited, but neither side could continue. The Southern troops simply held their ground.

At the other end of the battlefield area, the Union left flank under General Burnside had been trying to cross a bridge over Antietam Creek since 9:30 A.M. Burnside had four divisions, and they were held back by four hundred Georgia riflemen. Having this large number of men tied up and unable to reinforce Hooker in the northern sector of the battlefield certainly contributed to McClellan's defeat at Antietam. It was not until 1:00 P.M. that the Federal troops crossed what is now called Burnside Bridge (Site 7). After taking two hours to reform their lines, the Union force drove the Georgia troops toward Sharpsburg. Again, their two-hour delay proved costly. Just as the Confederate line was being turned back, additional reinforcements arrived—Gen. A. P. Hill's division from the Harpers Ferry area. The Federal army was driven back to the fateful bridge and did not attack again.

The Hawkins Zouave Monument marks the spot where the battle ended, at 5:30 P.M. on September 17. A footpath leads to this hillside monument, which provides a view over the entire battlefield. It's a good place to put the day's events into perspective. Directly in the line of vision is the Antietam National Cemetery, where 4,776 of the 12,410 Federal soldiers killed at Antietam are buried. Southern dead, numbering 10,700, lie elsewhere.

By late afternoon, the Battle of Antietam was over. Losses were overwhelming, and Lee had no more men to send into battle. McClellan, on the other hand, had twenty thousand fresh troops still in reserve. If the North had made a big push, the Southerners quite likely would have been defeated. But McClellan held back, and Lee withdrew his army, recrossing the Potomac into Virginia. The South would fight another day—and another.

Antietam National Battlefield Park covers twelve square miles. Park tours start at the visitor center. An audio-visual program helps put events at Antietam in perspective, and a twenty-six-minute film, *Antietam Visit,* is shown on the hour. The film focuses on President Lincoln's visit with Commander of the Army George B. McClellan after the battle. Lincoln reviewed the troops, visited the numerous wounded, and urged McClellan to pursue the Confederates into the South. The visitor center also has four large paintings done by Capt. James Hope from sketches he made on the battlefield. During the summer months, there are guided walks. The park is open daily from 8:30 A.M. to 6:00 P.M. in the summer and until 5:00 P.M. the rest of the year. It is closed on Thanksgiving, Christmas, and New Year's Day. A nominal admission is charged, and cassette tapes of the battlefield tour can be rented. For additional information, you can call (301) 432-5124.

Directions: Take Washington Beltway Exit 35 (I-270) to Frederick. Continue on Route 70 until it intersects with Route 34. Take Route 34 to Sharpsburg; the visitor center is north of Sharpsburg on Maryland Route 65.

Fredericksburg National Military Park

In the bitter and tragic story of America at war with herself, Fredericksburg was indeed inopportunely placed, being midway between the two capitals. On four occasions, the two sides fought bitterly in and around Fredericksburg. Within a seventeen-mile radius of this small Virginia town was a theater of war so intense and continuous that it is unequaled on the American continent.

After General McClellan's poor showing at Antietam, he was replaced by Gen. Ambrose Burnside. It was this gentleman's bushy cheek whiskers that prompted the term "sideburns." Burnside, recognizing that McClellan had been relieved of his command because he did not pursue Lee into the south after Antietam, was determined that the army under his command would advance to Richmond. Crucial to this plan was Fredericksburg. Burnside decided to cross the Rappahannock River by using pontoon bridges. When he arrived, anxious to leave Fredericksburg before the Confederate Army could unite and move up into position, there were no boats.

Although the pontoon boats arrived on November 25, Burnside had grown cautious and waited still longer—too long, as it turned out. The Confederates under General Lee moved into the area and positioned themselves in the hills behind Fredericksburg. On the night of December 10, the Rebel sentries on the town side of the river heard a voice from the other side yelling, "Yankees cooking big rations! March tomorrow!"

Before attempting to fight their way through the Confederate lines, the Union army turned their cannons on the town and inflicted a brutal bombardment. When they crossed into the city, they rampaged through the town, destroying the belongings in the empty Fredericksburg homes. The Confederates, lying in wait in a seven-mile line on the hills behind the city, did not leave their entrenched position

The real battle began on December 13, when 110,000 Union soldiers attempted to storm the Confederate-held hills west of the city. The Union army could not have picked a worse place to engage the enemy than Marye's Heights. At the foot of the heights was a sunken road with a stone wall in front of it. Behind this wall were Confederate soldiers, four deep.

Like soldiers in earlier European conflicts, the Yankees marched in neat rows beneath the cannons on Marye's Heights. It was a slaughter. They were mowed down as they came on throughout the long, bloody day. Line after line, column after column, and still they were ordered to advance up the deadly slope. Not one Union soldier got within thirty yards of the fateful stone wall. More than six thousand men were casualties in a matter of hours. After eight hours General Burnside had lost thirteen thousand men either wounded or dead and was still going to order another attack when his officers persuaded him not to demand the certain death of any more brave soldiers. Two nights later, Burnside recrossed the river using the protection of a heavy storm. The Battle of Fredericksburg, one of the most one-sided defeats in American military history, was over.

To gain an overview of Fredericksburg National Military Park, begin at the visitor center, where there are exhibits and a short slide show. Maps and brochures also help to orient visitors. Directly in front of the center is the Sunken Road, along which there is a well-marked walking route.

Across the Sunken Road is the **National Cemetery**, where fifteen thousand Union dead are buried. On a hill is a large painting of the Battle of Fredericksburg. A taped message will provide additional information. Continuing along the Sunken Road, which originally ran for four hundred yards along the edge of the Heights, visitors pass an area where the stone wall of the Southern fortifications has been reconstructed. A short segment of the original wall behind which the Confederates made their successful stand has been preserved. On the right is the Innis House, which stood directly on the Confederate front line. The house sustained damage from hundreds of bullets during the fighting on December 13. A few Confederates fired from the building itself. It was repaired, and today, a taped message continues the story of the battle.

There was another house next door, the Stephens House, which has since been destroyed. Martha Stephens did not leave her home in fear of the approaching battle like most Fredericksburg residents. According to tradition, she stayed and nursed the wounded soldiers outside her door. The night after this fierce battle, Federal wounded lay beneath the guns of both sides. A young Confederate sergeant from South Carolina, Richard Kirkland, moved by the Union soldiers' helpless cries for water, asked leave to bring the dying men water from the Stephens' well. Warned that no flag of truce could be shown and that he probably would be shot when he climbed the protecting stone wall, he nevertheless filled as many canteens as he could carry and jumped the wall to help the wounded Federal soldiers. A cheer came from the Union lines instead of the bullets he expected. Kirkland was called the "Angel of Marye's Heights," and today, the Kirkland Monument honors this brave, compassionate soldier.

One final spot to be noticed is the Marye House, built in 1830 and called Brompton. Confederate artillery officers used the building as their headquarters during the battle. The house itself is not open.

After completing the walking tour, take the self-guided battlefield auto route along Lee Drive. At Stop 2, there is a short trail to the top of Lee Hill. From this vantage point, Gen. Robert E. Lee directed the Confederate forces, consulting with subordinate officers Stonewall Jackson and James Longstreet. The guns that stand on Lee Hill are similar to those that were in place in December 1862 and that helped repulse the Union force. While Lee watched the battle, a shell fell at his feet but failed to explode.

The last major stop along the route is at the point of a major Federal breakthrough. Under Gen. George G. Meade, one division managed to break the Confederate line at least temporarily. They were driven back when Confederate reinforcements were brought in to augment General Gregg's command. Just a bit farther down Lee

Drive is Prospect Hill, where a large battery of Confederate guns assaulted the Federal line. Along the hilltop the fortifications constructed to protect the fourteen guns that once stood here can still be seen.

There are other sites of interest within Fredericksburg National Military Park. The stately home, Chatham (see selection), which was used as both headquarters and hospital can be visited. At Chatham, there is an overlook of the Pontoon Crossing Site. Other markers, monuments, and cannons can be viewed in the park, which is open daily at a nominal charge.

Directions: Take Exit 4 from I-495/95, the Washington Beltway. Take I-95 south to Fredericksburg. Signs provide directions to the Fredericksburg National Military Park.

Chancellorsville Battlefield

Lee's greatest victory, the Battle of Chancellorsville, was sadly diminished by the irreparable loss of Gen. Stonewall Jackson, who was inadvertently shot by his own men during the battle.

Lee's victory was a triumph of strategy over numbers and determination over vacillation. Actually, Gen. Joseph Hooker did come up with a good plan; he had to, as he was very much aware that he was replacing General Burnside, who made such a poor showing at Fredericksburg. So Hooker was determined to beat Lee. After reorganizing the 135,000 Union troops during the winter camp, he was ready. "My plans are perfect," said Hooker. "May God have mercy on General Lee, for I will have none."

His plan was to hold Lee's force at Fredericksburg with one part of the army while moving around Lee's left side with a larger force, thus compelling Lee to withdraw or surrender. But Lee, recognizing Hooker's intention, adroitly split his army and then executed the same maneuver on an army twice his size.

As Hooker moved to attack Lee's left flank with seventy-five thousand men, Lee left only ten thousand men under Gen. Jubal Early to hold Fredericksburg and moved the rest of the army, forty-five thousand strong, toward Chancellorsville.

When Hooker met the advancing troops, he halted and dug in rather than attacking the inferior force, thereby metaphorically digging his own grave and burying his hopes of victory over Lee.

When Lee arrived and discovered the Northerners dug in, he decided to attack. Planning with his trusted aide, General Jackson

(Stop 6, the Lee-Jackson Bivouac), Lee came up with a bold and daring maneuver. With less than half his already outnumbered force, he would hold the line, while Jackson, with thirty thousand men, would march around the Union force and envelop Hooker's right flank. This surprise move was enormously effective, caving in the Federal line for two and a half miles. It was at this time, however, that fate ceased smiling on the Confederates. Jackson, who had ridden out in front of his own line to reconnoiter the Federal position in order to continue the attack into the night, was badly wounded—fired on by his own men as he returned.

The Southern troops resumed their attack the next day, pushing Hooker back toward the river. Word had come in that a Northern attack had forced General Early to abandon Fredericksburg. Drastic measures were again called for. Lee left J. E. B. Stuart in Jackson's place and took twenty thousand men east to recapture Fredericksburg.

Though Chancellorsville was a Confederate victory, the cost was high. Lee lost twelve thousand men, plus the military genius of Jackson. Union losses were even higher, totaling seventeen thousand. At the Chancellorsville Visitor Center (Stop 5; Stops 1–4 are part of Fredericksburg Battlefield, ten miles east), exhibits and displays bring this stirring Confederate victory, at two to one odds, dramatically to life. There is also a twelve-minute film covering the conflict of May 1–4,1863. Maps available at the center direct visitors to all the stops.

Stop 6, Chancellorsville Inn, served as General Hooker's headquarters. In fact, as he leaned against one of the inn's porch pillars on May 3, he was painfully wounded by a Confederate shell. The shell did not prove as damaging as his earlier loss of nerve, which had prompted him to withdraw and dig in to a defensive position on May 1, abandoning the offensive to Lee.

When the Confederates took the area around Chancellorsville on May 3, they realized victory was in their grasp. At Stop 9 on the battlefield tour, fierce fighting occurred on May 3. One of the few high, open areas, Hazel Grove was the location of Confederate artillery and placed the Southerners in a location to batter the center of the Union lines.

The last major point of interest at Chancellorsville Battlefield is the clearly marked Jackson Trail, tracing the route Jackson took to attack Hooker's flank. This trail can be picked up at Stop 8, Catherine Furnace. Specific details of the drive are given on the map available at the visitor center.

An important footnote to the Battle of Chancellorsville is the small frame office building at Guinea Station. After being shot by his own men, Jackson's arm was amputated at Wilderness Tavern. He was then moved to Fairfield Plantation, where he contracted pneumonia and died on May 10, 1863. The area is now the **Stonewall Jackson Shrine**. Guinea Station is on Route 606 just fifteen miles south of Fredericksburg.

Directions: To reach the Chancellorsville Battlefield, take Washington Beltway Exit 4 (I-95) south to Fredericksburg, Exit 130B; then take Route 3 to Chancellorsville. Both Stops 5 and 6 are on Route 3.

Gettysburg National Military Park

The bloodiest battle in American History, the high watermark of the Confederacy, the turning point of the Civil War—all these are phrases that attempt to describe the indescribable: the Battle of Gettysburg in July 1863.

This was the second and last time Lee attempted to invade the North. His first effort failed in September of 1862 at Antietam, Maryland. After his victory at Chancellorsville, Lee was ready to try again. His goals were the same as those he had attempted to achieve the year before, to gain either a negotiated settlement with the North or, failing that, to secure from European allies aid in the continuing struggle.

In June 1863, to the utter consternation of officials in Washington, Lee, with the seventy thousand men of his Army of Northern Virginia, moved west and north from Fredericksburg into Pennsylvania. By late June, the Confederates held Chambersburg, York, and Carlisle. Advancing Southern troops were moving in on Harrisburg, the Pennsylvania capital.

Washington ordered General Hooker's Army of the Potomac to pursue Lee, who continued north with no real idea of how close the Union line was to his troops. His normal reconnaissance unit, J. E. B. Stuart's cavalry, was not with the main force, but had moved east.

It was thus purely accidental that the two armies ran into each other around Gettysburg on June 30, 1863. Hooker was no longer in command of the Northern forces. He, too, failed to measure up to Lee and had been replaced just two days before by Gen. George Meade.

The Battle of Gettysburg began on the morning of July 1, just beyond McPherson's Barn (Stop 1 on the Gettysburg Battlefield Auto Route). Gen. John Reynolds commanded the Union infantry that held this line. The Federal forces were outnumbered here and at Oak Ridge (Stop 3) but held out until the afternoon, when Jubal Early's

Confederates broke through the Federal line at Barlow Knoll. This collapsed the Federal line north of Gettysburg, and the Union forces were driven back to Cemetery Hill (Stop 14), south of Gettysburg, which ended the first day's fighting.

Dawn on July 2 found the two armies positioned one mile apart on two parallel ridges—the North on Cemetery Ridge and the South on Seminary Ridge. Lee's plan of attack called for Gen. Richard Ewell and Gen. A. P. Hill to make secondary attacks on the Union position while General Longstreet enveloped the left flank.

Longstreet was in position to attack by the afternoon of July 2, which gave the North time to reinforce their line. Once Longstreet's men began the attack, they cleared the Union troops from Devil's Den to the Peach Orchard (Stop 10). Between these two points was a wheat field (Stop 9), which was the scene of a great deal of the fighting that day. It was left strewn with dead and dying men.

By late afternoon, Longstreet's right flank began to climb two hills, Round Top and Little Round Top (Stop 8). These hills would give the South a commanding position from which to encircle the entire Federal line. But heavy artillery and infantry fire halted Longstreet's men before they reached the crest. The presence of two Union brigades at the peak of Little Round Top was the result of quick action on the part of General Warren, chief engineer of the Union army, who had watched the action and realized the crucial need for an adequate defense of the hilltop position. If Warren had not commandeered two brigades, the North could well have lost the Battle of Gettysburg on July 2.

Longstreet's drive on Little Round Top was halted at dusk. Longstreet had broken through General Sickles's line in the Peach Orchard, and Ewell's attack on Culp's Hill (Stop 13), though briefly successful, was pushed back.

July 3, 1863, was the last day of the Battle of Gettysburg. Lee had decided to attack the center of General Meade's line on Cemetery Ridge. In an effort to weaken the Federal position, 130 cannons bombarded the Union troops for two hours. As the smoke from this barrage cleared, the Northerners saw facing them a long line of Confederate soldiers, battle flags flying. As the infantrymen under George E. Pickett, J. J. Petigrew, and I. R. Trible began crossing the open field, they were met by a salvo from more than eighty-eight guns. Though some faltered and fell, they kept marching into this killing fire. Lee, who was watching (from Stop 5), realized he had made the worst mistake of his military career. In fifty minutes six thousand men were killed, wounded, or missing, and Pickett's Charge entered the pages of history.

For one brief moment during the charge, it seemed as if they might breech the Federal line. General Armistead, holding his black hat on his sword, urged the men on over the wall. When Pickett's Charge was turned back at the ridge, where the same copse of trees still stands, the tide turned irrevocably for the Southern cause. Never again would they come so close to victory. The war from then on would be a defensive attempt to hold out and wear the North down. There is a one-mile trail at the high water mark (Stop 15 on the Auto Route), which takes about an hour to walk but is worth the time. The chance to stand at the very spot where Pickett's Charge was repulsed, see the many poignant monuments to these courageous soldiers, as well as Leister House, which served as Meade's headquarters, should not be missed.

When Pickett's Charge failed, the Battle of Gettysburg was over. Losses for both sides were heavy; each side lost more than twenty thousand men. More Americans died than in any other single battle in American history.

The last stop on the auto tour, which takes two to three hours to cover adequately, is the **National Cemetery** (Stop 16). When the Army of the Potomac left Gettysburg, many Union soldiers did not. Remaining were the twenty-one thousand casualties and the eight thousand dead soldiers either lying unburied or covered over in shallow temporary graves. Pennsylvania governor Curtin was appalled at this carnage. He appointed a local attorney, David Wells, to establish a national cemetery. Only the 3,512 Union soldiers were buried there. The 3,320 Confederate dead were buried where they fell. After the war the Southern dead were removed to cemeteries in Richmond and other Southern capitals.

Reburial of Union soldiers began on October 27 and was less than half finished by November 19, 1863, when the Soldiers' National Cemetery was dedicated. Abraham Lincoln had accepted David Wells's invitation to attend the ceremonies. Lincoln spoke after the main address, which lasted over two hours. His remarks took only two minutes but are remembered to this day as the Gettysburg Address. In 1869 the **Soldiers' National Monument**, the first of thirteen hundred monuments that would be built at Gettysburg, was erected on the site where Lincoln delivered his simple message. The original, two-page, handwritten copy of the address is in the Library of Congress.

During the celebration of the seventy-fifth anniversary of the Battle of Gettysburg, soldiers who had fought here gathered for the last time. In their nineties, these eighteen hundred men listened while President Franklin Roosevelt dedicated the **Eternal Light Peace Memorial** (Stop 2).

The North Carolina State Monument, a masterpiece of the sculptor Gutzon Borglum, is located along West Confederate Avenue on the Gettysburg Battlefield. The battle at Gettysburg was the turning point of the Civil War; during it, more Americans lost their lives than in any other single battle in the country's history.

There is so much to see at Gettysburg National Military Park that the best way to begin a visit is at the visitor center. Auto route maps, hiking trail maps, and an electric map orientation program will help fill in the details of this three-day battle. There is a charge for the thirty-minute topographic map program.

Adjacent to the visitor center is the **Cyclorama Center**. In the large circular auditorium built to house the 356-foot cyclorama, painted in 1884 by Paul Philoppoteaux, there is a sound and light program. The twenty-six-foot-high oil painting of Pickett's Charge is remarkably dramatic. In the days before movies, cycloramas were very popular. The Gettysburg Cyclorama is one of only three in North America. It was purchased by the United States Government in 1942. A small admission is charged, but the Cyclorama Center should not be missed.

Park roads open daily from 6:00 A.M. to 10:00 P.M. The visitor center is open from 8:00 A.M. to 5:00 P.M., and Cyclorama opens at 9:00 A.M. and closes at 5:00 P.M. The buildings are closed Thanksgiving, Christmas, and New Year's Day.

Directions: Take Washington Beltway Exit 35 (I-270) to Frederick; then follow Route 15 to Gettysburg.

Wilderness Battlefield

West of Fredericksburg was a dense tangle of forest and underbrush called the Wilderness. Here the opposing armies engaged in "bushwhacking on a grand scale," to quote one old veteran.

In this overgrown terrain armies could not maintain regular lines, and many soldiers were accidentally shot by their own men or surrounded by the enemy. A further problem produced by the heavy but dry vegetation was that artillery shells set the tinder ablaze, leading to deadly infernos that killed both Union and Confederate soldiers.

Eighteen thousand Union men were shot or burned and an estimated eleven thousand Confederate men lost during the two-day Wilderness fighting. Lee could no longer accept that many casualties, as he had only half as many men as General Grant. So this marked the end of the costly Confederate charges that had turned the tide of the Second Battle of Manassas and again at Chancellorsville. General Lee now had to husband his dwindling army.

The Battle of the Wilderness ended when General Grant began evacuating his position on May 7, 1864. The Army of the Potomac had withdrawn from every encounter with Lee. As the lead column reached the intersection that would indicate either retreat or a continued battle, the men raised a rousing cheer to Grant because they realized they were heading farther south to engage Lee's force once again.

At the site of the Wilderness Battlefield, there are interpretive road signs and an exhibit shelter at Wilderness on Route 20, just 1.3 miles from the intersection with Route 3.The exhibit shelter will provide a picture of the position of the opposing armies. General Grant had attached himself to General Meade's Army of the Potomac to map an overall strategy to end the three-year conflict in Virginia. The Union army wanted to position their force between Lee and Richmond, cutting off supplies and gradually winnowing away his command. As the Union army moved from their Culpeper camp on May 4, 1864, they entered the Wilderness area and were in a vulnerable position, unable to master an organized defense. Lee moved in and engaged them. For two days the armies clashed.

Moving down Route 20 less than 0.1 mile from the exhibit shelter to Hill-Ewell Drive, you can turn left and drive along trenches built by the Confederates during the Wilderness Battle on May 5. From the intersection of Hill-Ewell Drive and Route 621, turn right (west) for 0.5 mile to an interpretive stop at Tapp Farm, where on May 6 Lee attempted to lead a counterattack after his line had been broken. Seeing Lee's purpose, the soldiers set up a cry, "Lee to the rear!" Lee heeded their cries, and his men succeeded in restoring the line.

Both sides indicated their loyalty to their commanding officer, and neither side suffered a decisive loss or stunning victory at the Battle of Wilderness. But still the young men died and the woods burned and the fighting moved on to Spotsylvania.

Directions: Wilderness Battlefield is a self-guided auto route. From the Washington Beltway, take Exit 4 (I-95) south to Fredericksburg, Exit 130B; then west on Route 3, approximately twelve miles to Route 20. Turn left and proceed two miles to the exhibit shelter.

Spotsylvania Battlefield

When Grant's soldiers cheered as they left the overgrown Wilderness Battlefield to engage Lee farther south, they did not envision the encounter at Spotsylvania Court House.

The Spotsylvania Exhibit Shelter will provide orientation for the brutal two-week stalemate that resulted in about thirty thousand casualties—twelve thousand Confederate and eighteen thousand Union soldiers. Heaviest fighting took place at the center of Lee's line, where it jutted into the Union position. At this point, called the "Bloody Angle," assault after assault was made. Fighting at times was hand to hand, with soldiers firing at point blank range, clubbing and bayoneting each other in savage frenzy. Spotsylvania's unfortunate distinction is that the Bloody Angle climax was the single worst twenty-four hours of the war. It was an unequaled, close-quarters death struggle.

To reach the Bloody Angle from the exhibit center, follow Grant Drive for 0.9 mile to a parking area. A thirty-minute loop trail covers the Bloody Angle fighting.

On the Spotsylvania Battlefield the sites of several houses used as headquarters are marked for visitors. The Landrum House ruins, from which Gen. Winfield S. Hancock directed the Union forces, is on the Bloody Angle trail. The McCoull House site served as headquarters for Confederate Gen. Edward "Allegheny" Johnson. On May 10, heavy fighting occurred around this house, and on May 12, Lee led a counterattack against Union forces near McCoull House.

Realizing finally that neither side could defeat the other, General Grant decided on May 21 to shift to a more southern position. He moved into the Richmond area toward confrontation at Cold Harbor, which would cost him dearly. Grant lost thirteen thousand men in the Battle of Cold Harbor, while Confederate losses numbered only three thousand.

There are two additional points of interest at Spotsylvania. The present courthouse stands on the location of the earlier structure, which was badly damaged during the Civil War. Also, the Spotsylvania Confederate Cemetery is here, where 570 soldiers who fell during this battle are buried.

Directions: Take Washington Beltway Exit 4 (I-95) south to Massaponax exit; travel north on Route 1 to Route 208. Then continue for twelve miles and turn left on Route 208 and follow to the junction of Route 613 (Brock Road). Go right on Brock Road and drive two miles farther to the battlefield entrance.

New Market Battlefield State Historical Park

The Battle of New Market is remembered as the first and only time in history that the entire student body of an American college marched into battle. The 257 brave cadets from the Virginia Military Institute joined Gen. John Breckinridge's troops. Some say that the older, battle-worn regulars of Breckinridge's command jeered as the young cadets joined the Confederate force at New Market in their newly issued uniforms. By the end of the battle, they had changed their tune and ended the day with loud cheers for the youngsters from VMI, who helped them win the last Confederate victory in the Shenandoah Valley.

By what set of circumstances did these fifteen- to seventeen-year-old boys get involved in actual combat? Lee and the Army of Virginia were bogged down at Spotsylvania Court House by Grant's Army of the Potomac. In an effort to gain control of the crucial Shenandoah Valley area, which not only provided wheat and livestock to provision the Confederate army, but also gave the Southern forces a line of invasion into the north, Federal military plans called for Maj. General Sigel, former German minister of war, to take seven thousand men and capture Staunton, Virginia.

To thwart the Northern plans, the South called on a latecomer to the Confederate cause, Gen. John Breckinridge. He was a senator from Kentucky when that state seceded and had made an unsuccessful bid for the presidency in 1860. He was also the youngest vice president, serving with James Buchanan when only thirty-five. Breckinridge waited until October 1861 to join the Confederate army, but he quickly made up for lost time. By 1864, he had seen service in more states than any other Confederate officer.

When Breckinridge gathered his force at Staunton, forty-five hundred Confederates were outnumbered by the Northern forces. To equalize the ranks, Breckinridge ordered the cadets of the Virginia Military Institute from their classrooms. After marching for four days through constant and sometimes torrential rain, the 257 students joined the seasoned ranks.

Early on May 15, 1864, the Battle of New Market commenced. The Confederate forces were on Shirley's Hill, and the Federal line on Bushong's Hill. To attack the Federal position, the long gray line, strung out so it would seem a more substantial force, had to advance up an open slope in the face of heavy artillery fire. Breckinridge himself led the assault. The Confederates won the first round with the courageous assistance of Woodson's Missouri Rangers, a crack, sixty-five-man company that, at the cost of sixty casualties, picked off the Federal gunners.

As the Confederate army prepared for the counterattack, it was obvious that they were short of men. The center of the line was weak, and there were no replacements, only the VMI cadets. When one of Breckinridge's staff, Maj. Charles Semple, advised putting in the cadets, General Breckinridge responded, "No, Charley, this will not do, they are only children and I cannot expose them to such fire as our center will receive." But time ran out, and it was the cadets or almost certain defeat. So asking God to forgive him, Breckinridge ordered the young boys into the center.

The cadets positioned themselves out in front of the line, along a fence by the Bushong farmhouse. Their actions along this line helped repulse Sigel's counterattack, meaning ultimate Confederate victory. A poignant footnote to this tale was added by the incessant rain. It created a virtual quagmire of the Bushong farm, which has come to be called "The Field of Lost Shoes"; the mud literally sucked off soldier's shoes as they tried to make their way through under lethal fire.

Though not a major battle in terms of the outcome of the Civil War, New Market is a battle that is not forgotten. It was the last Confederate victory in the Shenandoah Valley, and it was the first and only time the entire student body of an American college not only marched into battle, but also helped win the day.

The events of the May 15 battle are brought vividly to life at the **New Market Battlefield State Historical Park's** Hall of Valor Civil War Museum. As visitors peruse the letters written by cadets both before and after the battle to their parents and see their young faces in the photographs, the cadets become individuals with whom we all can identify. A penciled note from Cadet Merritt to his father reads: "Dear pa, I write you a few lines to let you know that I was wounded. I was in the battle here yesterday... " Cadet Merritt was one of forty-seven cadets wounded during the battle. There is a life-size portrait of Thomas Garland Jefferson, seventeen-year old cousin of President Thomas Jefferson, who died from a fatal chest wound. The short film *New Market—A Field of Honor* is particularly poignant as it follows the cadets from classroom to conflict. Each May 15, the entire corps of VMI in Lexington (see selection) calls the roll of the ten cadets killed at the Battle of New Market; it is indeed moving.

But this is certainly not a Southern museum. Both sides of the Civil War conflict are presented, as is the entire war from beginning to end, with photo murals and maps. The museum has a second film that focuses on Stonewall Jackson and the Valley Campaign, so highly regarded by military strategists. It gives the amateur historian an idea of what made this campaign noteworthy.

But this million dollar museum is just part of the 280-acre park. Also of interest is the Bushong Farm, which has been restored to provide a complete picture of a typical farm of the Civil War period. Nine dependencies of this nineteenth-century farm have also been reconstructed.

A park walking tour traces the path of the VMI cadets. A battery of Civil War cannons still stands on top of Bushong's Hill. Each year on the Sunday prior to May 15, the Battle of New Market is re-enacted.

New Market Battlefield State Historical Park is open daily 9:00 A.M. to 5:00 P.M., and is closed Thanksgiving, Christmas, and New

Year's Day. Admission is charged. Bushong Farm House is open from mid-June to Labor Day.

Directions: Take Washington Beltway Exit 9 (I-66) to Route 81. New Market Battlefield State Historical Park is on Route 81, one mile from the New Market Exit, 264. From the exit turn onto Route 211 west and then make an immediate right onto Route 305, the George Collins Parkway. Travel to the end of the parkway, 1.5 miles, to reach New Market Battlefield State Historical Park.

Monocacy National Battlefield

In July 1864, two years after General Lee experienced heavy losses while trying to carry the war into the North at the Battle of Antietam (see selection), Confederate troops fought again in the Frederick area. Although this time they won the battle, they were prevented from taking the capital. The last campaign to carry the war into the North failed.

Confederate troops under Gen. Jubal Early marched north to the fields outside Frederick in hopes that they could divert Union troops from their siege of Petersburg—the longest siege in American history. Grant had tried to break through Lee's defenses in June 1864, but the Confederates had held him off. Jubal's northward raid had the desired effect: Grant sent a division under General Ricketts, and then a full corps under Gen. H. G. Wright, to protect Washington.

Until these troops arrived, it was up to Maj. Gen. Lew Wallace (who would later write *Ben Hur*) and his twenty-three-hundred-man force, most of which had never seen battle, to stop Early's troops. They met in the fields outside Frederick on July 9, 1864. Wallace was not sure whether the Confederates were heading for Baltimore or Washington, so he entrenched his men at Monocacy Junction, three miles southeast of Frederick, where the major roads to both cities and the Baltimore & Ohio Railroad converged. If he could hold them at this junction, he could protect both cities.

Wallace positioned his men along a six-mile stretch of the Monocacy River, thus protecting the Georgetown Pike bridge leading to Washington and the bridge on the National Road to Baltimore, as well as the railroad bridge. Although his men were stretched thin, the higher bank on the river's east side provided a natural breastwork for at least some of them. Assistance came with the arrival of the twenty-five-hundred-man division under James B. Ricketts.

Confederate general Rodes's division encountered the troops

defending the National Road bridge and then General Ramseru's men, who were defending the Georgetown Pike bridge. These encounters prompted General Early to try a flanking operation using a cavalry attack. Some of the heaviest fighting occurred when these troops attacked Wallace's left flank. The numerically superior Confederate force, numbering around fifteen thousand men, forced the Union troops to sacrifice their position. Confederate brigades conducting a three-pronged attack on the Federal left flank kept up a steady barrage and forced them back still farther. Late in the day, the Federal troops began retreating to Baltimore, after 1,294 Union soldiers had been killed, wounded, or captured.

Confederate losses were between seven hundred and nine hundred killed, missing, or wounded. Equally damaging to their cause was the loss of a day's time. By the time Early's men arrived at the earthworks of Fort Stevens, which guarded Washington, they could see the Union troops under Wright's command marching into the fort. Early soon withdrew his troops across the Potomac River, and Washington survived its final test of the war.

Of the Monocacy battle, General Grant wrote, "General Wallace contributed on this occasion, by the defeat of the troops under him, a greater benefit to the cause than often falls to the lot of a commander of an equal force to render by means of a victory." Wallace recognized this. As he retreated from the battlefield, he ordered that the fallen men be buried on the battlefield and a monument erected, reading, "These men died to save the National Capital, and they did save it."

You can take a four-mile, round-trip auto tour of **Monocacy National Battlefield**. The tour starts at the small visitor center and makes three stops on the battlefield. At the center, an electric map will orient you to the battlefield, and you can pick up the auto tour map. Five monuments can be seen on the battlefield.

Monocacy National Battlefield is open daily, at no charge, from 8:00 A.M. to 4:30 P.M., Memorial Day to Labor Day. The rest of the year, it is open Wednesday through Sunday.

Directions: From Baltimore, take I-70 west to Frederick; then head south on Route 355, the Georgetown Pike. The visitor center is on the left, 0.1 mile past the Monocacy River Bridge.

Sailor's Creek Battlefield Historical State Park

Seventy-two hours before General Lee surrendered at Appomattox, he lost nearly a quarter of his army in the botched and bloody Battle of Sailor's Creek. Total Confederate losses were estimated at seventy-seven hundred, with six thousand taken prisoner—the largest number of men ever to surrender in a single action on this continent. Eight general officers also were captured, and almost all of Lee's dwindling supplies were lost.

What caused such a debacle? A combination of factors bedeviled Lee's ragged and starving army as they fled Petersburg and Richmond. Heavy spring rains caused frequent rerouting, and mud-soaked roads were often impassable for the wagons, resulting in loss of communication. The army was heading for Amelia Court House, where they hoped to be reprovisioned. When supplies did not arrive, a day was wasted on a fruitless search for food, which gave Union forces time to catch up and set the stage for the last major battle of the Civil War in Virginia.

On April 6, 1865, a third of Lee's army under General Anderson and General Ewell bogged down—literally—in the swampy bottom land of Little Sailor's Creek and were overtaken by Federal troops under General Wright. Though the Richmond clerks, sailors, and artillerymen who made up the Confederate forces repulsed the first attack, they came under the Union artillery batteries and were stopped. The entire force surrendered.

The wagon column under General Gordon that the Confederates were trying desperately to salvage had already crossed the creek, but here, too, they were stopped by superior Union forces commanded by General Humphries. While General Gordon and a few men escaped, the wagons and three-fourths of the column were captured.

The defeat of the Confederate army at Sailor's Creek was the first step to Lee's surrender of the Army of Northern Virginia. Three days later, Lee would admit defeat at Appomattox Court House.

Today, there is an interpretive auto route at the **Sailor's Creek Battlefield Historical State Park**. Overlooking the site of the Battle of Sailor's Creek is the Hillsman House, which was used as a field hospital by both North and South. The floors, marked even now by bloodstains from the operating tables, still bear silent testimony to the many wounded. The Hillsman House is open to the public from June through September. Interpretive signs and an audio program tell visitors the exciting story of this climactic encounter. Sailor's Creek Battlefield Historical State Park, open year-round, is operated by Virginia's Division of State Parks.

Directions: From the Washington Beltway, take Exit 4 (I-95) south to Petersburg. If you are northbound on I-95, take Exit 50D, Wythe Street. If you are southbound, take Exit 52, which is also Wythe Street, Route 460. If you have time you can take side roads off Route 460, which include most of the stops along **Lee's Retreat Driving Tour**, which highlights Lee's route from Petersburg to Appomattox. Or, you can stay on Route 460 until the intersection with Route 617 and head northeast on Route 617. The interpretive auto route at Sailor's Creek Battlefield Historical State Park is marked at intervals on Route 617.

Petersburg National Battlefield

Serving as the industrial and transportation hub of the Confederacy, Petersburg became a victim of its own success. Because of its commercial and strategic importance to the South, Grant felt that "the key to taking Richmond is Petersburg." After failing with the direct assault approach at Cold Harbor in June of 1864, the Union army turned south to Petersburg.

Their confidence undermined by the series of confrontations with Southern troops at Wilderness, Spotsylvania, and Cold Harbor, the Federal commanders did not press their assault. They also realized that a frontal assault on a well-constructed fortification was suicidal. This lapse gave Lee an opportunity to move his army to Petersburg from the Richmond area.

It also led to the longest siege in American history—no other American city has ever suffered through an ordeal of this length (see Siege Museum selection). Just maintaining the armies in the field was the largest military operation of the nineteenth century. At one point, there were more than a hundred thousand men in the Army of the Potomac. At the **Petersburg National Battlefield** Visitor Center, there is a seventeen-minute map presentation every half-hour that details events during the long siege, highlighting the battle in June of 1864, when Grant tried to break through the Confederate defense, and the climactic Confederate offensive in April 1865.

A short walk from the visitor center leads to a Confederate battery that fell into Union hands during the first day of the opening battle. It was here that a seventeen-thousand-pound Union mortar called the "Dictator" fired two-hundred-pound shells toward the city, only two and a half miles away.

Stops 1, 2, 3, 5, and 8 are near Confederate forts built to protect

Petersburg. They were areas of bitter fighting during the struggle to gain control of this Confederate stronghold. Stops 5, 6, and 7 were part of the Union siege line. In fact, Stop 5, Fort Stedman, was the last objective Lee attempted to seize. Realizing that the Northern stranglehold was growing even tighter as the railroad links with Petersburg were broken, Lee decided to attack Grant at Fort Stedman, hoping to force a Union shift to the eastern sector of the siege line, which would ease the pressure on the last Confederate railroad supply link into Petersburg. For a brief time, it looked as though Lee would succeed, but a strong Federal counterattack doomed the offensive.

Grant, seeing victory at last, ordered General Sheridan to attack seventeen miles west of Petersburg at Five Forks on April 1.Union victory here opened the way to cut the last supply line into the city and forced Lee to withdraw the next day.

Indeed, Lee would not have had the chance to evacuate his army were it not for the gallant stand of the 450 men left to hold back the Federal advance at Fort Gregg. It was 450 against 5,000, but they bought enough time for Confederate reinforcements to arrive. It would end for Lee seven days later at Appomattox. Fort Gregg is one of eleven forts on the sixteen-mile drive of the siege line that begins at the Crater.

The Crater is one of the most unusual strategic battle approaches employed during the Civil War, and it almost worked. The Battle of the Crater came in the early days of the siege, and the idea behind it was ingenious, although not unique. Grant had tunneled under the enemy position a year earlier at Vicksburg. Pennsylvania coal miners dug a tunnel under the Confederate line. Four tons of gunpowder were placed in the tunnel and literally exploded beneath the unsuspecting Southerners. When the explosion went off on July 30, 1864, it caused a crater 170 feet long, 60 feet wide and 30 feet deep. The idea was for an assault division from the Ninth Corps to lead the charge, penetrating the Confederate position through the gap left by the explosive, with the entire Ninth Army Corps to follow. Union concern, however, that the black division trained to carry out the mission might be lost, thereby leading to accusations that the Federal command was trying deliberately to kill black soldiers, prompted them to substitute an unprepared division for this all-important assault. Some Federal soldiers poured into the crater instead of going around the gap left by the explosion until they created a bottleneck and became perfect targets for the Southern troops to pick off. The Union lost more than four thousand men; the South, fifteen hundred. They also lost the chance to end the siege. The Crater was the greatest manmade explosion to occur before World War I.

One final point of interest at Petersburg National Battlefield is Stop 3, Meade Station, where a three-quarter-mile loop trail leads to this important stop on the US Military Railroad. During the siege, five hundred thousand tons of supplies were shipped on this line, providing the Army of the Potomac with food and uniforms to endure the coldest weather this area had experienced in years. Southern troops were not so fortunate, as the Union cut the city's vital supply link, railroad line by railroad line. The Meade Station Trail has interpretive markers to explain the role of the railroad in the siege of Petersburg. Maps of this walking tour and of the extended battlefield siege line drive are available at the visitor center.

During the summer months, visitors also can find the times for various artillery firing demonstrations and other living-history programs at the park. The men fire the twelve-pounder Napoleon field gun according to standard Civil War drill. Visitors should cover their ears, as the Napoleon makes a mighty noise. The twelve-pound balls fired from this gun can travel one mile.

Petersburg National Battlefield is open daily, except major holidays. An admission fee is charged.

Directions: Take Washington Beltway Exit 4 (I-95) south to Petersburg. Proceed east on Route 36 toward Hopewell. Turn left on Wythe Street and continue for two miles to the entrance to Petersburg National Battlefield.

City Point Unit and Appomattox Manor

During the American Revolution, George Washington received the rank of lieutenant general. This rank was not bestowed again until late in the Civil War, when on March 9, 1864, President Abraham Lincoln made Ulysses S. Grant general in chief of all Union armies, which included more than a half million soldiers across the United States.

Grant lost approximately eighteen thousand men at the Wilderness battlefield, roughly another nineteen thousand at Spotsylvania, where the fiercest twenty-four-hour period of the war occurred at the Bloody Angle, followed by about twelve thousand more at Cold Harbor near Richmond. Nevertheless, Grant decided to cross the James River and attack Petersburg, the railroad center of the Confederacy. Much of Gen. Robert E. Lee's supplies were brought from the deep South to his army through the Petersburg rail lines. Grant realized that if the rail lines were severed, Lee's supply line would be restricted, which might hasten Lee's defeat.

For four days in June of 1864, Grant's army hit hard at the Southern line just outside Petersburg. When the aggressive attack did not break the city's defenses, Grant decided to dig in and start siege operations. Thus began a nine and a half-month siege, the longest siege in American history. Grant's headquarters were located at **City Point**, which soon became the largest logistical and supply operation of the entire war. During the Siege of Petersburg, City Point was one of the world's busiest ports. Enormous quantities of war materials were off-loaded at the half-mile stretch of wharves along the James River. These supplies provisioned more than a hundred thousand Union troops and sixty-five thousand animals. Tons of supplies also were shipped to the army by the railroad, which had supply lines leading directly to the front.

Telegraph lines linked Grant to the battlefront, Washington, D.C., and other theaters of war. Seven hospitals were built at City Point; more than six thousand patients a day could be treated at the largest facility. Support facilities also included a bakery, which produced more than a hundred thousand rations of bread each day.

President Lincoln met with Grant at his City Point headquarters on two occasions. In March and April 1865, Lincoln spent two of the last three weeks of his life at City Point and nearby Petersburg and Richmond.

When you tour City Point, it is fascinating to discover that Grant refused the spacious accommodations available in the Eppes's **Appomattox Manor** and lived in a tent from June 1864 until a crudely constructed officers' cabin was completed that November. The cabin, which for a time stood in Fairmount Park, Philadelphia, has been moved back. It is located on the manor's east lawn, and you can view the interior through the front door and windows.

Appomattox Manor, the ancestral home of the Eppes family since 1763, serves as a visitor contact station. The east wing and portions of the west wing were added around the central portion before the Civil War. Although there are twenty-three rooms, only three are open to the public, and only two decorated with original Eppes's family furnishings. At the center, you can view a fifteen-minute video, shown every half hour, on Grant and the supply system established at City Point. The attractive porch offers a view of both the river and grounds, including several of the original outbuildings. There are six interpretive markers on the grounds.

The City Point Unit, which is part of the Petersburg National Battlefield, is open daily from 8:30 A.M. to 4:30 P.M. An admission fee is charged. It is closed on Christmas and New Year's Day. If you have time, you may want to take the Hopewell and City Point Historic District Walking Tour.

Directions: Take I-95 to the Hopewell Exit. Take Route 10 east into

Hopewell. Once you cross the Appomattox River, turn left at the second traffic signal onto Main Street, which will change into Appomattox Street. Follow Appomattox Street to Cedar Lane; turn left. At the end of Cedar Lane, turn left into the National Park Service parking lot.

Appomattox Court House National Historical Park

It was fitting, but still a magnanimous gesture, to end the fratricidal war that cost the lives of over a half-million soldiers, more Americans than were lost in World Wars I and II combined, in a manner that allowed the defeated to return to their homes with their horses and personal possessions, and so begin the job of restoring their lives and their country.

The surrender of Lee's Army of Northern Virginia, the Confederacy's most successful field army, at Appomattox Court House was a surrender made with honor and dignity. Grant's terms left the men not only with the means of resuming their civilian lives but also with the feeling that, though they had lost the battle, they were not disgraced. When the Confederates rode and marched between the Federal lines to lay down their arms, their former opponents saluted them. Responding to this unexpected tribute, the Confederates returned the salute in a moving moment on that day of formal surrender.

On a more practical level, when news of the Confederate surrender was passed among Federal camps, men emptied their haversacks to share their rations with the near-starving Confederate soldiers.

It had been a long road to Appomattox. Lee left the small Virginia town on the anniversary of the firing on Fort Sumter four years earlier. With his surrender, the Civil War was all but over, the hopes of the Confederacy ended. The unity of the United States was secure.

The last encounter of Lee and Grant came after the bitter Virginia campaign of 1864, when Lee halted Grant's drive toward Richmond. Grant, realizing it was futile to persist in his objective, shifted to attack Petersburg, and the long ten-month siege of that city began.

When the Petersburg defense finally cracked in April 1865, it was the beginning of the end for Lee and his men. There would be only seven days between their withdrawal from Petersburg and the surrender at Appomattox Court House. The savage fighting at Sailor's Creek on April 6 cost Lee nearly one-fourth of his army, and his oldest son was captured.

By the time Lee was camped outside the small village of Appomattox Court House on April 8, 1865, he was operating without supplies. The headquarters of this general of the Confederate Army had no tent, no chairs, no bed, or table. It was here, at the site marked Lee's Headquarters (a five-minute walk from the parking lot leads to the campsite), that the last council of war was held and Confederate options explored. Lee rejected the idea of continuing the conflict through guerrilla tactics. The officers decided to make one last attempt to break through the Union lines. General Gordon's veteran infantrymen were to try to crack the line early the next morning. After Gordon left, he realized he didn't know how far he should lead his men if he broke through. Sending a message back to Lee, he received this answer, "Tell him that I'd be glad for him to halt just beyond the Tennessee line."

But Lee realized that no hope really existed, and when he appeared before his startled officers on the morning of April 9, he was in full dress uniform, embroidered belt, and gold spurs. He believed that before the day was out he would be Grant's prisoner. When word came that Gordon had failed, Lee resigned himself to surrender, saying, "Then there is nothing left me to do but to go and see General Grant and I would rather die a thousand deaths."

Lee sent word to Grant and arrangements were made to meet at the McLean House. There is a certain irony to their choice as it had been the fighting at Manassas that prompted Wilmer McLean, a merchant and sugar importer, to move to this out-of-the-way Virginia town. He wanted a place where his family would be safe, where he could be near a railroad to conduct his business dealings, and where the armies would be unlikely to appear. The first battle of the Civil War occurred right near his house, and when the Second Battle of Manassas returned the fighting to his neighborhood, he felt compelled to seek a haven at Appomattox Court House, little dreaming that the war would come to an end in his parlor. Grant and Lee met and, observed by Grant's staff officers, agreed to surrender the Army of Northern Virginia. Lee was pleased with the terms of surrender and felt that it would do much toward conciliation of the defeated Southerners. When the Federal artillerymen began a hundred-gun salute to victory, Grant had them stop. "The rebels are our countrymen again," said Grant, "and the best sign of rejoicing after the victory will be to abstain from all demonstrations in the field."

If the leaders in Washington had followed Grant's generous approach to victory, the scars of this internecine war would have healed much more rapidly. But with Lincoln's assassination five days after the surrender at Appomattox, the hotheads inflamed rather than soothed the wounds of the country. There was even an attempt by a small group to hang Lee for treason, which was rebuffed by Grant's soldierly intervention. Lee went on to assume the presidency of Washington College in Lexington, Virginia. It was renamed Washington and Lee University after his death in October 1870. Grant went on to assume the presidency of the United States from 1869 to 1877.

Today, Appomattox Court House looks the same as it did in 1865, except for the absence of the people to fill the village streets, to tend the fields, and to enjoy a respite in the tavern. The quiet of Appomattox induces a reflective mood and a somber realization of how important this site really was for our country's future. Thirteen of the original buildings in the town are still standing and have been carefully restored. Fourteen other buildings, including the McLean House, have been reconstructed where they once stood.

Visitors to **Appomattox Court House National Historical Park** should start at the reconstructed courthouse, which serves as the park's visitor center. It was once a Confederate recruiting station. During the climactic events in April 1865, the courthouse played no role in the drama. Two fifteen-minute slide shows give different perspectives on the surrender of Lee's army. One is a chronological account of the events from April 1 through 12. The second, *Honor Answers Honor*, uses first-person accounts of the surrender to dramatize the formal surrender on April 12.

The village, with its major buildings and other sites, is easily covered on foot. Of paramount interest is the **McLean House**, where Lee surrendered to Grant. A few of the furnishings are original; most of the pieces in the parlor where the famous meeting occurred were bought as souvenirs immediately after the papers were signed. General Ord purchased the table where General Lee sat. The small oval table used by General Grant was sold to General Sheridan for twenty dollars. McLean didn't want to part with the chairs, but when he wouldn't sell them, they were taken by two cavalry officers. The painting by Louis Guillaume of this historic meeting has helped historians to reconstruct the room.

Outside the McLean House are a number of dependencies, including the log kitchen and slave quarters, the gazebo well in front of the house, and an icehouse on the side. Across the street are several commercial establishments, including Meek's Store, built in 1852 and one of the social centers of the community; the one-room frame law office of John Woodson; and the Clover Hill Tavern with guesthouse and tavern kitchen. It was here that many of the 28,231 individual Confederate paroles were printed. Also restored is the county jail, with the sheriff's office and quarters on the first floor and the cells on the top two floors. Four private residences that were part

The war that began in Wilmer McLean's front yard, along Bull Run, ended in his parlor at Appomattox Court House. Gen. Robert E. Lee surrendered his Army of Northern Virginia to Gen. Ulysses S. Grant on Palm Sunday, April 9, 1865, bringing an end to the Civil War.

of the local scene in 1865 have been restored. On the opposite side of the village from Lee's headquarters is the site of General Grant's headquarters.

Appomattox is symbolic of a new beginning for the United States. This obscure village marks the spot of one of the great watersheds in American history. It is open daily, except Federal holidays and Thanksgiving through Presidents Day. There is a entrance fee. During the summer months, interpretive programs are given.

Directions: Take Washington Beltway Exit 9 (I-66) west then Route 29 south to Amherst. At Amherst, take Route 60 east to Route 26, then south to Appomattox. Appomattox Court House National Historical Park is three miles north of Appomattox on Route 24. Or from I-95 in the Richmond area, take Route 360 west to Jetersville, then Route 307 to Route 460. Go west on Route 460 to Appomattox. Take Route 24 north for two miles to Appomattox Court House National Historical Park

Civil War Museums

The repositories of the mosaic of American history are the museums throughout the United States. Testifying to the enduring interest and popularity of the historical museums, approximately one new history museum opens every week in the United States. More than twenty-five hundred history museums exist throughout the country. Those described in this section relate to the Civil War.

The first museum in the United States opened in 1784, when noted portrait artist Charles Willson Peale opened his Philadelphia home so that the public could enjoy his work. This proved to be only the beginning. Undoubtedly the largest and most inclusive collection is housed in the more than 150-year-old Smithsonian Institution's thirteen museums, which contain an estimated seventy-eight million items, many of which languish in the vast storage space of never-visited rooms. The Smithsonian is often called the nation's attic.

Just as America's first museum was in Philadelphia, so was the first historical museum. Again, it was in a private home, this time that of amateur historian Pierre du Simitiere. In the 1780s, he opened his house so others could see his collection of historical artifacts, documents, and portraits.

There has been a boom in history museum attendance as a result of the interest in finding one's roots. To experience a sense of the past, the feeling of being part of a continuing series of events is essential. Museums like the Siege Museum in Petersburg vividly bring to life the courageous actions of everyday people with whom visitors can identify.

The best way to approach any museum is to discover its purpose and how it is laid out. Many museums are organized chronologically, and a visit that is begun haphazardly will not be as interesting or as informative. If the museum provides an orientation film, see it before touring. If not, try to obtain a brochure or, at the very least, question the museum attendant to obtain basic guidelines for getting the most out of the museum.

Virginia

Lee Chapel and Museum

On October 2, 1865, less than six months after the surrender at Appomattox, Robert E. Lee accepted the presidency of Washington College at an annual salary of fifteen hundred dollars. At fifty-eight, he was anxious for the chance to be of use to the "rising" generation.

Lee first lived in the president's house, which Stonewall Jackson had shared with his in-laws during his fourteen-month marriage to Elinor Junkin, whose father was the college's president (see Stonewall Jackson House selection). Soon after Lee arrived, he embarked on a building program.

His first project was the chapel that ultimately became known as the **Lee Chapel**. Lee lavished great enthusiasm on the chapel he requested the trustees build on campus. Work began in January 1867 under the close supervision of Lee and his son Custis, a professor at neighboring Virginia Military Institute. It was completed in time for the 1868 June commencement. From then until his death in 1870, Lee attended daily worship service at the chapel with his students.

Lee's son also helped him formulate plans for a new president's home. Although unhappy that the house cost more than the fifteen thousand dollars originally appropriated for it, Lee was pleased with several architectural details. The verandas were designed so that his wife, crippled with arthritis, could move her rolling chair across them. Lee also was happy to have his favorite horse, Traveler, nearby in a new brick stable adjoining the house. Reports from the 1860s indicate that Traveler certainly needed a refuge. Souvenir hunters had pulled out so much hair from his mane and tail that the warhorse shied away from people.

On the chapel's lower level, Lee established his office. He fashioned and furnished it, and it remains today as it was when illness forced him from his desk on September 28, 1870. The remains of Traveler are buried just outside the office. Today, the rest of the lower level is a museum where reminders of both Lee and Washington can be seen.

A letter dated 1796 thanks George Washington for his gift of stock, saving the school from bankruptcy. Washington endowed the school with fifty thousand dollars of James River Canal Company stock, which is still paying dividends. Students today each receive roughly three dollars a year in residuals. Many of Lee's personal belongings are included in the museum collection. The portraits bring famous figures from history to life. Paintings include the Charles Willson Peale portraits of Washington and Lafayette and the popular Lee portrait done by Theodore Pine.

The lower level also contains the Lee family crypt, where Lee is buried with his wife, parents, and seven children. Many visitors mistakenly believe Lee is buried in the chapel apse, beneath the impressive Edward Valentine statue. Lee's widow chose the recumbent pose; she wanted to remember him as if he were sleeping on the battlefield.

Robert E. Lee died on October 12, 1870. Later in the month, when George Washington Custis Lee was elected to succeed his father as president, the college name was changed to Washington and Lee University. Both the Lee Chapel and the Front Campus Colonnade of Washington and Lee University are National Historic Landmarks. There is no charge to visit the Lee Chapel and Museum. Hours are 9:00 A.M. to 4:00 P.M., Monday through Saturday from mid-October to mid-April and until 5:00 P.M. the rest of the year. Sunday hours are 2:00 to 5:00 P.M.

Directions: From I-95 in the Richmond area, take I-64/I-81 west to Lexington. Take the Route 11 exit off I-64 and travel south. Just outside Lexington, Route 11 will fork right onto Main Street. Follow Main Street to the Washington and Lee campus. From the south, if you are traveling on I-81, take Exit 188, Route 60 West. Follow Route 60 West to Main Street. Turn left to Henry Street, which will take you to the Washington and Lee campus. For information on this and all the Lexington attractions, stop first at the Lexington Visitor Center at 107 East Washington Street.

Pamplin Historical Park

It isn't surprising that most Civil War museums reveal the history of the war's leaders. They start their story at the top of the ranks, detailing the battle plans of generals and exhibiting memorabilia associated with such legendary military figures as Lee, Grant, Jackson, Sherman, Stuart, and a host of other easily recognizable names. Some museums include artifacts from the citizen-soldier, and New Market's Hall of Valor even has at its main thrust the schoolboy soldiers from Virginia Military Institute who fought on this battlefield. But on Memorial Day 1999 at **Pamplin Historical Park**, a new thirteen-million-dollar museum opened, one that focuses on a different dimension of the Civil War saga: the story of the three million rank-in-file soldiers who fought in the Civil War.

The Civil War killed more American soldiers than any war before or since, which isn't surprising because statistics include both side of the conflict. The **National Museum of the Civil War Soldier** reveals the story of ordinary soldiers from both North and South. Lieutenants and captains are included in this story because, for the most part, they were originally enlisted men and were elected by those they served. But officers from majors on up are not part of this story. You get the picture before you even set foot in the museum. Outside, you're greeted not by a soldier on horseback but by a statue of two tired foot soldiers (who could be from either side) taking a break from their long march.

It is amazing to think that the items in the museum just recently were acquired, albeit carefully authenticated. Pamplin Historical Park was built by Robert B. Pamplin, Sr., and Robert B. Pamplin, Jr., members of one of the four hundred richest families in America. They have spent over thirty million dollars on this 363-acre historic park located where General Grant broke through the Confederate defenses surrounding Petersburg on April 2, 1865. Grant's decisive action led to the fall of the Confederate capital and Lee's retreat to and surrender at Appomattox.

One of Pamplin's goals is to help young people understand what prompted the ordinary soldier to handle the hardships they endured during the Civil War. Each visitor chooses a "soldier comrade" before beginning the museum tour. There are twelve companions, all actual individuals who fought in the Civil War, whose experiences are well documented throughout the museum on customized, state-of-the-art interactive CD players. The CD players allow visitors to glean more information on exhibits by accessing the exhibit code on the CD keypad.

Visitors can customize their tour as they discover details about their soldier comrade, beginning with why he joined the army, then moving to what his life would have been like while stationed at a Civil War training camp. Against a gigantic backdrop mural, a Sibley tent is filled with various items a soldier might have in his possession. Soldiers were asked to carry only sixteen pounds (compared to the forty-pound pack of the Vietnam era). In the letters soldiers wrote home during the early days of the war, they frequently commented on the amazing array of food, arms, and equipment the army had on hand. Soldiers were issued thick wool uniforms, which they wore summer and winter. Each also had a rifle, six-round cartridge box, bayonet, canteen, boots, and blanket. Visitors are encouraged to pack a haversack in preparation for moving out.

An exhibit of an army on the march focuses on an array of original artifacts, including uniforms, flags, weapons, and equipment. Here the backdrop is a diorama of an army on the march, which tries to capture the sheer size of the long, trailing column of men on the move.

This brings the visitor to the museum's central attraction, an interactive exhibit called "Trial by Fire," which tries to capture the experience of a soldier's first battle, what the soldiers on both sides of the conflict called going to "see the elephant." Visitors feel the floor shake beneath their feet with the explosion of the guns, the air seems to vibrate with whizzing bullets, and video screens portray rows of soldiers firing at will. The intended effect suggests the chaos, confusion, and terror of this first experience.

Each battle had a number of possible outcomes for the individual soldier, and the fate of each soldier comrade is different. Photographs and artifacts reveal the possible results of death, a battle wound, capture, and survival. Being wounded in battle all too often resulted in a lingering, painful death as the battlefield hospitals were often stark, unsanitary facilities. A video re-creates a Civil War amputation, but it is not for the weak-stomached.

For those who survived the battles, there were long periods of inactivity, which also are captured at the museum. Inactivity was typical during the winter months, when troop movement was difficult. During these respites from armed engagements, the men re-evaluated their decisions to serve in the war—should they walk home when their enlistment ended or continue with their unit for the duration of the war. In the last gallery of the museum, visitors learn the fate of their soldier comrades.

The museum has a well-stocked museum store and restaurant. Outside, a demonstration area features living-history programs on such diverse topics as Civil War music, rifle firing, and other elements of the lifestyle of Civil War soldiers. On the grounds of Pamplin Historical Park is the 1812 Tudor Hall plantation home, owned by the Boisseau family during the Civil War and used as the brigade headquarters of Confederate general Samuel McGowan. The plantation house has been renovated and furnished to reflect the Civil War era, and several outbuildings, including slave quarters, have been reconstructed to complete the picture. A kitchen and herb garden provide an opportunity for additional living-history programming.

A 1.7-mile interpretative trail traces the April 2, 1865, action, when General Grant's forces broke through General Lee's Petersburg defense line. In a fierce twenty-minute fight, nearly eleven hundred Union soldiers were killed or wounded, achieving this hard-won ground. The siege of Petersburg lasted more than nine months. Once the Petersburg defenses were breached, the Confederates evacuated

Richmond, and within a week, Lee surrendered at Appomattox.

A battlefield center has exhibits focusing on the pivotal April 2 encounter. A military encampment suggests the quarters that soldiers used here from October 1864 through April 1865. Tents and winter huts replicate army issue equipment and are filled with articles to suggest the period. Living-history demonstrations and artillery demonstrations are conducted at this site.

Pamplin Historical Park is open year-round from 9:00 A.M. to 5:00 P.M. There are extended hours during the summer months. Admission is charged. For current living-history schedules and information on guided tours and special programs, including the anniversary weekend and Christmas at Tudor Hall, call (804) 861-2408 or toll-free at (877) 726-7546. You can also check their Web site at www.pamplinpark.org.

Directions: Take I-95 south of Richmond to the Petersburg area; then veer southwest on I-85. From I-85 take Exit 63A, Route 1 south for one mile to Duncan Road, Route 670. Pamplin Park is 0.5 mile on the left at 6523 Duncan Road.

Portsmouth Naval Shipyard Museum

In May 1862, after a year in which the number of Union ships blockading Southern ports had increased to seven hundred and reduced Southern trade to a mere trickle, a strange new vessel sailed out of Norfolk harbor. The South, with great ingenuity, had come up with a new weapon to fight the wooden ships of the North. Over the hulk of the federal steam frigate *Merrimack*, they had added an iron superstructure with a large ram. This formidable sailing weapon, now called the *Virginia*, easily sank two Union ships. Tremors were felt in the North, but the North wasn't the industrial center for naught; the next time the ultimate Confederate ironclad emerged, she was met by a federal ironclad, the *Monitor*, which was easier to manipulate than the *Virginia* and had guns on a revolving turret. The classic fight between these two behemoths lasted four hours, and, although neither scored a decisive victory, it resulted in ultimate triumph for the North. The Virginia never reappeared, while the North produced dozens of ironclads.

The **Portsmouth Naval Shipyard Museum** is home of the CSS *Virginia*, which was the original *Merrimack*. The details of its development, first foray, and climactic battle with the *Monitor* are outlined in the museum.

The range of the exhibits extends far beyond the years of the Civil War. Ship models, uniforms, weapons, and flags from the first naval ship through the Polaris missile are on display.

There is no charge to visit this museum, which is open Tuesday through Saturday from 10:00 A.M. to 4:00 P.M. and Sunday from 2:00 to 5:00 P.M.

Directions: Take I-495 exit 4, I-95 south, to Richmond, then Route 64 to Hampton. Take Route 17/258 across the James River and follow Route 17 into Portsmouth. The museum is on the waterfront of the Elizabeth River, at the foot of High Street.

Siege Museum

"You can still find the old city if you look, you can hear it if you listen," says Petersburg native Joseph Cotten as he narrates the inspiring movie shown at the **Siege Museum** about the ten months Petersburg was under siege. It was a time of courage and a time of fortitude; no other American city has endured such a long trial.

Petersburg became the Union target because Gen. Ulysses S. Grant believed it was "the key to taking Richmond." He felt that in order to take Petersburg, he needed to sever the five railroad lines that fed the city. At the Siege Museum, the civilians' side of the last great struggle of the War between the States is told. They suffered almost daily shelling.

The museum's exhibit of shells reveals that the never-ending bombardment left few buildings unmarked. Shells flew so thick and fast that they even met in midair, as you will discover. The relatively small size of most of the shells meant that almost all of the damage was repairable. Personal accounts from diaries and letters lend poignancy to the fear and hunger the townspeople endured. Although they had little to share, ladies smuggled what they could to the men protecting the city. They carried food, supplies, and messages beneath their crinolines. Miss Anne Pigman ran the blockade disguised as a poor market woman. Fortunately gallantry was observed by both sides. Had she been required to lift her skirts even an inch, she would have revealed not only smuggled goods, but also her sixty-dollar shoes, a sure giveaway. The expensive shoes are now on display in the museum.

The display "The City and Its People" re-creates a portion of a typical Petersburg parlor and an office from the Bank of the City of Petersburg. There's also a children's desk and school box indicative of the normal routines the citizens tried to follow.

A more comprehensive look at banking in Petersburg is given at the visitor center located in the **Farmers Bank Museum** in Old Towne, easily located by following the bright red Petersburg Tour markers. Banks in the 1800s were primarily for the wealthy, so the Farmers Bank was established to serve the common man. The bank museum has a cashier's office with a printing press used to print Confederate money, a teller's office with a small safe made at the Petersburg iron-works, plus a bank vault where you can see the hidden chamber beneath the regular vault. You'll learn that when customers applied for a loan, directors would vote with marbles. The black marble indicated a no confidence vote, hence the derivation of the term "blackball." The Farmers Bank Museum is closed October through March.

The visitors center and Siege Museum are located within a block of each other. Except for holidays, both are open daily, 10:00 A.M. to 5:00 P.M. There is a small charge for the Siege Museum. On your stroll from one to the other, you can browse through the boutiques and antique shops in Old Towne. Along the main street, there are several excellent places for lunch.

Directions: Take I-95 to Petersburg, Exit 52, Washington Street. Follow Washington Street to the fifth traffic signal and turn right onto Market Street. At the second traffic signal, turn right onto Bank Street. The Siege Museum is at 15 W. Bank Street, and free public parking is available behind the museum. For additional information on Petersburg call the Petersburg Visitor Center, (800) 368-3595.

Valentine Museum and Wickham House

Mann S. Valentine, Sr. (1786–1865), his son Mann S. Valentine II (1824–1892), and his grandson Granville Valentine (1860–1943) exemplify the **Valentine Museum's** theme: people create their own histories by what they chose to save and collect. As curator Jon Zachman explains, "The individual histories people developed were often transformed into museums." Certainly the Valentines were collectors.

The senior Mann amassed a fine arts collection, and the next two generations gathered archeological material. Their collections were exhibited privately and publicly. Granville took the histories and the items his family collected and established the Valentine Museum in 1898, then reorganized it in 1930.

Five interpretative periods in the history of the Valentine family are covered in the exhibit "Creating History." Over the years, the

Valentine Museum changed its definition of culture and its interpretation of history to reflect the changes in social assumptions and interpretations of the past. Items from the collection of each generation are included. A new gallery showcases the Valentines' nationally acclaimed costume and textile collection.

Valentine Museum docents also conduct tours of the adjacent **Wickham House**. John Wickham, prominent Richmond attorney, had this elegant, neoclassical, seventeen-room mansion built on the highest hill in the city in 1812 at a cost of seventy thousand dollars. Now a National Historic Landmark, the house has been restored to its 1820s splendor.

On entering the house, you'll see eighteen-inch brick walls overlaid with stucco to look like marble. The cantilevered staircase winds upward to an opening shaped like an artist's palette. The banister is carved with magnolia seed pods, dogwood blossoms, and periwinkle. The oval ladies' parlor is unusually beautiful. On its walls are paintings of scenes from Homer's *Iliad*, done during Wickham's residency and subsequently over painted. Only recently discovered, they have been carefully uncovered and restored. The restoration also re-created mantels of carved Italian marble and period window treatments.

Mr. Wickham conducted his law practice from his very masculine library. His most famous case was the successful defense of Aaron Burr in his trial for treason before Chief Justice Marshall at the Virginia State Capitol. The dining room has the original Wickham porcelain dining service, which arrived intact from China in 1814.

The grandeur on the first floor is not matched on the second floor. The upstairs rooms were bedrooms and work space for the thirty-one people who lived in the house (the extended family and servants). It was here that Mrs. Wickham bore many of her seventeen children. There are also work areas in the basement.

The garden is the oldest in continuous use in Richmond. It is maintained in accordance with the original landscape specifications. Within the garden, you'll find the sculpture studio of Edward V. Valentine, a noted nineteenth-century artist and brother of Mann Valentine. You'll see the tools of his trade and both completed and unfinished work. Valentine's best-known piece is the *Recumbent Lee* in the Lee Chapel on the Washington and Lee University campus (see selection).

The Valentine Museum, the Museum of the Life and History of Richmond, and Wickham House are open Monday through Saturday from 10:00 A.M. to 5:00 P.M. and Sunday from noon to 5:00 P.M. Admission is charged, but Historic Downtown Richmond block tickets can be purchased. These tickets encompass more than three dozen museums, historic houses, and other significant buildings.

Directions: From I-95 take Exit 74C, Broad Street west. Continue on Broad Street to 11th Street; turn right. Follow 11th Street to Clay Street and turn left. Make another left on 10th Street, and the Valentine Museum parking lot will be on your left. From I-64 take Exit 43, 5th Street south. Continue on 5th to Marshall Street and take a left. From Marshall, take another left on 11th and left again on Clay Street. Make a last left on 10th Street, and the parking lot will be on your left.

VMI Museum

On November 11, 1839, twenty-three men reported to the Franklin Literary Society Hall in Lexington. They became the first Virginia Military Institute cadets when their sole instructor, Maj. Francis Smith, assumed command of the old arsenal and established the nation's first state-supported military college. The history of **VMI** and its well-known graduates unfolds at the museum, which is located on the campus parade grounds.

For more than 150 years, VMI has trained citizen-soldiers who have made outstanding contributions to their respective communities. The young cadets live in spartan surroundings, as you can see from the museum's cadet exhibit room, which is just one part of the cadet life exhibit that details their surroundings and uniforms as well as VMI's sports, academic, military, ROTC, and spiritual programs. The collection of VMI rings dating from 1848 to the present is enormously popular.

The first graduates barely completed their college years before being called to serve in the Mexican War, 1846–48. A captured Mexican general's war chest with its silver goblets provides a look at what the Mexican high command considered "roughing it."

Three years after the Mexican War in 1848, Thomas Jonathan "Stonewall" Jackson resigned his army commission and joined the faculty at VMI. He found the peacetime army too tedious and unrewarding for a man anxious to make his reputation. As a teacher of natural philosophy (physics) and artillery tactics, his students found him dull, rigid, and severe (see Stonewall Jackson House selection). The blackboard from his classroom is part of other Jackson artifacts on display.

Jackson's genius became apparent when he led the Stonewall Brigade in the War between the States. The VMI Museum displays the uniform Jackson wore as a teacher as well as his battlefield raincoat, a poignant reminder of his mortal wounding at the Battle of Chancellorsville. Jackson was wearing the Indian rubber raincoat on May 3, 1863, when he was accidentally shot in the arm by one of his own men. The bullet hole is clearly visible; it seems too small to have caused such a big hole in the Confederate command. After his arm was amputated, Jackson contracted pneumonia and died within a week. It also is interesting to discover that while teaching at VMI, Jackson had escorted cadets to stand guard at the hanging of John Brown. A further historical footnote to that event, John Brown's lawyer was a VMI graduate. One of the museum's most popular items is Little Sorrel, Jackson's favorite horse. Little Sorrel died in 1886; whereupon his hide was preserved and mounted over a plaster of paris form. The saddle was made by H. Peat, saddler to the queen of England.

It was not only teachers who marched off to battle during the Civil War. The small butternut jackets on display remind visitors how young the boys were who were sent off to join General Breckenridge's battle-worn regulars. In May 1864, the Southern general was ordered to stop the Northern push into the crucial Shenandoah Valley. The Union troops, under the command of M. G. Franz Sigel, numbered six thousand and were up against Breckenridge's forty-five hundred. To augment the ranks, the 257 cadets at VMI were ordered out of the classroom into battle. A total of fifty-seven casualties included ten cadets who died as a result of the Battle of New Market (see New Market Battlefield selection).

Jackson is only one of the illustrious professors profiled in this museum. Following him so closely that he used the same microscope was physics professor Matthew Fontaine Maury (see Goshen Pass selection), noted for his marine charts. A small section of the Trans-Atlantic cable is exhibited. As Cyrus Fields, who laid the cable, explained, "Maury provided the brains, I provided the brawn." Another faculty member, John Mercer Brooke, designed the armor for the *Merrimack*, the ironclad the Confederates called the *Virginia*. Brooke also invented a device to bring up samples from the ocean floor. One of VMI's most gifted graduates was George Catlett Marshall (see George C. Marshall Museum selection), and his accomplishments are proudly noted.

Today, when cadets enter the barracks through the Jackson Arch, they are reminded of Stonewall's determination. Carved overhead are his time-honored words: "You may be whatever you resolve to be." The museum shows that many VMI graduates have followed his advice.

The museum is open at no charge daily from 9:00 A.M. to 5:00

P.M. Visitors who would like a free, cadet-escorted tour of the post may stop at the VMI Visitor Center in Lejeune Hall. They are given twice a day; call for specific times at (540) 464-7306. You also can pick up a walking tour map and wander the campus on your own.

Directions: From the Richmond area, take I-64 west toward Lexington. From I-64, exit on Route 11. Entering Lexington, Route 11 forks to the right; you need to make an immediate right onto Letcher Avenue. Follow Letcher Avenue the length of the VMI parade grounds, and the VMI Museum will be on your right at Jackson Memorial Hall.

The White House and Museum of the Confederacy

The two-story townhouse of Dr. John Brockenbrough at 12th and Clay streets in Richmond has survived the vicissitudes of time. The house has not, however, remained unchanged. In the 1850s, the Brockenbrough house was architecturally altered to include a third floor and a cupola; Victorian features were added to the interior. One of the finest in Richmond, the house was purchased by the city in June 1861 for Jefferson Davis, president of the Confederacy. When he would not accept it as a gift, the city rented it to the Southern states to be used as the **White House of the Confederacy**. The Davis family was in residence until April 1865, when Varina Davis and her four children fled.

During Reconstruction, 1865–70, the former White House was used as US Army headquarters for Military District Number 1. Alterations were made when it was converted to use as a public school, but by 1890 it was in such sad repair that the city considered tearing it down. It was saved by the Confederate Memorial Literary Society, a group that evolved from a ladies' organization devoted to tending the Confederate graves at Richmond's Hollywood Cemetery. The addition of the word "literary" gave justification for the transfer of this former city school to private hands. It also reflected the national interest in the South evoked by the late-nineteenth-century literary movement of southern authors.

The house was repaired and opened as a museum by the Confederate Memorial Literary Society in 1896. The very existence of this museum prompted donations from throughout the South, and the collection grew.

By 1976, a new Museum of the Confederacy had been built adjacent to the old Brockenbrough house. The personal effects of

395

Robert E. Lee, including the sword he wore at Appomattox, are the museum's most prized pieces. There are military weapons and uniforms belonging to Stonewall Jackson, J. E. B. Stuart, Joseph E. Johnston, and A. P. Hill. Many uniforms, letters, and mementos from the soldiers who fought the battles the generals planned are on display. Dresses, jewelry, and letters from the women who fought the battles at home are also prominently featured.

With the opening of the new museum, work began on restoring the White House to its appearance during the Davis residency. The ground floor houses an exhibit introducing visitors to the Jefferson Davis family. Above it, on the first floor, are the public rooms of the Executive Mansion, which served as the social center for the political and military leaders of the Confederacy. The second floor is restored to reflect the family quarters, with nursery, private office, and master bedroom. The third floor has administrative offices.

The neoclassical White House is included in the Historic Downtown Richmond block ticket. It, along with the Museum of the Confederacy, is open Monday through Saturday from 10:00 A.M. to 5:00 P.M. On Sunday it opens at noon. Admission is charged.

Directions: From I-95 or I-64 eastbound take Exit 74C, Broad Street. Go west on Broad Street. From Broad Street, turn right onto 11th Street and proceed two blocks to Clay Street. Turn right on Clay Street and go two blocks to 12th. You will see a parking deck straight ahead. Bring your parking ticket to be validated.

Maryland

National Museum of Civil War Medicine

During the four-year Civil War, the Union and Confederate armies lost hundreds of thousands of lives from battlefield wounds and disease. The battles fought around Frederick, Antietam, and Monocacy saw heavy losses on both sides. After the former, there were eight thousand wounded in the twenty-nine hospitals set up in Frederick. (This was at a time when the population of Frederick was also eight thousand.) In the heart of historic Frederick, in a 1832 building that was used as an embalming station after the Battles of Antietam and South Mountain, you can visit the **National Museum of Civil War Medicine** (NMCWM). This museum is the center for the study and interpretation of the medical history of the Civil War. You will discover that this wartime medicine brought changes in surgical techniques, reconstructive surgery, women's role in medicine, hospital care, triage, sanitation, and embalming.

There are self-guided and docent-led tours of the museum, and a docent-led Civil War Walking Tour every weekend from April through December 1. The museum is open Monday through Saturday from 10:00 A.M. to 4:00 P.M. and Sunday 11:00 A.M. to 4:00 P.M. From April through October, the museum stays open until 5:00 P.M. There is a nominal charge. You'll find educational items in the museum store.

Directions: From Baltimore, take I-70 west to Frederick. The NMCWM is in downtown Frederick—use the South Market Street exit from I-70. Go north on Market to Patrick; the museum is at 48 E. Patrick Street.

Recent History

From 1607 to 1865, the Middle Atlantic region had, for better or worse, a front seat in American history. Wars were fought in front yards; illustrious figures lived, shopped in, and frequented the growing towns. Those exploring our country's past will find spots here that highlight every aspect of these long-ago years.

When the Civil War ended, the stage shifted, and history happened someplace else. A new chapter opened. America spread beyond this section of the country. The United States developed and expanded westward, while in the east, big business began to rival the government in power.

This chapter suggests these epochal developments in modern American history. One of the greatest of the industrialists was John D. Rockefeller, who, after amassing his great wealth through shrewd business practices, went on to plow his money back into society. The Rockefeller Foundation was responsible for the restoration of Colonial Williamsburg and the Rockefellers' gracious home, Bassett Hall, which evokes the era of great wealth.

Concurrent with undisciplined economic growth was international expansion. The United States became involved in world politics. It is fortunate that the Civil War is the last conflict that permits us to walk the battlefields in the United States. Later conflagrations wrought far more havoc as war became more mechanized and death less personal. The role of the United States in the military struggles of the last 115 years is traced in various military museums throughout the mid-Atlantic. In no other part of the country is there the opportunity to explore such diverse aspects of the US military machine. The military museums included here all shed light on the US role in foreign affairs through the uniforms, equipment, and reminders of the deadly conflicts in which American soldiers have fought.

Woodrow Wilson, who was president during World War I, is represented twice in this section. His two homes reflect a man who was a pivotal figure not only in US history, but also in world history.

One of the most colorful periods from our past, the Roaring Twenties, is represented by the Blue Blazes Whiskey Still. And to bring this book up to date there is the Vietnam Memorial.

The Woodrow Wilson Birthplace

Thomas Woodrow Wilson was born in Staunton's Presbyterian manse on December 28, 1856, "at 12 3/4 o'clock at night," as his proud father recorded in the family Bible. The Bible is on display at his birthplace. When the Reverend Joseph Wilson accepted a call to be minister of the Staunton Presbyterian Church, he and his wife, Jessie Woodrow, and their daughters, Marion and Annie, moved into the manse.

The twelve-room, Greek Revival–style, brick house was less than ten years old when the Wilsons arrived in March 1855. The house was built for Mr. Wilson's predecessor, the Reverend Benjamin Mosby Smith. "The congregation has contracted to have a house built for Mr. Smith," it was recorded, "which it is said will be the best house in Staunton when it is finished. The lot on which it is to be built is one of the most beautiful situations in Staunton... " The total cost of construction was about four thousand dollars. Indicating how little some things have changed over the years, there is a notation in Mr. Smith's diary about his dissatisfaction with the poor work being done by the paperhanger. The reverend dismissed him and, with his wife's help, finished wallpapering the parlor and dining room himself.

Tommy Wilson, as the future president was called until his law school days, spent no more than a year in Staunton. His father's success led to a call from an even larger, more prosperous church in Augusta, Georgia. The Wilsons left Staunton in late 1857. Even though he spent only a year in Virginia as a child, Woodrow Wilson always considered himself a Virginian and returned to Staunton in 1912 to celebrate his birthday as president-elect.

The Woodrow Wilson Birthplace has been extensively restored, giving an accurate look at life in a middle-class minister's home in antebellum Virginia. Many of the furnishings belonged to the Wilsons; others are period pieces.

The manse tour includes three floors. The kitchen, workroom, servant's bedroom, and family dining room are on the ground floor. The master bedroom, where Thomas Woodrow Wilson was born, is on the main floor. His mother was attended by a physician, an unusual practice for this time and place, which was a measure of the social standing of the minister. The birth room was identified from a letter that Jessie wrote to her father, in which she tells him that both she and the baby are doing fine. In the front parlor the Wilson family Bible rests on the table. A silver service given to Mr. Wilson by his Augusta congregation and English flatware belonging to Jessie Woodrow's family are displayed in the dining room. You'll also see the pastor's study. The oldest piece in the house is the hall clock, crafted in Staunton in the 1790s. Bedrooms for the children and for guests are upstairs.

Augmenting the guided tour of the manse is a museum with seven exhibit galleries, which give an in-depth look at the accomplishments of Woodrow Wilson as an author, scholar, university president, governor, and statesman. Rare artifacts, photographs, and family and personal possessions help to narrate the fascinating history of Wilson the man and Wilson the leader in some of the most critical times of our nation and the world. A star attraction is President Wilson's 1919 Pierce-Arrow, used by him during his term and which he purchased for his retirement. The museum has seasonal tours and other special activities; call ahead for details and schedule at (540) 885-0897 or toll free (888) 4-Woodro.

The manse gardens, one of the earliest projects of the Garden Club of Virginia, make a delightful add-on to the house tour. They were laid out in 1934 with crescent and bowknot beds and a variety of ornamental trees on the terraced grounds.

The Woodrow Wilson Birthplace and Museum is open daily from March through October from 9:00 A.M. to 5:00 P.M. November through February, hours are Monday through Saturday 10:00 A.M. to 4:00 P.M. and Sunday noon to 4:00 P.M. It is closed on Thanksgiving, Christmas, and New Year's Day. Admission is charged. The President's Shop offers a wide variety of unique books, educational toys and games, as well as specialty gifts for the home and garden.

Historic Staunton Foundation offers guided walking tours that begin at the Woodrow Wilson Birthplace Reception House. Staunton has twenty-two properties included on the National Register of Historic Places. The walk will take you through Gospel Hill Historic District and in to see the Tiffany windows of Trinity Church, built in 1763 and the town's oldest church. Next you'll stroll through the oldest continually occupied residential area, now the Newtown Historic District. Of interest are an Eastlake-style house at 18 Church Street and the 1854 "Board and Batten" house, the oldest unaltered house in Staunton. From there you'll explore the Wharf Historic District, a significant Confederate supply depot during the Civil War. Tours last approximately an hour; for information call (540) 885-7676.

Directions: From I-95 in the Richmond area, take I-64 west to I-

81. Go north to Staunton, Exit 222, which is Richmond Road, Route 250. Take Route 250 into Staunton and turn right on Route 11; stay in the center lane. Go straight ahead onto Coalter Street. Approaching from the north on I-81, follow the signs from Exit 225. The Woodrow Wilson Birthplace and Museum is at 24 North Coalter Street.

Woodrow Wilson House

The high cost of living in Washington is nothing new. Those who would like to indulge their own knack for design should take heart—even ex-presidents have found the rates prohibitive. When Woodrow Wilson left the White House on March 4, 1921, one of his greatest hopes was to be able to build a home from his own plans. But even Wilson found he couldn't afford to realize his dream.

Though the Wilsons considered other cities for their retirement, they decided to remain in Washington, as the former president required the accessibility of the Library of Congress for his scholarly writing.

As with so many families, it was Edith Bolling Galt Wilson who did the house hunting. After weeks of searching, she chose a Georgian revival townhouse on S Street. She described it as "an unpretentious, comfortable, dignified house, fitted to the needs of a gentleman." She was surprised on their fifth wedding anniversary, when Wilson escorted her to the house and gave her the key to the front door and soil from the garden, an old Scottish custom. He had bought the house for her—it was the first house he ever owned.

Surprisingly, this is Washington's only presidential museum, and it looks remarkably the same as it did when the Wilsons lived here. Like a time capsule, the house preserves upper-middle-class life in the 1920s, with the very special addition of the mementos of Wilson's two terms as president. Wilson's favorite room, and the one that reveals most about his personal tastes, is the library. Here, this learned former president of Princeton University was surrounded by his personal collection of eight thousand books, all familiar to him. He was the author of nine books and numerous articles and, until sickness precluded it, continued to write during his retirement.

The library contains two poignant reminders of World War I—the pen Wilson used to sign the proclamation of a state of war between the United States and Germany and a microphone marking Wilson's last public address, from this room, on Armistice Day, November 10, 1923. Within three months, he would be dead.

But Wilson wasn't all work, and some of his recreational interests also are represented. Until his health confined him to the S Street house, he enjoyed Saturday night movies at the RKO Keith's. Once it became difficult for him to get out, friends provided a graphoscope, so that he could see movies at home. Just outside the library is a Victrola talking machine, which played records with a wooden needle. In the closet, which is still filled with Wilson's clothes and belongings, you see reminders of other recreational interests, like his golf clubs.

Many of the decorative items in the house were given to the Wilsons by other countries, reflecting the enormous role foreign relations played in Wilson's career and his tireless crusade for the formation of the League of Nations. A Gobelin tapestry made for the Wilsons was a gift of the French government; the Belgian royal family gave them hand-painted plates; and the Italian government, a painting and desk. There is even a baseball signed by King George of Great Britain, the only baseball ever signed by a British monarch.

Throughout the house Wilson's wife tried to re-create aspects of their White House life. Nowhere is this more evident than in Wilson's bedroom, which is an exact replica of his White House room. The bed is a copy of the Lincoln Bed, and over the mantel is an empty brass shell, which held the first shot fired by an American soldier in World War I.

Because of Wilson's semi-invalid state, the home was not only a residence but a refuge. It is clearly apparent as you tour the house that here is where the Wilsons spent most of their time. Mrs. Wilson continued to live in the house for thirty years after Woodrow Wilson died. When she died, in 1961, it became the property of the National Trust for Historic Preservation.

The home truly has been preserved. Even the green plants Edith Wilson so loved still infuse the house with life. The Woodrow Wilson House is open Tuesday through Sunday, from 10:00 A.M. to 4:00 P.M. Admission is charged.

Directions: The Woodrow Wilson House is at 2340 S Street, N.W., Washington, D.C. It is just off Embassy Row, four blocks from Dupont Circle Metro.

Frederick Douglass National Historic Site— Cedar Hill

Cedar Hill takes visitors to the threshold of the nineteenth century. Frederick Douglass's journey from fugitive slave to US marshal brought him to Washington in 1877. He was born in 1818, not too far from the capital in Easton, on Maryland's Eastern Shore. Although he was a slave, Frederick Douglass taught himself to read and write, despite his owner's objections. At age twenty-one, he was sent to Baltimore to learn ship caulking and, seizing his opportunity, Douglass escaped north. He then took his name, married Anne Murray, and began fighting for the abolitionist movement.

Frederick Douglass was such an articulate spokesman for the antislavery movement that many doubted he had once been a slave. He published his life story in 1845, even though this put him at great personal risk since he was still a fugitive slave. Compelled to flee the country, he moved his struggle for abolition to England, where he gained supporters who provided financing for the abolitionist newspaper *The North Star*, which Douglass began publishing after his return to the United States in 1847.

Douglass continued his newspaper work when he moved to Washington and edited the *New National Era*. Several years after arriving in the capital, he became the District's register of deeds. Eighteen months after his wife died, he married a secretary for the Office of the Recorder of Deeds who was a staunch supporter of black human rights. Theirs was an interracial marriage. After Frederick Douglass's death on February 20, 1895, his wife spent the rest of her life preserving their Washington home as a memorial to his life and work.

In 1962, the National Park Service took over the Cedar Hill property (also called the Frederick Douglass National Historic Site). The two-story brick house, built in 1855, sits on a hill overlooking the capital. The furnishings and grounds reflect the Douglass years, and many of his personal belongings fill the rooms. His one-thousand-volume library has been preserved. You'll see a brief film on Douglass's life before you begin exploring the house.

The house is open daily, except Thanksgiving, Christmas, and New Year's Day. From mid-April through mid-October, hours are 9:00 A.M. to 5:00 P.M. At other times, it closes at 4:00 P.M. Admission is charged, and reservations are required for all tours; call (800) 967-2283.

Directions: This historic house is inside the Washington Beltway in southeast Washington at 1411 W. Street, S.E.

Sewall-Belmont House

The **Sewall-Belmont House** has a history as diverse as its architecture. The land on which this Capitol Hill residence stands was granted by King Charles to Cecilius Calvert, second Lord Baltimore, in

1632. For a time, all of the Calvert lands were managed by Margaret Brent of the St. Mary's settlement (see Historic St. Mary's City selection). She was the executrix of the Calvert estate and also owned property. These two facts prompted her to ask for a voice in the General Assembly of the New Colony, but her request was refused. It is singularly appropriate that the land she once oversaw became the headquarters of the National Woman's Party, which achieved the vote for women so many years after Margaret Brent failed.

Though there was a house built on the land in the mid-1700s, it was not until after Robert Sewall purchased the land in 1798 that an impressive home was erected. Since the 1800 house incorporated the earlier structure, the Sewall-Belmont house is one of the oldest in Washington.

During the Jefferson and Madison administrations, Albert Gallatin, the secretary of the treasury, rented the house. It is thought that he arranged the financial details of the Louisiana Purchase from here. A year after Gallatin moved out, men from Commodore Barney's flotilla stationed themselves in the Sewall house and fired on the British, which is believed to be the only armed resistance the British experienced as they took Washington during the War of 1812 (see The 1814 British Invasion Route selection).

Generations of the Sewall family owned the house for a total of 123 years, after which it changed hands one more time before becoming the property of the National Woman's Party in 1929. The numerous owners, plus the fact that the house was partially burned by the British during the War of 1812, created a mixture of architectural styles. Some experts love it as an eclectic survey of architectural periods, encompassing as it does the early primitive colonial farmhouse, Georgian, Early American, Federal, Queen Anne, Classic Revival, Victorian, and French Mansard periods. Some view the house as devoid of architectural integrity because of the mingling of styles. None dispute its historical interest.

The Sewall-Belmont House's greatest historical significance is that it is a living monument to Alice Paul, who founded the National Woman's Party in 1913 and led women all across the country in support of the Nineteenth Amendment, which gave women the right to vote. In 1923, Alice Paul wrote the Equal Rights Amendment, which inspired generations of women.

After the 1929 purchase of the Sewall-Belmont House by the National Woman's Party, Alice Paul directed the fight for the Equal Rights Amendment from this house. It was her battle for equal rights and suffrage that led to the house being designated a National Landmark. It is the only house in the United States from which the contemporary women's movement can trace its roots.

The Hall of Statues at the house recognizes women leaders, from Jeanne d'Arc to American leaders like Lucretia Mott, Susan B. Anthony, Elizabeth Cady Stanton, and Alice Paul. If these names don't strike a responsive chord, then exploring this collection associated with the women's rights movement will provide a great deal of background.

Originally, the house was named for Alva Belmont, benefactor of the National Woman's Party, who made it possible for the party to purchase the house in 1929. When it was declared a National Landmark, the name was changed to the Sewall-Belmont House. Mrs. Belmont also provided funds for the organization's first headquarters in Lafayette Square. The dining room furniture is from the Belmonts' Long Island home. The furniture has interesting associations, as most of the pieces have been donated in memory of illustrious women activists.

The library collection was first opened in 1943, when it was dedicated as the Florence Bayard Feminist Library, the first feminist library in America. The library has been closed for several years, but is being reopened for serious research use.

The Sewall-Belmont House Museum and Shop are open Tuesday through Friday from 10:00 A.M. to 3:00 P.M. Tours are given at 11:00 A.M., noon, 1:00 and 2:00 P.M. On Saturday, it opens from noon to 4:00 P.M., with tours on the hour; the last is at 3:00 P.M. During the months of March (Women's History Month), November, and December, the museum and shop also are open from 1:00 to 4:00 P.M. Tours begin with the showing of a twenty-eight-minute film about the founding of the National Woman's Party and the fight for women's suffrage and continue for about twenty minutes with a tour through the two floors of the house that compose the museum.

Directions: The Sewall-Belmont House, 144 Constitution Avenue, N.E., Washington, D.C., is located at the corner of 2nd and Constitution Avenue, N.E. It is immediately adjacent to the Hart Senate Office Building.

Blue Blazes Whiskey Still

On quiet days in the mountains during the summer of '29, you'd occasionally hear the thump from the moonshiner's wooden keg; but on July 29, 1929, it was still. No noise betrayed its location.

Two men drove along Big Hunting Creek until they came to a narrow, rough road up the Mountainside draw. They parked, and toting an empty whiskey jug, started up the draw. Before they'd gone very far, they were halted by a rifle-toting still blockader (so called after the blockade runners of earlier seafaring days). They were told to "git," and git they did—but only long enough to assemble the rest of the posse. The raid on the **Blue Blazes Whiskey Still** was underway.

Stories are still told in Frederick County about the shoot-out that ensued. You'll learn all about this still from the park rangers who oversee the Blue Blazes Whiskey Still. (You might want to call ahead and obtain the park's calendar of events to see if there are any ranger-led programs, 301-663-9388.) The current still is not nearly as large as the operation raided back in 1929. The original was no fly-by-night setup. It was one of the biggest stills ever destroyed in Maryland, having produced over twenty-five thousand gallons of whiskey. Such big stills were called steamer stills and held roughly forty barrels of moonshine. The smaller apparatus operated at **Catoctin Mountain Park**, a unit of the National Park Service, since 1970 was originally a Smoky Mountain still seized by treasury agents, or revengers. But it wore out, so the usable parts were used to build another old-time model.

A self-guided nature trail leads from the National Park Service Visitor Center (301-663-9388) to the Blue Blazes Still. This is just one of the more than twenty-five miles of hiking trails within the Catoctin Mountain Park and **Cunningham Falls State Park,** directly across Route 77.

The most scenic spot in these two parks is Cunningham Falls. Handicapped visitors can negotiate the short walk from the accessible parking area on Route 77. There is a wooden boardwalk to the base of the falls. Other visitors park at the William Houck area. The Lower Cunningham Falls Trail is also easy, but the Cliff Trail, which also leads to the falls, is strenuous.

The cascading Cunningham Falls drop seventy-eight feet and offer many photographic possibilities, so be sure to bring a camera. If you have a zoom lens or binoculars, you'll be able to enjoy a close-up of the woodland birds. On hot summer days the falls might whet your urge for a swim, but remember, absolutely no swimming in the falls themselves is allowed. Head over to the forty-three-acre Hunting Creek Lake, where you'll find two sandy public beaches and a bathhouse for changing. On summer weekends, it's advisable to arrive by 10:00 A.M. if you want to find a parking spot. Those more interested in fishing than dipping can throw a line in the well-stocked lake or in Big Hunting Creek, a catch-and-return fly stream, which has native Brook trout.

Little Hunting Creek is for fishing with artificial lures. A license is required for anyone sixteen and over, and a trout stamp is required for anyone possessing or fishing the special regulation areas for trout.

Canoes can be rented during the summer and on some fall weekends. A fishing pier for the handicapped is accessible by wheelchair.

Other park options include camping, hunting, picnicking, cross-country skiing, horseback riding on designated trails, snowshoeing, sailing, and a half-acre playground made from recycled tires. On the second and third weekends in March, the park hosts a maple syrup program. Rangers demonstrate tree tapping and sap boiling and give talks every hour from 10:00 A.M. to 3:00 P.M. A sausage and pancake breakfast is served at the concession stand.

At the southern end of the Cunningham Falls State Park off Route 15, on Route 806, you'll see the remains of the Old Catoctin Furnace, one of three furnaces operated here from 1776 to 1903. The Mountain Tract, as the surrounding land was called, was issued to Benedict Calvert and Thomas Johnson for the purpose of erecting an iron works. In the last triumphant stages of the Revolution, this furnace supplied ten-inch shells for the Continental Army. The stack you see today is from the Isabella Furnace, built in 1867. Signs along the self-guided trail explain just how this furnace operated. There's a new visitor center at the adjacent Manor Area.

Directions: From Baltimore, take I-70 west to Frederick. Head north on Route 15 for thirteen miles to Catoctin Furnace. To get to the Houck Area of Cunningham Falls State Park continue north on Route 15 to Thurmont. Take Route 77 west, which leads to both the National Park Service Catoctin Mountain Park Visitors Center and the Houck Area, where you can pick up the trail to Cunningham Falls.

Dumbarton Oaks

From August to October 1944, world leaders met at the elegant Georgetown mansion **Dumbarton Oaks** to lay the groundwork for the United Nations. Their plans, submitted to the San Francisco Conference in April 1945, evolved into the United Nations Charter.

Dumbarton Oaks is more than a historical footnote; it is a gracious mansion surrounded by one of the loveliest formal gardens in the country. The sixteen acres of gardens were first landscaped in 1922 by Beatrix Ferrand. Its European style is epitomized in the perfect symmetry of the Pebble Garden and the Ellipse. Cherry Hill blooms with soft delicate pink blossoms in May. When the spring bulbs in the formal garden plots are spent, the summer annuals take their place.

The mansion contains an outstanding collection of Byzantine and pre-Columbian art as well as tapestries and antique furnishings. The estate is now a research center and museum owned by Harvard University. The museum galleries are open Tuesday through Sunday from 2:00 to 5:00 P.M. The gardens are open daily from April through October from 2:00 to 6:00 P.M. Admission is charged for the gardens in season; there is no charge from November through March, when they close at 5:00 P.M. Dumbarton Oaks is at 32nd and R Streets, N.W. The historic gardens located on a steep hillside may present challenges for some visitors with disabilities, as do some parts of the mansion. Call (202) 339-6410 on weekdays for accessibility information. Adjacent to this private estate is Dumbarton Oaks Park, another delightful getaway in the spring when the wildflowers are in bloom.

There are three additional historic landmarks in Georgetown: the C&O Canal, which starts one half block south of 30th and M Streets, N.W.; Oak Hill Cemetery, at 3001 R Street, a nineteenth-century garden park cemetery that blends natural gardens with monuments dating from the Civil War period; and Georgetown University, the oldest Catholic university in the country, at 37th and O Streets, N.W.

Directions: Dumbarton Oaks is within the Washington Beltway, in the Georgetown section of northwest Washington, bordering on the Potomac River, one block east of Wisconsin Avenue. The Business and Professional Association of Georgetown has produced an excellent brochure and map listing historic landmarks and more than fifty recommended shopping and dining spots. You can obtain it at numerous spots in Georgetown or at the Washington, D.C. Convention and Visitors Association at 1212 New York Avenue, N.W. You can call (202) 789-7000 for information.

Bassett Hall

On November 27, 1926, under an ancient oak tree behind the eighteenth-century home of Burwell Bassett (nephew of Martha Washington), John D. Rockefeller, Jr., and the Reverend W. A. R. Goodwin first met to plan the restoration of Williamsburg, the eighteenth-century capital of the colonies. As they strolled back to town, Rockefeller said if he came back to Williamsburg, he'd like to picnic beneath the oak.

It became easy for Rockefeller to picnic at Bassett Hall after he purchased the 585-acre estate in 1936. From this comfortable vantage point, the Rockefellers watched the rebirth of Williamsburg. John D. Rockefeller, Jr., ultimately spent sixty million dollars on the restoration of the venerable city, and contributions by other family members brought the figure to a hundred million dollars.

A tour of Bassett Hall reveals a great deal about the Rockefeller lifestyle. From the moment you enter the informal sitting room, the first room on the self-guided, audiotape tour, one decorative influence is immediately apparent—Mrs. Rockefeller's folk art collection. There are two hundred pieces from her extensive collection in this home, and more than four hundred pieces at the nearby Abby Aldrich Rockefeller Folk Art Center.

Bassett Hall represents a mix of decorating styles. In the hall passageway, which in colonial times served as the summer living room, you'll see a collection of Chinese export paintings. The paint was applied on the back side of the glass. Such paintings had to be carefully shipped, for if the glass broke, the picture was lost.

In the formal parlor another unusual style of painting, called mourning pictures, is on display. Painted by schoolgirls and much in vogue after the death of George Washington, these depict graveyard scenes full of tombstones. Additional examples of these morbid works are upstairs, though the master bedroom has stenciled pictures with cheerful subjects, such as flowers, fruits, and birds. Throughout Bassett Hall, you see objects acquired by Mrs. Rockefeller's sister, Lucy, on her travels. She purchased the crocheted bedspread in the master bedroom from the Royal School of Needlework in England. Mrs. Rockefeller herself was a talented needleworker, as a trunk full of rugs that were made by her attests.

In the sitting room of the new wing, an unusual painting of General Washington crossing the Delaware is on display. The faces of all the men in the boat resemble George Washington.

Back downstairs, you'll see the formal dining room, which Mrs. Rockefeller described in a letter to her son David as "the most pleasant room in the house." Although the dining room is quite elegant, when the heads of states from around the world attended the Summit of Industrialized Nations in May 1983, they enjoyed lunch in the garden overlooking the oak allée.

Explore the grounds before you end your tour of Bassett Hall. There are three original outbuildings: a smokehouse, kitchen, and dairy. A modern teahouse, or orangery, was added by the Rockefellers.

Bassett Hall is open daily, 9:00 A.M. to 4:45 P.M., except Wednesday, by appointment. When you visit, you join a distinguished array of guests, including the queen mother of England, President Lyndon Johnson, Vice President Hubert Humphrey, and Japanese Emperor Hirohito. Appointments can be arranged at any Colonial Williamsburg ticket office. Admission is by Colonial Williamsburg's Good Neighbor Card, Patriot's Pass, or Museums Ticket.

Directions: From I-95 in the Richmond area, take Exit 238, I-64 east, to Colonial Williamsburg. An alternate route is via Route 5 east from Richmond. You may want to stop at the Colonial Williamsburg Visitor Center upon arrival to obtain maps, brochures, and tickets.

College Park Aviation Museum

If you've been to the National Air and Space Museum in Washington, D.C., and long for the early days of flying, visit the **College Park Aviation Museum**, at the oldest continuously operated airport in the world.

After making the first motor-driven, heavier-than-air flight on December 17, 1903, Orville and Wilbur Wright were anxious to sell their flying machine to the US Army. They brought their plane to Fort Myer, Virginia, for test flights. The Wright plane was well built, but many problems still needed to be worked out. This became evident during one of the tests at Fort Myer, when the plane crashed and Orville broke his thigh. (His passenger, Lt. Thomas E. Selfridge, died, becoming the first military aviation fatality.) The army decided to accept the Wright plane despite this mishap. On August 2, 1909, it became Signal Corps Airplane #1 on the condition that the Wrights would instruct two officers in the art of flying.

In October of that year the army moved its operations to a field near the Maryland Agricultural College in College Park, and Wilbur began the training of the two army officers. From the earliest days, a succession of dramatic aviation firsts occurred at the College Park Airfield. The first flights by army officers and the first flight in the US with a woman passenger kept College Park in the news. After army specifications for the Wright plane had been met and the officers taught to fly, a minor accident damaged the machine. It was crated and sent to Fort Sam Houston, Texas. Money had not yet been appropriated by Congress for aviation, so army activities at College Park Airfield temporarily came to a halt with the departure of Signal Corps Airplane #1. Civilian aviators, however, have always kept the airfield busy, and it is recognized as the world's oldest continuously operated airport, the "Cradle of American Aviation."

One of the civilians working at College Park was Rexford Smith, who perfected one of the earliest biplanes. A private firm, National Aviation Company, began offering instruction at College Park on Wright, Curtiss, and Bleriot airplanes. With the civilian aviation market expanding, the government finally appropriated money for aviation, and in June 1911, a Signal Corps aviation school was established at College Park.

Records were again made at the airport. It was here that the first bomb-dropping devices were tried, the first mile-high flight was flown, and the first machine guns were fired from an airplane. This "aerodrome" was also the starting point for one of the first "long cross-country flights," from College Park, Maryland, to Frederick, Maryland. The two-man craft made it to Frederick without encountering any problems, but the pilots couldn't find their way back. When they landed to ask directions, the plane stalled on takeoff. The red-faced pilots ended up returning by train!

The US Post Office air mail flights that began in 1918 had their share of problems, too. Although official mail flights began at College Park, test flights were carried out by the army at Potomac Park in Washington. On May 15, 1918, the first delivery was scheduled to embark from Potomac Park. President Wilson was on hand, and he watched—and watched! When the pilot started his takeoff, the plane wouldn't go. Officials paced while mechanics checked out the engine for thirty minutes. Someone finally thought to check the fuel tanks—they were empty. This was far from the only hitch; once underway the pilot, perhaps rattled by his rocky start, flew southeast instead of north to Philadelphia. He had followed the wrong railroad tracks. On landing in Waldorf, Maryland, to ask directions, he broke the propeller. The 140 pounds of air mail were eventually delivered to Philadelphia by truck.

Another series of aviation experiments began at the airport in 1920; these involved vertical aviation. The father-and-son team of Emile and Henry Berlin began testing a machine that could rise vertically. After several years of testing and experiments, in 1924 the machine made what many consider to be the first successful controlled flights by a helicopter. The Berliner helicopter is currently on exhibit here (on loan from the Smithsonian Institution).

Yet another government agency became active at College Park between 1927 and 1935. Those were the years when the Bureau of Standards ran experiments on "flying blind," or on instrument, which led to the development of the first radio navigational gear and the blind landing equipment that today is standard.

The former College Park Airport Museum has a new name and a new facility designed to represent a wing of the Wright Flyer. Within are four galleries displaying photos of aviation firsts, aviation equipment, memorabilia from the earliest flying years, field aviation films, and a collection of early air mail items and photographs. An exciting new addition is a replica of the 1909 hangar with an animatronic Wilbur Wright that harkens back to the field's early history. There is a nominal admission charge. The museum is open daily from 10:00 A.M. to 5:00 P.M. It is closed on major holidays.

You may want to plan lunch at the adjacent **94th Aero Squadron Restaurant**, which looks like a French farm used by American forces during World War I. Adding to the atmosphere are tables overlooking the action on the still-active runways at College Park Airport. Some tables even have hook-ups so you can listen to the cockpit conversations.

Directions: From Baltimore, take Route 295, the Baltimore-Washington Parkway, to Greenbelt Road. Take Greenbelt Road toward College Park, then make a left onto Kenilworth Avenue. Head south on Kenilworth to the intersection with Paint Branch Parkway; make a right turn. Make another right at the first stoplight on Cpl. Frank Scott Drive for the College Park Aviation Museum. The entrance for the 94th Aero Squadron also is off Calvert Road, just before the museum entrance.

Eisenhower National Historic Site

Gettysburg, once so battle-scarred and bloodied, was quiet rolling farmland both before and again after the battle. The area around Gettysburg is still primarily farmland. One farm in particular draws visitor's attention, the farmhouse of Dwight and Mamie Eisenhower, and it is now the **Eisenhower National Historic Site.**

The Eisenhower's farm was originally settled in the 1750s and was acquired by them in 1950. This 189-acre farm on the edge of the Gettysburg battlefield was the only home Dwight David Eisenhower ever owned.

When the Eisenhowers were in the White House, they began planning the major reconstruction of their farm. The new, modified Georgian farmhouse incorporated the south portion of the old house in its design. The new house had eighteen rooms and eight baths. When it was completed in 1955, the farmhouse became Eisenhower's presidential retreat and temporary White House. After Ike's first heart attack in late 1955, he recuperated at his new home. When he left office on January 20, 1961, he retired to this haven and spent his last years here.

One of the nice things about visiting this farm is that it really does seem like a home. You'll get no museum feeling when you tour. Homey touches abound—like Ike's faded blue rocker and much-used easel. Seven of his oil studies hang on an upstairs wall. Mamie, too, had her pictures: Family photographic portraits are framed and massed on the grand piano, indicating her close family ties. The open door in Mamie's pink and green bedroom and the general's robe and slippers on the bed where he often napped give an illusion that the Eisenhowers have just stepped out and will soon be coming home.

One can imagine such distinguished guests as Winston Churchill, Charles de Gaulle, Nikita Khrushchev, and Jawaharlal Nehru getting a genuine look at real life in America while visiting the Eisenhowers at Gettysburg. A warm and friendly atmosphere still makes itself felt here.

A visit includes self-guided tours of the grounds, the skeet range, and the farm buildings. Black Angus cattle still graze in the pasture, and the Eisenhower's farm machinery is on display in the barns. Ranger-conducted talks and tours and living-history programs are offered in season. There is also a program for families called the Junior Secret Service Program, which lets children test their skills in activities that range from the searching for unauthorized objects and personnel with binoculars to the interrogation of some of the site's staff. Participants can see some of the actual security equipment used by agents to protect President Eisenhower in the 1950s and 1960s. A badge is awarded to those who complete this program; its design is based on the official badge worn by agents of the United States Secret Service. The program, offered at no charge from 9:00 A.M. to 3:00 P.M. daily, is available for children seven to twelve. The program takes about two hours. For more information call (717) 338-9114.

Tickets to the farm can be obtained at the Gettysburg National Military Park Visitor Center. Buses transport visitors from the center to the farm for a fee.

Directions: From I-76, the Pennsylvania Turnpike, take Exit 17, Route 15, south to Gettysburg. Once in Gettysburg, follow the signs to the Gettysburg National Military Park Visitor Center.

George C. Marshall Museum and Library

George Catlett Marshall, one of only a few professional soldiers to be awarded the Nobel Peace Prize, was both a military genius and an inspired humanitarian. His European Recovery Plan rehabilitated the economies of that war-torn continent.

As the son of a Kentucky Democrat living in Republican Union-town, Pennsylvania, young Marshall had no hope for an appointment to West Point. He chose instead to attend Virginia Military Institute, spending his spare time exploring Virginia's Civil War battlefields. He learned a great deal about the military strategies of legendary VMI instructor Stonewall Jackson.

Today at the **George C. Marshall Museum**, you'll see an exhibit covering Marshall's years as staff officer in France, 1917–19. Damon Runyan wrote a newspaper column about him entitled "American Sudan Drives According to Principles of Stonewall Jackson." Runyan was not the only one to discern the influence of Jackson. As early as 1913, while he was in the Philippines, Marshall was called upon to attack when his chief of staff fell ill. Marshall dictated the entire plan of battle without corrections. In commending the young lieutenant for his field orders, Maj. Gen. J. Franklin Bell said, "He is the greatest military genius since Stonewall Jackson."

Photo murals and personal mementos at the museum trace Marshall's outstanding military leadership. The course of World War II is detailed in a twenty-five-minute electric map presentation.

Marshall's career as statesman and diplomat is also thoroughly covered. In the postwar years, he served as President Truman's envoy to China with the rank of ambassador and as his secretary of state. It was in the latter capacity that he spoke at the Harvard Commencement program in June 1947 and outlined what has become known as the Marshall Plan. The Nobel Peace Prize, won in 1953 for the European Recovery Act, known as the Marshall Plan, is on display. At the age of seventy, by a special act of Congress, Marshall became Truman's secretary of defense during the Korean conflict.

America is not the only nation to recognize Marshall's achievements. The museum displays medals from sixteen countries, including the George VI's Honorary Knight of the Grand Cross, Military Division of the Order of Bath. One award did not go directly to Marshall, but to *Patton*, the movie about General Patton's drive across Europe. The producer of this Best Picture of the Year for 1970, Frank M. McCarthy, chose to have his Oscar displayed at the George C. Marshall Museum.

The museum has an innovative "Try on a Piece of History" program for young visitors. The Research Center houses an extensive archive containing the personal and private papers of General Marshall and other contemporaries as well as a library of more than twenty-five thousand volumes specializing in twentieth-century military and diplomatic history. The Research Center is accessible without charge to researchers of all ages.

The George C. Marshall Museum is open daily from 9:00 A.M. to 5:00 P.M. The Research Center is open weekdays from 8:30 A.M. to 4:30 P.M. Both are closed on Thanksgiving, Christmas, and New Year's Day. Admission is charged for the museum.

Directions: From I-95 in the Richmond area, take I-64 west to Lexington, then exit onto Route 11. Just outside Lexington, Route 11 forks to the right onto Jefferson Street. The first right off Jefferson up Letcher Avenue takes you to the VMI parade grounds and to the George C. Marshall Museum. From I-81, take the Route 60 exit and head north into Lexington on Nelson Street. Follow Main Street to Letcher Avenue.

Douglas MacArthur Memorial

When Douglas MacArthur was born January 26, 1880, in Little Rock, Arkansas, the Norfolk, Virginia, paper reported, "Douglas MacArthur was born... while his parents were away." This was not a medical first, simply a hometown paper commenting on a local personality. His mother, Mary Pinkney Hardy MacArthur, had been born in Norfolk, and since his father, Arthur MacArthur, was a peripatetic military officer, Norfolk was always their "home by choice."

Although Gen. Douglas MacArthur never actually lived in Norfolk, he nevertheless consented to the city's suggestion of a memorial in 1960 and helped plan the complex you'll see. Norfolk redesigned the 1850 city hall done by Thomas Walter, who is noted for his work on the US Capitol dome and its House and Senate wings. The **Douglas MacArthur Memorial** opened in 1964 on the general's eighty-fourth birthday. When MacArthur died on April 5, 1964, he was buried in the rotunda that he helped design; not in Washington, D.C., where he said he had never won a battle.

Begin your visit at the MacArthur Memorial Theater, where you'll see a twenty-two-minute newsreel compilation of footage that captures significant events in American history in which the general played a pivotal role. The film gives added life to the still photographs and memorabilia in the nine galleries surrounding the rotunda.

The first gallery contains exhibits that depict MacArthur's family, his youth, and his four years at West Point. You'll see reminders of the young MacArthur, who had the highest entrance marks to West Point and graduated with one of the highest averages in the academy's history.

Galleries two through seven cover MacArthur's service in the Philippines, World Wars I and II, and the Korean War. Photographs, uniforms, weapons, medals, and maps help tell the story. Large murals show MacArthur's return to the Philippines, his attendance at the Japanese surrender, and his address to Congress in 1951, after President Truman relieved him of command. Gallery eight reflects on MacArthur's twilight years, when his achievements in business, writing, and other pursuits are fully recorded.

Gallery nine contains the well-remembered corncob pipe, sunglasses, and visored cap identified with MacArthur. Two large cases of medals presented by countries around the world and by the US government also are displayed. His Congressional Medal of Honor is prominent among the latter; his receipt of it made the MacArthurs the only father and son in American history to receive the award. This very dramatic display also contains the general's desk and chair, plus a special video presentation that highlights MacArthur's career and his impact on world history.

Be sure to see the changing exhibit galleries in the theater and the large gift shop, where the general's sedan is on display.

The MacArthur Memorial is open at no charge, 10:00 A.M. to 5:00 P.M., Monday through Saturday, and 11:00 A.M. to 5:00 P.M. on Sunday. It is closed Thanksgiving, Christmas, and New Year's Day.

Directions: From I-95 in the Richmond area, take I-64 to Norfolk; then take I-264 and exit on City Hall Avenue. Proceed three blocks west. Parking is available in several nearby City of Norfolk garages. Take your ticket to the museum receptionist for validation.

Paul E. Garber Facility

Aircraft conservators responsible for taking old planes apart prior to restoration at the Smithsonian's **Paul E. Garber Facility** have discovered some unusual messages from the past. Staffers working on the Enola Gay, the B-29 that dropped the uranium bomb on Hiroshima, found one of the three original arming plugs behind a piece of heavy equipment. In a Chance Vought F4U Corsair, the US Navy carrier-based fighter plane that first exceeded four hundred miles per hour, a conservator was dismantling the engine when he found a faded scrap that probably was placed there by a fun-loving crew chief during a 1940s maintenance check. It read: "What in the hell are you looking for in here, you silly... "

At the Paul Garber Facility, you can readily see what it is they're looking for in these old planes—the blueprints of past designs. In the five buildings open to the public at Silver Hill, the Smithsonian has roughly 140 aircraft on display, compared to seventy-five at the museum on the Mall in downtown Washington. The remainder of the 322 aircraft in the collection are on loan, in storage, or undergoing restoration. In an average year two or three aircraft are restored, each requiring between five thousand and thirteen thousand man-hours of labor.

Touring the Garber warehouses gives you an inside look at the world of aviation. A typical tour group of fifteen to thirty will consist mainly of pilots and aviation buffs. The conversation tends to sound like Hollywood outtakes, with talk of "auguring in," the "outside of the envelope," and "hangar queens." No two tours are exactly alike because the docents tailor the two-and-a-half- to three-hour tours to the participants.

Grown men become enthusiastic youngsters as they crowd around vintage biplanes and one-of-a-kind experimental models. A frequently asked question is "Can these planes fly?" Many can, but none do. Once the Smithsonian acquires a plane, it is grounded to prevent additional damage.

As you tour the workshop, you'll see planes still unrestored and in some cases wonder how what appears to be rubble can be restored to mint condition. Providently, aviation developed simultaneously with photography, and there was always someone with a camera to rush out to the field when a barnstorming show came to town. Thus, excellent photo documentation exists of even the earliest aircraft. All restorers need is one small piece that is clearly visible in a photo, and the remaining pieces can be drawn to scale. Another factor that helps restorers is that if only parts from one side of a plane survive, the other still can be duplicated.

At the Smithsonian the planes are restored exactly as they were; if the insignia had been painted on with a brush, a brush will be used, not a spray gun. On the Bellanca CF every screw head on the wooden section has the slots lined up just as they once were. Such a lineup enabled the pilots to tell when a screw was loose. If restorers cannot locate an original part, it is made to match; then carefully labeled to indicate that it is not authentic. Old-timers have come through the Garber Facility and commented that the planes here look better than the originals.

In addition to learning a good bit of aviation history, you'll discover why the early pilots wore flowing white scarves, why the Messerschmitt killed more friends than foes, what single airplane was on the military inventory the day WWII started and the day it ended, and why German fighter pilots had an edge over the WWII Lightning.

After a visit, you may agree with the Ernest Hemingway quote prominently displayed over a desk in the reception area: "You love a lot of things if you live around them, but there isn't any woman and there isn't any horse... that is as lovely as a great airplane."

To arrange a visit, call (202) 357-1400 weekdays between 9:00 A.M. and 5:00 P.M. Or write the Tour Scheduler, NASK Smithsonian Institution, Washington, D.C. 20560. Free tours are given Monday through Friday at 10:00 A.M. and on weekends at 10:00 A.M. and 1:00 P.M. Wear comfortable walking shoes and note that the cavernous warehouses have neither heat nor air-conditioning.

Directions: From Baltimore, take I-95 south to the Washington

Beltway (I-495/95) and go south on I-95 to Exit 7B (Branch Avenue, Route 5, Silver Hill). After exiting, make a left on Auth Road and proceed one block to the traffic fight at the junction with Route 5. Make a right and follow Route 5 north for one mile to St. Barnabas Road, Route 414. Make a right on St. Barnabas and go 0.5 mile to the Paul Garber Facility, on the right directly across the Silver Mill Road intersection.

Marine Corps Air-Ground Museum

The **Marine Corps Air-Ground Museum** is across Route 1 from the Prince William Forest Park. You need no advance reservations to visit this museum. The Marine guard at the sentry booth will check your driver's license when you enter the base and issue you a visitor's pass.

For many years, the museum was limited primarily to Marine aviation, but now the scope is broader and includes ground equipment and weapons. Currently, there are three hangars open to the public. The first covers the "Early Years" of the air-ground team (1900–1941), the second covers World War II, and the third hangar focuses on the Korean War.

Quantico's association with aviation goes back to the Civil War, when hot air balloons were used for reconnaissance over the Potomac River nearby. Dr. Samuel Pierpont Langley launched a twenty-five-pound, thirteen-foot flying model from the roof of a wooden houseboat moored in the river. He believed that the water would make recovery of the craft more likely. Langley models were the forerunners of the Wright brothers' airplane, and Langley tried two unsuccessful manned flights before the Wright brothers succeeded at Kitty Hawk.

Langley's flying machine is on display in the main lobby of the National Air and Space Museum in Washington, but the Marine Corps Air-Ground Museum exhibits some of his early models in the first hangar. Included in this exhibit are a Curtiss airplane "Pusher" and World War I vintage aircraft: a Thomas-Morse "Scout" advance trainer and a DeHaviland D.H. 4B fighter bomber of the type flown by Marine pilots in France. There also are two Boeing fighter planes from the late 1920s and 1930s, as well as a Stearman N25-3 primary trainer. A Wright J-5 "Whirlwind" engine on display is the same type that powered Lucky Lindy's *Spirit of St. Louis*.

In addition to the airplanes, there are track and wheeled vehicles, artillery, small arms, uniforms, personal equipment, photographs, and art—all part of the story of the Marine Corps's air-ground attack and defense.

The museum is open April through the third Sunday in November, from 10:00 A.M. to 5:00 P.M. Tuesday through Saturday, and from noon to 5:00 P.M. on Sunday. It is closed on Mondays and Easter Sunday. Guided tours are provided for groups by prior arrangement; call (703) 784-2606. No guided tours begin after 4:00 P.M.

One other museum in the area is the **Weems-Botts Museum**, just up Route 1 in Dumfries. Parson Weems was a physician, preacher, and traveling bookseller. In the early 1800s, Parson Mason Locke Weems wrote the first biography of George Washington. His apocryphal anecdotes, including the cherry tree story, have become part of American folklore.

Weems purchased this story-and-a-half house in 1798 to use as a bookstore. In 1802, Benjamin Botts purchased the house to use as his law office. Benjamin Botts was the youngest lawyer on Aaron Burr's defense team during Burr's 1807 trial for treason. It is good that Botts achieved early fame, for he met a tragic death, along with his wife, the governor of Virginia, and 162 other patrons who perished in the Richmond Theater fire of 1811. An addition to the Weems-Botts house built in the mid-1800s by the Merchant family now houses artifacts from the Dumfries area. The museum hours are 10:00 A.M. to 4:00 P.M. Tuesday through Saturday.

Directions: From I-95 south of Alexandria, take Exit 150, the Quantico-Triangle exit. For the Marine Corps Air-Ground Museum take Route 619 east for about a mile. For the Weems-Botts Museum take Exit 151 off I-95 and follow signs to the museum.

Quartermaster Museum

One of the world's most complete military uniform collections can be seen at the **Quartermaster Museum** at Fort Lee. The uniforms date from the 1700s to the present and include boots, helmets, and all kinds of special gear, such as fearsome looking gas masks and padded dog-training suits.

Many well-known military leaders are remembered. The museum has Gen. George S. Patton's 1944 jeep with its "steamboat trombones," or air horns, and Gen. Dwight D. Eisenhower's 1940 mess jacket and his "pinks and greens" dress uniform. Amid the many presidential banners used by Taft, Wilson, Harding, Truman, and both Roosevelts is the original fifty-star flag presented to President Eisenhower.

The museum reveals the diverse functions of the Army Quartermaster Corps, which range from providing housing, food, clothing, and transportation to arranging funerals. You'll learn how much the rations of the US soldier, now considered the best in the world, have changed from the fire cakes and water that were standard fare at Valley Forge.

The Corps also quarters and equips animals used by the military. There's a delightful old recruitment poster that tells potential soldiers, "Join the Cavalry and Have a Courageous Friend... The Horse is Man's Noblest Companion." The era of the horse soldier is illustrated by a display on the Ninth and Tenth Cavalry, whose Black ranks were known as the "Buffalo Soldiers." You'll also see a reconstructed saddler's workshop and a blacksmith shop.

In the military funeral exhibit, look for the elaborate black caisson used in the funeral of Gen. George Pickett in 1875 and Jefferson Davis on May 31, 1893. There is also the architect's original model for the Tomb of the Unknown Soldier at Arlington Cemetery. A somber black drum used in the funeral cortege of John F. Kennedy causes many a visitor to stop and stand solemnly before it.

There is so much to see that visitors with special interests can spend hours. The Hall of Heraldry alone has thousands of examples of crests, patches, plaques, and flags. Special exhibits and selections from the stored collection make this is an interesting spot to revisit. The QM, as it is called, is open Tuesday through Friday from 10:00 A.M. to 5:00 P.M. and on weekends from 11:00 A.M. to 5:00 P.M. It is closed on Thanksgiving, Christmas, and New Year's Day. There is no admission charge.

Directions: From I-95 in the Petersburg area, take the Fort Lee Exit (signs also indicate directions to the QM Museum). The QM is located on Route 36, east between Petersburg and Hopewell. The museum is just inside the main gate of Fort Lee. You do not need a special pass; Fort Lee is an "open post."

Navy Yard Museums

From the moment visitors drive through the gates, the Navy Yard captures their attention. First, there are the omnipresent uniformed personnel. Willard Park, located in front of the **Navy Museum**, has a collection of captured guns, Civil War cannons, shipboard missile launchers, tanks, and a huge propeller from the battleship *South Dakota*.

Building 76, which houses the indoor exhibits, was originally the Breech Mechanism Shop of the old Naval Yard Gun Factory. The Navy Yard began operation in 1799 and built the first ships for the young American navy. This cavernous building (at six hundred feet, the longest hall in Washington) is often called the Navy's attic. The military pieces that fill the huge space offer young visitors a chance to climb on cannons, into the bathyscaphe and look through submarine periscopes. When youngsters sit behind the barrel of the massive cannon, they can crank the heavy brass wheel to swing the barrel. Kids are apt to provide their own sound effects, as they quickly realize this isn't the kind of museum where they must talk in whispers.

While younger visitors man the guns, older visitors can read the fascinating commentary that accompanies the exhibits. There is a simulated gun deck from the *Constitution*, the oldest commissioned ship in the Navy, which explains the origin of the nickname "Old Ironsides." The seven-inch oak timbers from which the hull was constructed were so thick that cannon balls seemed to bounce off. The museum also has the fully rigged foremast of the *Constitution*, taken off the ship when it was overhauled in 1976.

It would take hours to fully appreciate all the items included in the collection. Among the more interesting pieces is Admiral Byrd's Antarctic hut, a nineteenth-century cat-o'-nine-tails, a full-size submersible, a model of an Apollo spacecraft, and a collection of ship models.

The models range in size, from exquisite ivory miniatures to oversize battleships. Old World crafts include early Viking ships, Spanish galleons, Korean tortoise boats, and ancient Chinese fighting boats. There are models of distinguished ships of the United States Navy, including the *Tennessee*, *Panay*, *Ranger*, *Fletcher*, *Missouri*, and *Forestal*. The models and artifacts fill cases, walls, and corners. They even hang from the ceiling, like the World War II *Corsair* and the huge underseas exploration vehicle *Trieste*.

If you're visiting with children, be sure to pick up the scavenger hunt brochure and the activities booklet when you enter the museum, as they make exploring even more fun. A computer game to decode messages is sure to challenge older children. The game also teaches players the history of cryptanalysis.

There is still more to see in the Navy Art Gallery in Building 76, a one-room collection of thirty-two paintings by Navy combat artists. The Navy Museum is open Monday through Friday from 9:00 A.M. to 4:00 P.M. and in the summer and on weekends and holidays from 10:00 A.M. to 5:00 P.M. The Navy Art Gallery is open Wednesday through Sunday from 9:00 A.M. to 4:00 P.M. All are free. Guided tours of the Navy Museum are available; call ahead at (202) 433-4995. For general information call (202) 433-4881 or visit their Web site at www.history.navy.mil.

There is one more *must* stop, and that is the USS *Barry*, a destroyer decommissioned in 1982 that has been on visiting duty at the Navy Yard for over seven years. Launched in 1956, the *Barry* was on active duty during the Cuban missile crisis and in the Vietnam War. As you tour the 424-foot ship (remember, the difference between

A view of ship guns on display at the Navy Memorial Museum at the Navy Yard. R. W. McDILL, OFFICIAL US NAVY PHOTOGRAPH

ships and boats is that ships carry boats, like the life boats, whale boat, and captain's gig aboard the *Barry*), it's hard to imagine a crew of 315 enlisted men and 22 officers operating in this small space. The officers' quarters are spartan, yet they look more appealing after a visit to the compartment that sixty-three crewmen shared. They called the three-tiered bunks "coffin racks." Once you see the mess, where the men not only ate meals—in fifteen-minute shifts—but also watched movies and played cards, you'll realize that there is not a single place to be comfortable aboard ship. There is no lounge area, and only the officers' chairs have backs.

There is, however, some very sophisticated equipment. When your tour reaches the captain's bridge and the combat information center, the brains of the ship, you'll be impressed by the array of hardware. You'll see a terminal that controls launchings; this will mean more to you when you arrive on the stern and see the antisubmarine launcher that fires the RTTs, or rocket-thrown torpedoes. Like all military personnel, your Navy guide speaks in acronyms, he or she explains during the twenty-minute tour of the ship. The *Barry* can be boarded at no charge on weekdays from 9:00 A.M. to 4:00 P.M. and on weekends and holidays from 10:00 A.M. to 5:00 P.M. During the summer months hours are from 9:00 A.M. to 5:00 P.M.

If you have more time, visit one more museum at the Navy Yard, the **US Marine Corps Historical Center and Museum** in Building 58. Although this museum is not hands on, it still appeals to both young and old visitors, particularly its corridor of "Marines in Miniature." Lighted dioramas capture a series of battles and confrontations from 1800 to 1918. You'll see reminders of nearby conflicts, like the Battle of Bladensburg during the War of 1812, and more far-flung missions, like the June 10, 1918, Battle of Belleau Woods, where Gunnery Sergeant Dan Daly led his men forward with the shout, "Do you want to live forever?"

Daly was decorated for his valor. Other Marine heroes and officers are remembered in a display along another wall. A collection of uniforms, weapons, and other artifacts represents all the major conflicts in which the Marines have fought since the Revolution. On your way out you'll see an exhibit featuring the Pulitzer Prize-winning photograph Joe Rosenthal shot at Iwo Jima.

The Marine Corps Historical Center and Museum is open at no charge, Monday through Saturday from 10:00 A.M. to 4:00 P.M. and Sundays and holidays from noon to 5:00 P.M.

Directions: The Washington Navy Yard is inside the Washington Beltway at 9th and M Streets, S.E.

Baltimore Maritime Museum

Three very different ships constitute the **Baltimore Maritime Museum** at the Inner Harbor's Pier 4. The USS *Torsk* was the head of a submarine wolf pack; the *Chesapeake* was a floating lighthouse; and the USCG *Taney* is the last surviving ship from the Japanese attack on Pearl Harbor.

On August 14, 1945, the *Torsk* sank two Japanese men-of-war. The next day, word came that the war had ended. Thus it was the *Torsk* that fired the last torpedoes of World War II. The submarine holds another record: It is the "diving-est" ship in the world, with 11,884 submersions.

After World War II, the *Torsk* was converted to a snorkel-equipped GUPPY submarine, which was involved in operations during the 1960 Lebanon crisis and the naval blockade of Cuba in 1962. The *Torsk* was transferred to Maryland in 1972 and now affords visitors a real feel for life aboard a submarine.

Visitors may find even a short stay claustrophobic in the crew's fourteen-by-thirty-foot quarters. It is sobering to realize the conditions under which twenty-six men lived; no movie or book adequately conveys the entombed feeling you'll get as you explore this submarine. You'll leave with a new respect for submariners.

The second ship of the Baltimore Maritime Museum is the lightship *Chesapeake,* built in Charleston, South Carolina, in 1930. Lightships were used where traditional lighthouses could not be constructed, near harbors or channel entrances. Seven years before the *Chesapeake* was built, a lightship began guarding the approach to New York Harbor.

The *Chesapeake* is on the National Register of Historic Places, but it's a "place" that doesn't stay put. This is one of the few lightships that is still operational, and it visits other cities as a representative of the city of Baltimore. When the *Chesapeake* is in port, it can be toured on a combination ticket with the *Torsk.*

The *Taney's* fifty years of naval service included serving as command ship at Okinawa and serving as fleet escort in the Atlantic and Mediterranean. Before being decommissioned in 1986, the *Taney* provided medical relief during Vietnam. She also has the distinction of being the last ship afloat that participated in the search for Amelia Earhart. There is a museum store aboard the *Taney.*

Included in the museum's collection is the seven-foot **Knoll Lighthouse,** which marked the entrance to the Baltimore Harbor for 135 years before it was moved to the Inner Harbor. Built in 1855, this is the oldest "screwpile" lighthouse in the state.

The Baltimore Maritime Museum, operated by the Living Classrooms Foundation, is open daily, 9:30 A.M. to 4:30 P.M. Admission is charged.

While you're in the area, take the elevator to the top of the World Trade Center for a view of the Baltimore Maritime Museum, the harbor area, and indeed the entire city. The panoramic gallery is called the "Top of the World," and it affords one of the best views in Baltimore. Telescopes and detailed maps help you pinpoint the city's main attractions. The World Trade Center at Pier 2 is the tallest pentagonal building in the United States. It is open 10:00 A.M. to 5:00 P.M. and admission is charged.

Directions: From I-95, take Exit 53 (I-395, Downtown). From this exit, bear left, following signs to the Inner Harbor. Continue in the left or center lane until the third light. Make a right onto Pratt Street and continue four blocks to the Inner Harbor. The three ships of the Baltimore Maritime Museum are docked at Pier 3, next to the National Aquarium at the Inner Harbor. When you leave the Inner Harbor to return to I-95, take Pratt Street to President Street and turn left. Continue for one block to Lombard Street and turn left. Take Lombard for nine blocks to Howard Street, following signs for I-395, Stadium. Make a left onto Howard Street, which will become I-395. Continue on I-395 to I-95.

Chesapeake Bay Maritime Museum

The shipbuilding heritage of **St. Michaels** stems from colonial days. There is a marvelous, but perhaps apocryphal, story about how this quaint town managed to survive the second American-British confrontation unscathed. Before dawn on August 10, 1813, the British navy anchored offshore and began firing at St. Michaels. Residents hung lanterns high in the trees, thus tricking the British into overshooting the town, which thereafter called itself "the Town That Fooled the British."

For more St. Michaels, as well as Chesapeake Bay, history, visit the multidimensional **Chesapeake Bay Maritime Museum**. It's a sixteen-acre complex that includes an 1879 lighthouse, small boat exhibit, bell tower, bandstand, and several museum outbuildings.

Few can resist heading directly to the stilt-legged **Hooper Strait Lighthouse**. This is one of only three remaining "cottage" lighthouses. Great screw pile supports almost literally screwed these structures into the muddy bay bottom. The lighthouse's spartan furnishings remind visitors that even these watermen, who never fished, lived a rugged life tending the warning lights. The light keeper's family was allowed to spend only two weeks a year at the lighthouse, although the keeper did get periodic leave.

From the top of the lighthouse you'll have a sweeping view of the bay and harbor. Every day, unless weather makes the bay unnavigable, oystermen, crabbers, and fishermen sail in and out. One skipjack that is no longer part of the work fleet is the *Rosie Parks*, now a museum exhibit. In the boat shop, craftsmen restore and repair the museum's fleet of historic workboats. St. Michaels's builders are credited with crafting the first Baltimore Clipper and the first racing log canoe. The techniques and tools of boat-building are explained, and finished products can be seen at the nearby small boat shed, which has yachts, workboats, and hunting skiffs.

You can move from hunters' boats to their guns and decoys, on display in the Waterfowling Building. In the autumn, the shores around St. Michaels are crowded with the migrating fowl so painstakingly duplicated by decoy carvers. Sportsmen not only hunt, they also fish these waters, and for a look at what they are likely to catch, visit the museum's **Waterman's Wharf**.

The wharf features interactive stations, and in them you can roll up your sleeves, get your hands wet, and be a waterman for a day. You can help tend the crab tank, pull up an eel pot, or wind a heavy oyster dredge by hand. If you haven't tried to catch large oysters in shallow water, this is your chance. You'll also learn how to set a fishing net. A replica of a waterman's shanty features a tool shed and work room. You'll gain a new empathy for what it is like to earn a living on the unpredictable waters of the bay.

Docked alongside Waterman's Wharf is the museum's floating fleet. *Martha*, a Hooper Island draketail used primarily for oystering and crabbing, dates from 1934. There is also a Potomac River dory boat with a wide hull designed for harvesting herring and shad as well as oysters. You'll also see the small, easily maneuverable pot pie skiff with a tuck stern used to trotline for crabs.

To put everything you've seen in perspective, stop at the museum's Chesapeake Bay Building. It traces life back to the formation of the bay during the last Ice Age. In the prehistoric period this region was part of the valley of the Susquehanna River, but as the glaciers melted it became a "drowned river." The story continues with the advent of pre-colonial Indians, who fished and traveled the region. The bay's role in the American Revolution, War of 1812, and Civil War is reviewed, as is the life of the watermen who've worked the bay for centuries.

The museum has numerous special exhibits and many traveling shows from other maritime history museums, as well as paintings of the Chesapeake Bay by significant artists. One permanent exhibit in the steamboat building centers on propulsion and features a collection of antique steam and gas engines. In the boatyard, craftsmen demonstrate such skills as blacksmithing, sailmaking, trapmaking, and operating a steam-powered engine. Children's programs include fish painting, beginner's sailing, and meteor shower cruises. One of the favorite exhibits for youngsters is the life-size sculpture of a bay retriever; it can be touched and climbed.

The Chesapeake Bay Maritime Museum is open daily from 9:00 A.M. to 5:00 P.M. and closed on Thanksgiving, Christmas, and New Year's Day. Admission is charged.

Be sure to save time to stroll the quiet streets of St. Michaels. Along Talbot Street you'll find an assortment of boutiques, antique shops, and specialty stores, plus a deli and the town saloon. The harbor area boasts three popular restaurants: the Crab Claw, Longfellows, and the Town Dock. There are also several bed-and-breakfasts in town.

Directions: From Baltimore, take Route 2 south to Route 50, cross the Chesapeake Bay Bridge, and continue on Route 50 to Easton. From Easton take Route 33 west to St. Michaels. In St. Michaels, turn right on Mill Street for the museum, which is at the end of the street at Navy Point.

The Mariners' Museum

You know the feeling. You read a book, hear a joke, eat a fine meal—and can't wait to share your find. That's the reaction you'll have when you visit the **Mariners' Museum** in Newport News. Although the museum was founded in 1930, it's still a relatively undiscovered treasure.

The treasures here are the varied ships that ride the seas. The "jewels" of the collection, spotlighted in a darkened room, are the sixteen miniature ships crafted by August F. Crabtree. These exquisite models represent the labor of a lifetime—each is a work of art. August Crabtree was born into an Oregon shipbuilding family in 1905. He worked for a time in a shipyard in Vancouver but enjoyed carving models more than building full-size ships. When Crabtree worked in Hollywood, he created the model of Lord Nelson's ship in the movie *That Hamilton Woman.*

The Mariners' Museum purchased Crabtree's models in 1956. His work is exact in every detail. To outfit the tiny prehistoric men on the raft and dugout canoe, Crabtree trapped a mouse and used its fur. The models reveal the artistry inherent in the construction of such ships as those of Queen Hatsheput's Egyptian fleet, circa 1480 B.C., and a Roman merchant ship, circa 50 A.D.

Some of the models have historical significance. One is the *Mora,* on which William the Conqueror invaded England in 1066; Christopher Columbus's *Santa Maria* and *Pinta* are also here. Others are so intricately carved you'll need to use the magnifying glass attached to the display case to see the details. The hull on a 1687 English fifty-gun ship is carved with 270 human, animal, and mythological figures. An 1810 American brig is noted for its elaborate rigging.

The last of Crabtree's models was the first of Cunard's red-and-black funneled passenger steamers, the *Britannia.* One of the early passengers was Charles Dickens, who complained that his cabin was "an utterly impracticable, thoroughly impossible, and profoundly preposterous box."

Entrancing as the models are, they fill only one of the museum's fourteen galleries. The museum is also noted for the boardroom models, done on a scale of one-quarter inch to a foot. These models were made by the shipbuilders for the ship owners' boardrooms. Many cruise ships are represented, including the S.S. *Rotterdam* and the *Queen Elizabeth I.* The latter is done on a scale of three-eighths inch to a foot and is over twenty-eight feet long. The room in which these models are displayed has as its centerpiece the steeple-type engine from the *William Stewart;* only a foghorn could add to the ambience.

A ship modeler works several days each week in the Carvings Gallery, surrounded by more than thirty lifelike figureheads, including a polar bear from the vessel used in Admiral Richard Byrd's Antarctic expedition. The museum has quite a collection of these carvings, which once graced the bows of tall ships. As you enter the museum you'll see one of the most striking: the 1½-ton gilded eagle with an 18½-foot wingspan from the U.S. Navy frigate *Lancaster*. There are some unusual figures among the more traditional buxom female figureheads, such as an imperial-looking Queen Victoria, a threatening Hindu with a spear, and even the Apostle Paul. When the Paul figurehead was purchased in Providence, Rhode Island, it was transported in an open rumble seat. Wrapped in a blanket to prevent damage, the figure looked so real that passersby took it for a dead body and called the police.

It takes a separate building to house the small craft, the most complete international collection in the Western Hemisphere. The oldest range from primitive skin boats to dugouts from Louisiana, Jamaica, and the Congo. There are experimental racing yachts like the *Dilemma*, a Dutch yacht called a jotter, a Brazilian raft, a Chinese sampan, a Norwegian four-oared boat, a Venetian gondola, a Spanish sardine boat, and a Portuguese kelp boat. The museum has expanded its Antique Boats Gallery to include additional boats, engines, and photographs. Its setting suggests a 1930s dealer showroom. It showcases three original Chris-Craft boats, including the twenty-six-foot *Miss Belle Isle*, one of the oldest surviving Chris-Crafts.

Another gallery honors William Francis Gibbs, the architect who designed more than six thousand naval and commercial vessels. He is best known for designing the superliners SS *United States* and SS *America*. The gallery features a re-creation of Gibbs's glass-enclosed New York office that includes many authentic personal effects, such as his drafting table, books, and certificates. Photographs and memorabilia from his superliners are displayed.

The museum owns more than thirty-five thousand items. Among them are many decorative pieces with nautical themes: Liverpool creamware, Staffordshire figures, Sevres and Derby ceramics, and lovely scrimshaw work. Photographs, weapons, uniforms, and ship models tell the story of important military confrontations at sea. The Chesapeake Bay Gallery covers fishing and boating on the bay from the time before European settlers first arrived.

For those with a scholarly interest in the sea, the museum has a seventy-five-thousand-volume library as well as maps, journals, and some 530,000 photographs. It is an amazing facility set in a 550-acre park and wildlife sanctuary. Within the park is 167-acre Lake Maury. There are fishing boats, athletic fields, picnic tables, and the five-mile Noland Trail around the lake and through the woods.

The Mariners' Museum is open daily from 10:00 A.M. to 5:00 P.M. It is closed on Christmas. Admission is charged.

Directions: From I-95 in the Richmond area, take I-64 east to Exit 258A at Newport News. Then take Route 17, J. Clyde Morris Boulevard, to the museum entrance. The route is well marked.

Norfolk Naval Base

The **Norfolk Naval Base**—the world's largest naval base—certainly demonstrates the magnitude of America's military strength. The long line of destroyers, aircraft carriers, submarines, and support ships tied up at Norfolk is truly an impressive sight.

Norfolk's naval significance dates from the Civil War, when the famous battle of the ironclads, the *Monitor* and the *Merrimack*, occurred in Hampton Roads harbor. Today, there are a hundred ships, thirty-two aircraft squadrons, and thirty-five shore-based activities in the South Hampton Roads command. The Norfolk Naval Base extends over thirty-four hundred acres and provides a great deal of interesting information and sights.

Tours leave daily between 9:00 A.M. and 2:00 P.M. from the Naval Base Tour Office at 9809 Hampton Boulevard. They leave on the half-hour during the summer months and take about forty-five minutes. The schedule changes in the off-season, so be sure to call (757) 444-7637 in advance for current times. There is a fee, but no reservations are required.

It seems everything is bigger at the Norfolk Naval Base. Fleet Industrial Supply Center boasts that it is the "World's Largest Store." It is open daily, year-round, and employs 1,605 civilians and 53 military personnel. It's easy to see why this Norfolk facility has a forty-eight-million-dollar federal payroll.

Near the top of the military payroll are the flag officers. Along "Admiral's Row," you'll see replicas of famous homes from various states built in 1907 for the Jamestown Exposition, which now are used as officers' homes. For example, the Georgia House is a copy of the summer home of Franklin Delano Roosevelt's mother, known for a time as the "Little White House." A typical colonial homestead represents Delaware. A lovely porticoed Virginia plantation house is the quarters of the supreme allied commander of NATO. Along this fascinating drive, there is also a scaled-down replica of Independence Hall.

Based at Norfolk are Sea King, Sea Knight, and Sea Sprite helicopters. All-weather early warnings, surveillance coordination, search and rescue missions, and numerous other functions are carried out by the Eighth Carrier Airborne Early Warning Squadrons, home ported at Norfolk. You are sure to see some of the Hawkeye planes they fly.

What's a military installation without confusing shorthand? On the tour you pass both the FASOTRAGRULANT and the NCTAMSLANT. The former is a sophisticated flight simulator facility. The latter is the largest and most complex communication station in the world.

All of the above is just icing on the cake for most visitors, who come primarily to see the ships—and there are plenty to see! As you enter the two-mile waterfront area, the first you see are the world's largest warships, berthed along Pier 12. You'll learn how to tell the difference between the nuclear-powered and conventional-powered ships. (Just a hint: it has to do with the color of the antennas.) You may see a nuclear-powered aircraft carrier, such as the *America* or the *Eisenhower*. These massive ships are eighteen stories high and as long as three football fields, plus an extra hundred feet at both ends. Their size sinks in when you learn that each link in the anchor chain weighs three hundred and fifty pounds. Each warship carries more than sixty-two hundred men. Due to recent changes in the laws, women can now serve in combat on board aircraft carriers. The USS *George Washington* already has a contingent of women.

Next, at the Cargo Ship Pier, you'll see twenty-three types of boats and ships: destroyers, cruisers, amphibious ships, helicopter ships, fleet oilers, and tugs. On weekends, from 1:00 to 4:30 P.M., you can usually board two ships, although these rarely include aircraft carriers and submarines. The final part of the harbor portion of the tour takes you past the workhorses of the Atlantic Fleet—more destroyers and cruisers, plus submarines and submarine tenders.

Directions: Take the I-295 loop around Richmond and pick up I-64 east to Norfolk. After you cross the Hampton Roads Bridge Tunnel, take Exit 564 for the naval base. Follow this to the very end, where it intersects with Gate 2, which is the main entrance to the naval base.

US Army Ordnance Museum

As you wander up and down the museum's rows of tanks, armored cars, howitzers, and associated artillery, you're likely to overhear stories recounted by visiting veterans about the days when their lives depended on these weapons. Such stories are more than matched by the legends and lore associated with field pieces in the **US Army Ordnance Museum** collection at the Aberdeen Proving Ground.

Anzio Annie, a major piece in the collection, is the name the Allies on Anzio gave the German Leopold gun that held them pinned to a sandy beachhead. The Allied high command was mystified by it; they couldn't imagine how a gun large enough to fire a 550-pound shell could escape their bombing and naval attacks. But the Leopold survived numerous raids. The puzzle was solved when the Allies broke from their beach position. The Germans retreated, leaving Anzio Annie hidden in a mountain tunnel. The gun was mounted on twenty-four railroad wheels and was only rolled out to be fired. Annie is the only German railroad gun known to survive World War II.

Another massive weapon is the atomic cannon introduced in the early 1950s. This 166,638 pound weapon fired both conventional and atomic munitions at targets up to eighteen miles away. These are just some of the more than 250 pieces in the outdoor exhibit, which, when combined with the indoor displays, forms the world's most complete weapons collection. The weapons have more than historic value; they also are highly useful for research, enabling engineers to develop and modify existing models, as well as learn how to defend against various weapons.

As you enter the museum, you'll see the Civil War–era Gatling gun, which illustrates the research value of this collection. Between 1902 and 1904, experiments were done with the Gatling gun to develop a more rapid firing weapon. At that time the need for speed was not critical, so the experiment was discontinued. When aircraft armaments were needed in the 1940s, the Ordnance Museum supplied information from the earlier tests, and the Gatling gun principle was used to develop the Vulcan, an aircraft weapon.

The museum's exhibits include the history and development of ammunition and examples of every kind of rifle imaginable. There is case after case of rocket launchers, machine guns, and submachine guns.

The US Army Ordnance Museum is open at no charge, Monday through Sunday from 10:00 A.M. to 4:45 P.M. It is open on selected national holidays. The museum is open on Armed Forces Day, Memorial Day, Veterans Day, and Independence Day.

Directions: From the Baltimore Beltway, I-695, take I-95 north twenty-one miles to Exit 85, Route 22. Turn right on Route 22 and proceed to the Aberdeen Proving Ground Military Police Gate. The museum is one mile beyond the gate, on the right.

Virginia Air and Space Center and Hampton Roads History Center

The **Virginia Air and Space Center**, on the Hampton waterfront, has been informing and entertaining visitors since its opening in April 1992. With its immense, glassed exhibit space soaring skyward, the official visitor center for NASA Langley Research Center is visually striking. This highly successful design conveys a sense of space that is very appropriate to the museum's themes.

To get the most out of your visit, start by watching the short video at the Orientation Theater, where you'll get a brief summary of the museum's history and an overview of the exhibits. The self-guided tour begins in a large open space where an array of small models traces the evolution of the airplane from its earliest days. Full-size airplanes hang suspended from the ceiling. Many of the planes hanging in the enclosed space had to be brought in before the final walls were put in place.

The suspended planes include a prototype YF-16 Fighting Falcon, like those the Air Force precision Thunderbirds fly, and a Chance Vought F4U-ID Corsair, a huge aircraft with a thirty-eight-foot wingspan. An F-4E Phantom II, which saw combat in Vietnam, is also exhibited. A Langley Aerodrome, Schleiche ASW-12 Glider, the world's largest paper airplane, and an applications technology Satellite 6, as well as eight other planes, can be viewed from several levels; you can even look down on them from a gantry that crosses high above the museum's ground floor. The gantry also provides a bird's-eye view of the Apollo 12 Command Module, which has a proud place on the main floor.

On the ground floor is the **Hampton Roads History Center** (which is slated to move to a new downtown location) and a three-hundred-seat IMAX theater with a giant five-story projection screen and sixteen thousand watts of wrap-around sound. Both are entertaining and educational.

Hampton was an official royal port for the Virginia colony. A wharf exhibit focuses on the importance of trade and tobacco to the area. In colonial times, the Bunch of Grapes Tavern stood on the site of this museum. It was in this tavern that irate patriots gathered to discuss their unhappiness with English rule. An audiovisual program brings the statuary customers to life so that you can hear a conversation that might have occurred in this tavern. Ship building was significant in this area; you'll see exhibits detailing the struggle to create a navy and defend the shores against the British in the American Revolution and War of 1812. Hampton Roads is forever associated with the dueling ironclads, and there is a full-size replica of the casement of the *Merrimack* (also called the *Virginia*). There is also a large-scale portion of the *Monitor*. It surprises many visitors to discover that the *Merrimack*, at 275 feet in length, was more than twice the size of the space shuttle. Continuing the Hampton story, there are exhibits on the local watermen and on the navy's influence in the area, including replicas of carriers and models of aircraft carriers. This museum is hands on, and with a push of a button you can experience the sights and sounds of US naval aviation.

The space gallery is on the second floor; at the exhibit entrance is a cradle with an infant dressed not in traditional bunting, but in a space suit. Over the cradle a quote from the "Father of Soviet Rocketry," Konstantin Tsiolovsky, reads, "Earth is the cradle of mankind, but we cannot live in the cradle forever." Space research has been conducted at NASA Langley Research Center since 1917—early strides and future goals are encompassed in the gallery. Achievements are recognized with items like the moon rock, the Viking orbiter and lander, and the space shuttle exhibit. Interactive displays let you play at being an "astronaut for a minute." There is also a simulated space launch. Other topics covered include rockets, satellites, aerospace research exhibits, and the role of space in science fiction. Level three has an observation gantry for an overview of the hanging exhibits and an observation deck for a panoramic view of the Hampton Harbor.

The center is open during the summer from Monday through Wednesday, 10:00 A.M. to 5:00 P.M.; Thursday through Sunday until 7:00 P.M. Winter hours are Monday through Sunday, 10:00 A.M. to 5:00 P.M. Admission is charged to the exhibits and the IMAX performances. Two IMAX movies usually are shown on the five-story-high screen; for additional information call (800) 296-0800. You should allow at least an hour to explore the museum and forty-five minutes for an IMAX movie.

Directions: Take I-64 east from the Richmond area to Exit 267, Settlers Landing Road, which will take you to downtown Hampton. The Virginia Air and Space Center is on the left. Parking is available across from the center.

Arlington National Cemetery

The use of Arlington House (see selection) grounds to bury slain soldiers was initiated by happenstance. In May 1864, President Lincoln and General Meigs were visiting the wounded in the tent hospital on the Arlington grounds. They realized that, with the number of Civil War fatalities mounting daily, a new burial site would be needed. So they decided to bury the dead at Arlington. Meigs's intention was to punish Lee for joining the Confederate army. Thousands would rest there before the end of the Civil War.

Buried at **Arlington National Cemetery** are the known and unknown, the famous and the ordinary citizen-soldier. All of our country's wars are represented, including the American Revolution, the War of 1812, and the Mexican War. Since Arlington officially began during the Civil War, veterans of these earlier conflicts were disinterred and reburied. Subsequent military deaths in the Indian campaigns, Spanish-American War, the Philippine Insurrection, World Wars I and II, the

Korean Conflict, Vietnam, and the Persian Gulf are represented by soldiers who lie at Arlington National Cemetery.

There are special memorials to soldiers who died in battle and could never be identified; the most famous is the Tomb of the Unknowns. On October 22, 1921, four unknown American soldiers were exhumed from separate military cemeteries in France where slain soldiers from World War I were buried. A highly decorated soldier, Army sergeant Edward F. Younger, placed a spray of white roses on one casket on October 24, 1921, and this became the unknown soldier of World War I. The following month, on Armistice Day, November 11, President Warren G. Harding headed the dignitaries on hand to officially inter the soldier at the plaza of the Arlington National Cemetery Memorial Amphitheater.

During the Eisenhower administration, on Memorial Day 1958, unknown soldiers from World War II and Korea were interred at Arlington. Americans from all across the country come to Arlington to pay tribute to these valorous soldiers, who are guarded around the clock by the tomb guards from the US Army 3rd US Infantry (the Old Guard). The impressive changing of the guard ceremony takes place every thirty minutes during summer hours, every hour during the winter.

The Tomb of the Unknowns was not the earliest monument honoring unknown soldiers at Arlington. The first unidentified battle dead came from Northern Virginia battlefields, most from the fields of Bull Run. There are about 2,111 unknown soldiers from the Civil War in a vault beneath a massive sarcophagus south of Arlington House. The mast of the battleship USS *Maine* is adjacent to the burial spot of 167 unidentified men who went down with the ship in Havana Harbor during the Spanish-American War.

Names from the pages of American history are found throughout Arlington National Cemetery: Pierre Charles L'Enfant, Oliver Wendell Holmes, Philip H. Sheridan, William Jennings Bryan, Robert Todd Lincoln, John J. Pershing, George C. Marshall, Walter Reed, Robert E. Peary, Richard E. Byrd, James V. Forestal, John Foster Dulles, Virgil Grissom, Roger B. Chaffee, and two presidents of the United States. William Howard Taft, chief justice of the US Supreme Court and the twenty-seventh president, is buried at Arlington.

A special memorial with an eternal flame marks the spot where John Fitzgerald Kennedy, the thirty-fifth president, is buried. The walls of the plaza are inscribed with excerpts from President Kennedy's inaugural address, including his moving words "Now the trumpet summons us again... " Two children who pre-deceased their father also are buried at the Kennedy grave site. Jacqueline Lee Bouvier Kennedy Onassis was buried next to the president in 1994. Robert Kennedy's nearby grave is marked by a small white cross and the sound of water flowing over a fountain spillway.

Arlington National Cemetery is open October through March from 8:00 A.M. to 5:00 P.M. and April through September until 7:00 P.M. Maps at the visitor center orient visitors and indicate specific burial sites. The cemetery is not open to vehicular traffic. Cars must be parked at the visitor center parking lot, but tour buses are available (for a fee) for those who do not want to walk.

North of the Arlington National Cemetery on Arlington Boulevard is the often-photographed **US Marine Corps Memorial**, also known as the Iwo Jima Statue, which was carved to duplicate the photo of the Marines raising the US flag on Mount Suribachi during World War II. The seventy-eight-foot sculpture is imposing, the largest ever cast in bronze. On Tuesday evenings during the summer months, the Marines have a dress parade and color ceremony at this memorial. Near the memorial is the Netherlands Carillon. The carillon tower and bells were a gift from the people of the Netherlands in gratitude for American assistance during and after World War II. The bells are played every Saturday from April to September, starting at 2:00 P.M.

Directions: Take I-95 to the perimeter of Washington; at the intersection with the Washington Beltway (I-495/95) and I-395, take the latter and head toward the city. Then exit at Memorial Bridge/Rosslyn exit onto Route 110 north. From Route 110, exit at Memorial Bridge/Washington. At the top of the exit turn left onto Memorial Drive, which goes directly to the entrance of Arlington National Cemetery and Arlington House.

Vietnam Veterans Memorial

One of the criteria for the design of the **Vietnam Veterans Memorial** was that it make no political statement about the war. The Vietnam conflict created a schism in America's body politic, and when the concept of a tangible symbol of recognition was conceived in 1979, it was hoped controversy could be avoided—but debate did ensue, not over the issue of US policy in Vietnam, but over the design itself.

Jan C. Scruggs, a wounded and decorated infantryman from Columbia, Maryland, was the leader of a Vietnam Veterans group determined to provide an appropriate monument for the men and woman who had served in Vietnam. It took nearly three years from the time Scruggs and his group incorporated as a charitable organization on April 27, 1979, until work started on the two-acre plot on the National Mall on March 26, 1982.

The veterans working on this project had hoped from the onset to have a prominent site in a large parklike area, and the western end of Constitution Gardens near the Lincoln Memorial was ideal. In addition to being nonpolitical, the veterans wanted the memorial design to be contemplative in character, to fit in with the other memorials on the Mall, and, finally, to have the names of all the servicemen and women who died, or remained missing, in the Vietnam War.

The Vietnam Veterans Memorial Fund raised $8.4 million to build the monument. Contributions came in from more than 275,000 individuals, organizations, corporations, foundations, and unions. The money was all privately donated; no federal funds were used. When the VVMF announced a nationwide design contest in October 1980, they had more than 2,573 registrants, making this the largest competition of its kind ever held in this country. By the March 1981 deadline, 1,421 designs had been submitted to the jury of eight international artists and designers. The panel's unanimous winner was Maya Ying Lin of Athens, Ohio, a twenty-one-year-old senior at Yale University.

Originally controversial, with time, Maya Lin's design has come to be admired. Her concept was to have a park within a park. The mirrorlike reflection of the surrounding trees and monuments in the polished black granite of the memorial links this monument with others honoring individuals from different eras of our country's past. Lin explained that she wanted the memorial to be "a place where something happens within the viewer. It's like reading a book. I purposely had the names etched ragged right on each panel to look like a page from a book." As the design consultant and architect of record, she chose to list the names in the chronological order of the date of casualty. Thus, in its totality, the walls tell the story of the Vietnam War as an endless series of human sacrifices—and each of these sacrifices is noted and is given a place in history.

There are two walls, the west and the east. Each is 246 feet, 8 inches long, and they meet at an angle. The east wall points to the northeast corner of the Washington Monument, and the west wall points to the Lincoln Memorial, bringing the Vietnam Veterans Memorial into a strong historical connection with the past. Each wall has seventy separate inscribed panels of varying sizes. The largest panel has 137 names; the shortest, only one. At the time of the dedication in 1982, there were 57,939 names, but more have been added since that time. With the exception of one casualty from 1957, the names are from 1959 to 1975, with the dates given from the point of injury, not necessarily the date of death. The names of the earliest casualties start at the top of East Panel 1, with the date and name given from left to right on down the panel, and then continuing on to the panel to the right. A symbol is used to designate status: a diamond indicates that the death was confirmed, while a cross indicates individuals who were missing or taken prisoner. For those prisoners whose remains were returned to this country, a diamond is placed over the cross, and in those instances where the serviceman returned home alive, a circle is inscribed around the cross. Eight women, all nurses, are included on the Memorial.

Initial reaction to the memorial was mixed, with many objecting to its stark lines and unconventional look. A short time after its completion, a flag and sculpture were added. Frederick Hart, who came in third in the original contest to design the memorial, was invited to create a realistic sculpture of a Vietnam serviceman. Called **The Three Servicemen**, or The Three Fighting Men, it depicts three men, dressed in Vietnam-era uniforms, carrying infantry weapons. One of the men was modeled after a young Marine stationed in Washington in 1983; the second soldier, who carries a machine gun, is based on a Cuban-American; and the third is a composite of several African Americans. To some, they seem to have the "thousand-yard stare" of combat soldiers. Others interpret their looks as those of men on patrol, while some feel that they are searching for their own names on the panels of the memorial.

A **Vietnam Women's Memorial**, like the memorial itself, was the result of the vision of a Vietnam veteran. Army nurse Diane Carlson Evans wanted recognition given to the women who volunteered for duty in Vietnam, risking their lives to care for the wounded and dying in a war that was often unpopular at home. Evans founded the Vietnam Women's Memorial Project in 1984 and worked toward the goal of adding a statue commemorating the courageous women who served in Vietnam. Her dream became a reality when Glenda Goodacre's statue of three women helping a wounded serviceman was added to the Vietnam Veterans Memorial and dedicated on Veterans Day 1993.

The Vietnam Veterans Memorial is the most visited memorial in D.C. Approximately 2,500,000 people visit annually, and smaller versions of the wall have traveled around the country.

Directions: The Vietnam Veterans Memorial is inside the Washington Beltway at Constitution Avenue and Henry Bacon Drive in Northwest Washington.

Geographical
Cross-Reference

DELAWARE

Corbit-Sharp House
Fort Delaware State Park
Hagley Museum
Historic Batsto Village
John Dickinson Mansion
Meeting House Galleries
Rockwood
Wilson-Warner House
Zwaanendael Museum

MARYLAND

C&D Canal Museum
    (Cecil County)
Chesapeake Bay Maritime
    Museum (Talbot County)
Chestertown (Kent County)
Dr. Samuel A. Mudd House
    Museum (Charles County)
Ellicott City B&O Railroad Station
    Museum (Howard County)
Furnace Town (Worcester County)
Smallwood's Retreat (Charles
    County)
Thomas Stone National Historic
    Site (Charles County)
Union Mills Homestead and
    Gristmill (Carroll County)
US Army Ordnance Museum (Har-
    ford County)

Annapolis

Chase-Lloyd House
Hammond-Harwood House
London Town Publik House and
    Gardens
Maryland State House and Old
    Treasury Building
Victualling Warehouse and Tobacco
    Prise
William Paca House and Garden

Baltimore

Baltimore Maritime Museum
B&O Railroad Museum
Fort McHenry National Monument
    and Historic Shrine
Hampton National Historic Site
Mount Clare Mansion
Star-Spangled Banner Flag
    House
US Frigate *Constellation*

Frederick

Barbara Fritchie House & the Home
    of Roger Brooke Taney
Blue Blazes Whiskey Still
Fort Frederick
Monocacy National Battlefield
National Museum of Civil War
    Medicine
Rose Hill Manor and Schifferstadt
    Architectural Museum

St. Mary's

Historic St. Mary's City
Historic St. Mary's
    Governor's Field
Point Lookout State Park
Sotterley Plantation

Western Maryland

Antietam National
    Battlefield Park
C&O Canal National Historical
    Park (Upper)
The Cumberland Road
George Washington Headquarters &
    Fort Cumberland Tunnels
Hager House
La Vale Toll Gate House
Maryland Heights and Kennedy
    Farm

NEW JERSEY

Morristown National
    Historical Park
Rockingham
Wallace House
Wheaton Village

PENNSYLVANIA

Lancaster/Pennsylvania Dutch Country

Conrad Weiser Homestead
Cornwall Iron Furnace
Daniel Boone Homestead
Eisenhower National
    Historic Site
Ephrata Cloister
Gettysburg National
    Military Park

Golden Plough Tavern
Hans Herr House
Historic Rock Ford Plantation
Hopewell Furnace
Robert Fulton Birthplace
Strasburg Rail Road
Wheatland
Wright's Ferry Mansion
York County Colonial
    Court House

Philadelphia

Betsy Ross House
Carpenters' Hall
City Tavern
Cliveden
Congress Hall & Old City Hall
Declaration House
Ebenezer Maxwell Mansion
Fort Mifflin
Franklin Court
Historic Bartram's Gardens
Independence Hall and the Liberty
    Bell Pavilion
Stenton
Thaddeus Kosciuszko National
    Memorial
Todd House and Bishop White
    House
Wyck

Philadelphia Countryside

Bethlehem Historic District
Brandywine Battlefield Park
The Colonial Pennsylvania
    Plantation
George Taylor House
Graeme Park
The Grange
Historic Yellow Springs
Hugh Moore Historical Park and
    National Canal Museum
Mercer Museum
New Hope Mule Barge Company
    and New Hope & Ivyland

Railroad
Pennsbury Manor
Peter Wentz Farmstead
Valley Forge National
    istorical Park
Washington Crossing
    Historic Park

Western Pennsylvania

Bushy Run Battlefield
Fort Ligonier
Fort Necessity National
    Battlefield
Fort Pitt Museum

VIRGINIA

Alexandria

Boyhood Home of Robert E. Lee
Christ Church
Fort Ward Museum and Historic
    Site
Gadsby's Tavern
Lee-Fendall House
Ramsay House and
    Carlyle House
Stabler-Leadbeater
    Apothecary Shop

Central Virginia

Appomattox Court House National
    Historical Park
Booker T. Washington National
    Monument
Henricus Historical Park
Montpelier
Quartermaster Museum
Red Hill, The Patrick Henry
    National Memorial
Sailor's Creek Battlefield Historical
    State Park

Charlottesville/Lynchburg

Ash Lawn–Highland
Michie Tavern, ca. 1784
Monticello
Thomas Jefferson's Poplar Forest

Fredericksburg

Chancellorsville Battlefield
Chatham
Fredericksburg National Military
    Park
Hugh Mercer Apothecary Shop
Kenmore Plantation and Gardens &
    Mary Washington House
The Monroe Presidential Center
Rising Sun Tavern
Spotsylvania Battlefield
Wilderness Battlefield

Hampton/Norfolk/Tidewater

Adam Thoroughgood House
Douglass MacArthur Memorial
Fort Monroe and the Casemate
    Museum
Fort Wool
The Mariners' Museum
Moses Myers House
Norfolk Naval Base
Pamunkey and Mattaponi Indian
    Reservations
Portsmouth Naval Shipyard
    Museum
Smith's Fort Plantation and Bacon's
    Castle
Virginia Air and Space Center and
    Hampton Roads
    History Center
Willoughby-Baylor House

James River Plantations

Berkeley
Sherwood Forest
Shirley Plantation

Lexington

George C. Marshall Museum

and Library
Lee Chapel and Museum
Stonewall Jackson House
VMI Museum

Northern Neck

George Washington Birthplace
    National Monument
Stratford Hall

Northern Virginia

Arlington House
Arlington National Cemetery
Colvin Run Mill
George Washington's Gristmill
    Historical State Park
Gunston Hall Plantation
Manassas National
    Battlefield Park
Marine Corps Air-Ground
    Museum
Morven Park
Mount Vernon
Oatlands
Pohick Church
Sully Historic Site
Woodlawn

Richmond/Petersburg/Hopewell

Centre Hill Mansion
City Point Unit and
    Appomattox Manor
Flowerdew Hundred Plantation
James River & Kanawha Canal
John Marshall House
Old Blandford Church
Pamplin Historical Park
Petersburg National Battlefield
Richmond National
    Battlefield Park
Scotchtown
St. John's Church
        and St. Paul's Church
Siege Museum
The Valentine Museum and

Wickham House
Weston Manor
The White House and Museum
    of the Confederacy
Wilton and Tuckahoe

Shenandoah Valley

Abram's Delight
Belle Grove
McCormick Farm and Historic
    Museum
Museum of American Frontier
    Culture
New Market Battlefield State
    Historical Park
Stonewall Jackson's
    Headquarters
Virginia's Explore Park
Woodrow Wilson Birthplace

Williamsburg/Colonial Triangle

Bassett Hall
Bruton Parish Church
Capitol in Williamsburg
Carter's Grove and Wolstenholme
    Towne
George Wythe House
Governor's Palace
Jamestown Settlement
Jamestown, The Original Site
    (Colonial National
    Historical Park)
Nelson House
Peyton Randolph House and the
    Brush-Everard House
Public Hospital—Williamsburg
Williamsburg's Taverns
Yorktown Colonial National
    Historical Park
Yorktown Victory Center

WASHINGTON, DC

Decatur House
Dumbarton Oaks
Ford's Theatre National Historic Site
and Petersen House
Frederick Douglass National
Historic Site—Cedar Hill
Navy Yard Museums
Octagon House
The Old Stone House
Sewall-Belmont House
Vietnam Veterans Memorial
The White House
Woodrow Wilson House

WASHINGTON SUBURBS

The Accokeek Foundation
National Colonial Farm and
Ecosystem Farm
Beall-Dawson House

C&O Canal National Historical
Park (Lower)
Clara Barton National
Historic Site
Claude Moore Colonial Farm at
Turkey Run
College Park Aviation Museum
Fort Marcy
Fort Washington
John Wilkes Booth Escape Route
Montpelier Mansion
Moyaone
Paul E. Garber Facility
Piscataway Park
Riversdale
The Surratt House
The 1814 British Invasion Route

WEST VIRGINIA

Harpers Ferry National Historical
Park

Index

445

Jane Ockershausen became a best-selling author by concentrating on the popular weekend travel market. She has written ten travel guides to the Mid-Atlantic region and Eastern seaboard states, including **One-Day Trip Books** on Virginia, Maryland, North Carolina, South Carolina, Georgia, Pennsylvania, and the District of Columbia. This long-awaited revision of her best-selling guide to historic destinations in the Mid-Atlantic region includes new sites and categories based on extensive travel over the course of twenty years.

Ockershausen has been a correspondent for the *National Geographic Traveler*, and her byline has appeared in the *Washington Post*, the *Baltimore Sun*, the *Chicago Tribune*, the *Buffalo News*, the *Dallas Times Herald*, the *Oregonian*, the *Pittsburgh Press*, and the *Pittsburgh Post Gazette*. She has also written for the *Washingtonian*, *Mid-Atlantic Country*, *Historic Preservation*, *Mid-Atlantic Weekends*, and *Pennsylvania Heritage Magazine*. She has addressed numerous statewide conferences on travel and journalism and lectured at the Smithsonian Institution in Washington.

Jane is a member of the board of directors of the Society of American Travel Writers and was the organization's president in 1999. She is also a member of the American Society of Journalists and Authors.